THE NEW LEFT

A Collection of Essays

THE NEW LEFT

A Collection of Essays

Priscilla Long, Editor

Introduction by Staughton Lynd

Extending Horizons Books

Porter Sargent Publisher

11 Beacon Street

Boston, Mass. 02108

This book is set in Bodoni Book, a modern type-face introduced to
the United States in 1910. It is not a copy of the types of the great
Italian, Giambattista Bodoni, but rather a version retaining his
principle of modern letter design.

Cover design by Flynn Donovan

Index by Keith Maillard

For

Edward Oquendo

EDITOR'S PREFACE

Another collection of essays . . . hopefully this one will help to move our movement along . . . to concisely bring together our somewhat diverse outlooks . . . to advance our theoretical basis . . . to share our ideas and strategies.

If you are new to the New Left, I ask you to read the four hundred-odd pages here, to read, to think and consider. Then, if you find that there is any truth in these pages, I urge you to do something about it. Look around you, you will see the needs . . . find a way to begin.

If I were to thank everyone who helped this book into being, the list would be very long, as I would have to begin with those who, very patiently, some six years ago, began my education as a radical. So I will be content to thank here, in particular, Michael Ferber, Bill Hunt and Noam Chomsky for their suggestions when the book was first taking form, Howard Zinn for his constant help, Floyd B. Barbour, Esther Doughty and Claire Joseph for their technical and intellectual assistance and for their constant encouragement, and F. Porter Sargent for making the book possible. I would especially like to thank my husband, Peter Irons, who spent the last two years in prison instead of making a book.

P. L. I.

Boston, 1969

ACKNOWLEDGEMENTS

For permission to reprint copyrighted material acknowledgements are gratefully made to the following:

New Left Review, London, for "Letter to the New Left" by C. Wright Mills. Copyright © 1961 by *New Left Review*.

Martin Secker and Warburg Limited, London, for excerpts from *Anarcho-Syndicalism* by Rudolf Rocker. Copyright © 1902 by Secker & Warburg.

Beacon Press for "No Rights, No Duties" which first appeared as Chapter Three of *The Right of Revolution* by Truman Nelson. Copyright © 1968 by Truman Nelson.

Harper and Row for "The National Security Bureaucracy and Military Intervention" by Richard Barnet, which first appeared in *No More Vietnams?* edited by Richard Pfeffer. Copyright © 1968 by Harper & Row.

News and Letters, 415 Brainard St., Detroit, Mich., for excerpts from the pamphlet "Workers Battle Automation" by Charles Denby. Copyright © 1960 by *News and Letters*.

Radical Education Project, Box 625, Ann Arbor, Mich., for "Getting by with a Little Help from Our Friends" by Barbara and Al Haber. Copyright © 1967 by Radical Education Project.

Random House, Inc. for "A New Community" which is chapter 6 of *Communitas* by Percival and Paul Goodman. Copyright © 1947, 1960 by Percival and Paul Goodman. Reprinted by permission of Random House, Inc.

Viet-Report and John McDermott, for "Thoughts on the Movement," first published in 1967 in *Viet-Report*. Copyright © 1967 by John McDermott.

W. H. Ferry and The Ad Hoc Committee on the Triple Revolution for "The Triple Revolution."

Philip Morris Inc. for their Virginia Slim advertisement. Copyright © by Philip Morris Inc.

Wayne Stayskal of *The Chicago American* for his Mme. Binh cartoon.

"Evolution of the ERAP Organizers" by Richard Rothstein appeared in an earlier version in *Radical America*, Vol. II, No. 2. (Mar.-Apr. 1968).

"Racism in The United States" by Frank Joyce appeared in an earlier version in *The Paper Tiger* in the Spring of 1968.

"Consumption: Domestic Imperialism" by Dave Gilbert is a follow-up to his pamphlet on *Imperialism* which is available from *The Old Mole*, 2 Brookline Ave., Cambridge, Massachusetts. Dave Gilbert wishes to emphasize that "Consumption: Domestic Imperialism" is not intended as a final analysis but as a beginning.

The authors of "A Woman is a Sometime Thing" recognize that *The Guardian* has changed its viewpoint on Women's Liberation.

CONTENTS

TOWARDS A HISTORY OF THE NEW LEFT

Staughton Lynd

I. F. Stone once wrote that United States counter-insurgency experts, trying to imitate Mao's formula of the guerrilla as a fish-in-the-sea-of-the-people, resembled an aquarium visitor watching fish through a plate glass window. In somewhat the same way, many Americans have watched the growth of the New Left without comprehending it. These observers may be familiar with major events in the New Left's history, such as the Montgomery, Alabama bus boycott of 1955-1956; the founding of the Student Nonviolent Coordinating Committee (SNCC) and the Students for a Democratic Society (SDS) in 1960; the culmination of the Southern civil rights movement in the Mississippi Freedom Summer and Selma, Alabama march in 1964-1965; the call for "black power" in spring 1966; the "student power" movement, highlighted by the Free Speech Movement (FSM) at the University of California in Berkeley in 1964-1965 and the Columbia University rebellion of April-May 1968; the intensifying protest against the war in Vietnam; and so on.[1] Knowing these things, the spectator may still feel that he is on the outside looking in, separated from the experience of "the Movement" by a gap as resistant as the side of the aquarium tank.

The writings gathered in this book will help the non-participant to place himself imaginatively within the experience of the white New Left.[2] Like any collection of writings, it is only the first step toward an adequate history. The story of a social movement, even a movement largely made up of students, is difficult to tell because so little of what happened is likely to be preserved in writing. Memory is therefore an indispensable resource: memory set down as quickly as possible before the past fades and is re-

interpreted in the light of subsequent events. This requirement in
turn implies that the history of the Movement must be the collective product of the Movement itself. What Regis Debray says of
the Cuban Revolution is also true of the American New Left, that
its history "can come to us only from those who organized and
participated in it."[3] In contrast to conventional history, written
by a single authority about events he did not experience primarily
on the basis of texts, the history of the New Left will be a "guerrilla
history" as different from conventional history as guerrilla theater
is different from the theater of Shakespeare.

Accordingly, it must be clearly understood that the following
remarks about the history of the New Left can only be tentative
and preliminary. Work on a guerrilla history of the New Left has
only begun.[4] This introduction is part of that beginning.

I

Clark Kissinger has remarked that every one dates the Movement from the year he entered it. But there would probably be
general agreement that a history of the New Left should begin in
1956.

Were the New Left considered merely as an American phenomenon, 1960 might seem a more logical point of departure. Actually,
however, the American New Left is part of an international
political tendency.[5] Differences in form notwithstanding, recent
student movements in the United States, Western Europe, and
Japan share certain common concerns: rejection both of capitalism
and of the bureaucratic Communism exemplified by the Soviet
Union; anti-imperialism; and an orientation to decentralized
"direct action," violent or nonviolent. And clearly such movements in the so-called free world are related to the heretical Com-
munisms of Tito, Mao Tse-tung and Fidel Castro, to the libertarian
currents in Eastern Europe, to various versions of "African socialism." 1956 is the obvious year of beginnings for this international
tendency.

That was the year of Khruschev's condemnation of Stalin at
the twentieth congress of the Communist Party of the Soviet
Union, and of the Soviet invasion of Hungary. These events put
an end to the hegemony of Soviet Communism in the world
radical movement. Response was immediate. In France, Jean-
Paul Sartre broke with the French Communist Party when it

supported Soviet intervention in Hungary. "From every point of view," he wrote, "the intervention was a crime. It is an abject lie to pretend that the workers are fighting side by side with the Soviet troups. . . . The Red Army opened fire on an entire nation. . . . What the Hungarian people teach us with their blood is the complete failure of socialism as a merchandise imported from Russia." According to Sartre this meant that in France, where for twelve years he had engaged in dialogue with the Communists for the sake of unity on the Left, those who thought as he did must return to the opposition. "Alliance with the Communist Party as it is and intends to remain can have no other effect than compromising the last chances for a common front."[6]

In England, ex-Communists and other radicals created the journals *Universities and Left Review* and *The New Reasoner*, later merged as *The New Left Review*. In China, Mao Tse-tung "suddenly changed course"; according to a possibly-apocryphal anecdote now current in Peking, "he made his decision after his journey to the USSR where he was appalled by the ideological level of foreign Communist leaders, and realized the ravages that bureaucratization had made in the Communist elite of the European socialist countries."[7]

The same year, 1956, contrasting New Left charismas were launched in the Western Hemisphere. Fidel Castro and his handful of followers landed from the *Granma* to conquer their Cuban homeland, and Martin Luther King led the successful Montgomery bus boycott.

So much, both political and intellectual, having happened during 1956 and immediately thereafter, the question arises why the upsurge of American student activity waited until 1960. What was happening in the American New Left between 1956 and 1960?

So far as black radicalism is concerned, Vincent Harding has written that the Southern Christian Leadership Conference formed by Dr. King after the Montgomery boycott "could not maintain the dynamic level of Montgomery. . . . Perhaps this was partly because SCLC was made up not of black radicals but for the most part of Negro Baptist ministers." In August 1958, according to Martin Oppenheimer, the NAACP Youth Council of Oklahoma City initiated the first sit-in by predominantly black students, and during the next year and a half there were several sporadic and unpublicized sit-ins in other border states.[8] Mass action, of course, began only with the Greensboro, North Carolina sit-in on February

1, 1960 and the formation of SNCC the following April.

Among white radicals the most significant political activity in the years 1956-1960 was a series of initiatives by pacifists grouped around A. J. Muste. Other leaders were Bayard Rustin, later coordinator of the March on Washington for Jobs and Freedom in August 1963, and David Dellinger, subsequently chairman of the National Mobilization Committee Against The War In Vietnam, which organized the Pentagon confrontation of October 1967. These men were involved in the creation of the Committee for Nonviolent Action (CNVA) in 1957, the 1958 voyage of the vessel *Golden Rule* into the forbidden nuclear testing zone of the Western Pacific, and a nonviolent "invasion" of the Omaha, Nebraska missile base in 1959.

Miniscule when compared with the marches and confrontations of the following decade, these political skirmishes of the late 1950's nonetheless helped to dispel the fear and apathy left behind by McCarthyism. Meantime New Left ideas were making their way to the United States from Europe, and C. Wright Mills, Paul Goodman, and William Appleman Williams were publishing their most influential books (*The Power Elite* and *Growing Up Absurd*, 1956; *The Tragedy Of American Diplomacy*, 1959). By the time the American New Left emerged as a political force in the early 1960's it was possible to speak, if not of a New Left ideology, at least of certain well-defined New Left intellectual attitudes. Such essays as Mills' "Letter to the New Left," Sartre's "Ideology and Revolution," or Che Guevara's "We Are Practical Revolutionaries," all three published in 1960 by the new radical journal *Studies on the Left*, exhibit common themes which have continued to characterize New Left thought.

The most important of these themes might be termed utopian activism. Mills expresses it in the first document in this volume, his "Letter to the New Left," which ends with a hymn of praise to young radicals the world over who, in the face of the pessimism of theorists, nevertheless act:

"But it's just some kind of moral upsurge, isn't it?" Correct. But under it: no apathy. Much of it is direct non-violent action, and it seems to be working, here and there. Now we must learn from their practice and work out with them new forms of action.

"But it's all so ambiguous. Turkey for instance. Cuba, for instance." [Mills refers to the victory of the Cuban Revolution in January 1959, and the overthrow of the Menderes government in Turkey in April 1960.] Of course it is; history making is always ambiguous; wait a bit; in the meantime, *help* them to focus their moral upsurge in less ambiguous political ways; work out with them the ideologies, the strategies, the theories that will help them consolidate their efforts: new theories of structural changes of and by human societies in our epoch.

"But it's utopian, after all, isn't it?" No — not in the sense you mean. Whatever else it may be, it's not that. . . .

In another essay in this volume, Howard Zinn defends New Left activism with equal eloquence:

> In an era when it is easy to feel helpless, we need the Existentialist emphasis on our freedom to act. The Marxist-Existentialist debate on freedom and determinism seems to me to be an empty one — an academic one. To stress our freedom, is not the result of ignorance that we do have a history, that we do have an oppressive environment. But knowing of these pressures on us, we should be existentially aware that there is enormous indeterminacy in the combat between us and the obstacles all around. We never know exactly the depth or shallowness of the resistance to our actions — until we act. We never know exactly what effect we will have. Our actions may lead to nothing except changing ourselves and that is something. They may have a tiny cumulative effect, along with a thousand other actions. They may also explode. . . .[9]

The actions which created the New Left were just such unpredictable explosions: a Montgomery seamstress refusing to go to the back of the bus; Hungarian workers hurling bricks at Soviet tanks; a handful of Cuban exiles embarking for revolution in a fishing boat; four black students sitting down in a lunch counter. Little wonder that New Left theorists protested against theories in which (in the words of Edward Thompson of England) "events seemed to will men, not men events" or which presented the human condition (in the words of Jean-Paul Sartre) "as if it were smothered in this world by inflexible laws."[10] The commitment to action, in the knowledge that the consequences of action can never be fully predicted in advance, has survived all changes in political fashion and remains the single most characteristic element in the thought-world of the New Left. Overseas, one finds it both in the Marxist Che Guevara, observing that the influence of *Das Kapital* "to a certain extent obscure[s] the objective fact that it is men who are the actors on the stage of

history," and in the anarchist Daniel Cohn-Bendit, defining the
task of a political vanguard as "to light the first fuse and make
the first breakthrough" by exemplary acts.[11] In the United States,
the existential mood is still equally evident in the rhetoric of the
nonviolent draft resister, David Harris, or in these words of Huey
Newton, Minister of Defense of the Black Panther Party:

> The large majority of black people are either illiterate or semi-literate.
> They don't read. They need activity to follow. . . . The same thing
> happened in Cuba where it was necessary for twelve men with a leadership
> of Che and Fidel to take to the hills and then attack the corrupt ad-
> ministration. . . . They could have leafleted the community and they
> could have written books, but the people would not respond. They had
> to act and the people could see and hear about it and therefore become
> educated on how to respond to oppression.
> In this country black revolutionaries have to set an example.[12]

Perhaps the New Left required an incubation period from 1956
to 1960 precisely because it was in such large measure neither the
implementation of a preconceived theory nor a response to material
deprivation, but an improvised act of will. In America during
those years the "beat" writings of Jack Kerouac and Allen Gins-
berg helped young people to take the first groping steps toward a
psychological freedom from convention which, in 1960, suddenly
found political expression.

II

The years after 1960 are crowded so thickly with events that
any summary seems arbitrary. Particularly dangerous are general-
izations about the collective state of mind of the Movement, or
any part of it, at a particular moment. Often the leadership of an
organization is composed of old members with a sophisticated
(even over-sophisticated) analysis which the majority of newer
members lack. As a result, it may appear to an observer that over
a period of time the organization as a whole is forever re-learning
the same lessons. Consider internationalism. Early SDS members
could hardly have been unaware of radical movements in other
countries. The Sharpesville massacre, the Aldermaston march,
student overthrow of the governments of Turkey and Korea, mass
visitation by American students to revolutionary Cuba, and the
publication of Mills' *Listen, Yankee!* all occurred the year SDS

was founded. Nor is it accurate to say that SDS lacked awareness of American imperialism at the time it called for the first mass protest against the Vietnam War in April 1965: shortly before that demonstration, SDS also sponsored a sit-in at the Chase Manhattan Bank in New York City to protest the bank's investments in South Africa. What is true, nonetheless, is that many of the students who joined SDS after it launched the Vietnam protest initially opposed the war as a phenomenon in isolation, and became conscious of the imperialist context for the war only, say, when they read Carl Oglesby's *Containment And Change*, published in the spring of 1966. Thus internationalism was a state of consciousness which had to be repeatedly achieved. (It is also true, of course, that the content of internationalism has itself changed; a sense of solidarity with Lord Russell's Committee for Nuclear Disarmament has developed into a sense of solidarity with the National Liberation Front. The intellectual development of the Movement resembles neither a straight line nor a circle, but a spiral.)

James O'Brien has boldly attempted a periodization of New Left history from 1960 to 1968. His scheme is as follows:

First was a period in the early 1960s when liberal issues were dominant: segregated public accommodations, nuclear testing, the House Committee on Un-American Activities, and scattered violations of academic freedom. This was a period above all of single-issue movements and a pervasive mistrust of political ideologies. The largest student protest organization was the Student Peace Union, which was so closely identified with the issue of nuclear testing that it almost entirely collapsed after the signing of a limited test-ban treaty in 1963.

Then came a period, perhaps roughly delineated by the years 1964 and 1965, when the issue of participatory democracy came to the fore in the new radical movement. SNCC and SDS emerged as the two most vital groups, and both of them put great stress on building a movement that would give ordinary people a real voice in the decision-making process. The Federal Government's liberal bureaucracy, as typified by the Justice Department and the War on Poverty, was viewed with increasing impatience and distrust. The new radicals came to regard the liberal style as a series of back-room deals among "leaders," in which decisions were made without the participation of the governed.

The third phase was one which lasted for about a year after the intensification of the Vietnam War in early 1965. At this time the War itself, rather than the Draft or overall US foreign policy, was the focus for radical activity. . . .

The fourth phase is one which may be dated from the spring and early summer of 1966, when SNCC formulated the Black Power concept and campus sit-ins took place against the furnishing of draft boards with class rank information. During this period . . . student radicals have come to feel, as Greg Calvert has expressed it, that they are engaged in an effort to liberate themselves through an overall transformation of society.[13]

This summary could probably be improved by distinguishing more clearly between the experiences of the white and black movements. The development of the white movement typically followed that of the black movement with a lag of one or two years. Thus SNCC turned its attention to off-campus community organizing in the fall of 1961, when it decided to shift emphasis from student sit-ins against social segregation to voter registration in southwest Georgia and Mississippi; SDS initiated the comparable Economic Research and Action Project (ERAP) in 1963-1964. Again, the SNCC staff decided to support draft resistance in December 1965, the SDS National Council following a year later in December 1966. And the Democratic Convention of 1964 represented a watershed or dividing line in the development of the black New Left which the white Left reached, perhaps, only at the next convention four years later.

From 1960 to 1964 most black activists sought allies in the white community so that full integration into American society might be achieved by peaceful means. After 1964 black radicals sought allies in the revolutionary movements of the Third World so that a socialist transformation of American society might be achieved by any means necessary. The Mississippi Freedom Summer and Democratic Convention of 1964 symbolized the failure of white allies to produce when push came to shove.[14] A half year later came the bombing of North Vietnam and the assassination of Malcolm X; a year later, the Watts rebellion. In the spring of 1966, SNCC elected a new chairman, Stokely Carmichael, who popularized the ideas of Malcolm as Black Power. The next summer, 1967, Carmichael enacted his own version of Malcolm's trip to the Near East and Africa by traveling to Havana and Hanoi.

The white New Left, too, became disillusioned with white liberalism, but more slowly and ambivalently. The first eight years of the existence of SDS coincided with Democratic administrations in Washington. Many a hard-core Leninist of 1968 had wondered about joining the Peace Corps in 1961 and cried when John Kennedy was killed in 1963. When early hopes of quick advance toward racial equality and international peace began to fade, the white New Left, again taking a cue from Mills,[15] began to denounce the "corporate liberalism" which covered the sordid quest for power and profit with liberal rhetoric.

Carl Oglesby, then president of SDS, put it this way to an anti-war demonstration in Washington, D. C. late in 1965:

> We are here to protest against a growing war. Since it is a very bad war, we acquire the habit of thinking that it must be caused by very bad men. But we only conceal reality, I think, to denounce on such grounds the menacing coalition of industrial and military power, or the brutality of the blitzkrieg we are waging against Vietnam, or the ominous signs around us that heresy may soon no longer be permitted. We must simply observe, and quite plainly say, that this coalition, this blitzkrieg, and this demand for acquiescence are creatures, all of them, of a government that since 1932 has considered itself to be fundamentally *liberal*.

Corporate liberalism, Oglesby went on, justifies corporate exploitation. "It performs for the corporate state a function quite like what the Church once performed for the feudal state. It seeks to justify its burdens and protect it from change."[16]

Corporate liberalism, then, came to be understood by white radicals as an instrument of mystification, which solicits the oppressed to accept their oppression willingly because oppression describes itself as freedom. Accordingly, the celebrated New Left revolt against authority is especially a revolt against paternalistic, indirect authority which hides the hand of power in the glove of verbal idealism. Black Power was the result of the discovery of this hypocrisy in the area of race relations, where talk of "progress" concealed unenforced laws and court decisions, and an unchanging relationship of the economic power of blacks to that of whites. It was a similar recognition concerning foreign policy which, as Oglesby said in Washington, "broke my liberal heart."

The white New Left discovered corporate liberalism not only in the oppression of American blacks and Vietnamese guerrillas, but in their own lives as well. Educational institutions at all levels were perceived as part of the system. At universities, Mario Savio declared, "students are permitted to talk all they want so long as their speech has no consequences."[17] In primary and secondary schools, Goodman, John Holt and A. S. Neill argued, "progressive educators" had abandoned overt coercion only to substitute for it (in Holt's words) "the idea of painless, non-threatening coercion."[18]

As white students began to be drafted for Vietnam in 1966 and 1967, recognition grew that the Selective Service System not only oppressed the young men it conscripted but also "channeled" those not drafted into occupations considered most important by the government. Here again was the experience of veiled coercion, which in this instance the government itself was brazen enough to describe as "pressurized guidance" and "the American or indirect way of achieving what is done by direction in foreign countries where choice is not permitted."[19] Understandably the Movement began to wonder whether its own protest activity was part of a process which kept it under control. In *One-Dimensional Man*, Herbert Marcuse suggested that traditional forms of protest are "perhaps even dangerous because they preserve the illusion of popular sovereignty."[20]

A final area of life in which the white movement, as of early 1969, was uncovering concealed oppression, was the relationship between men and women. A women's liberation movement emerged to denounce male chauvinism not only in the larger society but among radicals, too.

As the Democratic Convention of 1964 signified a turning-point in the development of the black New Left, so the Democratic Convention of 1968 was the high-water mark of the white New Left's endeavor to expose corporate liberalism. But the transition from liberal optimism to a more militant, sophisticated radicalism has been harder for whites than for blacks. Black radicals readily reinterpreted "participatory democracy" to mean control of black communities by the black people who live in them. The transition from the rhetoric of Martin Luther King to the rhetoric of Malcolm was effected without losing the dimension of fraternal solidarity: organizers who spoke before 1964 of an integrated "blessed community" now excluded white people and called one another "soul brother." Among white radicals it was different. As participatory democracy, like nonviolence, came to seem the product of a naive early stage of protest before the magnitude of the Movement's task was fully recognized, white radicals drifted back toward the political style of the Old Left.

Thus the tendency in the second half of the 1960s was away from the distinctive atmosphere of humor, emotional expressiveness, experimentation, and (as it seemed to some) chaos, which had characterized the early years of the white New Left. Decision-making by consensus gave way to caucusing, factional polemics, and voting. Those who sought to preserve the older atmosphere often became a-political, often with the help of drugs. Especially after the entry into SDS of the youth contingent of the Marxist Progressive Labor Party, in the spring of 1966, a split gradually widened between "political" activists who usually stayed in SDS, and "moral" activists who typically left SDS to start new groups, focussed on draft resistance.

The disunity of the white New Left is the more disturbing because of the new danger of rightwing repression. It seems to me that American New Left theory makes the implicit assumption that capitalism in the United States will not turn to overt authoritarianism. It overlooks the possibility that the very success of the New Left in unmasking corporate liberalism, the very growth of a serious internal opposition, may change the character of the situation and force upon the governing class a felt need for more rigorous controls. Like black radicals in 1965, white radicals in 1969 must find ways to cope with an oppression greater than they had supposed to exist.

III

Whatever the future holds for the New Left in the United States, it will deserve to be remembered. In the century of Auschwitz, Hiroshima, and the Moscow purges, in the midst of the most powerful society in the history of the world, young men and women found the courage to resist. As Camus says at the beginning of *The Rebel*, this "no" implies a "yes," the affirmation of a limit indicates that there is something this side of that limit which is precious and to be guarded.

In the writings collected in the following pages the "yes" of the New Left is given many names: participatory democracy, anarcho-syndicalism, workers' control, community. Elsewhere in the literature of the Movement it has still other names. Marcuse speaks of liberated reason, Fanon of an end to crimes "committed in the heart of man," Guevara of man as "an unfinished product."

An attractive aspect of the American New Left is that it has found its own idiomatic, understated form for these worldwide ideas. Its history is summarized in the words of its favorite buttons: "There's a change gonna come"; "Let the people decide"; "Resist"; "Join us."

Notes

[1] A helpful chronology of events in the history of the New Left through the end of 1965 may be found in *The New Radicals: A Report With Documents*, ed. Paul Jacobs and Saul Landau (New York, 1966). James P. O'Brien provides a very full bibliography in three articles in *Radical America*, May–June 1968, pp. 1–25; Sept.–Oct. 1968, pp. 1–22; Nov.–Dec. 1968, pp. 28–43.

[2] For the story of the black New Left as told by four participant observers, see Howard Zinn, *SNCC: The New Abolitionists* (Boston, 1964); Stokely Carmichael and Charles V. Hamilton, *Black Power: The Politics Of Liberation In America* (New York, 1967), chapters four and five; Vincent Harding, "Black Radicalism: The Road From Montgomery," in *Dissent: Explorations In The History Of American Radicalism*, ed. Alfred F. Young (De Kalb, Illinois; 1968), pp. 321–354.

[3] Regis Debray, "Revolution In The Revolution? Armed Struggle And Political Struggle In Latin America," trans. Bobbye Ortiz, *Monthly Review*, July–August 1967, p. 16. In this as in so much else Che Guevara set an example. He began his *Reminiscences Of The Cuban Revolutionary War*, trans. Victoria Ortiz (New York and London, 1968) with the word (p. 29): "For a long time we have wanted to write a history of our Revolution which would encompass all its many facets and aspects. Many of the leaders of the Revolution have often privately or publicly expressed their desire to write such a history, but the tasks are many, the years pass, and the memory of the insurrection is dissolving in the past. . . ."

[4] Jack Newfield, *A Prophetic Minority* (New York, 1966), is most valuable when dealing with aspects of the early history of SDS which Newfield himself experienced. *The New Student Left: An Anthology*, ed. Mitchell Cohen and Dennis Hale (Boston, 1966), is important in preserving a number of early position papers, but one journal (*The Activist*) is over-represented and the experiential context for these documents is not provided. Illustrative of the kind of history are Richard Rothstein, "ERAP: Evolution Of The Organizers," *Radical America*, March–April 1968, pp. 1–18, a document which appears in slightly revised form in the present volume, and C. Clark Kissinger, "Starting In '60 Or From SLID To Resistance," *New Left Notes*, June 10–July 8, 1968.

[5] In the following paragraphs, and in portions of the introduction dealing with the New Left's philosophy, I have drawn heavily on my "The New Left," an essay written for a forthcoming volume of the Papers of the American Academy of Political and Social Science.

[6] Articles in *L'Express*, November 9, 1956 and *Les Temps Modernes*, November 1956–January 1957, quoted in Michel-Antoine Burnier, *Choice Of Action: The French Existentialists In Politics* (New York, 1968), pp. 104–107.

[7] K. S. Karol, "Two Years Of The Cultural Revolution," in *The Socialist Register 1968*, ed. Ralph Miliband and John Saville (New York, 1968), p. 60.

[8] Harding, *op. cit.*, p. 327; Martin Oppenheimer, "The Southern Student Movement: Year I," *The Journal Of Negro Education*, Fall 1964, pp. 396–398.

[9] It goes without saying that an immense literature has arisen concerning the relationship between what I have called the "utopian activism" of the New Left, and Marxism. Two thoughtful comments on the question are Gabriel Kolko, "The Decline Of American Radicalism In The Twentieth

Century," *Studies On The Left*, September–October 1966, pp. 9–26, and Leo Huberman and Paul M. Sweezy, "Lessons Of Soviet Experience," *Monthly Review*, November 1967, pp. 9–21.

10 Edward P. Thompson, "Outside The Whale," in *Out Of Apathy* (London, 1960), p. 184; Jean-Paul Sartre, "Ideology And Revolution," in *Sartre On Cuba* (New York, 1961), p. 148. Mills' "Letter to the New Left" was a response to the publication of *Out Of Apathy*.

11 "On The Budgetary System Of Financing" [1964], in *Venceremos! The Speeches And Writings Of Ernesto Che Guevara*, ed. John Gerassi (New York, 1968), p. 293; interview between Jean-Paul Sartre and Daniel Cohn-Bendit, quoted from *Le Nouvel Observateur*, May 20, 1968, by Liberation News Service, May 30, 1968.

12 Interview with Huey Newton, *The Movement*, August 1968.

13 O'Brien, "The New Left, 1967–68," *Radical America*, November–December 1968, pp. 42–43.

14 See Harding, *op. cit.*, pp. 338–339, and Carmichael and Hamilton, *op. cit.*, chapter four.

15 In the next-to-last chapter of *The Power Elite*, on "The Conservative Mood," as well as in his "Letter to the New Left," Mills described the use of liberal rhetoric to defend conservative reality.

16 Speech of November 27, 1965, *The New Radicals*, pp. 258, 265.

17 Speech on the steps of Sproul Hall, c. December 1964, *ibid.*, p. 232. Sometimes the de-mystifiers are themselves bemused. Witness the fact that the foreword to the only collection of New Left writing edited by student radicals themselves, published in 1966, illustrates the mood of radical youth with a long quotation from a commencement address by — President Grayson Kirk of Columbia University! (*The New Student Left*, viii–ix.)

18 John Holt, *How Children Fail* (New York, 1964), p. 179.

19 The quoted phrases are from a Selective Service System memoradum, withdrawn after its discovery by the New Left; the memorandum is reproduced in *Ramparts*, December 1967.

20 Herbert Marcuse, *One-Dimensional Man: Studies In The Ideology Of Advanced Industrial Society* (Boston, 1956), pp. xii, 256.

I

NEW LEFT THEORY

LETTER TO THE NEW LEFT

C. WRIGHT MILLS

When I settle down to write to you, I feel somehow "freer" than usual. The reason, I suppose, is that most of the time I am writing for people whose ambiguities and values I imagine to be rather different from mine; but with you, I feel enough in common to allow us "to get on with it" in more positive ways. Reading your book, *Out of Apathy*, prompts me to write to you about several problems I think we now face. On none of these can I hope to be definitive; I only want to raise a few questions.

It is no exaggeration to say that since the end of World War II in Britain and the United States smug conservatives, tired liberals and disillusioned radicals have carried on a weary discourse in which issues are blurred and potential debate muted; the sickness of complacency has prevailed, the bi-partisan banality flourished. There is no need — after your book — to explain again why all this has come about among "people in general" in the NATO countries; but it may be worth while to examine one style of cultural work that is in effect an intellectual celebration of apathy.

Many intellectual fashions, of course, do just that; they stand in the way of a release of the imagination — about the cold war, the Soviet bloc, the politics of peace, about any new beginnings at home and abroad. But the fashion I have in mind is the weariness of many NATO intellectuals with what they call "ideology," and their proclamation of "the end of ideology." So far as I know, this began in the mid-fifties, mainly in intellectual circles more or less associated with the Congress for Cultural Freedom and the magazine *Encounter*. Reports on the Milan Conference of 1955 heralded it; since then, many cultural gossips have taken it up as a posture and an unexamined slogan. Does it amount to anything?

Its common denominator is not liberalism as a political philosophy, but the liberal rhetoric, become formal and sophisticated and used as an uncriticized weapon with which to attack Marxism. In the approved style, various of the elements of this rhetoric appear simply as snobbish assumptions. Its sophistication is one of tone rather than of ideas: in it, the *New Yorker* style of reportage has become politically triumphant. The disclosure of fact — set forth in a bright-faced or in a dead-pan manner — is the rule. The facts are duly weighed, carefully balanced, always hedged. Their power to outrage, their power truly to enlighten in a political way, their power to aid decision, even their power to clarify some situation — all that is blunted or destroyed.

So reasoning collapses into reasonableness. By the more naive and snobbish celebrants of complacency, arguments and facts of a displeasing kind are simply ignored; by the more knowing, they are duly recognized, but they are neither connected with one another nor related to any general view. Acknowledged in a scattered way, they are never put together: to do so is to risk being called, curiously enough, "one-sided."

This refusal to relate isolated facts and fragmentary comment with the changing institutions of society makes it impossible to understand the structural realities which these facts might reveal; the longer-run trends of which they might be tokens. In brief, fact and idea are isolated, so the real questions are not even raised, analysis of the meanings of fact not even begun.

Practitioners of the no-more-ideology school do of course smuggle in general ideas under the guise of reportage, by intellectual gossip, and by their selection of the notions they handle. Ultimately, the end-of-ideology is based upon a disillusionment with any real commitment to socialism in any recognisable form. *That* is the only "ideology" that has really ended for these writers. But with its ending, *all* ideology, they think, has ended. *That* ideology they talk about: their own ideological assumptions, they do not.

Underneath this style of observation and comment there is the assumption that in the West there are no more real issues or even problems of great seriousness. The mixed economy plus the welfare state plus prosperity — that is the formula. US capitalism will continue to be workable; the welfare state will continue along the road to ever greater justice. In the meantime, things everywhere are very complex, let us not be careless, there are great risks . . .

This posture — one of "false consciousness" if there ever was one — stands in the way, I think, of considering with any chances of success what may be happening in the world.

First and above all, it does rest upon a simple provincialism. If the phrase "the end of ideology" has any meaning at all, it pertains to self-selected circles of intellectuals in the richer countries. It is in fact merely their own self-image. The total population of these countries is a fraction of mankind; the period during which such a posture has been assumed is very short indeed. To speak in such terms of much of Latin America, Africa, Asia, the Soviet bloc is merely ludicrous. Anyone who stands in front of audiences — intellectual or mass — in any of these places and talks in such terms will merely be shrugged off (if the audience is polite) or laughed at out loud (if the audience is more candid and knowledgeable). The end-of-ideology is a slogan of complacency, circulating among the prematurely middle-aged, centered in the present, and in the rich Western societies. In the final analysis, it also rests upon a disbelief in the shaping by men of their own futures — as history and as biography. It is a consensus of a few provincials about their own immediate and provincial position.

Second, the end-of-ideology is of course itself an ideology — a fragmentary one, to be sure, and perhaps more a mood. The end-of-ideology is in reality the ideology of an ending: the ending of political reflection itself as a public fact. It is a weary know-it-all justification — by tone of voice rather than by explicit argument — of the cultural and political default of the NATO intellectuals.

All this is just the sort of thing that I at least have always objected to, and do object to, in the "socialist realism" of the Soviet Union.

There too, criticism of milieux are of course permitted — but they are not to be connected with criticism of the structure itself: one may not question "the system." There are no "antagonistic contradictions."

There too, in novels and plays, criticisms of characters, even of party members, are permitted — but they must be displayed as "shocking exceptions": they must be seen as survivals from the old order, not as systematic products of the new.

There too, pessimism is permitted — but only episodically and only within the context of the big optimism: the tendency is to confuse any systematic or structural criticism with pessimism itself. So they admit criticisms, first of this and then of that: but engulf them all by the long-run historical optimism about the system as a whole and the goals proclaimed by its leaders.

I neither want nor need to overstress the parallel, yet in a recent series of interviews in the Soviet Union concerning socialist realism I was very much struck by it. In Uzbekistan and Georgia as well as in Russia, I kept writing notes to myself, at the end of recorded interviews: "This man talks in a style just like Arthur Schlesinger Jr." "Surely this fellow's the counterpart of Daniel Bell, except not so — what shall I say? — so gossipy; and certainly neither so petty nor so vulgar as the more envious status-climbers. Perhaps this is because here they are not thrown into such a competitive status-panic about the ancient and obfuscating British models of prestige." The would-be enders of ideology, I kept thinking, "are they not the self-coordinated, or better the fashion-coordinated, socialist realists of the NATO world?" And: "Check this carefully with the files of *Encounter* and *The Reporter*." I have now done so; it's the same kind of . . . thing.

Certainly there are many differences — above all, the fact that socialist realism is part of an official line; the end-of-ideology is self-managed. But the differences one knows. It is more useful to stress the parallels — and the generic fact that both of these postures stand opposed to radical criticisms of their respective societies.

In the Soviet Union, only political authorities at the top — or securely on their way up there — can seriously tamper with structural questions and ideological lines. These authorities, of course, are much more likely to be intellectuals (in one or another sense of the word — say a man who actually writes his own speeches) then are American politicians (about the British, you would know better than I). Moreover, such Soviet authorities, since the death of Stalin, *have* begun to tamper quite seriously with structural questions and basic ideology — although for reasons peculiar to the tight and official joining of culture and politics in their set-up, they must try to disguise this fact.

The end-of-ideology is very largely a mechanical reaction — not a creative response — to the ideology of Stalinism. As such it takes from its opponent something of its inner quality. What does it all mean? That these people have become aware of the uselessness of Vulgar Marxism, but not yet aware of the uselessness of the liberal rhetoric.

But the most immediately important thing about the "end of ideology" is that it *is* merely a fashion, and fashions change.

Already this one is on its way out. Even a few Diehard Anti-Stalinists are showing signs of a reappraisal of their own past views; some are even beginning to recognize publicly that Stalin himself no longer runs the Soviet party and state. They begin to see the poverty of their comfortable ideas as they come to confront Khrushchev's Russia.

We who have been consistently radical in the moral terms of our work throughout the post war period are often amused nowadays that various writers — sensing another shift in fashion — begin to call upon intellectuals to work once more in ways that are politically explicit. But we shouldn't be merely amused — we ought to try to make their shift more than a fashion change.

The end-of-ideology is on the way out because it stands for the refusal to work out an explicit political philosophy. And alert men everywhere today do feel the need of such a philosophy. What we should do is to continue directly to confront this need. In doing so, it may be useful to keep in mind that to have a working political philosophy means to have a philosophy that enables you to work. And for that, at least four kinds of work are needed, each of them at once intellectual and political.

In these terms, think — for a moment longer — of the end-of-ideology:

1. It is a kindergarten fact that any political reflection that is of possible public significance is *ideological:* in its terms, policies, institutions, men of power are criticized or approved. In this respect, the end-of-ideology stands, negatively, for the attempt to withdraw oneself and one's work from political relevance; positively, it is an ideology of political complacency which seems the only way now open for many writers to acquiesce in or to justify the *status quo.*

2. So far as orienting *theories* of societies and of history are concerned, the end-of-ideology stands for, and presumably stands upon, a fetishism of empiricism: more academically, upon a pretentious methodology used to state the trivialities about unimportant social areas; more essayistically, upon a naive journalistic empiricism — which I have already characterized above — and upon a cultural gossip in which "answers" to the vital and pivotal issues are merely assumed. Thus political bias masquerades as epistemological excellence, and there are no orienting theories.

3. So far as the *historic agency of change* is concerned, the end-of-ideology stands upon the identification of such agencies with

going institutions; perhaps upon the piecemeal reform, but never upon the search for agencies that might be used or that might themselves make for a structural change of society. The problem of agency is never posed as a problem to solve, as our problem. Instead there is talk of the need to be pragmatic, flexible, open. Surely all this has already been adequately dealt with: such a view makes sense politically only if the blind drift of human affairs is in general beneficent.

4. So far as political and human *ideals* are concerned, the end-of-ideology stands for a denial of their relevance — except as abstract ikons. Merely to hold such ideals seriously is in this view "utopian."

But enough. Where do *we* stand on each of these four aspects of political philosophy? Various of us are of course at work on each of them, and all of us are generally aware of our needs in regard to each. As for the articulation of ideals: there I think your magazines have done their best work so far. That is *your* meaning — is it not? — of the emphasis upon cultural affairs. As for ideological analysis, and the rhetoric with which to carry it out: I don't think any of us are nearly good enough, but that will come with further advance on the two fronts where we are weakest: theories of society, history, human nature; and the major problem — ideas about the historical agencies of structural change.

We have frequently been told by an assorted variety of dead-end people that the meanings of Left and Right are now liquidated, by history and by reason. I think we should answer them in some such way as this:

The Right, among other things, means — what you are doing, celebrating society as it is, a going concern. Left means, or ought to mean, just the opposite. It means: structural criticism and reportage and theories of society, which at some point or another are focused politically as demands and programs. These criticisms, demands, theories, programs are guided morally by the humanist and secular idea of Western civilization — above all, reason and freedom and justice. "To be Left" means to connect up cultural with political criticism, and both with demands and programs. And it means all this inside *every* country of the world.

Only one more point of definition: absence of public issues there may well be, but this is not due to any absence of problems or of contradictions, antagonistic and otherwise. Impersonal and structural changes have not eliminated problems or issues. Their absence from many discussions — that *is* an ideological condition, regulated in the first place by whether or not intellectuals detect and state problems as potential *issues* for probable publics, and as *troubles* for a variety of individuals. One indispensible means of such work on these central tasks is what can only be described as ideological analysis. To be actively Left, among other things, is to carry on just such analysis.

To take seriously the problem of the need for a political orientation is not of course to seek for A Fanatical and Apocalyptic Vision, for An Infallible and Monolithic Lever of Change, for Dogmatic Ideology, for A Startling New Rhetoric, for Treacherous Abstractions — and all the other bogeymen of the dead-enders. These are of course "the extremes," the straw men, the red herrings, used by our political enemies as the polar opposite of where they think they stand.

They tell us, for example, that ordinary men can't always be political "heroes." Who said they could? But keep looking around you; and why not search out the conditions of such heroism as men do and might display? They tell us we are too "impatient," that our "pretentious" theories are not well enough grounded. That is true, but neither are they trivial; why don't they get to work, refuting or grounding them? They tell us we "don't really understand" Russia — and China — today. That is true; we don't; neither do they; we are studying it. They tell us we are "ominous" in our formulations. That is true: we do have enough imagination to be frightened — and we don't have to hide it: we are not afraid we'll panic. They tell us "we are grinding axes." Of course we are: we do have, among other points of view, morally grounded ones; and we are aware of them. They tell us, in their wisdom, we don't understand that The Struggle is Without End. True: we want to change its form, its focus, its object.

We are frequently accused of being "utopian" — in our criticisms and in our proposals; and along with this, of basing our hopes for a New Left *politics* "merely on reason," or more concretely, upon the intelligentsia in its broadest sense.

There is truth in these charges. But must we not ask: what now is really meant by utopian? And: is not our utopianism a major source of our strength? "Utopian" nowadays I think refers to any criticism or proposal that transcends the up-close milieux of a scatter of individuals: the milieux which men and women can understand directly and which they can reasonably hope directly

to change. In this exact sense, our theoretical work is indeed
utopian — in my own case, at least, deliberately so. What needs
to be understood, and what needs to be changed, is not merely
first this and then that detail of some institution or policy. If there
is to be a politics of a New Left, what needs to be analysed is the
structure of institutions, the *foundation* of policies. In this sense,
both in its criticisms and in its proposals, our work is necessarily
structural — and so, *for us*, just now — utopian.

Which brings us face to face with the most important issue of
political reflection — and of political action — in our time: the
problem of the historical agency of change, of the social and
institutional means of structural change. There are several points
about this problem I would like to put to you.

First, the historic agencies of change for liberals of the capitalist
societies have been an array of voluntary associations, coming to a
political climax in a parliamentary or congressional system. For
socialists of almost all varieties, the historic agency has been the
working class — and later the peasantry; also parties and unions
variously composed of members of the working class or (to blur,
for now, a great problem) of political parties acting in its name —
"representing its interests."

I cannot avoid the view that in both cases, the historic agency
(in the advanced capitalist countries) has either collapsed or become most ambiguous: so far as structural change is concerned,
these don't seem to be at once available and effective as *our* agency
any more. I know this is a debatable point among us, and among
many others as well; I am by no means certain about it. But
surely the fact of it — if it be that — ought not to be taken as an
excuse for moaning and withdrawal (as it is by some of those who
have become involved with the end-of-ideology); it ought not to
be bypassed (as it is by many Soviet scholars and publicists, who
in their reflections upon the course of advanced capitalist societies
simply refuse to admit the political condition and attitudes of the
working class).

Is anything more certain than that in 1970 — indeed this time
next year — our situation will be quite different, and — the
chances are high — decisively so? But of course, that isn't saying
much. The seeming collapse of our historic agencies of change
ought to be taken as a problem, an issue, a trouble — in fact, as
the political problem which *we* must turn into issue and trouble.

Second, is it not obvious that when we talk about the collapse of agencies of change, we cannot seriously mean that such agencies do not exist. On the contrary, the means of history-making — of decision and of the enforcement of decision — have never in world history been so enlarged and so available to such small circles of men on both sides of The Curtains as they now are. My own conception of the shape of power — the theory of the power elite — I feel no need to argue here. This theory has been fortunate in its critics, from the most diverse points of political view, and I have learned from several of these critics. But I have not seen, as of this date, any analysis of the idea that causes me to modify any of its essential features.

The point that is immediately relevant does seem obvious: what is utopian for us is not at all utopian for the presidium of the Central Committee in Moscow, or the higher circles of the Presidency in Washington, or — recent events make evident — for the men of SAC and CIA. The historic agencies of change that have collapsed are those which were at least thought to be open to *the left* inside the advanced Western nations: those who have wished for structural changes of these societies. Many things follow from this obvious fact; of many of them, I am sure, we are not yet adequately aware.

Third, what I do not quite understand about some New Left writers is why they cling so mightily to "the working class" of the advanced capitalist societies as *the* historic agency, or even as the most important agency, in the face of the really impressive historical evidence that now stands against this expectation.

Such a labor metaphysic, I think, is a legacy from Victorian Marxism that is now quite unrealistic.

It is an historically specific idea that has been turned into an a-historical and unspecific hope.

The social and historical conditions under which industrial workers tend to become a-class-for-themselves, and a decisive political force, must be fully and precisely elaborated. There have been, there are, there will be such conditions; of course these conditions vary according to national social structure and the exact phase of their economic and political development. Of course we can't "write off the working class." But we must *study* all that, and freshly. Where labor exists as an agency, of course we must work with it, but we must not treat it as The Necessary Lever — as nice old Labor Gentlemen in your country and elsewhere tend to do.

Although I have not yet completed my own comparative studies of working classes, generally it would seem that only at certain (earlier) stages of industrialization, and in a political context of autocracy, etc., do wage-earners tend to become a class-for-them-selves, etc. The "etcs." mean that I can here merely raise the question.

It is with this problem of agency in mind that I have been study-ing, for several years now, the cultural apparatus, the intellectuals — as a possible, immediate, radical agency of change. For a long time, I was not much happier with this idea than were many of you; but it turns out now, in the spring of 1960, that it may be a very relevant idea indeed.

In the first place, is it not clear that if we try to be realistic in our utopianism — and that is no fruitless contradiction — a writer in our countries on the Left today *must* begin there? For that is what we are, that is where we stand.

In the second place, the problem of the intelligentsia is an ex-tremely complicated set of problems on which rather little factual work has been done. In doing this work, we must — above all — not confuse the problems of the intellectuals of West Europe and North America with those of the Soviet bloc or with those of the underdeveloped worlds. In each of the three major components of the world's social structure today, the character and the role of the intelligentsia is distinct and historically specific. Only by detailed comparative studies of them in all their human variety can we hope to understand any one of them.

In the third place, who is it that is getting fed up? Who is it that is getting disgusted with what Marx called "all the old crap"? Who is it that is thinking and acting in radical ways? All over the world — in the bloc, outside the bloc and in between — the an-swer's the same: it is the young intelligentsia.

I cannot resist copying out for you, with a few changes, some materials I've just prepared for a 1960 paperback edition of a book of mine on war:

"In the spring and early summer of 1960 — more of the returns from the American decision and default are coming in. In Turkey, after student riots, a military junta takes over the state, of late run by Communist Container Menderes. In South Korea too, students and others knock over the corrupt American-puppet regime of Syngman Rhee. In Cuba, a genuinely left-wing revolu-tion begins full scale economic reorganization — without the dom-ination of US corporations. Average age of its leaders: about 30 —

and certainly a revolution without any Labor As Agency. On Taiwan, the eight million Taiwanese under the American-imposed dictatorship of Chiang Kai-Shek, with his two million Chinese, grow increasingly restive. On Okinawa — a US military base — the people get their first chance since World War II ended to demonstrate against US seizure of their island: and some students take that chance, snake-dancing and chanting angrily to the visiting President: "Go home, go home — take away your missiles." (Don't worry, 12,000 US troops easily handled the generally grateful crowds; also the President was "spirited out the rear end of the United States compound" — and so by helicopter to the airport.) In Great Britain, from Aldermaston to London, young — but you were there. In Japan, weeks of student rioting succeed in rejecting the President's visit, jeopardise a new treaty with the USA, displace the big-business, pro-American Prime Minister, Kishi. And even in our own pleasant Southland, Negro and white students are — but let us keep that quiet: it really *is* disgraceful.

"That is by no means a complete list; that was yesterday; see today's newspaper. Tomorrow, in varying degree, the returns will be more evident. Will they be evident enough? They will have to be very obvious to attract real American attention: sweet complaints and the voice of reason — these are not enough. In the slum countries of the world today, what are they saying? The rich Americans, they pay attention only to violence — and to money. You don't care what they say, American? Good for you. Still, they may insist; things are no longer under the old control; you're not getting it straight, American: your country — it would seem — may well become the target of a world hatred the like of which the easy-going Americans have never dreamed. Neutralists and Pacifists and Unilateralists and that confusing variety of Leftists around the world — all those tens of millions of people, of course they are misguided, absolutely controlled by small conspiratorial groups of trouble-makers, under direct orders straight from Moscow and Peking. Diabolically omnipotent, it is *they* who create all this messy unrest. It is *they* who have given the tens of millions the absurd idea that they shouldn't want to remain, or to become, the seat of American nuclear bases — those gay little outposts of American civilization. So now they don't want U-2's on their territory; so now they want to contract out of the American military machine; they want to be neutral among the crazy big antagonists. And they don't want their own society to be militarized.

"But take heart, American: you won't have time to get really bored with your friends abroad: they won't be your friends much longer. You don't need *them*; it will all go away; don't let them confuse you."

Add to that: in the Soviet bloc, who is it that has been breaking out of apathy? It has been students and young professors and writers; it has been the young intelligentsia of Poland and Hungary, and of Russia too. Never mind that they've not won; never mind that there are other social and moral types among them. First of all, it has been these types. But the point is clear — isn't it?

Thats why we've got to study these new generations of intellectuals around the world as real live agencies of historic change. Forget Victorian Marxism, except whenever you need it; and read Lenin again (be careful) — Rosa Luxemburg, too.

"But it's just some kind of moral upsurge, isn't it?" Correct. But under it: no apathy. Much of it is direct non-violent action, and it seems to be working, here and there. Now we must learn from their practice and work out with them new forms of action.

"But it's all so ambiguous. Turkey for instance. Cuba, for instance." Of course it is; history-making is always ambiguous; wait a bit; in the meantime, *help* them to focus their moral upsurge in less ambiguous political ways; work out with them the ideologies, the strategies, the theories that will help them consolidate their efforts: new theories of structural changes of and by human societies in our epoch.

"But it's utopian, after all, isn't it?" No — not in the sense you mean. Whatever else it may be, it's not that: tell it to the students of Japan.

Isn't all this, isn't it something of what we are trying to mean by the phrase, "The New Left"? Let the old men ask sourly, "Out of Apathy — into what?" The Age of Complacency is ending. Let the old women complain wisely about "the end of ideology." We are beginning to move again.

Yours truly,

C. Wright Mills

CONSUMPTION: DOMESTIC IMPERIALISM

Dave Gilbert

Human history is a record of groups of men struggling to control their environment, in order to meet human needs — needs which are developed and defined in the context of that struggle, and which constantly change. Human needs change quantitatively: as population increases, a greater scale of production is required to sustain it. And they change qualitatively: the introduction of new technology creates a need for new kinds of tools, skills, services. The pressure of new needs creates a demand for new technology: new technology creates new needs.

Human activity is socially organized. The social organization of labor and the technical apparatus that men use to manipulate their environment comprise the notion of *production*. The *means of production* is the human labor and technical apparatus that men have at their disposal in the struggle to control their environment. The means of production changes historically; new tools and machines are introduced and human labor is consequently reorganized. Changes in the means of production lead to new social needs, to new forms of social organization and production, and to new forms of social stratification.

As feudalism develops into capitalism and the country/agricultural productive base develops into an urban/industrial base, the structure of society accordingly changes: a new class structure develops. For *class* most simply refers to who controls (and who does not control) the means of production in any historical situation. Class includes also the whole spectrum of differentiated social roles and differential access to power, both of which ultimately flow from control of means of production and concomitant division of labor (cf. Marx and Engels, *The German Ideology*).

26

Modern American capitalism fits this general historical model. But in one important area — the interaction of new technology and new needs — the historical process has been distorted. Instead of human needs providing the impetus for the development of new technology, the needs emerging from new technology are consciously manipulated to serve the survival needs of the capitalist system. This distortion is the result of a qualitative change in the means of production: the introduction of cybernated technology, which provides the basis for new forms of exploitation and which also creates historically new potentials for human liberation.

The Economic Dynamic of Modern Capitalism

In modern American capitalism, the control of most industries is in the hands of a few large corporations. This economic form of control is called *oligopoly*. Oligopolistic firms tend to eliminate price competition. Although historically price competition was largely responsible for the introduction of new technology, other incentives for technological development still remain. One: Intra-industry competition — technology is introduced to enhance profits and the size of the market share, within a given industry with a given price structure, by lowering costs through higher productivity. Two: Inter-industry competition — technology is introduced in order to expand into new markets through new products and processes produced at lower costs. Three: International competition — technology is introduced to compete for markets with other capitalist countries through higher productivity and innovation. Four: The cold war — technology is used to compete with rising productivity in the socialist countries and, at the same time, to secure the continuing loyalty of the domestic population by offering them a higher standard of living.

All these incentives allow for the *partial* development of technology. The long term trend of modern capitalism is towards automation and cybernation (cybernation is the automated control of automation). The *rate* of introduction of new technology under modern capitalism is far slower, in terms of human needs, than it ought to be, and in terms of what is *technologically* possible far slower than it need be. But full cybernation is not possible under the social form of capitalism.

For the nature of capitalist society inhibits the trend towards automation and cybernation. Introduction of new technology means greater productive capacity. When this increase in production is not met with a simultaneous increase in consumption, capitalism faces the threat of an *underconsumption* crisis. Because there is no social control over production and consumption, the corporations will retard the growth of productivity in order to avoid underconsumption. The tension between the need to introduce new technology (inter- and intra-industry competition, etc.) and the restrictions that the threat of underconsumption place on that need is a central contradiction of modern capitalism.

The Sources of Underconsumption

The cost structure of production in modern capitalism is highly vulnerable to the threat of underconsumption. A corporation employs new technology in order to increase productivity — lower costs per unit produced. Costs *per unit* decline as a function of total volume produced. If consumer demand slackens, machines cannot be laid off (as workers can be): machines are fixed, as opposed to flexible, costs. The more dependent production is on technology, as it tends to be, the greater proportion of fixed to flexible costs. A firm must cover basic fixed costs of production before it can start to realize profits; the breakeven point rises as a function of the introduction of new technology.

Harvard Business Review (Sept.–Oct. 1967, p. 8) puts it this way: "One of its [technology's] 'side effects' will be on costs. Costs inevitably become stickier and breakeven chart curves flatten out when capital is substituted for labor. As a result, business will have an even greater incentive to maintain continuously higher levels of output. . . ." What this clearly implies is that business has a great incentive to maintain continuously higher levels of *consumption*, for if output produced is not bought, profits evaporate.

But there is, under modern capitalism, an apparently irresolvable impediment to domestic consumption: *maldistribution of wealth*, which is a structural feature of modern capitalism for several reasons. 1. The accumulation of capital for investment is done privately. 2. Control over the means of production is based partially on private ownership (i.e. wealth). 3. Social privileges are partially realized through relative wealth. The maldistribution of wealth affects the economic structure of modern capitalism in two ways: 1. a disproportionate relationship of investment funds to consumption funds; and 2. inability to fully utilize consumption funds. The first problem results in what are called *underconsumption cycles*; the second in *discretionary income*.

Underconsumption Cycles

The goal of modern capitalism is profit. Profit, by and large, is made available for reinvestment, in order to achieve and maintain a competitive market position necessary to continue realizing profit (see the section on the economic dynamic of capitalism). The high proportion of the value of a product taken as profit is not available for workers' wages which, by and large, are devoted to consumption. The social structure and values of capitalism, then, result in a disproportionate income devoted to investment funds as opposed to consumption funds. Investment (purchase of machinery, new processes, research, etc.) is used to increase the production of consumer goods. Hence profitable utilization of investment funds is dependent on the level of consumption. But consumption, as stated above, is constricted by the high proportion of profit to wages. Hence a cycle of underconsumption tends to emerge. The inability to use investment funds leads to laying off workers in the production of machinery (producer goods). This in turn leads to a further slack in demand for consumer goods, which in turn leads to underutilization of investment funds, which leads to laying off workers . . . and so the cycle goes.

Discretionary Income

Secondly, under modern capitalism, the problem of maintaining and increasing sufficient consumer demand is aggravated by maldistribution of wealth within the consumer sphere. Maldistribution of wealth means that on one end of the spectrum there is a group of people with very low (or no) income; while on the other end there is a group of people with very high income. The group with high income has great consumer buying power; the group with low income has the least consumer buying power. But the low income group is under much more pressure to spend its *full* income — it must, simply to meet survival needs. The high income group is under no necessary pressure to spend its full income.

After survival needs have been met, it can choose to spend or to save. Over and above the survival level, it enjoys *discretionary income*. If people with discretionary income choose not to buy as many consumer goods as they potentially could, there is at least short term underconsumption.

Furthermore, discretionary income is rising. *Fortune's* (Dec. 1967) figures on discretionary income — defined as the sum of all family income above $7500 — indicate that it now constitutes about one third of all personal income. *Fortune* estimates that it will grow to about 37% by 1975. (Since the definition of discretionary income is somewhat arbitrary, these figures provide only general orders of magnitude and growth.)

Correlated with the growth of discretionary income is the increased proportion of durable goods (cars, household appliances, sports equipment) and luxuries on the consumer market. With these goods, a consumer has a good deal of leeway to defer consumption decisions by repairs, disregarding style changes, choosing to do without. The growth of discretionary income and the growth in the proportion of durable goods and luxuries relative to other consumer goods have served to make consumption very flexible.

Thus the general tendency is for production costs to become more and more rigid, while consumption becomes more flexible. As this tendency continues, the potential for economic crisis is clear. Under particular political-social circumstances, demand can contract violently (people can choose not to spend their discretionary income), while producers have very little leeway to respond, since they are committed to a structure of high fixed costs.

How Modern Capitalism Deals With Underconsumption

An interesting aspect of a potential underconsumption crisis is that Keynesian techniques are largely irrelevant. Measures to increase income (welfare, negative income tax, guaranteed minimum income) do not raise consumption and investment in a situation where a significant proportion of consumers have sufficient income but neither need nor want to spend it. Economic reforms are still available. The government can and does create demand *directly* (although most of the important "multiplier effect" would be lost in this situation) and can attempt limited redistribution of wealth. But as the potential magnitude of this sort of crisis grows, there are definite limits to what can be done within a capitalist structure. Relative maldistribution of wealth and the exploitation of labor is systemic to capitalism. It is necessary to maintain class privileges. Further, the type of social situation likely to precipitate such a crisis (e.g. wide-spread urban rioting) might well limit the government's flexibility.

In addition to limited redistribution of wealth and demand creation, modern capitalism deals with the problems of under-consumption through its policy of imperialism, both foreign and domestic. Foreign imperialism is becoming more and more a policy of extending markets: securing the investment and consumer potential in other countries. This policy holds true especially in Western Europe; the resultant political and social tensions give rise, for example, to the nationalistic politics of Gaullism. Even more impressive is American foreign policy of the sixties, which encourages internal economic growth in the Third World, both in order to improve market possibilities and to create a native bourgeoisie that serves as a bulwark against socialist revolution (i.e. stabilizes the investment and consumer markets, to use State Department jargon). In fact, securing markets and encouraging a certain kind of economic growth, while preventing revolution, is the essence of corporate liberal foreign policy. The meaning of Vietnam is underscored by the fact that the danger of under-consumption is heightened every time a successful socialist revolution cuts off another area from U.S. economic domination.

The other form of imperialism has to do with the ways capitalism deals with the problem of insufficient consumption domestically. First, capitalism has to make sure that a certain proportion of investment funds are used in ways other than increasing true productivity. Simply put, these funds are used to create new industries whose specific purpose is to create the desire to consume more. These industries include communications media that extend corporate influence and control to every sector of the population, and advertising that not only distorts and manipulates real needs, but also creates the desire for a quantitative increase in consumption. Similarly, funds invested in new technology are used to create waste and obsolescence: style changes, planned breakdown, gimmick products.

Paralleling the deflection of technological innovation into non-productive channels is the growth of the various industries that contribute to the management of demand. The way to insure

that demand does not fall below a certain level is to manipulate
and distort people's needs, to *make* them consume more and more
and more. Market research and advertising are the key demand-
managing industries, but others contribute — it is not an entire
accident that maxiskirts finally made it into the consumer market
the month after *Bonnie and Clyde* hit the movie houses. (The
fashion industry had been pushing maxiskirts unsuccessfully for
two years.)

But modern capitalism and its policy of imperialism have
aroused political responses which have the potential to destroy it.
The response to America's attempts to secure markets abroad is,
increasingly, the emergence of national liberation movements.
Similarly, waste production and the management of demand
(domestic imperialism) seems to be leading to the development of a
large-scale domestic movement (a New Left) reacting against
meaningless jobs and manipulative consumption. In fact, the
development of some of the industries which are key to the survival
of modern capitalism (e.g. mass media, mass education) themselves contain the roots of its potential destruction. For people —
especially the young and the blacks — are becoming more and
more aware of the gap between potential social wealth and the
reality of their own lives, whether in the ghetto, in the classroom,
or on the job.

Commodities and Men

In capitalist society, wealth is measured in terms of the accumulation of commodities (products), with money serving as the
universal commodity, the medium of exchange. In earlier periods
of history, products were directly consumed by the producers and
their overlords. Commodities are distinguished from non-com-
modities by the fact that commodities have a market (or exchange)
value, in terms of which they can be traded for other commodities
or for money. In a capitalist system, commodities include the
majority of *men*, since the majority of men must sell their labor
power on the market in order to live.

The more commodities men produce, the greater is man's control
over nature and the greater is the potential for human liberation.
But at the same time, every extension of commodities is a negation
of human freedom. The key to this contradiction is the position
of the majority of men as commodities. Men who sell their labor

power do not conceive, create and consume their own products for their own purposes. Rather, they produce according to the needs of the capitalists who hire them for the purpose of making profits. Thus, a worker confronts his own product not as an extension of himself and his control over his environment, but as an alien object outside himself. The more man produces, the greater the power of these alien objects. Moreover, capitalism constantly creates (*must* create) new needs and new products, thus extending this alien power over him. (Marx, *The Economic and Philosophical Manuscripts of 1844; Capital,* Vol. 1. Chap. 1.)

Under modern capitalism, the process of creating — or more accurately, the channeling into commodity form — of basic human needs has reached a qualitatively new phase. Of course the natural process of the extension of human needs with the overall development of society has continued. But the high productivity now possible with the introduction of automated technology, and the correspondingly shorter labor time required, has made cultural activity and other social needs — *non-commodity needs* — important, and increasingly important in proportion to purely material needs.

Simultaneously, the economic dynamic of modern capitalism, as discussed earlier, demands a constant rise in consumer (commodity) sales. Thus those who control production must consciously develop needs for specific commodities, in order to increase consumption. They must even create life styles defined by consumption, to assure that higher income levels don't permit sudden, capricious drops in demand. Leisure time becomes consumption time. Sports and culture are not extensions of human social activity, but are commodities for which we buy a $2 ticket, or enjoy at home via television (consumer durable good) while watching beer commercials and drinking beer.

The basis for creating and manipulating consumer needs is the use and redirection of real human needs, associating them with a given commodity. Thus the needs for sex, love, personal identity and creativity, etc., are used to sell products with which they have no necessary connection. Thus, not only do man's products become an alien power outside himself; at the same time, his own (socially formed) inner needs are turned against him, to make him desire those same alien products.

The logical extension of this process is man defined and delimited by the commodities outside himself. Man becomes defined by what he has, rather than what he is and does. A magazine ad announces: "Your clothes *are* you." Masculinity is a red convertible with a stick shift. Security is a house in the suburbs. Love is a warm blanket.

Exploitation, traditionally, has been defined as the difference between what a worker produces and what he receives. The difference goes to the person who bought the labor of the worker, in the form of profits, rents, etc. The quantitative aspect of a commodity's social value is derived from the amount of human labor that went into it. The costs of producing a given commodity, other than the direct application of human labor — things such as raw materials and machinery — are themselves products of labor. This notion of exploitation fitted the context of early industrial capitalism, where the direct material wealth associated with human labor could be fairly easily measured and thus the exploitation of the working class fairly accurately assessed.

Before attempting to reformulate exploitation in terms of modern conditions, it will be useful to distinguish carefully between *oppression* and exploitation — terms that have often been confused with each other. Exploitation refers to a class situation — the degree to which a man's labor is appropriated — under a given productive system. Oppression refers to the situation of a social domination in the context of the total environment, not simply to men's labor. How a man is oppressed can be seen by the difference in the conditions of his life relative to the conditions of the most privileged group in the society — the oppressors. The conditions of life include material wealth, physical environment, culture, etc. In a given society, the exploited and the oppressed are not identical, although they certainly overlap. Thus, in modern America, a technically skilled worker might be the most exploited (given his relative labor value), and a ghetto dweller the most oppressed (given the relative misery of the total conditions of his life). This distinction is important for any critique of society (e.g. this one) which attempts to include class conditions as well as environmental conditions within its scope.

The traditional approach to exploitation made sense when most of the commodities consumed by the working class went to the physical sustenance of the worker and his family according to minimal social conditions. The worker consumed in order that he continue to work. This was defined as the social reproduction of labor. But the pattern of working class consumption has changed significantly under modern capitalism. On one level, the growth and complexity of capitalist society has resulted in a rise in the cost of the social reproduction of labor (higher standard of living). Secondly, qualitatively new processes involving such things as a sixteen billion dollar advertising industry, planned obsolescence, and frequent style changes (to all of which a worker is of course subject) have assumed importance with respect to the notion of exploitation. These new processes, discussed earlier in connection with the management of demand, can be defined in relation to exploitation as *waste production*.

As described earlier, management of demand is crucial to the survival of modern capitalism. Waste production concomitant with the management of demand amplifies the notion of exploitation as appropriation of labor, and extends the notion of exploitation into the sphere of consumption. Here is how it works: part of a worker's labor goes into the production of waste. For example, a worker produces a light bulb. Some of his labor is utilized to make sure that the light bulb will burn out sooner than it should (planned obsolescence). Not only is that amount of his labor wasted; the worker will have to buy two, three, many light bulbs (instead of one that would last and last), thus helping to fulfill the capitalist system's need for people to consume, consume, consume.

The amount of time the worker expends on waste production is part of the social costs of production: the social costs of maintaining the irrational capitalist system which entails the necessity of constantly increasing consumption. Early industrial societies also had their share of the social costs of production (for example, expenditures for the state and defense). But these costs have been increased so drastically by modern capitalism that the quantitative change verges on a qualitative change: exploitation extends to the consumer sphere. Thus the notion of exploitation proper to modern capitalism must include not only the difference between what one produces and what one receives, but also the difference between what one ought to be able to produce (were it not for waste production) and what one ought to receive (enough, but not an addictively increasing enough). In short, exploitation under modern capitalism is the difference between potential social productivity and overall quality of life (including both work and consumption). This new and total form of exploitation is important in the way it has affected class structure, consciousness, and the potential for creating a new society in contemporary America.

Class, Constituency and Consciousness

The class structure of a society is based on men's relations to the means of production in a given historical period. The key aspects of these social relations are: 1. the control or non-control of the means of production; and 2. the expropriation of value (men's labor) — the dynamic of profits and exploitation. The means of production and the concomitant forms of exploitation are constantly changing, and with them, the class structure of society changes. Therefore, during the last half of the nineteenth century, with the emergence of factory labor and the early crude industrial plants, the industrial working class became potentially the most revolutionary class, because of its essential relation to production coupled with its being the most *exploited* group in the society. Yet the industrial working class always constituted a minority of the population.

For a class to develop revolutionary action, it must achieve a certain degree of class consciousness. Consciousness develops out of experience, life activity, which for the working class was primarily *direct* activity in production (directly productive work). And it was *shared* experience, based on a common relationship to the means of production. With the perception of common interests, political organization and revolutionary activity can follow.

In modern American capitalism, certain quantitative and qualitative changes have occurred within the class structure. These changes can be traced to the way technological change has affected the economic structure and the form of exploitation. Fundamentally, these changes have led to an alteration in the productive system itself. Production has become increasingly *socialized*. This means two things: 1. the extension of commodities into all spheres of human activity besides those directly connected with material needs (everything ranging from cultural and educational industries to defense); and 2. a restructuring of work because of the tremendous growth of jobs that no longer relate directly to material production (more and more jobs that have to do with the machines that turn out products rather than with products directly; there has been a huge increase in jobs that deal with the social aspects of production — e.g., accounting, advertising, social services).

The restructuring of work has produced a series of new contradictions in capitalism. First, there is the tendency toward increasing job specialization and fragmentation, for which technology is responsible, and which capitalism desires. Whereas the technological trend towards cybernation creates the *potential* for integrated (rather than alienated) jobs, and for the greater involvement of each person's work with the overall development and benefit of society. Secondly, it is technologically possible to eliminate the waste production which is created by the social irresponsibility of capitalism — waste production which stands in the way of the creative and meaningful work that we are taught (both in school and through corporate advertising) to seek.

Any examination of the American class structure must integrate these new contradictions. Because of the increasing socialization of production, the American ruling class not only is defined by those who control the means of production and directly profit from the labor of others, but also includes the people who control such non-productive sectors as education and communications. The changes in class structure in the working class and underclass — those who do not control the means of production and are not included in the nonproductive sectors which contribute to the maintenance of the capitalist system — have been more complicated.

The socialization of production which has led to a restructuring of the work force differentiates various strata within the American working class. The oldest and most recognizable of these strata is the *traditional working class*, which is still a crucial force in production and constitutes about 30% of the work force. This group works directly on production. Because the technological trend is toward automation and cybernation, the traditional working class will possibly diminish. But because of the internal contradictions of capitalism, automation is introduced at an uneven rate, allowing the traditional working class to survive and to play an important role.

The traditional working class, as well as other strata of the working class, has been affected by the rise in the domestic standard of living. They, as well as everyone else, feel the brunt of new forms of exploitation in their role as *consumers*. It is this fact more than anything else that can potentially link the traditional working class with other groups.

Since the other strata of the working class are more directly affected by the changes in the nature of *work*, they can be defined, for lack of a better term, as the *new working class*. This group can be subdivided into three kinds of work: technical work, human service work, and white-collar (middle sector) work.

Technical work: With the growth of technology and automation, more and more laborers work directly on machines, which in turn produce a product. Such jobs include inventing, designing, building, programming, repairing and supervising machines — jobs generally for technicians and engineers. Although workers of this type existed in the early stages of capitalism, they have by now become a special stratum because of their tremendous growth in numbers and their importance in the new technology. Although still a small percentage of the work force, it is the fastest growing sector.

There are several aspects of technical workers' experience that relate to political consciousness. Their high pay, relatively privileged positions, and possible promotion into management all militate against radical political consciousness. These factors, however, tend to diminish as technical workers come to constitute a larger percentage of the work force. On the other hand, their relatively great rate of exploitation (stemming from high labor value plus exploitation through waste consumption) enables them to perceive first hand the nature of waste production and could lead to radical consciousness. This radical consciousness is based on the perception of the gap between potential and reality: the central contradiction of capitalist production. The potential of modern technology in the service of creative and rational control of production includes the elimination of waste production and the possibility of integrated, creative work responsible for the development of the whole society. The reality of capitalist production is meaningless (if not destructive) and boring work, and the manipulated consumption of waste.

Human service work: With socialized capitalist production, more and more jobs are created that deal with people (including their physical environment and culture) as commodities. These jobs include teaching, social work, city planning, medicine, law, architecture, communications, and entertainment (which used to be called culture). Usually classified under the general rubric of professional work, the essential contradiction in these jobs has to do with the quality of life in America, with its manipulated passivity and misery. "Professionals" are turned against their clients;

to the extent that this is effective, service workers do not develop radical consciousness. The development of radical consciousness comes when a "professional" realizes that the system of which he is an instrument, and through which he victimizes his clients, is in fact victimizing him. A teacher, for example, realizes that his role in the educational system is the socialization — brutalization and channeling — of children into the "American way of life." The teacher wants to be a creative educator; he is in fact a cop in the classroom. The recognition of this contradiction can turn him against the system itself.

White collar and middle sector work: These jobs fall in the area of the social costs of production. They include workers in sales, advertising, accounting and clerical work. This group is the largest sector of the work force, constituting more than a third of the total.

The question of consciousness here is blurred by ambiguous class positions (class being based on relation to the means of production). These workers sell their labor power on the market, yet do not directly create value. Essentially, their function is to help the capitalists appropriate surplus value (realize profits). Their wages, however, do not come from direct expropriation of other workers: they are not capitalists. Rather, the middle sector is paid according to the prevailing market and social standards to perform labor necessary to the capitalists for realizing profits. The middle sector is essentially a special sector of the working class (cf. Marx's discussion of the "mercantile wage worker" in *Capital*, Vol. III, pp. 289–300). Further, the middle sector workers are highly exploited in terms of our new definition of exploitation, in that they realize little value compared to their expenditure of time and energy.

Historically, this sector has shown both socialist and fascist potential. The revolutionary potential of middle sector workers today is dependent on their ability to perceive their exploitation as *consumers*, relying on leadership exerted by other strata of the working class.

Strategy for the New Left

As has already been clearly indicated, changes (and coming changes) in the work force imply new strategic directions. Unlike in the Thirties, strategy can no longer be based on material demands alone (wage demands in reaction to economic crisis). Rather, it must be based on a more encompassing projection of the social and economic alternatives to the status quo. Briefly, we propose a strategy that posits, on the one hand, a critique of the reality of meaningless jobs, manipulated consumption and growing maldistribution of wealth, and on the other hand, a vision of the liberating potential of a fully automated, fully communist society.

Two vanguard groups have emerged in America: youth and the underclass, specifically blacks. The underclass includes the chronically poor and unemployed. They are the most oppressed. Further, they have been treated more and more as commodities within the service sector of production. And as they are socialized by the service sector, they are brutalized — to which systemic racism contributes. The most radical demands they can raise — which go beyond the demand to be included in the system — can force the whole society to confront itself. They have the potential of developing a nonmarketable culture, nonmarketable because it could include elements antipathetic to the system as a whole. But if black people are forced to develop in isolation from the rest of society (cut off by racism when they can't be bought off by liberalism), their potential power will be limited because of their non-relation to production.

Youth, and particularly students, can also reject the system as a whole. As trainees in a system of exploitation, their rejection of the role of trainee is not simply a rejection of the specific task they are being trained for, but also of the process as a whole. This includes a rejection of consumer culture and manipulative consumption as well as the rejection of meaningless work which they refuse to participate in (e.g. the hippies). It can extend — has begun to extend — to a global critique of American capitalism's role both at home and abroad.

Youth, being the object of intense socialization through education, is best able to perceive the potential that socialized production contains. Yet they are being trained for individual roles as workers and consumers that are boring, uncreative, wasteful. The perception of this fundamental gap between potential and reality leads youth to radical consciousness. And we have already begun to develop alternatives to the existing system. In the liberated buildings of Columbia, in the dropout communities of New York, San Francisco, and dozens of other cities, we are beginning to build our own commonwealth, our own culture.

This class analysis is more static than the current situation in fact is. With the growth of technology, production comes to be based more on the general productivity and technical level of society as a whole than on any particular group of workers. In other words, while technology has tended to fragment job structure, it has also socialized production as a whole, creating the basis for the perception of a unity of interests among all sectors of the working class and the underclass. Exploitation through consumption provides a further basis for socialization and unity of interests. While there are different styles of consumption among different classes, the mass culture developing out of advertising and mass media provides a partial basis for common experience within the working class.

In the short run, job fragmentation will necessitate constituency politics as a prelude to a full class politics. Potential constituencies might include the sectors and sub-sectors of the working class already discussed, as well as groups such as students, women and consumers, which constitute overlapping constituencies. To avoid reformism, and even fascism, such constituency politics must be based on relating the concerns of each constituency to the central contradictions of capitalism and imperialism. Through the experience of common struggle against exploitation and oppression, the constituencies can develop into a full class movement, a movement to abolish class.

Technology, Repression and Liberation

The opening paragraphs of this paper pointed out the distortion of the historical relationship between needs and production under modern capitalism. Production is held back because of the threat of underconsumption which in turn stems ultimately from the maldistribution of wealth. And yet, were it not for the irrational and anti-human organization of production necessitated by modern capitalism, modern technology provides the real potential for a post-scarcity economy for the first time in history. (For an excellent discussion of the economics of "fully automated full communism," see E. J. Nell's article "Automation and the Abolition of the Market" in *New Left Notes*, Aug. 1967.) Further, cybernation points to a mode of production that can abolish the necessity of externally imposed labor. Only through the elimination of material scarcity and division of labor can the basis of social domination be abolished. Then, man's activity becomes defined by his own, consciously determined needs, not by external necessity. This potential, embodied in the increasingly socialized means of production, creates the basis for communist revolution and a new quality of human relationships.

ANARCHO-SYNDICALISM

RUDOLF ROCKER

Ideology of Anarchism

Anarchism is a definite intellectual current of social thought, whose adherents advocate the abolition of economic monopolies and of all political and social coercive institutions within society. In place of the capitalist economic order, Anarchists would have a free association of all productive forces based upon co-operative labor, which would have for its sole purpose the satisfying of the necessary requirements of every member of society. In place of the present national states with their lifeless machinery of political and bureaucratic institutions, Anarchists desire a federation of free communities which shall be bound to one another by their common economic and social interests and will arrange their affairs by mutual agreement and free contract.

Anyone who studies profoundly the economic and political development of the present social system will recognize that these objectives do not spring from the utopian ideas of a few imaginative innovators, but that they are the logical outcome of a thorough examination of existing social maladjustments, which, with every new phase of the present social conditions, manifest themselves more plainly and more unwholesomely. Modern monopoly-capitalism and the totalitarian state are merely the last stages in a development which could culminate in no other end.

The portentous development of our present economic system, leading to a mighty accumulation of social wealth in the hands of privileged minorities and to a constant repression of the great masses of the people, prepared the way for the present political

and social reaction and befriended it in every way. It sacrificed
the general interests of human society to the private interests of
individuals, and thus systematically undermined a true relationship between men. People forgot that industry is not an end in
itself, but should be only a means to insure to man his material
subsistence and to make accessible to him the blessings of a higher
intellectual culture. Where industry is everything, where labor
loses its ethical importance and man is nothing, there begins the
realm of ruthless economic despotism, whose workings are no less
disastrous than those of any political despotism. The two mutually
augment one another; they are fed from the same source.

Internally, our modern social system has split the social organism
of every country into hostile classes, and externally it has broken
up the common cultural circle into hostile nations; both classes
and nations confront one another with open antagonism, and by
their ceaseless warfare keep the communal social life in continual
convulsions. Two world wars within half a century and their
terrible after-effects, and the constant danger of new wars, which
today dominates all peoples, are only the logical consequences of
this unendurable condition which can only lead to further universal
catastrophes. The mere fact that most states are obliged today
to spend the better part of their annual income for so-called
national defense and the liquidation of old war debts is proof of
the untenability of the present status; it should make clear to
everybody that the alleged protection which the state affords the
individual is certainly purchased too dearly.

The ever-growing power of a soulless political bureaucracy
which supervises and safeguards the life of man from the cradle to
the grave is putting ever greater obstacles in the way of co-opera-
tion among human beings. A system which in every act of its life
sacrifices the welfare of large sections of the people, of whole
nations, to the selfish lust for power and the economic interests of
small minorities must necessarily dissolve social ties and lead to a
constant war of each against all. This system has merely been the
pacemaker for the great intellectual and social reaction which finds
its expression today in modern Fascism and the idea of the totalitarian state, far surpassing the obsession for power of the absolute
monarch of past centuries, and seeking to bring every sphere of
human activity under the control of the state. "All for the state;
all through the state; nothing without the state!" became the
leitmotiv of a new political theology which has as its counterpart the

various systems of ecclesiastical theology which say that God is everything and man nothing; so for this modern political creed the state is everything and the citizen nothing. And just as the words the *will of God* were used to justify the will of privileged castes, so today there hides behind the *will of the state* only the selfish interests of those who feel called upon to interpret this will in their own sense and to force it upon the people.

In modern Anarchism we have the confluence of the two great currents of thought, Socialism and Liberalism, which before and since the French Revolution have found such characteristic expression in the intellectual life of Europe. Modern Socialism developed when profound observers of social life came to see more and more clearly that political constitutions and changes in the form of government could never get to the root of the great problem that we call the *social question*. Its supporters recognized that an equalizing of social and economic conditions for the benefit of all, despite the loveliest of theoretical assumptions, is not possible as long as people are separated into classes on the basis of their owning or not owning property, classes whose mere existence excludes in advance any thought of a genuine community. And so there developed the conviction that only by the elimination of economic monopolies and by common ownership of the means of production does a condition of social justice become feasible, a condition in which society shall become a real community and human labor shall no longer serve the end of exploitation, but assure the well-being of everyone. But as soon as Socialism began to assemble its forces and become a movement, there at once came to light certain differences of opinion due to the influence of the social environment in different countries. It is a fact that every political concept from theocracy to Caesarism and dictatorship have affected certain factions of the socialistic movement.

Meanwhile, two other great currents in political thought had a decisive influence on the development of socialist ideas: Liberalism, which had powerfully stimulated advanced minds in the Anglo-Saxon countries, especially Holland, and in Spain, and Democracy in the sense to which Rousseau gave expression in his *Social Contract*, and which found its most influential representatives in the leaders of French Jacobinism. While Liberalism in its social theories started off from the individual and wished to limit the state's activities to a minimum, Democracy took its stand on an abstract collective concept, Rousseau's *general will*, which it

sought to fix in the national state. Liberalism and Democracy
were pre-eminently political concepts, and since most of the
original adherents of both did scarcely consider the economic conditions of society, the further development of these conditions
could not be practically reconciled with the original principles of
Democracy, and still less with those of Liberalism. Democracy
with its motto of *equality of all citizens before the law*, and Liberalism
with its *right of man over his own person*, both were wrecked on
the realities of capitalist economy. As long as millions of human
beings in every country have to sell their labor to a small minority
of owners, and sink into the most wretched misery if they can find
no buyers, the so-called equality before the law remains merely a
pious fraud, since the laws are made by those who find themselves
in possession of the social wealth. But in the same way there can
be no talk of a right over one's own person, for that right ends
when one is compelled to submit to the economic dictation of
another if one does not want to starve.

In common with Liberalism, Anarchism represents the idea that
the happiness and prosperity of the individual must be the standard
in all social matters. And, in common with the great representatives of liberal thought, it also has the idea of limiting the functions of government to a minimum. Its adherents have followed
this thought to its ultimate consequences, and wish to eliminate
every institution of political power from the life of society. When
Jefferson clothes the basic concept of Liberalism in the words:
"That government is best which governs least," then Anarchists
say with Thoreau: "That government is best which governs not
at all."

In common with the founders of Socialism, Anarchists demand
the abolition of economic monopoly in every form and shape and
uphold common ownership of the soil and all other means of
production, the use of which must be available to all without
distinction; for personal and social freedom is conceivable only on
the basis of equal economic conditions for everybody. Within the
socialist movement itself the Anarchists represent the viewpoint
that the struggle against capitalism must be at the same time a
struggle against all coercive institutions of political power, for in
history economic exploitation has always gone hand in hand with
political and social oppression. The exploitation of man by man
and the domination of man over man are inseparable, and each is
the condition of the other.

As long as a possessing and a non-possessing group of human beings face one another in enmity within society, the state will be indispensable to the possessing minority for the protection of its privileges. When this condition of social injustice vanishes to give place to a higher order of things, which shall recognize no special rights and shall have as its basic assumption the community of social interests, government over men must yield the field to the administration of economic and social affairs, or, to speak with Saint-Simon: "The time will come when the art of governing men will disappear. A new art will take its place, the art of administering things." In this respect Anarchism has to be regarded as a kind of voluntary Socialism.

This disposes also of the theory maintained by Marx and his followers that the state, in the form of a proletarian dictatorship, is a necessary transitional stage to a classless society, in which the state, after the elimination of all class conflicts and then the classes themselves, will dissolve itself and vanish from the canvas. For this concept, which completely mistakes the real nature of the state and the significance in history of the factor of political power, is only the logical outcome of so-called economic materialism which sees in all the phenomena of history merely the inevitable effects of the methods of production of the time. Under the influence of this theory people came to regard the different forms of the state and all other social institutions as a "juridical and political superstructure on the economic edifice" of society, and thought that they had found in it the key to every historic process. In reality every section of history affords us thousands of examples of the way in which the economic development of countries was set back for centuries by the state and its power policy.

Before the rise of the ecclesiastical monarchy, Spain, industrially, was the most advanced country in Europe and held the first place in economic production in almost every field. But a century after the triumph of the Christian monarchy most of its industries had disappeared; what was left of them survived only in the most wretched condition. In most industries they had reverted to the most primitive methods of production. Agriculture collapsed, canals and waterways fell into ruin and vast stretches of the country were transformed into deserts. Princely absolutism in Europe, with its silly "economic ordinances" and "industrial legislation," which severely punished any deviation from the prescribed methods of production and permitted no new inventions, blocked industrial progress in European countries for centuries, and prevented its natural development. And even now after the horrible experiences of two world wars, the power policy of the larger national states proves to be the greatest obstacle to the reconstruction of European economy.

In Russia, however, where the so-called dictatorship of the proletariat has ripened into reality, the aspirations of a particular party for political power have prevented any truly socialistic reorganization of economic life and have forced the country into the slavery of a grinding state-capitalism. The proletarian dictatorship, which naive souls believe is an inevitable transition stage to real Socialism, has today grown into a frightful despotism and a new imperialism, which lags behind the tyranny of Fascist states in nothing. The assertion that the state must continue to exist until society is no longer divided into hostile classes almost sounds, in the light of all historical experience, like a bad joke.

Every type of political power presupposes some particular form of human slavery, for the maintenance of which it is called into being. Just as outwardly, that is in relation to other states, the state has to create certain artificial antagonisms in order to justify its existence, so also internally the cleavage of society into castes, ranks and classes is an essential condition of its continuance. The development of the Bolshevist bureaucracy in Russia under the alleged dictatorship of the proletariat — which has never been anything but the dictatorship of a small clique *over* the proletariat and the whole Russian people — is merely a new instance of an old historical experience which has repeated itself countless times. This new ruling class, which today is rapidly growing into a new aristocracy, is set apart from the great masses of the Russian peasants and workers just as clearly as are the privileged castes and classes in other countries from the mass of the people. And this situation becomes still more unbearable when a despotic state denies to the lower classes the right to complain of existing conditions, so that any protest is made at the risk of their lives.

But even a far greater degree of economic equality than that which exists in Russia would be no guarantee against political and social oppression. Economic equality alone is not social liberation. It is precisely this which all the schools of authoritarian Socialism have never understood. In the prison, in the cloister, or in the barracks one finds a fairly high degree of economic equality, as all the inmates are provided with the same dwelling, the same food, the same uniform and the same tasks. The ancient Inca state in Peru and the Jesuit state in Paraguay had brought equal economic provision for every inhabitant to a fixed system, but in spite of this the vilest despotism prevailed there, and the human being was merely the automation of a higher will on whose decisions he had not the slightest influence. It is not without reason that Proudhon saw in a "Socialism" without freedom the worst form of slavery. The urge for social justice can only develop properly and be effective when it grows out of a man's sense of freedom and responsibility, and is based upon it. In other words, *Socialism will be free or it will not be at all.* In its recognition of this fact lies the genuine and profound justification of Anarchism.

Institutions serve the same purpose in the life of society as physical organs do in plants and animals; they are the organs of the social body. Organs do not develop arbitrarily, but owe their origin to definite necessities of the physical and social environment. Changed conditions of life produce changed organs. But an organ always performs the function it was evolved to perform, or a related one. And it gradually disappears or becomes rudimentary as soon as its function is no longer necessary to the organism.

The same is true of social institutions. They, too, do not arise arbitrarily, but are called into being by special social needs to serve definite purposes. In this way the modern state was evolved, after economic privileges and class divisions associated with them had begun to make themselves more and more conspicuous in the framework of the old social order. The newly arisen possessing classes had need of a political instrument of power to maintain their economic and social privileges over the masses of their own people, and to impose them from without on other groups of human beings. Thus arose the appropriate social conditions for the evolution of the modern state as the organ of political power for the forcible subjugation and oppression of the non-possessing classes. This task is the essential reason for its existence. Its external forms have altered in the course of its historical development, but its functions have always remained the same. They have even constantly broadened in just the measure in which its supporters have succeeded in making further fields of social activities subservient to their ends. And, just as the functions of a physical organ cannot be arbitrarily altered so that, for example, one cannot at will hear with one's eyes or see with one's ears, so also one cannot at pleasure transform an organ of social oppression into an instrument for the liberation of the oppressed.

Anarchism is no patent solution for all human problems, no Utopia of a perfect social order (as it has so often been called), since, on principle it rejects all absolute schemes and concepts. It does not believe in any absolute truth or in any definite final goals for human development, but in an unlimited perfectibility of social patterns and human living conditions which are always straining after higher forms of expression, and to which, for this reason, one cannot assign any definite terminus nor set any fixed goal. The greatest evil of any form of power is just that it always tries to force the rich diversity of social life into definite forms and adjust it to particular norms. The stronger its supporters feel themselves, the more completely they succeed in bringing every field of social life into their service, the more crippling is their influence on the operation of all creative cultural forces and the more unwholesomely does it affect intellectual and social development. This is a dire omen for our times, for it shows with frightful clarity to what a monstrosity Hobbes' *Leviathan* can be developed. It is the perfect triumph of the political machine over mind and body, the rationalization of human thought, feeling and behavior according to the established rules of the officials, and consequently the end of all true intellectual culture.

Anarchism recognizes only the relative significance of ideas, institutions and social conditions. It is therefore not a fixed, self-enclosed social system, but rather a definite trend in the historical development of mankind, which, in contrast with the intellectual guardianship of all clerical and governmental institutions, strives for the free unhindered unfolding of all the individual and social forces in life. Even freedom is only a relative, not an absolute concept, since it tends constantly to broaden its scope and to affect wider circles in manifold ways. For the Anarchist, freedom is not an abstract philosophical concept, but the vital concrete possibility for every human being to bring to full development all capacities and talents with which nature has endowed him, and turn them to social account. The less this natural development of man is interfered with by ecclesiastical or political guardianship, the more efficient and harmonious will human personality become, and the more will it become the measure of the intellectual culture of the society in which it has grown. This is the reason why all great culture periods in history have been periods of political weakness, for political systems are always based upon the mechanizing of, rather than the organic development of social forces. State and Culture are irreconcilable opposites. Nietzsche, who was not an Anarchist, recognized this very clearly when he wrote: "No one can finally spend more than he has. That holds good for individuals; it holds good for peoples. If one spends oneself for power, for higher politics, for husbandry, for commerce, parliamentarism, military interests — if one gives away that amount of reason, earnestness, will, self-mastery which constitutes one's real self for one thing, he will not have it for the other. Culture and the state — let no one be deceived about this — are antagonists: the *Culture State* is merely a modern idea. The one lives on the other, the one prospers at the expense of the other. All great periods of culture are periods of political decline. Whatever is great in a cultured sense is non-political, is even antipolitical."

When the influence of political power on the creative forces in society is reduced to a minimum, culture thrives the best, for political rulership always strives for uniformity and tends to subject every aspect of social life to its guardianship. And in this, it finds itself in unescapable contradiction to the creative aspirations of cultural development, which is always on the quest for new forms and fields of social activity, and for which freedom of expression, the many-sidedness and the continual changing of things, are just as vitally necessary as rigid forms, dead rules, and the forcible suppression of ideas are for the conservation of political power. Every successful piece of work stirs the desire for greater perfection and deeper inspiration; each new form becomes the herald of new possibilities of development. But power always tries to keep things as they are, safely anchored to stereotypes. That has been the reason for all revolutions in history. Power operates only destructively, bent always on forcing every manifestation of social life into the straitjacket of its rules. Its intellectual expression is dead dogma, its physical form brute force. And this unintelligence of its objectives set its stamp on its representatives also, and renders them often stupid and brutal, even when they were originally endowed with the best talents. One who is constantly striving to force everything into a mechanical order at last becomes a machine himself and loses all human feelings.

It was from this understanding that modern Anarchism was born and draws its moral force. Only freedom can inspire men to great things and bring about intellectual and social transformations.

The art of ruling men has never been the art of educating and inspiring them to a new shaping of their lives. Dreary compulsion has at its command only lifeless drill, which smothers any vital initiative at its birth and brings forth only subjects, not free men. Freedom is the very essence of life, the impelling force in all intellectual and social development, the creator of every new outlook for the future of mankind. The liberation of man from economic exploitation and from intellectual, social and political oppression, which finds its highest expression in the philosophy of Anarchism, is the first prerequisite for the evolution of a higher social culture and a new humanity.

The Political Struggle — Anarcho-Syndicalist View

Political rights do not originate in parliaments; they are rather forced upon them from without. And even their enactment into law has for a long time been no guarantee of their security. They do not exist because they have been legally set down on a piece of paper, but only when they have become the ingrown habit of a people, and when any attempt to impair them will meet with the violent resistance of the populace. Where this is not the case, there is no help in any parliamentary opposition or any Platonic appeals to the constitution. One compels respect from others when one knows how to defend one's dignity as a human being. This is not only true in private life; it has always been the same in political life as well.

All political rights and liberties which people enjoy today, they do not owe to the good will of their governments, but to their own strength. Governments have always employed every means in their power to prevent the attainment of these rights or render them illusory. Great mass movements and whole revolutions have been necessary to wrest them from the ruling classes, who would never have consented to them voluntarily. The whole history of the last three hundred years is proof of that. *What is important is not that governments have decided to concede certain rights to the people, but the reason why they had to do this*. Of course, if one accepts Lenin's cynical phrase and thinks of freedom merely as a "bourgeois prejudice," then, to be sure, political rights have no value at all for the workers. But then the countless struggles of the past, all the revolts and revolutions to which we owe these rights, are also without value. To proclaim this bit of wisdom it hardly was necessary to overthrow Tsarism, for even the censorship of Nicholas II would certainly have had no objection to the designation of freedom as a "bourgeois prejudice."

If Anarcho-Syndicalism nevertheless rejects the participation in the present national parliaments, it is not because they have no sympathy with political struggles in general, but because its adherents are of the opinion that this form of activity is the very weakest and most helpless form of the political struggle for the workers. For the possessing classes, parliamentary action is certainly an appropriate instrument for the settlement of such conflicts as arise, because they are all equally interested in maintaining the present economic and social order. Where there is a common interest, mutual agreement is possible and serviceable to all parties. But for the workers the situation is very different. For them the existing economic order is the source of their exploitation and their social and political subjugation. Even the freest ballot cannot do away with the glaring contrast between the possessing and non-possessing classes in society. It can only give the servitude of the toiling masses the stamp of legality.

It is a fact that when socialist labor parties have wanted to achieve some decisive political reforms they could not do it by parliamentary action, but were obliged to rely wholly on the economic fighting power of the workers. The political general strikes in Belgium and Sweden for the attainment of universal suffrage are proof of this. And in Russia it was the great general strike in 1905 that forced the Tsar to sign the new constitution. It was the recognition of this which impelled the Anarcho-Syndicalists to center their activity on the socialist education of the masses and the utilization of their economic and social power. Their method is that of direct action in both the economic and political struggle of the time. By direct action they mean every method of the immediate struggle by the workers against economic and political oppression. Among these the outstanding are the strike in all its gradations, from the simple wage struggle to the general strike, organized boycott and all the other countless means which workers as producers have in their hands.

One of the most effective forms of direct action is the *social strike*, which was hitherto mostly used in Spain and partly in France, and which shows a remarkable and growing responsibility of the workers to society as a whole. It is less concerned with the immediate interests of the producers than with the protection of the community against the most pernicious outgrowths of the present system. The social strike seeks to force upon the employers a responsibility to the public. Primarily it has in view the protection of the consumers, of which the workers themselves constitute the great majority. Under the present circumstances the workers are frequently debased by doing a thousand things which constantly serve only to injure the whole community for the advantage of the employers. They are compelled to make use of inferior and often actually injurious materials in the fabrication of their products, to erect wretched dwellings, to put up spoiled foodstuffs and to perpetrate innumerable acts that are planned to cheat the consumer. To interfere vigorously is, in the opinion of the Anarcho-Syndicalists, the great task of the labor syndicates. An advance in this direction would at the same time enhance the position of the workers in society, and in larger measure confirm that position.

Direct action by organized labor finds its strongest expression in the general strike, in the stoppage of work in every branch of production in cases where every other means is failing. It is the most powerful weapon which the workers have at their command and gives the most comprehensive expression to their strength as a social factor. The general strike, of course, is not an agency that can be invoked arbitrarily on every occasion. It needs certain social assumptions to give it a proper moral strength and make it a proclamation of the will of the broad masses of the people. The ridiculous claim, which is so often attributed to the Anarcho-Syndicalists, that it is only necessary to proclaim a general strike in order to achieve a socialist society in a few days, is of course just a ludicrous invention of ignorant opponents. The general strike can serve various purposes. It can be the last stage of a sympathetic strike, as for example in Barcelona in 1902 or in Bilbao in 1903, which enabled the miners to get rid of the hated truck system and compelled the employers to establish sanitary conditions in the mines. It can also be a means for organized labor to enforce some general demand, as for example in the attempted general strike in the U.S.A. in 1886, to compel the granting of the eight-hour day in all industries. The great general strike of the English workers in 1926 was the result of a planned attempt by the employers to lower the general standard of living of the workers by a cut in wages.

But the general strike can also have political objectives in view, as for example the fight of the Spanish workers in 1904 for the

liberation of the political prisoners, or the general strike in Cata-
lonia in July 1909 to force the government to terminate its criminal
war in Morocco. Also the general strike of the German workers
in 1920, which was instituted after the so-called Kapp *putsch* and
put an end to a government that had attained power by a military
uprising, belongs in this category. In such critical situations the
general strike takes the place of the barricades of the political uprisings of the past. For the workers, the general strike is the logical
outcome of the modern industrial system, whose victims they are
today, and at the same time it offers them their strongest weapon
in the struggle for their social liberation, provided they recognize
their own strength and learn how to use this weapon properly.

MARXISM AND THE NEW LEFT

Howard Zinn

My intention in this paper is not to define the radicalism of the New Left but to redefine it. By a remarkable coincidence, that is, I believe, in the spirit of Marxism — to declare what something *is* by declaring what it should be — Marxism assumes that everything — including an idea — takes on a new meaning in each additional moment of time, in each unique historical situation. It tries to avoid academic scholasticism, which pretends to dutifully record, to describe — forgetting that to merely describe is to circumscribe. (The pretense of passive description is what Herbert Marcuse in *One-Dimensional Man* called *operationalism*.)

Marxism is not a fixed body of dogma, to be put into big black books or little red books, and memorized, but a set of specific propositions about the modern world which are both tough and tentative, plus a certain vague and yet exhilarating vision of the future, and, more fundamentally, an approach to life, to people, to ourselves, a certain way of thinking about thinking as well as about being. Most of all it is a way of thinking which is intended to promote action.

The New Left — that loose amalgam of civil rights activists, Black Power advocates, ghetto organizers, student rebels, Vietnam protestors — has been exciting because it has been acting. In that circle of encounter where the spirit of Marxism and the action of the New Left intersect, the New Left will take from Marxism — if it is wise — not all of its exact propositions about the world Marx and Engels lived in (a world which is partly the same today and partly different), but its approach. This approach demands a constant redefinition of theory in the light of immediate reality, and an insistence on *action* as a way of both testing and reworking theory.

56

One of the most quoted, and most ignored, in practice, of Marx's statements is the eleventh point of his *Theses on Feuerbach* (about 1845): "The philosophers have only interpreted the world in various ways; the point however is to change it." Since any body of ideas is part of the world, this suggests our job is not merely to interpret Marxism and the New Left, but to change them. Earlier in these *Theses*, Marx criticized Feuerbach's emphasis on "the theoretical attitude." He said: "Social life is essentially practical. All mysteries . . . find their rational solution in human practice."

In their best moments, thinking revolutionaries agree with this. When Mao Tse Tung was in Yenan, after the Long March, he gave his lecture "On Practice," where he talked of the primacy of experience in knowledge, of uniting perceptual knowledge with rational knowledge, rationalism with empiricism. He said: "The Marxist recognizes that in the absolute, total process of the development of the universe, the development of each concrete process is relative; hence in the great stream of absolute truth, man's knowledge of the concrete process at each given stage of development is only relatively true." That spirit is somehow different than what one encounters in the *Peking Review* these days, with its litany: Long Live Chairman Mao.

To try for a moment to act out the Marxist approach: look at the academic setting in which we live. We find that so much of what is called "intellectual history" is the aimless dredging up of what is and was, rather than a creative recollection of experience pointed at the betterment of human life. We are surrounded by solemn, pretentious argument about what Marx or Machiavelli or Rousseau really meant about who was right and who was wrong — all of which is another way the pedant has of saying: "I am right and you are wrong." Too much of what passes for the theoretical discussion of public issues is really a personal duel for honor or privilege — with each discussant like the character in *Catch-22* who saw every event in the world as either a feather in his cap or a black eye — and this while men were dying all around him.

This scholasticism, oddly enough, has been typical both of the Old Left and of the academic journals, journals which would be horrified at being called Left or Right, and which indeed could hardly be accused of moving in any identifiable direction. Because the New Left is a successor to the Old Left in American history, and because it comes to a large extent out of the academic world (whether the Negro colleges of the South or the Berkeleys of the North), it is always being tempted by theoretical irrelevancies. Fortunately, the young people of today seem more nimble than their predecessors in avoiding this trap.

The contributions of the Old Left — and they were considerable — came not out of its ideological fetishism but out of its action. What gave it dynamism was not the classes on surplus value but the organization of the CIO, not the analysis of Stalin's views on the National and Colonial Question, but the fight for the Scottsboro boys, not the labored rationale for dictatorship of the proletariat, but the sacrifices of the Abraham Lincoln Battalion. I am not arguing here against theoretical discussion, or against long-range principles, or the analysis of sub-surface realities, but I am asserting that theory must be informed by observation and expressed in action. It must, in other words, be relevant.

A materialist approach — in the Marxian sense — makes suggestions rather than demands. One of these is that we look for the situational circumstances behind the behavior and thought of men, if we want to affect both. A dialectical approach — in the Marxian sense — suggests that we evaluate a situation not as fixed, but as in motion, and that our evaluation itself affects that motion. Dialectical materialism asks awareness that we are creatures of limited vision, in eyes and brain, and so must not assume that what we see or perceive is all — that conflicting tendencies often lie beneath the surface of any event.

These are not just academic observations: such an approach should make it easier for us to understand what is wrong when the government says to a penniless Negro in the Mississippi Delta, we have passed a bill and you are now free. Such an approach should help us to sense, in walking past the tenements of a city, temporarily quiet, the element of a violent insurrection. Marx's emphasis on the tyranny of economics can't tell us *how much* economic motivation there is behind any specific political act, but it can lead us to look for it. And so the New Left might go overboard in stressing economic interests in Southeast Asia as an explanation for escalation in Vietnam — but it might be devilishly right in noting the connection between U.S. economic interests in Latin American nations and the pro-American votes of these nations in the U.N.

Marxism, in other words, doesn't tell us *exactly* what we will find beneath the surface — it does suggest what we should look for —

and it certainly insists that we look. A Marxist would have given Lysenko his microscope; but it was a Stalinist who told him — or created an atmosphere that told him — what he must find beneath it.

And if someone says this isn't dialectical materialism or Marxism — this is common sense, or rationalism, or pragmatism, or empiricism, or naturalism — why deny that, or argue? Who cares about credit? True, the Old Left didn't like to admit relations with any other ideology. It remained virginal and lonely. The New Left seems different.

There has been much talk about a Christian-Marxist dialogue — but if such a dialogue is to be useful perhaps it should begin with the idea that God is dead and Marx is dead, but Yossarian lives. This is only a way of saying: let's not spend our time arguing whether God exists or what Marx really meant, because while we argue, the world moves, while we publish, others perish, and the best use of our energy is to resist those who would send us — after so many missions of murder — on still one more.

A new radicalism should be anti-ideological, I believe, in the sense I have discussed. But it also should be — and here it has been inadequate — concerned with theory. I see three essential ingredients in such a theory. First we need a vision of what we are working toward — one based on transcendental human needs and not limited by the reality we are so far stuck with. Second, this theory should analyze the present reality, not through the prism of old, fixed categories, but rather with an awareness of the unique here and now and of the need to make the present irrationality intelligible to those around us. Finally, such a theory would explore — in the midst of action — effective techniques of social change for the particular circumstances we find at the moment.

Let me speak now about the first requirement of this theory, the vision of the future. Here the Marxian vision is useful. True, it is vague. But what better guard is there against dogmatism than vagueness? Uncertainty is not a virtue in depicting the facts of the moment; it may not only be tolerable, but desirable, in trying to portray the future.

I stress this as a Marxian vision, even though many non-Marxists have held the same vision — because while it's necessary to emphasize to the Left that it does not monopolize either compassion or insight, it is necessary to remind everyone else — the Christians, the Jews, the Buddhists, the Humanists, and anyone else — that they share certain aims with Marxism. No one of these groups is going to revolutionize the world by itself, and so all need to be reminded of a certain consensus of humanistic values that has developed in the modern world. Marxists and liberals at their best (and they have not usually been at their best) share this theoretical consensus, here and abroad. Indeed, one of the great contributions of the New Left has been to remind both Marxist countries and liberal capitalist countries how far is their behavior from the values they claim.

In *The Holy Family*, one of the early writings of Marx and Engels (about 1845) they say man needs to be "not negatively free to avoid this or that event" but "positively free to express his true individuality." They say this requires arranging the empirical world around us so that "man experiences and assimilates there what is really human, that he experiences himself as a man." Rather than punishing individuals for their crimes, we should "destroy the social conditions which engender crime, and give to each individual the scope which he needs in society in order to develop his life." This speaks to the so-called socialist countries of today which imprison writers who criticize the state. It also speaks to a country like the United States, which gives people the negative freedoms of the Bill of Rights, but distributes very unequally the scope in which people can develop their individuality, can exercise their freedom — so that some children can roam in little suburban mansions surrounded by gardens, and others are equally free to play in rat-infested tenements. While every one "has" freedom of speech, the corporation with a million dollars to spend on television time can speak to thirty million people, and the individual who can afford a soap box can speak to thirty people. What makes the New Left so critical of the wealthiest nation in the world is its acute consciousness that freedom means not only legal permission to occupy space, but the resources to make the most of this.

The New Left has not even begun to figure out how to explain this complex problem of freedom to all those people in the United States brought up on high school history books and American Legion essay contests. What can make the New Radicalism really new, and really pertinent to here and now, is to be able, without recourse to the stale slogans about "bourgeois freedom," to do justice to the degree of freedom that does exist for people in the United States — while noting that it *is* a matter of degree, that freedom in America is like wealth, plentiful, and very unequally distributed.

Let me turn to another element in the Marxian vision. There is still a widespread popular belief, heavily stressed on the *Reader's Digest* level that Marxism believes in the supremacy of the state over the individual, while democracy believes the opposite. In fact, the existence of oppressively overbearing states in the world, which call themselves Marxist, reinforces this idea. But a true radicalism would remind people in both socialist and capitalist countries of Marx's and Engels' hope, expressed early in the *Manifesto*, that some day "the public power will lose its political character" and "we shall have an association in which the free development of each is the condition for the free development of all." This is not just a youthful aberration (there is a fad about the young romantic Marx and the old, practical Marx) because twenty-seven years later, Marx, in his *Critique of the Gotha Program*, says: "Freedom consists in converting the state from an organ superimposed upon society into one completely subordinate to it." Here also he says, on the subject of the state giving education to the people, "the state has need, on the contrary, of a very stern education by the people." And Engels, a year after Marx's death, in 1884, writes in his *Origin of the Family, Private Property and the State:*

> The society that will organize production on the basis of a free and equal association of the producers will put the whole machinery of state where it will then belong: into the musum of antiquities, by the side of the spinning wheel and the bronze ax.

Their attitude to the state is made even clearer and more specific in Marx's book on the *Civil War in France*, and Engels' *Introduction* to it, where, both of them point admiringly to the Paris Commune of early 1871. The Commune almost immediately abolished conscription and the standing army, declared universal suffrage and the right of citizens to recall their elected officials at any time, said all officials, high or low, should be paid the same wage as received by other workers, and publicly burned the guillotine.

The New Left is anti-authoritarian; it would — I expect — burn draft cards in any society. It is anarchistic not just in wanting the ultimate abolition of the state, but in its immediate requirement that authority and coercion be banished in every sphere of existence, that the end must be represented immediately in the

means. Marx and Bakunin disagreed on this, but the New Left
has the advantage over Marx of having an extra century of history
to study. We see how a dictatorship of the proletariat can easily
become a dictatorship over the proletariat, as Trotsky warned, as
Rosa Luxemburg warned. The New Left should remind the
socialist states as well as the capitalist states of Marx's letter of
1853 to the *New York Tribune* saying he didn't know how capital
punishment could be justified "in a society glorying in its civilization."

In America, both liberalism and radicalism were beguiled into
cheering for state power because under F.D.R. it seemed beneficent: it enacted certain economic reforms, and it waged war
against Hitler. The New Left, hopefully, will recognize that the
state cannot be trusted, either to carry reforms far enough, or to
drop bombs only on Nazi invaders and not on Asian peasants in
their own country. It will therefore create constellations of power
outside the state to pressure it into humane actions, to resist its
inhumane actions, and to replace it in many functions by voluntary
small groups seeking to maintain both individuality and co-opera-
tion. Black Power, in its best aspects, is such an endeavor.

The New Left in America needs to show people how the state,
whether a proletarian dictatorship or a sophisticated welfare capitalism, constitutes a special interest of its own which deserves not
unthinking loyalty, but criticism, resistance, and (even in its better
moments) watchfulness. This New Left attitude toward the state
expresses a more general attitude — against making instruments
into absolutes or means into ends — against the deification of any
party, any nation, any ideology, any method.

Now another point about the Marxian vision. Perhaps nowhere
does Marx speak more directly to our mass society today, and
therefore to the new radicals in mass society, than in his *Economic
and Philosophical Manuscripts* of 1844. The estrangement of man
described there is pertinent not only to the classical proletariat of
his time but to all classes in every modern industrial society — and
certainly to the young people of this generation in the United
States. He talks of men producing things alien to themselves,
which become monsters independent of them (look all around us,
at our automobiles, our television sets, our skyscrapers, even our
universities). People find no satisfaction in working. He points
to the irony that in man's specifically human functions (working,
creating) he feels like an animal, while only in his animal functions

(eating, sex) does he feel like a human being. Our activity becomes not enjoyable in itself, but just a means to keep alive. Activity *is* life — what else is life? — and yet it becomes in modern society only a means to life.

So, we become estranged from what we produce, from our own activity, from our fellow men, from nature (here Marxism must share credit with Taoism), and finally from ourselves — because we all find ourselves living another life, not the one we really want to live. The New Radicals of today are desperately conscious of this and try to escape it. They want to do work which is congenial to them — so they go to Mississippi or move into the ghetto — or they don't work at all rather than work at hateful or parasitic jobs. They often try to create relationships with one another which are not warped by the rules and demands of the world around them. The crucial cause of all these forms of estrangement is that people's activities are coerced rather than free, and so the young people today are defiant. This is not easy, but the very act of attempting it is a free act.

From all this it is quite clear what Marx's values were; the free man, in his individuality, in his sociality, in his oneness with nature. The New Left is in accord here. Where it parts, I think, is in Marx's claim — although some attribute this to Engels (one of those academic disputes I spoke about) that this vision of unalienated man springs not from a wish, but from an observation — from a scientific plotting of a historical curve which moves inevitably in the direction of man's freedom.

Surely we don't have such confidence in inevitabilities these days — we've had too many surprises in this century. (Simone de Beauvoir says in her book *The Ethics of Antiquity* that there is no inevitable proletarian uprising — the movement may go in six different directions.) We are unabashed in declaring our subjective wants and desires — without needing a "scientific" basis for such wants. Here again, the discussion of whether ethical norms are grounded in empirical science is one of those academic discussions which lead us nowhere in actuality. Surely, most people agree on the gross necessities of life — food, sex, peace, freedom, love, dignity, self-realization. Our energy should be spent in working toward them, not in discussing their metaphysical meaning.

I suggested above that the second requirement of a pertinent theory is an analysis of the *particulars* of today's reality. One of Marx's great perceptions was that there is a material basis for man's alienation and unhappiness — the scarcity of goods which he and society need, producing conflict, exploitation, coercion. Thus, abundance is a prerequisite — though not a guarantee — of man's freedom. In the United States, we face this paradox, that the state with the most enormous productive apparatus, indeed the only state in the world which has the technological capacity to have communism, and where a communist society would have the greatest chance of preserving the freedom of the individual (because the *socialist* societies are plagued by scarcity) gets apoplectic at the very mention of the word.

It is here in the United States that the slogan "to each according to his need" can have meaning. We have enough doctors and hospitals to give adequate medical care to whoever needs it, without rationing this according to wealth. We grow enough food in this country without insisting that people without money do with very little food. We can — if we want to — build enough homes in this country to eliminate slums. And so on. There is room for some scholarly work here: economists could sit down somewhere and work out a specific plan for free food in America, also for free college tuition and allowances. What the New Left needs to show, and in specific detail, is where the resources are in this country, what they *are* being used for, and what they *could* be used for.

The Marxian economic categories have long provided material for academic controversy — and I doubt that Marx intended this. But he was only human and perhaps he too succumbed to the temptations of the intellectual: his research, his curiosity, his passion for scheme-building and for scientific constructions ran away with him. I confess that I cannot see how his dense Volume II of *Das Kapital* on the "Circulation of Commodities" or his long expositions of absolute rent and differential rent are essential to revolutionary theory. Does it really matter if Böhm-Bawerk was right or wrong on the relationship between aggregate surplus value and aggregate prices of production?

Even so brilliant a theory as that of surplus-value — how relevant is it to social action? Has the militancy of workingmen in history required such an analysis to sustain it? Has such militancy been transformed into revolutionary consciousness anywhere by the comprehension of the distinction between the use value and exchange value of labor power? The Baran-Sweezy notion of a surplus (in *Monopoly Capital*) comprised of waste, military expenses, and unused capacity, is more fruitful, I think, as a theoretical prod to revolutionary action.

James Bevel is right when he says you can only organize large numbers of people around issues that are obvious or that can easily be made obvious. So instead of discussing the falling rate of profit, or the organic composition of capital, I would concentrate on what is readily observable — that this country has enormous resources which it wastes shamefully and distributes unjustly. A country that produces 200 billion dollars worth of goods and services a year, and this is not our full capacity, should not have ten million families living below the $3000 a year level. All the Chamber of Commerce pronouncements, the fancy *Fortune Magazine* charts about our progress, the confident State of the Union Addresses fall apart when you take a long walk through any major American city: through Harlem or Roxbury or Chicago's South Side.

The most useful Marxian statement about capitalist society is the largest one — that in an era when production is a complex, world-wide social process, and requires rationality, our system is incredibly irrational. This is because corporate profit, not human need, governs what is produced and what is not produced. It is also because there is a huge vested interest — economic, military, political, psychological — in the production of present and future corpses, on which we spend seventy billion dollars a year. We spend about twenty billion dollars a year on public relations, advertising, promotion. We build too many cars, too many highways, too many office buildings, produce too many cigarettes, too much liquor, too many gadgets and not enough homes, schools, hospitals. Corporate profits after taxes amount to forty billion dollars a year — enough to raise every $3000 a year family to $7000 a year. The New Left, instead of getting involved in theoretical discussions about economic categories, needs to find ways to make clear to Americans how wasteful, irrational, and unjust is our economy.

With a vision of how man should live, with some perception of how men do live (and so many of us need to be *shown*), the most urgent theoretical problem for the New Left — and the one where traditional Marxism gives the least guidance — is: how do we change society? How do we redistribute the power in society in order to redistribute the wealth? How do we overcome those who are enjoying power and wealth and won't give it up? How do we

stop the fanaticism of both civilian and military leaders who feel
it is America's duty to establish its power, or its puppets, wherever
possible in the world — and don't care how many people, Americans or others — they kill in the process?

The traditional Marxian idea of a revolution taking place because of a breakdown in the capitalist mechanism and an organized,
class-conscious proletariat taking over, is hardly tenable today.
Where socialist revolutions have taken place in the world, they
have taken place mostly because war has weakened or destroyed
the state and created a vacuum in which organized revolutionaries
could take over. The traditional liberal idea of a gradual evolution
towards freedom, peace, and democracy through parliamentary
reform is also hardly tenable. We see that poverty and racism can
be institutionalized, with only token steps taken to assuage their
worst aspects; that by creating a contented, bloated middle class,
by introducing state regulatory mechanisms in the economy, the
status quo can be maintained. And furthermore, in foreign policy,
it has become accepted that the President and a small group of
advisers make foreign policy, while the mass communications
industry creates a nation of sheep who give assent.

Certainly, in the United States, the traditional idea that the
agent of social change will be the proletariat needs re-examination,
when the best-organized of the workers are bribed into silence with
suburban houses and automobiles, and drugged into compliance
with mass entertainment. Perhaps unorganized workers — the
bulk of the labor force — may play a part, but these consist of
white collar workers, domestic workers, migratory and farm
laborers, service industry workers, and various kinds of people
who are the hardest to organize. Recent experience suggests that
Negroes — and perhaps Negroes in the ghetto — may be the most
powerful single force for social change in the United States. Marx
envisioned the industrial proletariat as the revolutionary agent
because it was in need, exploited, and brought face to face in the
factory. The Negro is in need, exploited and brought together in
the ghetto. And since Berkeley and the teach-ins, there is some
evidence that students — especially as they are pushed more and
more toward the mouth of the cannon — may be another important agent of change. Perhaps some peculiar combination,
unpredictable at this moment, will be formed in a time of national
crisis.

How will change come about? By tactics short of violent revolution, but far more militant than normal parliamentary procedure, it seems to me. Even the demonstrations of the civil rights movement were not enough to achieve more than tokens of change: a few laws, a few high appointments, and LBJ reciting "We Shall Overcome." Spontaneous uprisings in the ghetto are alarm signals, but do not produce change in themselves. It will take systematic, persistent organizing and education, in the ghettos, in the universities, plus co-ordinated actions of various kinds designed to shock society out of its lethargy.

The New Left's idea of parallel organizations, as a way of *demonstrating* what people should do, how people should live, has enormous possibilities: freedom schools, free universities, free cities — remember how these grew up in medieval times outside the feudal system — self-controlled communities. But also, free, active *pockets* of people inside the traditional cities, universities, corporations. In military combat, guerilla warfare arose as an answer to overwhelmingly centralized military power. Perhaps we are in need of political guerrilla tactics in the face of mass society — in which enclaves of freedom are created here and there in the midst of the orthodox way of life, to become centers of protest, and examples to others. It is in techniques of organization, pressure, change, community-building — that the New Radicals need the most thought, and the most action. It may take an ingenious combination of energy and wit to carry through a new kind of revolution.

Action *is* preferably organized, thought-out action, but there should be room for whatever kinds of action any individual or group feels moved to undertake. In an era when it is so easy to feel helpless, we need the Existentialist emphasis on our freedom to act. The Marxist-Existentialist debate on freedom and determinism seems to me to be an empty one — an academic one. To stress our freedom is not the result of ignorance that we do have a history, that we do have an oppressive environment. But knowing of these pressures on us, we should be existentially aware that there is enormous indeterminacy in the combat between us and the obstacles all around. We never know exactly the depth or the shallowness of the resistance to our actions — until we act. We never know exactly what effect we will have. Our actions may lead to nothing except changing ourselves, and that is something. They may have a tiny cumulative effect, along with a thousand other actions. They may also explode.

What the fact of indeterminacy suggests is that we should not be preoccupied with prediction or with measuring immediate success — but rather should take the risk of acting. We are not totally free but our strength will be maximized if we act *as if* we are free. We are not passive observers, students, theorizers; our very thoughts, our statements, our speeches, our essays, throw a weight into a balance which cannot be assessed until we act. This Existentialist emphasis on the necessity for action — based on conscience, avoiding that cool and careful weighing of "the realities" — is one of the most refreshing characteristics of the New Radicalism in America.

Along with the Existentialist emphasis on freedom there is responsibility. To the extent that we feel free, we feel responsible. There is something about our time which makes it difficult for us not only to feel free but to feel responsibility. Contemporary life is complicated, and evil comes at the end of a long assembly line with a division of labor so intricate it is impossible to trace; everyone has responsibility and no one has responsibility. But if we are to feel our own freedom, we must feel our responsibility, not for anyone else's actions, but only for our own; not for the past and without any pledge to the future — but at this moment, now, where we stand.

NONVIOLENCE AND RADICAL
SOCIAL CHANGE

BARBARA DEMING

Is nonviolence a relevant — a practical — discipline for those
who want to bring about radical social change? I believe it is the
most practical discipline. What revolutionaries speak of bringing
into being is a new world in which men will treat each other with
true respect. Those who accept the discipline of nonviolence try
to bring this world into being immediately, by acting out that
respect *now*, even toward the men with whom we are struggling.

Some would object: that's all very fine, but can you actually win
when you fight this way? Some would object that when we are
nonviolent we may respect the enemy, but we don't respect ourselves — we don't stand up for ourselves. They would agree with
Stokely Carmichael's and Carl Oglesby's definition of nonviolence
— that it is essentially a kind of prayer, a humble petition to those
who are in power to be good to us. By petitioning them, we
actually reinforce their authority — when we should be challenging
their authority. And our petition is based on the naive assumption
that the powers that be victimize us only because they are not
fully aware of how unhappy we are. If we let them know this — in
a nice way — they will of course do something to change things
for us. As Carmichael put it to the white power structure: we
have found you out; you are not the nice guys you are supposed
to be. And he concludes, we've found out therefore that nonviolence does not work.

I agree very much that one cannot simply petition those in
power for change — one cannot simply expect to touch the con-
sciences of men. It isn't that easy. One has to confront those in
power with power on *our* part. But here I differ with Carmichael
and others because I believe that in nonviolent struggle one can

do just this — one can confront them with such power. Too often those who believe in nonviolence have limited their actions to petition, but we needn't limit ourselves in this way. We can go very much further — and must.

What is the power of nonviolence? Radical nonviolence, if it is really employed as it can be, relies on the application of two kinds of pressure — two pressures which are particularly effective in combination.

The pressure which those describing nonviolence tend always to omit from the description is the pressure of our refusal to co-operate with a system which denies us our freedom — but which exploits us, that is to say which *relies* on our cooperation. This is how we stand up for ourselves nonviolently; we refuse the authorities our labor, we refuse them our money (our taxes), we refuse them our bodies, to fight in their wars. We strike. We go even beyond this and block and obstruct and disrupt the operation of that system in which we cannot feel like free men. Those who are committed to nonviolence have simply never gone as far as they could in this direction. (Though they went furthest perhaps under Gandhi — went far enough to enable them to throw the British out of India without killing a single Englishman.) One can make life as usual, business as usual, simply impossible for our antagonists.

But I've spoken of a combination of pressures. And this is crucial in defining the power of nonviolence. Noncooperation, disruption, can of course be nonviolent or violent. When it is non-violent I believe it is immensely more powerful in the long run. Because one has then, as it were, two hands upon the adversary. With one hand one shakes up his life drastically, makes it impossible for him simply to continue as he has been. With the other hand we calm him, we control his response to us. Because we respect his rights as well as ours, his real, his human rights — because we reassure him that it is not his destruction that we want, merely justice — we keep him from responding to our actions as men respond to violence, just mechanically, blindly. We force him to think — to ask all kinds of questions of himself, about the nature of our actions and our grievance, about the real issues involved, about what others watching the struggle will think, about where his own real long-term interests lie — whether they don't lie in adjusting himself to change.

When we fight this way, we can count on suffering, in the long run, many fewer casualties. (Though it may not feel that way at first, because we are suffering all of them and the other side none.) But the antagonist cannot, beyond a point, escalate violence against us when we are using none. Conscience quite aside, it won't look right to others.

If he does continue to escalate violence, unreasonably, he will begin to lose the sympathy of allies and supporters on whom he depends. We will begin to gain them. (The genius of guerilla warfare is to make it impossible for the other side to make full use of its weaponry. We carry this principle even further.)

In brief, men have barely begun to experiment with the power there is in noncooperation and disruption; and they have barely begun to experiment with the control they can wield over an antagonist's response to these if one remains strictly nonviolent, treating the other always with basic respect.

Of course, I had better stress, in struggle of this sort, though one can expect fewer casualties finally than in violent struggle, one has, nevertheless, to expect them — one has to take the psychological step of entering real battle. One can't withdraw when one does begin to get hurt. One has to learn that if we are taking casualties — even though we're not hurting anyone on the other side — it doesn't mean that something is going wrong. This is battle.

Experiment with nonviolent struggle has barely begun. But in a world where violent battle can escalate into nuclear warfare, it is an experiment that is absolutely necessary to push to its furthest limits.

NO RIGHTS, NO DUTIES

Truman Nelson

Thomas Jefferson, when queried about the authority, legal and otherwise, for his revolutionary assertion that people have a right to overthrow their government under certain conditions, said:

All its authority rests then on the harmonizing sentiments of the day, whether expressed in conversation, in letters, printed essays, or the elementary books of public right, as Aristotle, Cicero, Locke, Sidney, etc. . . . it was intended to be an expression of the American Mind.

It was just as plainly understood by the founding fathers that all government is a contract, and if it gives no rights, or even diminished rights, you owe it no duties. What allegiance, really, can this government demand of a group commonly known as *second-class citizens?* The same is true of *paupers* and *minors.* They are never given the equal protection of the laws. The poor are confined by economic attrition in slums where violations of housing and health codes are carried on with impunity every day. They could not exist as slums, otherwise. The minors, healthy young boys under voting age, are forced into an involuntary servitude in the military establishment, which demands of them that they kill or be killed in countries far away for purposes which they consider irrelevant to the point of madness. As minors, they have no rights that a legislator needs to respect.

The American people as a whole, even the affluent, seem to have lost control over their own politics. They know that faceless men at the levers of power in the Pentagon can throw a switch to oblivion for the world without even considering asking for the consent of the governed. Many of us are finally getting this straight in our heads, but they have got to us lower down and made us political eunuchs. We are so squeezed by our "responsibility to the free world" that we cannot have a free thought but what we are warned that the whole "free world" will go down if we act on it.

Political emasculation is not our only organic change. The simple facts of the Newark rebellion reveal that the total organism of American life is rotting faster and faster into putrefaction. The stinking decay grows in our guts, and when we try to cure it, they break in our hands. One of our most sacred rights, that of the individual, *individualism*, forsooth, is now debased and swept away with the full connivance of the elected powers.

The crimes, if any, in Newark, were carried out by individuals. A few armed men, estimated by the police as not over ten men, with names, personalities, and motives of their own (men feeling perhaps, that they owed no more duty to this government than the Irish did to the British Government in the beginning of their revolution) fired at our police and our soldiers. A whole people was punished for this. Mortal punishment in a rain of fire went sweeping into the apartment houses and killing the innocent.

It is nowhere known for certain if any snipers were killed by the police, and it never will be known because the police have moved into simple warfare where the trajectory of function is to find the locus of the enemy and flush him out with firepower. And to act, with the greatest immediacy, not against a suspected individual, but against a flawed totality. Thus our nationalism has reached its apogee. No longer can a man stand and bargain with his government over the extent of his rights and duties, his innocence or guilt, as our forefathers did, even with their God.

This new point of view, the consciousness now formed which demands that we punish collectively for individual guilt, we are acting out all over the world. The most important task assigned to us as a nation, the leading and generating fact of our lives, is the war we are carrying on in Vietnam, a war against a total people, wherein it is a routine function to bomb and burn a whole village because it is suspected that one or two of the active enemy are located there, or have always lived there.

How can we think that in performing this, which even our apologists characterize as a cruel and *dirty* war, that our actions will not stain through our whole consciousness and benumb and degenerate us in our wholeness and make us act toward ourselves as we do toward others?

The fact is, what the rich man does to the poor man, what the landlord does to the tenant, what the merchant does to the consumer, what the boss does to the worker, what the policeman does to the suspect, what the jailor does to the helpless criminal in his power is only a local reflection of what we are doing as a nation abroad with our armies. And as the merchants, police, judges, landlords, bosses, jailors increase at home, while our soldiers escalate their presence abroad, so does the scope and intensity of their action against their victims.

And all the time we are told that to suffer this is part of the *duty* we must pay for our *rights*. That these acts which they say they perform only as a cruel necessity are saving us from being the victims of evil men, somewhere else, or evil systems, over there . . . who will only use us for their gratification. That if they let up for a moment their heavy-handed control of our lives, it will provide the vicious and unprincipled a chance to oppress the innocent. So, although some individuals may question some of the acts performed by those in power . . . they must continue to rule us for the greater good.

This means that they, our overlords, are all virtuous, all compassionate, all understanding public servants who took up the cross to suffer and sacrifice in carrying out their tasks and duties to us . . . that it is their duty to curtail our rights because they are carrying out a responsibility to law and order and the greatest good.

We, on the other hand, have to accept their acts of usurpation and control as our *duty* and promise on our oaths that we will unquestioningly obey their commands as spoken and enforced by their myriads of overseers, spies, interrogators, and whippers-in, from the President to the local draft board and social worker. And cheerfully recognize their rights to the lion's share of our daily labor so they can carry out their duty to control us with a maximum efficiency and have a gracious surrounding in which they can unwind, after a wearisome day of holding us in an appropriate system of checks and balances.

And we must carry out, proudly and cheerfully, our right to mark, every four years, a cross beside some names printed on a ballot . . . names of men either completely unknown to us, or only too well known as scoundrels, windbags, and embezzlers who have lived all their lives on the public payrolls and prospered well beyond the million mark. And although we know, from the experiences of ourselves, our fathers, and grandfathers, that regardless of the inane speeches they utter, promising change, they will do the same as the men in office before them and before them and before them, and they will plead the same crises of the Republic, plead the same urgencies and imperatives about the obscene Vietnam War of 1967 as they did about the obscene Mexican War of 1847, and in about the same words.

We must also perform the right and duty of serving voluntarily in the courts, and sitting in judgment on other frail humans; knowing that by the time the government prosecutor and the government judge get through with the case we will still not know much about the guilt or innocence of the accused or be able to do anything about it if we did. All we have to do is be the face of the rubber stamp which the clerk pounds on the face of the man on trial which says, The people find you guilty and sentence you to prison and torture for your life's duration.

And finally, we must always consider it part of our rights and duties that, no matter how decent, how politically and economically advanced, how humane, gentle, and loving we know people in other nations to be, and no matter if the cause they are fighting and dying for is to overthrow the yoke of centuries of exploitation and despotism, we must be prepared at a moment's notice to look on them as deadly enemies threatening the very foundations of our homes and be prepared to burn them, starve them, torture them, kill them, and do the same to all others who do not regard them as deadly enemies because of government fiat, even though these others may be our own sons, brothers, fathers, lovers, and friends. Laws, lawmakers, or law-enforcers who do this are not to be considered laws, nor lawmakers, nor law-enforcers, and should be resisted as any usurpation or usurper should be, at all times.

The self-evident American right of revolution lies in this: that an unconstitutional law is not a law. An unconstitutional law can be defined, in revolutionary terms, as one against the people en masse, and for special privilege. It should be just as opposable when it is against *a people*, living within the confines of the United States. It is thus clearly not agreed on by all the people.

An officer of the government is as any officer "of the law" only when he is proceeding according to law. When he is killing a woman in an apartment house that may or may not be the location of a sniper, he is not acting in a lawful way. The moment he ventures beyond the law he becomes like any other man. He forfeits the law's mantle of immunity and protection. He may then be resisted like any other trespasser. A law that is palpably against the peace and security of all the people, such as all the racist laws on the books of the Southern States, laws limiting the rights and privileges of privacy and movement of the blacks in the Northern states, the laws against the Indians in the Western States, and those against the poor in all the states, is really not a law at all, constitutionally, and is thus void and confers no authority on anyone, and whoever attempts to execute it, does so at his own peril.

Common sense, the conscience of the mass, will tell you if this doctrine is not valid; then anyone with police power can usurp authority, and sustained by these unconstitutional laws, can treat people as he pleases. Many have already done this, are doing this, and still we wonder why we can't get these usurpers off our backs. A self-proclaimed "law-making body" or "law-enforcing agency" can beat, rape, torture or kill at will — as such bodies do now, in Mississippi, and have for over a century — and the people have no right to resist them. It simply does not make sense. The best of our founding fathers wanted the law to make sense . . . wanted a "government and policy on such plain and obvious general principles, as would be intelligible to the plainest rustic. . . ."

The true revolutionary, then and now, holds that the Declaration and the Constitution contemplate no submission by the people to gross usurpation of civil rights by the government, or to the lawless violence of its officers. On the contrary, the Constitution provides that the right of the people to keep and bear arms shall not be infringed. This constitutional right to bear arms implies the right to use them, as much as the constitutional right to buy and keep food implies the right to eat it.

The Constitution also takes it for granted that, as the people have the right, they will also have the sense to use arms, whenever the necessity of the case justifies it; this is the only remedy suggested by the Constitution, and is necessarily the only remedy that can exist when the government has become so corrupt that it can offer no peaceful solution to an intolerable way of life.

It is no answer to this argument on the right of revolution to say that if an unconstitutional act be passed, the mischief can be remedied by a repeal of it, and that this remedy can be brought about by a full discussion and the exercise of one's voting rights. The black men in the South discovered, generations ago, that if an unconstitutional and oppressive act is binding until invalidated by repeal, the government in the meantime will disarm them, plunge them into ignorance, suppress their freedom of assembly, stop them from casting a ballot and easily put it beyond their power to reform their government through the exercise of the rights of repeal.

A government can assume as much authority to disarm the people, to prevent them from voting, and to perpetuate rule by a clique as they have for any other unconstitutional act. So that if the first, and comparatively mild, unconstitutional and oppressive act cannot be resisted by force, then the last act necessary for the imposition of a total tyranny may not be.

The right of the government "to suppress insurrection" does not conflict with this right of the people to resist the execution of laws directed against their basic rights. An insurrection is a rising against the law, and not against usurpation. The actions, for example, of native facist groups can be demonstrated by their own public acts and statements to be designed for privilege for themselves and to be defamatory and oppressive to other groups among the people. The black people don't want the police to shoot into white working-class apartments either.

The right of resistance to usurping laws is in its simplest form a natural defense of the natural rights of people to protect themselves against thieves, tyrants, monomaniacs, and trespassers who attempt to set up their own personal, or group, authority against the people they are supposed to serve. It is the threat of the power of the people to remove them by force that keeps officeholders from perpetuating themselves. Not that they are any worse than other men, but the rewards are great and most of them act as though they were trying to discover the utmost limit of popular acquiescence to their self-exploitation and small tyrannies. In sum, if there is no right of revolution there is no other right our officials have to respect.

By no means am I saying that this is the prevailing concept of our organic law among the leaders and pundits of the country. Although they might, if pressed hard enough, give lip service to it. Arthur Schlesinger said in the *Atlantic Monthly* that the American concept of the right of revolution was the greatest idea we have given to the world:

First and foremost stands the concept of the inherent and universal right of revolution ... proclaimed in the Declaration of Independence: the

doctrine that "all men are created equal . . . possessing inalienable rights
to life, liberty and the pursuit of happiness" with the corollary that governments derive their just powers from the consent of the governed and that
therefore the people have a right to supplant any government "destructive
of these ends" with one they believe most likely to effect their safety and
happiness. True, the history of England provided precedents to the men
of 1776, and the Age of Enlightenment supplied intellectual support; but
the flaming pronouncement, followed by its vindication on the battlefield,
made the doctrine ever afterwards an irrepressible agency "in the course
of human events." Europe was the first to respond . . . A series of revolts
overturned, or strove to overturn, illiberal governments through most of
the Continent, and hastened popular reforms in other lands to forestall
popular upheavals. These convulsions all had their internal causes but
in every instance the leaders derived inspiration from America's achievement of popular rule, as well as from its freely expressed interest in their
similar aspirations.

"The Declaration of Independence is our Creed," Supreme
Court Justice Douglas said, in an article on "The U.S. and the
Revolutionary Spirit." He said we should not be afraid to talk
revolution and to voice our approval of it. He tells us to become
the active protagonist of the independence of all people. Go up
against the darkness and pain of continuing feudalism. "There is
a political feudalism where a dynasty has the trappings of a parliamentary system but manipulates it for the benefit of a ruling
class . . . Revolution in the twentieth century means rebellion
against another kind of feudalism . . . economic feudalism . . . the
United States should promote democratic revolutions against these
conditions of economic feudalism."

Going back, we find John Locke's dictum, in his essay on government, that when the natural rights of man are violated, the people
have the right and the duty of suppressing or changing the government. "The last recourse against wrongful and unauthorized force
is opposition to it."

It is the massiveness of the display of force against them that has
brought the black people to their revolutionary flash point more
than anything else. They know, as soon as they hear the sounds
of masses of police sirens that their little insurrection, or their little
rebellion, or their small act of resistance will turn into a massacre,
not of the enemy, but of themselves. But yet they go on resisting
until the local police sirens are replaced by the clank of tanks, or
personnel carriers; the clubs, the police revolvers are superseded

by bayonets and death-spitting machine guns. And still their exultation grows, an exultation that is absolutely inexplicable to the whites, seeing them surrounded by the massacre of their own people. Sartre speaks of this; of how the Frenchmen of the Resistance never felt freer than when they were under the attacks of the Nazi S. S. How the more they were condemned to silence, the more they felt that they were approaching liberation.

These rebellions by the blacks are a minority action: they cannot succeed militarily, and nobody thinks they will. The whole process is a *telling* revolution, a way of stating something buried under centuries of apathy and indifference far worse than omnipresent opposition. A *Life* magazine interview with a black sniper reveals this. He is not trying to kill cops and Guardsmen. When they are struck down it is by accident. He is trying, he says, to tell "our people we are here." And in the process, "the firing of five or six shots in the air is enough to draw cops thick as fleas on a dog and still give time to get away." Then the people take what they want.

But it is much more than that: the black insurrection-white massacre method of telling revolution is in some ways comparable to the Buddhists burning themselves to tell of their to-the-death commitment to their country's revolution.

I always felt that an enormous amount of time, money, and effort was wasted in the last years of the civil-rights crisis, while the leaders, black and white, were trying to convince the American black man that he was really a downtrodden Hindu, a palpitating mass of ingrained and inborn submission, a victim of a caste society which stretches back, almost to prehistory. The Hindu, or to be more specific, the followers of Gandhi, were victims in a land so impoverished and barren that a lifetime of starvation was, and still is, their common lot . . . a land where living is so hard that men want a God so they can hate him as the father and ordainer of their degradation.

The American black man is a citizen in a rich land, with a citizen's rights and duty to resist, resist all attempts to deprive him of its manifold blessings. Even if he doesn't *want* to resist, he must; it is his duty, as it is the duty of all honest whites to urge him and support him in the process. Why should he have been urged to go through all this Hinduizing to regain the rights he already had in 1776? He was here then and fought alongside of the whites out of the same revolutionary morality, for the same

revolutionary rights he is dying for right now . . . the idea that
men before the law are exactly equal and that no man can take
away these equalities except as forfeiture for a crime adjudged and
confirmed by ancient and democratic due process.

Legally he has always had these rights. They were taken away
from him by force and fraud. When the racist laws were written
and enforced and then upheld finally by the Supreme Court of the
United States, it was the lawbreaker and should have been resisted.
The black man did resist these racist laws, but in vain. Police,
militia, Federal troops beat him until he went down, over and over
again, a victim of blood and violence, his land looted, his home
burned, his daughter raped, his son lynched, his babies starved,
his progeny for generations suffering automatically the same fate.

When he was finally handed the weapon of "soul force" he tried
it; no one can deny that he honestly gave it a try. But we are
living in a lunatic society, a racist society that will never stop hiring
cops and soldiers to beat him until he stops them . . . or we stop
the hiring. If we say the black man is a citizen, then he has a clear
duty to resist tyranny and dictatorship, legally and peacefully if
he can, forcibly if he must. He is the birthright possessor of the
same rights we have. He cannot give them up if he wants to. He
was not born to be a victim to test the longevity of our desire to
oppress him.

Take a good look at the *Life* magazine for July 28, 1967. Look
at it before it lies dog-eared in the dentist's office, or slides to
oblivion in the trash trucks. Before the eyes of one of its reporters
and cameramen, a police cruiser drew up on a littered street, surrounded by stores so gutted and debased that they are simply
valueless: they are not stores anymore, they are piles of trash. A
twenty-four-year-old black man took a six-pack of beer from one
of them. He saw the cops. He had been arrested before, so he ran.

A yellow-helmeted cop with a shotgun leaped out of the cruiser.
He aimed the gun with *his kind* of all deliberate speed and shot the
black man dead . . . for a six-pack of beer! And the spreading
pellets from the murderous blast tore their way into the soft flesh
of Joe Bass, Jr., a black shoeshine boy, twelve years old, with
nothing in his hands. He was struck in the neck and the thigh and
fell bleeding to the pavement, his eyes open and staring straight
ahead, his body almost finding a restful embrace in the dirty
asphalt.

The Newark policeman, his shotgun still at the ready, turns

away from the murdered Billy Furr, the looter of a six-pack of beer. There is no anguish in his face, his mouth is relaxed, almost soft as he reaches into the side pocket of his blue shirt for a cigar. The story is told accurately and compassionately, even to the point of telling how when little Joey was struck down fifty sobbing black men and women tried to get to him, to help him, and were clubbed back by a small squad of police with rifle butts. But the name of the murderer in the blue uniform shirt is not reported. And it is possible he will never be known, and his face will be forgotten, for the police in this country, when they are acting against the black people, are usually faceless and nameless and omnipotent, infallible and unpunishable, like Yahweh.

There was the Boston Massacre and there was the Newark Massacre. The last took place yesterday, in our time, in our country; the men who carried it out bore our faces, the bullets that found their way anonymously into black bodies were paid for, in part by us. It is our consciousness, our heritage, vibrating in the air we breathe.

Let us examine again the rules we live by . . . the life, liberty and pursuit of happiness guarantees. These rules say, if these guarantees are not forthcoming . . . "that whenever any form of government shall become destructive of these ends, it is the right of the people to alter or abolish it, and to institute a new government."

Certainly, no one in his right mind will deny that this form of government has been highly destructive to the life, liberty, *et cetera* of the black people. This, above all things, is self-evident. The black people are still in a social, economic, and political bondage. After a great war was fought to free them, they are not free. There is no excuse for the brute fact that our parliamentary system has not been able to bring them into the mainstream of American life. Not only that, their story can only be told in times of upheaval and self-slaughter. And even after these take place, the only comment made on it, or the only ones asked about it, are old crocks like Senator Dirksen, someone who is supremely irrelevant to what is going on, anywhere, and who yet is considered one of the two or three leading spokesmen of our government. All he can say is that we, the whites, are "getting impatient with this disregard of law and order." This fact alone, that Dirksen is speaking for it, shows the complete idiocy and futility of the Congress.

We say over and over again that the solving of the race question will take time, but there is no excuse for this. We establish new forms of government because it took too much time before, in the old form, to resolve an accursed question of human suffering. New governments are not to create a continuation of the same wrongs and social stultifications that made the new form a bloody imperative. We have had long enough . . . enough, enough to see ourselves as white-skinned racists creating and maintaining a society where some get all the good of it while others deeply suffer . . . where the good of one comes out of the evil put upon another . . . where we exist in a prison of our white skin as inescapable as that of our black neighbors. What we do to the black people, daily, makes me want to secede from the white race! It makes me, down deep, hate myself, and my color. All decent whites especially the young whites, abhor having to bear the burden of racist guilt their fathers have placed upon them.

And they hate white racist America and their own fathers for sustaining it, for stealing from them what should have been a birthright of human brotherhood, alienating them from young blacks by white cruelty to them, in their white image. For setting up impassable barriers between young whites and young blacks, areas of suspicion coming from a constant betrayal. They want to clasp hands with the blacks, if only in admiration of the dignity, patience, and restraint they have shown up to this breaking point. If we let them alone they will offer them love and support for their bloody struggle to rise to a level of liberation and privilege which whites accept as due to them by their birth alone.

And we adults: we hate white racist America because it has blocked out of the culture of our time the unfettered expression of the wisdom of a people to whom the meaning of life has had to be privation, suffering and alienation, but who have lived, somehow, with moments of ecstasy, with spurts of infectuous and inexplicable joy. White racist America makes me ashamed of my own country, which not only presents to a vibrant, revolutionary world the complacent facade of a sluttish society whose mass ideal is the unlimited consumption of all possible goods and services . . . but has lost all of its revolutionary virtues in an hour when the darker people are finally climbing into the light, and are forced to seek elsewhere the encouragement which some of our revolutionary fathers meant for us to bestow upon mankind. And in the losing of this revolutionary virtue, we have turned despicably into our opposites and are murdering revolutionaries all over the world.

And all the time we are doing this we are telling the little white children, and some of the little black children, that Abe Lincoln said in 1848: "Any people anywhere being inclined and having the power, have the right to rise up and shake off the existing government, and form a new one that suits them better. This is a most valuable and sacred right, a right we hope and believe is to liberate the world."

And we are teaching high school students, black and white, that Abe Lincoln, the great emancipator, said, in his First Inaugural Address: "This country, with its institutions, belongs to the people who inhabit it. Whenever they shall grow weary, of the existing government, they can exercise their constitutional right of amending it, or their revolutionary right to dismember, or overthrow it."

They tell us that we have this great and basic right, but if we so much as suggest the use of it, we are punished . . . we are imprisoned. So that it serves as an entrapment, a vicious provocation to smoke out radicals and revolutionaries. Why do they say this . . . why do they so piously quote the forefathers and then blame and hurt people under an unforgivable longevity of oppression . . . obviously getting worse instead of better . . . for trying to act under it?

The United States House of Representatives has just demonstrated its imbecility and outright betrayal of the Bill of Rights, which it has sworn to uphold, by passing a bill which makes traveling from one state to another and saying anything that might be, after the fact, twisted into a connection with a riot, a criminal offense. It carries a fine of ten thousand dollars or imprisonment for five years, or both.

It was written by a white racist from Florida and forced onto the floor by the white racist from Mississippi, who said, the insurrections in the black ghettos were "organized conspiracies backed by the Communists . . . if you vote against this bill, what are you going to say when you go home and meet the policeman and fireman who risked their lives, and in many instances, lost them. . . ." As if it was not already clear that the lawless, conspiratorial, rioting element in the community is the police themselves.

This does not mean that the Southern racist congressmen were responsible for the bill. Charles W. Sandman, Jr., a Republican from New Jersey, was one of its most ardent supporters and said the police in Newark had told him that rioters had crossed the Hudson River in buses, were picked up in cars and taken to the

84

center of Newark, where the trouble occurred. There is no proof
in existence that this did occur, while on the other hand it is well
known that the police will say anything that will develop their
own positions. So the bill was passed by a vote of 347 to 70 . . . and
they were not all Southern congressmen who voted for it.

This is how we put off, again and again, truth and resolution for
some dishonest and shoddy solution. And then we snivel and
hurt the helpless when the chickens come home to roost. It was
not outside agitators behind the guns of Newark . . . it could be
the inflammatory boasts and texts of our daily education. Now
they will have to prevent Thomas Jefferson, in the form of his
writings, from crossing state lines, for he said: "What country can
preserve its liberties if their rulers are not warned from time to
time that this people preserve the spirit of resistance. Let them
take arms. . . ."

Or if the agitator from New Jersey crosses the line into Pennsylvania, he will find the Pennsylvania Declaration of Rights already
there, saying: "The Community hath an indubitable, inalienable,
and indefeasible right to reform, alter or abolish government in
such manner as shall be by that community judged most conducive
to the public weal."

Henry Clay of Kentucky, the Great Commoner, said: "An oppressed people are authorized, whenever they can, to rise and break
their fetters."

John Adams, the second President of the United States, said:
"It is an observation of one of the profoundest inquiries into human
affairs that a revolution of government is the strongest proof that
can be given by a people, of their virtue and good sense."

His son, also a President of the United States, said: "In the
abstract theory of our government, the obedience of the citizen is
not due to an unconstitutional law: he may lawfully resist its
execution."

And Henry D. Thoreau, a good revolutionary, an artist of the
revolutionaries, said: "All men recognize the right of revolution,
that is the right to refuse allegiance to and to resist, the government where its tyranny or its inefficiency are great and unendurable."

In Maryland its Declaration of Rights reads: "Whenever the
ends of government are perverted, and public liberty manifestly
endangered, and all other means of redress are ineffectual, the
people may, and of right ought to, reform the old or establish a

new government; the doctrine of non-resistance against arbitrary power and oppression is absurd, slavish and destructive of the good and happiness of mankind."

General and President U. S. Grant said: "The right of Revolution is an inherent one. When people are oppressed by their government, it is a natural right they enjoy to relieve themselves of the oppression if they are strong enough, either by withdrawing from it, or by overthrowing it and substituting a government more acceptable."

And Emerson, talking of affairs in Kansas, when white settlers in 1856 had to knuckle down to racist tyrants and live like people in the black ghettos today, said:

I think there never was a people so choked and stultified by forms. We adore the forms of law, instead of making them vehicles of wisdom and justice. Language has lost its meaning in the universal cant. . . . *Representative Government* is really misrepresentative. *Democracy, Freedom,* fine names for an ugly thing. They call it attar of roses and lavender, — I call it bilge water. They call it Chivalry and Freedom; I call it the stealing of all earnings of a poor man and the earnings of his little girl and boy, and the earnings of all that shall come from him his children's children forever. But this is union and this is Democracy, and our poor people, led by the nose by these fine words, dance and sing, ring bells and fire cannon, with every new link of the chain which is forged for their limbs by the plotters in the Capital. . . . What are the results of law and Union? There is no Union. The judges give cowardly interpretation to the law, in direct opposition to the known foundation of all law, *that every immoral statute is void!* If that be law, let the ploughshare be run under the foundations of the Capitol — and if that be government, extirpation is the only cure. I am glad that the terror at disunion and anarchy is disappearing. . . .

Now I submit that somewhere, every day in this country, some schoolboy is reading about these men; that their words, revolution and all, are passing into their consciousness. This being undeniably true . . . how can we stop these dangerous thoughts from crossing state lines, color lines, or lines of any kind? We could not stop them from entering the icy legal mind of Mr. Justice Jackson, late of the Supreme Court, who gave, in 1950, the most concrete modern juridical opinion of the right of revolution based on the Declaration of Independence.

. . . we cannot ignore the fact that our own government originated in revolution, and is legitimate only if overthrow by force can sometimes be justified. That circumstances sometimes justify it is not Communist doctrine, but an old American belief. The men who led the struggle forcibly to overthrow lawfully constituted British authority found moral support by asserting a natural law under which their revolution was justified, and they bravely proclaimed their belief in the document basic to our freedom. Such sentiments have also been given ardent and rather extravagant expression by Americans of undoubted patriotism.

So there it is, deep in the hide of the Republic, and you can talk about it all you want, having a revolution, that is, just as long as it is in a classroom, and you are white. But don't say it, as William Epton did, on the streets of Harlem before a group of silent men, whose eyes have a tiny glow like the stirring of a long-banked fire.

II

Issues

THE NATIONAL SECURITY BUREAUCRACY AND MILITARY INTERVENTION

RICHARD BARNET

I

Although it is too early for full-scale postmortems, the pathological character of America's descent into the mire of Vietnam has begun to inspire some exploratory dissection of the policy-making process itself. How could Vietnam have happened? The calamity of the involvement is attributed by some critics to a series of mistakes — misperceptions, self-delusions, and false analogies. Well-meaning officials in the State Department and the Pentagon blinded themselves to the truth and then to protect their reputations felt driven to mislead the country. James C. Thomson, for example, describes a bureaucratic climate in which the "politics of inadvertance" thrives. Informed judgment and decent instinct are stifled. Good men become prisoners of their own rhetoric, seeking escape by promising to do tomorrow with increased vigor what so clearly failed yesterday.

Other critics prefer to explain the fact that the United States is now engaged in a war that threatens to tear apart American society as well as Vietnamese by blaming the specific individuals who with phenomenal tenacity have continued to define the Vietnam "commitment" for the rest of us. Dean Rusk, Walt Rostow, William Bundy, Maxwell Taylor, and Robert McNamara are indeed primarily responsible for implicating the rest of us in a moral and political disaster. They have counseled and helped carry out the commission of offenses against the law of nations, against our own constitution, and against elementary morality. For this alone, those of them who are still in office should not serve another day. But it is wildly optimistic to think that the overdue retirement of a group of individuals will in itself produce a change of policy. "Throw the rascals out" is a good American political slogan but it does not carry us very far towards a political analysis of what has happened to the United States in the Vietnam War. Nor does it provide any assurance that we will avoid future Vietnams.

It is the thesis of this paper that the roots of the Vietnam failure lie more in the structure and organization of the national security bureaucracy than in the personality of the President or the idiosyncracies of the particular group of foundation executives, military commanders, Rhodes Scholars, and businessmen who have been the President's principal advisors during the escalation of the Vietnam commitment into the Vietnam War. As Tom Wicker's recent study makes clear, the President's personal role is crucial, but he operates within limits set by the vast foreign policy machinery of government. The President may decide, but the bureaucracy structures the decisions by setting out the choices. If the basis of the American commitment to take on revolutionary movements around the world is institutional, then we cannot hope to avoid future Vietnam-like adventures in other places merely by shifts in personnel or even by changes in general policy pronouncements. We could write a National Security Council directive to avoid large-scale military interventions in the future, but if we do not change the institutions which push us toward intervention, such a paper will have as much effect in keeping us out of future Vietnams as our United Nations commitments have had on the present involvement.

The interventionist thrust of postwar U.S. foreign policy from Greece in 1947 to the Dominican Republic and Vietnam in the 1960's has been its most striking characteristic. On an average of once every eighteen months the United States has sent military and para-military forces into other countries either to fight guerrilla movements or to overthrow governments considered to be Communist or Communist-leaning. In addition to the major campaigns in such places as Iran, Guatemala, Dominican Republic, British Guiana, and Cuba the United States maintains counterinsurgency forces and intelligence operations for manipulating internal politics in most of the other underdeveloped countries of the world. The intervention in Vietnam is not an aberration. It is part of a continuing pattern. Indeed, the same analysis and techniques that were applied to Vietnam are now being applied to Thailand and to Guatemala, to name only two of the most likely candidates for the next major interventions. (There are more U.S. counter-insurgency forces in Thailand today than there were in

Vietnam in early 1965). What is aberrational about Vietnam is that the extraordinary concentration of killing power directed at America's enemies (as well as her friends) in that small country has not produced the results we have been able to obtain elsewhere. For a variety of historical reasons mainly concerned with the fact that Ho Chi Minh has gained a certain proficiency through practice, having won the same war before, the Vietnamese intervention is a failure. This accounts for much of the criticism of the present policy. In cost-effectiveness terms the war makes no sense. I have spoken to several people in the Pentagon who favor settlement of the war on whatever terms we can get on the ground that it is the right war in the wrong place.

It is not my purpose here to argue the merits of an interventionist policy. I have discussed elsewhere why America's arrogation of a "responsibility" to suppress revolutionary movements in the name of anti-communism brutalizes and corrupts not only the societies which we are attempting to set right but our own. My starting point is that the "overmilitarization" of our foreign policy, as George Kennan calls it, combined with the interventionist itch is our greatest national problem.

Another premise is that national policy cannot be defended simply by pointing to official characterizations of foreign threats. During the past twenty years we have ignored or excused a variety of revolting acts carried out by people on the public payroll including invasions, assassinations, coups, crop destructions, and village burnings by telling ourselves that the Soviet Threat or the Chinese Threat or the Guatemalan Threat required them. We have institutionalized in the office of the Deputy Director for Plans of the CIA an operation which Agency employees themselves like to refer to as the "Department of dirty tricks." To justify its activities, however outrageous, it has been necessary only to point to the world-wide espionage activities of the Soviet Union.

It is foolish to deny that the world is in fact a dangerous and anarchic place or that other nations do not behave in similar ways — although because of their limited resources not usually to the same extent. But threats in international politics can be apprehended not by revelation but by judgment. The threats which are triggers of national policy are intellectual constructs developed by bureaucracies whose function is to discover and deal with threats. Neither the Secretary of State nor the Chief of Staff of the Air Force has the gift of infallible political insight. They must

guess. Over the past twenty years there has been a marked tendency to guess in certain ways rather than others about the nature
of the threats facing the United States and what should be done
about them. Put simply, the official world view provides an ideological justification of the ever-growing use of force as an instrument of national policy. The intelligence bureaucracies knowingly
err on the "conservative" side in discovering enemies and esti-
mating their intentions. If they do not turn out to have the vast
armies and limitless guile which are attributed to them, then, so
these bureaucracies argue, no harm is done. It's better to be
prepared for the worst, and this means taking on new military
"requirements." Sometimes, however, threats are minimized in
order to justify a seemingly rational policy based primarily on the
use of military power. Thus North Vietnam can be beaten in a
few months, the advocates of military intervention argued. China,
according to the disciples of victory through air power, can be
eliminated as a world power by simply "taking out" her atomic
installations.

It must be said that many of the threats to which we have
responded have been consistently exaggerated. The Soviet invasion
of Western Europe of the nineteen forties, the missile gap of the
nineteen fifties, and the world-wide campaign for wars of national
liberation orchestrated in Moscow are all examples of threats discovered by the national security bureaucracy which in retrospect
we know were nothing like what the national security bureaucracy
proclaimed them to be at the time. Yet each was the inspiration
for major decisions to increase military commitments and inter-
ventionary behavior. The purpose of this paper is to examine
some of the characteristics of the national security bureaucracy
which lead it to identify threats in the way they do and to influence
U.S. policy in the direction of intervention.

II

The Vietnam experience illustrates the crucial role of bureaucratic momentum. When President Kennedy was considering putting 16,000 troops in Vietnam in 1963, George Ball is reported to
have told him that it would take 300,000 to get them out. The
President himself completely understood that deployments are
themselves commitments and that a military presence must be
protected by a greater presence. "The troops will march in; the

bands will play," he told his advisors, "then we will be told to send in more troops. It's like taking a drink. The effect wears off and you have to take another." Yet he was unable to resist stepping onto the escalator. Once troops are committed and some are killed, then those who advocate escalation can use the irresistible rhetoric of redemption. We must commit more to justify what we committed already. Each stage of the commitment is looked upon as an experiment. Each bureaucracy specializing in a different technique for controlling the internal development of South Vietnam asks for the chance to show what it can do. The Special Forces argue that six months of pacification efforts will break the back of the insurgency. A few thousand troops are sent. But the political situation in Saigon has come close to collapse. Therefore, the Air Force argues, let us make a dramatic commitment of our overwhelming air power and bomb the north. The Navy has its solution and the Army also. Because of the variety of military and para-military techniques at the disposal of the United States, the apparent weakness of the enemy, and the low risk of massive intervention by the Soviet Union and China, the proponents of escalation can argue that the costs of experimentation are low. Unlike a major war where the United States itself is endangered, the consequences of failure of any particular military operation against a distant underdeveloped country appear limited. The bureaucracy falls prey to the illusion that they are able to control events because they are free of the fear of retaliation. They feel they have all the options and they can try them one by one. The great preponderance of power of the United States also relieves them of any responsibility to think through the process of escalation to the end and attempt to calculate the final costs and benefits. They are convinced that the United States is willing and able to "pay any price" or "bear any burden" to carry through what it started. As the commitment increases, so of course does the psychological investment in the objective for which the commitment is presumably made. The preservation of an American sphere of influence in Vietnam looks far more crucial *after* the massive installations at Cam Ran Bay and Danang are built than before.

The National Interest in small countries where Americans have few ethnic ties or business interests is determined by the national security bureaucracies themselves. They define both the tasks and the techniques to be employed. They are, understandably, not prone to underestimate the importance of what they are doing nor are they reticent in calculating the support they need. If they are operating a base, it is the most important bastion of the Free World to be protected at all costs. It matters little that the base was built before the present intercontinental weapons system and in purely military terms is obsolete. To lose it, the interested bureaucrats argue, would be a political defeat. To them, the National Interest and the Air Force's Interest are identical despite the fact that most Americans have never heard of the irrelevant base and would sleep no less soundly if it were gone.

Once an American presence is established in another country, experience suggests that it is unlikely that the U.S. will limit that presence in either size or character to its original commitment. In Greece, Lebanon, the Dominican Republic as well as Vietnam non-military interventions escalated into major military efforts. In each case American soldiers were sent because the non-military bureaucracies were inadequate to maintain American interests as they had been defined. (In Greece, U.S. officers under General Van Fleet ended up running the war for the Greek Government despite explicit assurances to Congress to the contrary. In Lebanon the Marines landed to extricate the United States from a disastrous involvement in internal Lebanese politics largely engineered by the CIA.) The progression from aid missions to counter-insurgency "advisors" to expeditionary forces takes on a kind of Parkinsonian inevitability. This is not true everywhere, to be sure. There is evidence that the U.S. would not have resorted to a military invasion to keep Indonesia from going communist simply because the task was so obviously formidable. But where the resources of the U.S. appear adequate to suppress insurgent movements, the result is predictable. In Latin American countries, for example, where the United States maintains a Little America with the familiar Military Advisory Group, the contingent from the Office of Public Safety to train and equip the police, and an array of agricultural and educational specialists, we have been ready to expand the national commitment to meet the threat as these bureaucracies define it. In Guatemala the role of the Special Forces has dramatically increased to keep pace with the rising insurgency. Given the assumptions underlying the original intervention — the necessity to prevent leftist insurgent movements from taking power — the decision whether to escalate the effort from non-military to para-military to overtly military means depends on the adversary's toughness, not American self-restraint. It may be logically possible to impose self-limits on the scale of intervention in a particular country but it is usually not politically possible. Because the increments in the scale are small — "What's the matter with sending a few more advisors?" — they are hard to resist. Since insurgent movements are growing in both numbers and strength in Asia, Africa, and Latin America, the present bureaucratic entities which owe their existence to an ideological commitment to oppose them have little incentive to resist new occasions for testing the National Will in exotic places.

III

The dynamism of the myriad bureaucratic empires dealing in national security assures not only the escalation of U.S. commitments but their progressive militarization as well. While the responsibility is his, President Johnson should not be judged too harshly for choosing in late 1964 two drastic military techniques to solve the Vietnam problem, for there were only military alternatives proposed to him. The national security bureaucracies were divided as to the specific techniques to use. The Air Force promised good results from bombing. The Army recommended an expeditionary force. Roger Hilsman reports that he wanted to send in rangers to act as counter-guerrillas. The Chemical Corps suggested certain chemical agents. From the idea-men in the Pentagon, the CIA and the State Department, there was funnelled up toward the White House a steady stream of proposals for burning, bombing, blasting, and poisoning the Vietnamese enemy. Most of the proposals were turned aside by the civilian leadership but a certain percentage were of course accepted.

Virtually no energy was spent in those crucial days on finding a political solution to the Vietnamese crisis so convinced was the whole national security establishment — especially the State Department — that only a military solution was possible. Roger Hilsman notes that as early as 1961 Secretary Rusk "regarded Vietnam as essentially a military problem." Proposals for settlement by U Thant, the Soviet Union, and de Gaulle, and peace feelers from Hanoi in 1964 were all dismissed. "We do not believe in conferences to ratify terror, so our policy is unchanged," the President announced. The national security bureaucracy was unready to take the risks of peace-making because they knew so little about the process. The classic political arts of negotiation and compromise, which are far harder to master than even the logistical skill entailed in moving a half million men into battle positions ten thousand miles away, were not in high demand in the State Department. Indeed, the one high official of the Kennedy Administration, Chester Bowles, who took the time and energy to plan a negotiated settlement of Vietnam involving the neutralization of Southeast Asia was rewarded for his efforts by a transfer to obscurity.

Thus, while the Pentagon bureaucracy churned out dozens of recommendations for making the life of the Vietnamese more miserable in imaginative new ways, no comparable energy was spent on thinking through the national interests of the United States in the area, other than how we could impose our will on the Viet Cong and North Vietnam. No staff work of any consequence was devoted to the kind of peace settlement we ultimately wanted or had reasons to expect, and how we could get it. There was no thought given to how the U.S. might relate peacefully to Southeast Asia. The alternatives were seen simply as "losing Southeast Asia" or crushing the Viet Cong. There were contingency plans on file with the Chiefs of Staff on what to do in the event of war with Cambodia or Brazil, but no body of bureaucratic wisdom on how to obtain a peace settlement in Vietnam by political means. Because the reality in Vietnam was far more complex and the position of the U.S. considerably less noble than our White Papers would have it, national security officials were quite ready to talk themselves into believing that negotiation was unnecessary. Knowing that negotiation would produce a result considerably short of a U.S. victory, the leaders of the Pentagon and State Department sought to avoid the personal risk of association with what political opponents would be sure to call a "sell-out." Thus they beguiled themselves with the thought that they could end the war by the application of military power alone. "The guerrillas will simply fade away," an Under-Secretary of State told me in early 1966.

The failure to treat Vietnam as a political rather than military problem has been extremely costly for the United States. By any military analysis the world's greatest military machine should have brought an already war-weakened nation of huts to its knees long ago. The lack of confidence in the U.S. government within our own population and among most foreign countries stems from the failure to accomplish this. Because the national security bureaucracy did not understand or admit to itself the real reasons people were fighting in Vietnam the very military strategy we employed increased our vulnerability. The more divisions we sent, the more we suffered casualties and the more the political costs mounted. We did not understand enough of Vietnamese politics or world politics to realize that the enemy would not only continue to fight but with the outside help he was sure to get would actually grow in economic and military strength.

Once again the National Security Managers — those in charge of the State Department, the Pentagon, and the White House staff — had reduced a complex political reality to a test of the American will. Because they had neither sufficient knowledge of Vietnamese history nor empathy with the tragedy of that land or its politics, they saw it only as a symbol of a larger struggle. The war in Vietnam was another of the great confrontations that the communists have arranged, as Walt Rostow has put it, to challenge "the nerve and will of the West." Along with Korea and Berlin it was another "test case." In this egocentric view of the universe other nations exist to serve as sparring partners for the United States. So fascinated by the confrontation model of world politics are the national security bureaucrats that they see even relatively minor procedural issues in the same heroic terms. One official greeted the preliminary skirmish over a site for "contacts" with North Vietnam as if it were Armageddon. "There we were right off the bat — eyeball to eyeball," he told a *New York Times* reporter, "on a question of prestige as well as procedure. And they're the ones who blinked. Now we're one up."

Because the national security bureaucracy tends to squeeze political problems into the confrontation mold, it favors using instruments of violence to solve them. Even where the essentially political nature of the problem is recognized, as in Vietnam where for years official analyses have stated that the war was primarily one for "hearts and minds" that had to be won on the "political battlefront," the military effort completely engulfed the non-military strategies. When the American expeditionary force overran villages and the Air Force obliterated them through bombing, Special Forces pacification teams found the campaign to win their political support by being nice to children and old people somewhat compromised. The national security bureaucrats explain the familiar phenomenon of the military strategy overtaking and rendering ineffective the non-military strategies by noting "that's the way the world is." The official view that guerrillas are part of a world-wide army intent on humiliating and defeating the United States rather than political rebels reacting to local political conditions cannot, however, be explained by reference to an "objective reality." Again and again the State Department has misread the politics of guerrilla movements in order to make them fit the preconceived military model. Thus the Greek guerrillas in 1947 were Stalin's agents carrying on, as Ambassador Loy Henderson put it at the time, "the red tide of invasion." In fact, Stalin was trying to stop the insurgency. According to William Bullitt who was influential in setting U.S. Vietnam policy in 1947, Ho Chi Minh was a Chinese agent. And in 1951, in his oft-quoted analysis, Dean Rusk pronounced Mao's China to be a "Russian Manchukuo."

These are not random "mistakes"; they are part of a consistent official ideology which cannot be explained by stupidity, for the national security elite are on the whole a group that excels on law school examinations. They are rationalizations for committing America's military power. The peculiar mental set of the national security bureaucrat is the product of certain biases which I would contend are inherent in the bureaucratic structure itself. Put simply, for almost thirty years the United States government has been organized for war. Since 1940, we have spent from 50% to 75% of the national budget on military and para-military bureaucracies. We have staffed them with bright energetic people who define their goals in the traditional terms of *Machtpolitik* and use military means to carry them out. The impact of the Second World War on the subsequent militarization of American policy is so crucial that we must look at it in some detail.

IV

Under the impact of war, the position of the federal bureaucracy in American society changed radically in two ways. First, government agencies came to control the creation and disposition of a significant share of the national wealth. Second, the balance of power within the federal bureaucracy shifted decisively to those agencies which concerned themselves with foreign and military affairs. In 1939 the Federal government had about 800,000 civilian employees, about 10% of whom worked for national security agencies. At the end of the war, the figure approached four million, of which more than 75% were in national security activities. The last pre-mobilization defense budget represented about 1.4% of the Gross National Product. The lowest postwar defense budget, an interlude of about 18 months between demobilization and re-mobilization for the Cold War, took 4.7% of the Gross National Product. Defense spending alone for fiscal year 1948 (the year of the lowest postwar Defense budget) exceeded by more than one billion the entire budget of the federal government for the last prewar year. Once postwar remobilization was underway, defense spending seldom dipped below 8% of the GNP.

The phenomenal increase in the size and importance of the national security bureaucracies was accompanied by major transformations in their character. The State Department and the military agencies came out of the war with views of their functions and roles that differed substantially from their prewar self-images. In large part, this metamorphosis was attributable to a generation of new men, schooled in war, who now stood ready to take over the swollen machinery of government.

Only for a few fleeting moments in her history had the United States attached high importance to the diplomacy of negotiation or awarded more than ceremonial status to the men who practiced it. In the earliest days of the Republic, Jefferson, Jay, and Franklin, the political and intellectual leaders of the United States, had shrewdly carved a place for the new nation as an adjunct of the European state system. In the weakness of infancy, the U.S. relied heavily on persuasion and political maneuver to protect herself. But the Monroe Doctrine, which marked the divorce of America from European politics, also marked the shift of American diplomacy from cosmopolitanism to parochialism. The focus of the State Department turned from negotiating with equal or stronger powers to servicing the process of expansion. In most of the world the American ambassador limited his role to that of a reporter or a scout for commercial opportunities. The Department in Washington devoted its energies principally to economic, consular, and trade matters. The diplomatic career was a pleasant life for the rich man's son, the dilettante, or the retired financier who did not mind being outside the mainstream of politics and commerce. It hardly taxed one's intellect or initiative, and the salary Congress was prepared to appropriate for the diplomat reflected the value it placed on his services. In the late nineteenth century, the top ambassadorial posts began to go to prominent businessmen. The embassy, like the honorary degree, had become a ritualized reward for commercial success.

The alternative conception of diplomacy was imperialism. From the Monroe Doctrine to the Truman Doctrine, American diplomats spent much of their time helping the army to wrest control of the continent from the Indians and extending the U.S. sphere of influence to Latin America and the island prizes of the Spanish-American war. While he was a passive agent of American interests in the great courts of Europe, the American diplomat was an active and vigorous defender of U.S. business interests among more backward peoples and an engineer of territorial expansion through purchase and war.

Nothing American diplomats had done in the prewar period equipped them to deal with the fantastic problems and opportunities that faced America across the ruins of war. The situation in the world was unprecedented: one nation had been restored and strengthened by the war that had ravaged most of the rest. How the United States should relate to a starving, seething planet was a task for which the diffident socialites who had graced the European embassies and the pro-consuls who had managed U.S. interests in Latin America were equally ill fitted. Most of the prewar generation of diplomats soon disappeared from the scene. A generation of career Ambassadors, like Norman Davis, as well as the leading administrators of the State Department in the New Deal period, Cordell Hull and Sumner Welles, did not survive the war in office. Despite repeated reorganizations during the war, the State Department's staff continued to reflect the prewar conception of its function. It was far stronger in economic, trade and consular matters than in the practice of international politics. Even three years after the war the Department had a total of only 336 officers supposedly dealing with political questions out of a total complement of 5,906.

Franklin D. Roosevelt, who loved to play both the soldier and the diplomat, helped finish off the feeble prewar foreign policy bureaucracy with a series of blows. First, he appointed as Secretary of State a decent, old-fashioned moralist who bored him utterly. When he felt compelled to communicate with the State Department at all, he usually did so privately through Sumner Welles, the old school-mate he had appointed as Under-Secretary. Throughout his memoirs, Hull complains about being left in the dark on the great issues. With the outbreak of war, communication between the White House and the State Department broke down almost entirely. "Don't tell anybody in the State Department about this," the President told Robert Murphy, then a junior foreign service officer about to leave on a presidential mission to North Africa. "That place is a sieve." To insure against State Department interference in his foreign policy, Roosevelt carried on his most important correspondence in Navy Department codes.

The State Department's prestige and power in government declined in other ways as well. Many foreign service officers were drafted. It was not considered an essential occupation. Thus while the officer corps of the military services grew astronomically, the ranks of the professional diplomatic service were depleted. At the same time the professionalism of the foreign service was further challenged. New foreign policy bureaucracies responsible to other, more powerful agencies, such as the Departments of Agriculture, Treasury, and Commerce, as well as the emergency agencies, came increasingly to overshadow the State Department. At the height of the war, forty-four separate government agencies had representatives stationed at the American Embassy in London. At the end of the war the Manpower Act of 1946 encouraged the "lateral entry" of military officers into the top foreign service grades, thus diluting the old club atmosphere and bringing in a new breed of diplomat fresh from the war. Veteran diplomats mourned the passing of the good old days when a half-dozen men would gather in the Secretary's office and talk over the state of the world.

The early postwar spy scandals further weakened the prestige of the older foreign affairs bureaucracy. Then, before McCarthy, came McCarthyism. Alger Hiss, the old China hands, the Poland losers, the Czechoslovakia losers, and the other "vendors of compromise" in the State Department, as Senator John F. Kennedy would later call them, became tabloid celebrities before Senator McCarthy produced the blank piece of paper that supposedly listed 205 known Communists in the State Department. The army eventually triumphed over McCarthy, but the State Department suffered further casualties in the war. A former police reporter, FBI agent, and administrative aid to Senator Styles Bridges, Scott McLeod, believed generally to be a McCarthy man, took over as the Security Officer of the State Department, bringing with him an Elbert Hubbard motto for his desk: "An ounce of loyalty is worth more than a pound of brains." Full field investigations were conducted on veteran foreign service officers all over the world. Dulles encouraged the house cleaning, demanding "positive loyalty" from his diplomats. John Paton Davies, who years earlier had come up with so unpopular a prediction as Mao's victory in China, was found to be "lacking in judgment" and was dismissed despite repeated clearances from various loyalty boards.

V

In the war years, the President turned increasingly to his generals and admirals for foreign policy advice not only because his primary focus was on winning the war but, perhaps more important, because Marshall and his associates inspired confidence as Hull did not. The Joint Chiefs, not Hull, attended the Big Three meetings at Cairo, Teheran, and Casablanca. At Yalta, Roosevelt threw aside the voluminous briefing books the State Department had provided him because he thought they were, in general, too equivocal on the future of the British, French, and Dutch Empires, and too hostile to the Soviet Union. When the subject came to China, he banished the State Department representatives from the room. At the outset of the war, Hull himself accelerated the State Department's decline by renouncing interest in vital political matters on the grounds that they sounded like "technical military" affairs. He refused even to look at the "ABC" papers, the strategic directives drafted by U.S. and British military leaders in the months preceding Pearl Harbor. On November 27, 1941, Hull "washed his hands" of the Japanese negotiations and turned the problem over to Stimson and Knox — the Army and the Navy. The Joint Chiefs of Staff were the most resourceful agency in the government in obtaining information. They received copies of the Roosevelt-Churchill correspondence "on a strictly personal basis" from the top British general in Washington, Sir John Dill. The military aide in the map room at the White House also smuggled out for his colleagues in the Pentagon memoranda prepared by FDR. All of these were of course quite unavailable to the State Department.

The power of the military services grew swiftly once the President turned his major attention from economic recovery to preparation for war. In December 1941 shortly after his first wartime meeting with Churchill, Roosevelt created the Joint Chiefs of Staff. This bureaucratic innovation, which was based on neither congressional legislation nor an executive order, greatly strengthened the position of the uniformed military and profoundly affected the future course of American diplomacy. The purpose of the decision was to create a counterpart for the British Chiefs of Staff who sat with the American officers on combined planning boards and to discourage inter-service rivalry. The effect was to create the most efficient structure in the government for the planning and implementation of national security policy. The Joint Chiefs acquired a huge staff and drew also on the Operations Division of the War Department, which for a while was headed by General Dwight Eisenhower. They had direct access to the President, a relationship strengthened by Admiral William Leahy who had an office in the White House and served as Ambassador between the military chiefs and the President. The military leaders saw the President far more frequently in the war than did their civilian superiors. F.D.R. who had enormous respect for General Marshall — "I feel I could not sleep at night with you out of the country" — rejected the advice of JCS no more than two or three times.

Perhaps most important, the military supplied the conceptual framework for thinking about foreign relations for the rest of the government. Walter Millis has summarized this major development in these words:

Because the State Department was so effectively sidetracked, because the military establishment had such a dominant institutional position, and because American experience furnished so little in the way of precedents for guidance, the inherited and ingrained American military doctrines about war and the functions of force in national policy became unusually important.

Thus, the major decisions of the war with the greatest obvious political impact were made by the President, the Joint Chiefs of Staff and Harry Hopkins. The Chiefs prepared for diplomatic conferences, negotiated with the allies, and in the war theatres the Commanders, Eisenhower and MacArthur were supreme. Each obtained the power to pass on all civilians sent to their theatres and to censor their dispatches. "Through these controls of overseas communications," Millis observes, "JCS was in a position to be informed, forewarned, and therefore, forearmed, to a degree no civilian agency could match."

Not only did the war radically shift the balance of power in the Federal bureaucracy, catapulting the military from a marginal institution without a constituency to a position of command over the resources of a whole society, but it also redefined the traditional tasks of the military. We have seen how in practice the traditional semantic barriers between "political" and "military" functions were eroded; in the development and execution of strategy the military were deep in politics. As the war ended, the generals and admirals themselves, but, more important, the civilian leaders in the Pentagon, were at work on an ideology which would assure a permanent place in American foreign relations for the military outlook, military personnel, and military techniques for achieving international objectives.

In the New Deal days military officers had been brought into a few civilian agencies. Major General Philip Fleming had been Federal Works Administrator. There was usually a military officer on the Maritime Commission. In the diplomatic corps, middle grade officers served as military attaches, which were largely ceremonial assignments. But for the most part civilian government was beyond the reach of the Army and the Navy. Indeed there was a wall of separation between the government of peace and the government of war.

As the war ended, it was unthinkable that the military would ever revert to their former role. They had achieved enormous prestige with the whole country. In public speeches they had taught again and again that weakness invites aggression. The generals made their postwar plans on the assumption that force would continue to be the primary instrument of American diplomacy. "We have tried since the birth of our nation to promote our love of peace by a display of weakness," General George Marshall wrote in his final report as Chief of Staff. "The world does not seriously regard the desires of the weak. . . . We must, if we are to realize the hopes we may dare to have for peace, enforce our will to peace with strength." That principle, as Harry Truman made clear in his first major postwar foreign policy speech as President, had been fully accepted. Speaking from the bow of the nation's mightiest battleship on Navy Day, he reminded the world that the United States was the greatest naval power on the planet and that American strength would enforce the peace.

At a time when Stalingrad was still under siege and it would have taken a lively imagination to conjure up a Soviet threat of world domination, U.S. military planners had already begun planning a huge postwar military machine. As the war ended, the Army demanded a ground force capable of expanding to 4.5 million men within a year. General Marshall hoped that Universal Military Service would be swiftly enacted to meet this "requirement." The

Navy thought it wanted to keep 600,000 men, 371 major combat ships, 5,000 auxiliaries, and a little Air Force of 8,000 planes. The Air Force also had specific plans. It wanted to be a separate service and to have a 70-group force with 400,000 men. With these plans, the top military officers made it clear that they were through being fire-fighters called in when the diplomats had failed. From now on they intended to be a continuing influence in U.S. foreign relations.

Their civilian chiefs in the Pentagon, James V. Forrestal, the Secretary of the Navy, and Robert P. Patterson, who succeeded Stimson as Secretary of War, were the military's advocates. In the fall of 1945, Ferdinand Eberstadt prepared a report for Forrestal urging the creation of a National Security Council which would, as Forrestal put it, "guarantee that this Nation shall be able to act as a unit in terms of its diplomacy, its military policy, its use of scientific knowledge, and finally of course in its moral and political leadership of the world." The military, Forrestal asserted, must be permitted to have its say on all important foreign policy questions. There were no wholly "military" or wholly "political" questions. Since war and peace were part of a continuum, not separate categories, the administrative machinery for conducting foreign relations must reflect that reality. "Our military policy," Harry Truman declared, "should be completely consistent with our foreign policy." While this commendable purpose lay at the heart of the National Security Council proposals, the power of the Pentagon combined with the weakness of the State Department, meant that the military often defined the terms of American foreign policy for the diplomats rather than the other way around.

The National Security Council symbolized at the apex of government a development that was taking place throughout the foreign policy machinery. The problem of diplomacy and international relations were becoming redefined as problems of National Security. This meant not only that military criteria for judging policies became more important and the processes of diplomatic adjustment less so, but that personnel from the military departments, both uniformed and civilian, came to play a much more prominent role.

While the war was still on, some of the key individuals who ran the emergency government that had descended on Washington were planning to integrate it permanently into American life. Under the pressure of war entire new techniques for manipulating the politics of other countries had been developed; those who had put together the bureaucratic structures for operating these tech-

niques fought to preserve their life. In the postwar world, they
argued, the U.S. would need them whatever the political environment would look like. The world-wide deployment of U.S. forces
at the end of the war represented an opportunity for projecting
power that a great country could not be expected to renounce.
Thus the Joint Chiefs of Staff argued successfully for retaining
most of the network of bases acquired in the war. The Research
and Development Program, the Public Relations and Propaganda
Networks, the Military Assistance Program, and the Subversion
and Intelligence Apparatus, which hardly existed in 1940, continued to be the major recipients of government funds after peace
returned. The thinking of General William Donovan, the creator
of the wartime OSS, as peace dawned, offers an insight into the
indestructibility of bureaucratic instruments. His assistant Robert
H. Alcorn has described his views:

> With the vision that had characterized his development of OSS, General
> Donovan had, before leaving the organization, made provision for the
> future of espionage in our country's way of life. Through both govern-
> ment and private means he had indicated the need for a long-range,
> built-in espionage network. He saw the postwar years as periods of con-
> fusion and readjustment affording the perfect opportunity to establish
> such networks. We were everywhere already, he argued, and it was only
> wisdom and good policy to dig in, quietly and efficiently, for the long pull.
> Overseas branches of large corporations, the expanding business picture,
> the rebuilding of war areas, government programs for economic, social,
> and health aid to foreign lands, all these were made to order for the infiltra-
> tion of espionage agents.

Thus before the Soviet spy revelations of 1946, before the first
clashes of the Cold War, decisions were made to use "for the long
pull" the instruments of subversion fashioned in war.

The emergence of a dominant national security bureaucracy was
a prime legacy of war. The power which these institutions wield
to set national priorities and to define the threats and opportunities
facing the nation has a decisive impact on the direction of policy.
It is not surprising that essentially military bureaucracies define
the principal threats to national security as the military threats
for these are the only kind they are equipped to handle. We see
the same phenomenon in domestic life. If the technology to produce a supersonic transport plane becomes available, a new
national goal is suddenly discovered and the machine will be built

regardless of how dubious its ultimate social utility. The forces in command of the technology are able to create a political reality within which it is impossible to say no to "progress." Similarly, the development of techniques for influencing political behavior of other countries accelerates the interventionist thrust of foreign policy. Having come into the possession of esoteric knowledge or esoteric techniques which can give it status and power, a bureaucracy fights to use it. If you can fly over another country or infiltrate its labor unions or destroy its crops, it's not hard to find a convincing reason to do it. The fascination with technique is almost irresistible. According to Stewart Alsop, President Eisenhower agreed to the U-2 flights over the Soviet Union after being shown a photograph of the Augusta golf course. "Every detail of the familiar well-loved course was clear to the President, who delightedly picked out a golf ball on a green." So a new capability spawned a new requirement and it became necessary to overfly the Soviet Union.

VI

Harold Lasswell once described the bureaucrat as a man with "an infinite capacity for making ends of his means." Robert Merton made the same point when he suggested that for the bureaucrat an "instrumental value becomes a terminal value." James V. Forrestal illustrated this fascination with technique rather than purpose when as Secretary of the Navy he learned of the spectacular capture and flag-raising ceremony on Mount Suribachi, Iwo Jima, and exclaimed, "This guarantees the continuation of the Marine Corps for 500 years!" The authentic experience is the professional activity; the higher purposes, the abstract causes for which the bureaucracy exists, become symbols to be manipulated in pursuing a career. Indeed, the bureaucrat is comfortable only when his choices are instrumental. To challenge the assumptions behind a policy is to take on the system which is the source of his power and status.

Being "in on the action" is the supreme status symbol in a life where the rewards are measured in the perquisites of office rather than in great differentials in cash. For the career bureaucrat, a secretary in the outer office, a couch, a rug, a title, or a water pitcher are the currency of success. For the National Security Managers at the top the goal is making something happen which, hopefully, history will smile upon, but which on no account, will lose him the respect of his peers on Wall Street or Detroit. For the bureaucrat at the top and just below the top, activity of recognized importance is the highest reward.

The running of a bureaucracy is a collective experience. Participation is a goal in itself and exclusion a bitter punishment. This phenomenon is not limited to the national security bureaucracy or even to government. It is common to all large organizations whose purposes are so complex or obscure that the individual loses grasp of the meaning of his own work. In discussing commercial as well as governmental bureaucracies, Robert Presthus points out that "the acquisition of status and prestige becomes an end in itself rather than a derivative of some significant achievement." The validation of one's efforts is a nod from the bureau chief or the privilege of attending the next meeting with the Secretary. "I'm sorry, he's with the President," the receptionist smiles. For the bureaucrat the invitation to participate is the significant event.

In complex national security issues there are few objective criteria for judging successes and failures. Was the operation in Greece in 1947 a success? Was NATO a success? It depends what you think the alternatives were and what time frame you use for making the judgment. If, as historians are coming increasingly to believe, Stalin and Malenkov would have settled for a reunified Germany in 1952 and 1953, then NATO was not, in my judgment, a success. If the contemporary problems of Greece have their roots in the unresolved political issues temporarily obscured by the counter-insurgency campaign in Greece in 1947, then the Truman Doctrine was something less than a success. But bureaucrats for very practical reasons do not concern themselves with long term results. Twenty years of stability and order is itself, in their view, a great accomplishment — indeed all that one can expect. They view themselves as custodians rather than problem-solvers because they are conscious of their brief authority. Dean Rusk once said that his personal ambition as Secretary of State was to hand over the major problems to his successor in no worse shape than he found them. The Assistant Secretary on a two-year tour of duty in Washington or the Foreign Service Officer awaiting reassignment is even more susceptible to this "keep the balls bouncing" view of statecraft. The canny bureaucrat is sustained by the faith that when the policy collapses he will be somewhere else.

This sort of approach to statecraft itself favors the recommendation of military measures. First, a military move can usually be presented as "buying time." To order in a few troops looks like a way of postponing difficult political decisions, although actually such an act, as the Vietnam experience shows, is itself a critical decision which circumscribes future choices. Second, a military initiative is much easier to arrange than a political initiative. The bureaucracy excels at deployment and logistics. If a man can define his professional responsibilities as moving troops or bombing targets he is not likely to make an immediate professional blunder. If, however, he sets his goal as reconciling conflicting political interests he has given himself a thankless task and will probably fail. Ordering the killing of Vietcong is much easier than attempting to reconstruct Vietnamese society. For a powerful country fighting comes far more naturally than negotiating.

The self-defined business of a bureaucracy, therefore, is to dispose of means and techniques. The man who questions not how the techniques are to be used, but whether they should be, makes himself a candidate for reassignment. Audiences roared when the Air Force general in *Dr. Strangelove*, prompted by his pride in the penetration capabilities of the B-52, forgot momentarily that the whole government was trying to prevent an errant bomber from reaching Moscow, and triumphantly assured the President that the plane would get through. The meeting David Lilienthal describes in his diaries at which Secretaries Forrestal and Royall urged President Truman to turn over the atomic bomb to military control is reminiscent of the same capacity to look at the big picture. "You have to understand that this isn't a military weapon," Truman began. "It's used to wipe out women and children and unarmed people, and not for military uses." "But, Mr. President," Forrestal argued, "as an old weaponeer yourself, you know how important it is to get used to handling a new weapon." "Yes," agreed the Secretary of the Army, "We have been spending 98% of all the money for atomic energy for weapons. Now if we aren't going to use them, that doesn't make any sense."

The tragic proclivity of a bureaucracy to avert its collective eyes from the consequences and meaning of its acts is illustrated by the history of two of the greatest government-ordered slaughters of the innocent carried out in this century. The Final Solution of the Jewish Problem and the Dropping of the Atomic Bomb. They are distinguishable in magnitude and context but as examples of the amorality of bureaucracy they are strikingly similar.

At the meeting SS Chief Heydrich called at the peaceful Berlin suburb of Wannsee on January 20, 1942, "to clear up the fundamental problems" of the projected genocide, fifteen high-ranking representatives of various ministries and agencies discussed various ways and means of carrying out the job, but not one challenged the effort. Similarly, a committee of distinguished Americans temporarily brought into the bureaucracy, including the President of Harvard, the President of the Massachusetts Institute of Technology, the President of one of the largest insurance companies, a former Supreme Court Justice, and a former Secretary of State, recommended unanimously "that the bomb be used against the enemy as soon as it could be done . . . without specific warning and against a target that would clearly show its devastating strength." They were not asked to give an opinion whether the bomb should be used as a terror weapon nor did they volunteer one.

We are accustomed to thinking of the Nazi bureaucrats as monsters. For this reason Hannah Arendt's argument that Eichmann's evil was "banal" and hence replicable in other societies was profoundly disturbing to many Americans. But James Conant, Vannevar Bush, William Clayton, Henry Stimson, and, finally, Harry Truman were not monsters nor notably less humane than Dwight Eisenhower, John Foster Dulles, or Pope Pius XII, all of whom subsequently deplored the decision to use the weapon on a population center without first having demonstrated its lethal effect somewhere else. What separated the first group from the second was their bureaucratic responsibility.

The hierarchical structure of the national security bureaucracy discourages speculation about purpose rather than technique. The man who asks "Why are we doing this" rather than "How can we do it better" is guilty of what Dean Acheson once called "re-examinationism." He invites the whispers of his colleagues and superiors that he is not quite as "responsible" as he used to be. The "re-examinationist," according to Acheson, is like the farmer who pulls his carrots out by the roots to see how they are growing.

The pressure to stay within the accepted framework of policy and to take the premises of policy as given are common to all bureaucracies. In the national security bureaucracy old premises take on a particularly sacred character because proponents of the *status quo* have carefully wrapped it in the flag. For a bureaucrat to suggest in the early nineteen sixties that Diem was something

less than a democrat or that torture was a more important instrument of his rule than charisma was to leave himself open to the
charge of "parroting the Communist line," a charge that was both
true and irrelevant, as well as highly effective in stifling self-
criticism.

Robert Presthus has observed that all big organizations "place
a high value upon power, status, prestige, order, predictability,
easy acceptance of authority, hard work, punctuality, discipline,
and conventionality." It is also clear that many of these qualities,
so necessary for bureaucratic success, constitute the ideological
goals of American foreign policy. Order and stability, however
unjust or undemocratic their base, are to be preferred to political
turmoil or revolution. It is better to support Trujillos, Batistas,
or General Ky's than to take a chance on the deluge that might
follow them. Non-military intervention is to be preferred to
military intervention, but the United States must be prepared to
use force rather than lose control over the political development
of countries where we have declared an interest. The bureaucrat
with his strong personal commitment to established order and
authority believes that the capacity to control the politics of other
countries is essential to American national security. An uncon-
trolled environment in his view is a threatening environment. The
politics of liberation frightens him for a revolution, however spontaneous, leads to chaos and to possible domination by other outside
powers. It is an article of faith that if events are allowed to unfold
without American interference, they will end up badly for the
United States.

The urge to intervene rests as much on psychological anxiety as
on hard-headed calculations of economic interest. Indeed, the fear
of losing control is more important than the fear of losing resources.
Projecting his own hierarchical view of the world, the National
Security Manager tends to discount spontaneity in others. Where
people act, they are acting under orders. Thus the Greek guerrillas
had no motives of their own to seize political power. They were
directed by a conspiracy, as were the Guatemalans, the Dominicans
and the Viet Cong. In the bureaucrat's view of the world, conflict
itself is distressing, for the continued supremacy of the United
States depends upon the maintenance of order. Early in the Cold
War, Walter Lippman alluded to the American "refusal to recognize, to admit, to take as the premise of our thinking the fact that
rivalry, strife, and conflict among states, communities and factions

are the normal condition of mankind." In the American ideology "the struggle for existence and the rivalry for advantages are held to be wrong, abnormal, and transitory." The Foreign Service Officer and the national security bureaucrat are especially troubled when others resort to violence, which they view as a disease to be eradicated, rather than a technique of change which throughout history all but the very rich have felt the need to use.

Despite extensive travels, the national security bureaucrat is peculiarly isolated from political events in other countries. His information comes from the client government we may be defending against an insurgency or from the local American bureaucracy. These intelligence sources have little incentive to supply information or interpretations that will disturb present policy or their superiors who make it, particularly when the health of their own bureaucratic empires varies directly with the gravity of the threat they are reporting.

The bureaucrat's lack of empathy for the human motivations behind political change — he has little feel for the politics of his own city in the United States much less in Africa or Vietnam — lead to tragic miscalculations. Where events cannot be squeezed into the bureaucratic vision, as where a Buddhist priest chooses self-immolation over political castration or thirteen-year-old boys and grandmothers do battle with U.S. Marines, there must be a sinister, hierarchical cause. And the response must be the classic hierarchical response, the punishment of the offender. Here is a prime example of many heads being more foolish than one. Individually, the national security bureaucrat knows that life is more complicated than is dreamed of in his White Papers. He does not like napalming villages and knows that "aggression" is not the key to understanding what has happened in Vietnam. But bureaucratic truth is different from personal truth just as collective morality differs from personal morality. As Harry Stack Sullivan has noted, the value system of the group provides the intellectual and moral framework for the individual . The individual conforms to the group "because of the extremely unpalatable, extremely uncomfortable experience of anxiety" he feels when he thinks or acts in deviant ways. Becoming a successful bureaucrat involves a learning process not unlike the educational experience of a child. He learns what it takes to become an accepted "team player" and what he must avoid. The bureaucracy socializes and forms basic political attitudes because it is the chief source of rewards and punishments. Membership in the community can bring the individual the prestige and personal satisfaction of important activity and access to important people. It can assure financial and psychological security. But it can also wield the parent's priary weapon: rejection. "Shape up or ship out" is the army's succinct way of expressing the bureaucratic commandment.

Arthur Schlesinger, Jr., offers insight into the anxieties of the bureaucrat and what he does to overcome them. In his account of the decisions leading up to the Bay of Pigs affair, he attempts to explain why, having written lucid memoranda opposing the invasion for the President, he failed to speak up at meetings where the final decisions were taken. Pointing out that he was a "college professor fresh to the government," who found it difficult to oppose the institutional judgment of the State Department, the Defense Department, and the CIA, he went on to make a more fundamental point:

> The advocates of the adventure had a rhetorical advantage. They could strike virile poses and talk of tangible things — fire power, air strikes, landing craft, and so on. To oppose the plan, one had to invoke intangibles — the moral position of the United States, the reputation of the President, the response of the United Nations, 'world public opinion' and other such odious concepts. These matters were as much the institutional concern of the State Department as military hardware was of Defense . . . I could not help feeling that the desire to prove to the CIA and the Joint Chiefs that they were not soft-headed idealists but were really tough guys, also influenced State's representatives at the Cabinet table.

If, as Veblen argues, the education of a bureaucracy is a "trained incapacity," the prime instrument of collective self-deception is official rhetoric. We have noted some of the characteristics of the bureaucratic system which make it difficult to correct errors or to ventilate the policy-making process. Language plays an enormously important role in assuaging guilt, suppressing criticism, and otherwise removing impediments to the smooth functioning of a bureaucracy on the move. Hannah Arendt has noted how the affectless language of the Nazi bureaucrat made it easier for him to accept the fact that he was in the genocide business. In the same way, the rhetoric of "pacification" or the "surgical strike" evoking the images of a Quaker meeting or the operating room served the purpose of rescuing the Vietnam policy-maker from a

human confrontation with the consequences of his acts. Bureaucratic detachment, as James Thomson has called it, feeds on the
"sanitized" truth of the mimeographed page, and such emotional
disengagement makes it easier to treat other nations and their
people as objects rather than neighbors.

Another characteristic of bureaucratic language is its abstraction
and lack of concrete referents. The use of such terms as "power
vacuum," "stability" or "balance," draws heavily from concepts
of Newtonian physics. They are good for describing rather simple
mechanical models like a see-saw but quite inadequate in the era
of post-Newtonian physics to describe the physical environment,
much less the political environment. The use of such a metaphor
helps to avoid a difficult discussion of the relationship of ends and
means. How do you decide whether there is or is not a "power
vacuum" in the Indian Ocean as Paul Nitze discovered a few days
after becoming Secretary of the Navy? The term "power vacuum"
when applied to a country, as it often is in the national security
bureaucracy, conceals a crucial political premise. There is a
"vacuum" when the local government is in effective control of the
country and is not a client of one great power or another. By using
the term a bureaucrat writes off the impossibility of national independence without even being aware of it.

The structure of language itself thus influences bureaucratic
choices by reinforcing a particular view of the world political
environment. Bureaucratic language is a ready-made instrument
for perpetuating error because the realm of discourse is so far
removed from the ordinary life experience of the human beings who
make up a bureaucracy. Official truths cannot be validated or
invalidated by personal experience. The global canvas which the
national security bureaucrat confronts is so vast and psychologically so separate from his own life that his analysis is dependent
upon metaphor and historical analogy. But making "grand designs" for other nations when you have neither personal loyalties
nor indeed personal relationships of any kind with them puts an
unbearable strain on the processes of human judgment. This
inherent limitation in the capacity of human organizations to
govern at a distance offers a clue as to why empires eventually fail.
As long as the business of foreign policy is seen essentially as a game
in which the objective, "security," is defined as making sure that
the rest of the world is sufficiently intimidated and that other
countries do not develop in ways we do not like, military inter-

ventions will continue. As long as the legitimacy of unilateral military intervention is accepted, the only restraint on the commitment of American power to future Vietnams is the national security bureaucracy's own assessment of the limits of our national power. Because the national security bureaucrat has in many ways been a stranger in his own country, he is likely once again to misunderstand and misuse the strengths of the nation. If the national security institutions themselves continue to define our national purpose, we will be taught once again that what is good for the Air Force or the CIA is not necessarily good for America.

ON REPRESSIVE INSTITUTIONS AND THE AMERICAN EMPIRE

PETER IRONS

The repressive nature of domestic social institutions in the United States flows directly from the demands of the imperialistic foreign policy of the American Empire in the 20th century, which in turn is a consequence of the structure of monopoly capitalism. Any effective attack on these institutions, any attempt to construct a new society which meets human needs rather than repressing them, necessarily depends on the destruction of American imperialism. The nexus of domestic repression and imperialism is so tightly woven that each becomes the product of the other; no critical analysis can separate one from the other. This essay is based on the assertion that the emergence of the United States as an imperialistic power, especially since the enunciation of an overtly imperialist foreign policy in the Open Door Notes of 1899-1900, has thwarted any effective movement to reform and restructure our domestic institutions.

Although I will describe the links between domestic repression and imperialism, our ultimate concern is with the developing consciousness of these links and the transformation of this consciousness into action and involvement. This analysis is based on the foundation laid by Marx and Engels, who stated in *The German Ideology* that "The production of ideas, of conceptions, of consciousness, is at first directly interwoven with the material activity and the material intercourse of men, the language of real life. Conceiving, thinking, the mental intercourse of men, appear at this stage as the direct efflux of their material behavior. The same applies to mental production as expressed in the language of the politics, laws, morality, religion, metaphysics of a people."[1]

Marxism acutely perceived the direct relationship between the structure of social institutions and "the material intercourse of

114

men." Ideas and institutions do not develop in a vacuum; they are products of the material world and reflect the most basic division in society, upon which all social institutions are built, that of social class. Classes, the historic product of the clash of interests between those who control property and those controlled by it, provide each of us with a world-view and broadly control our place in the social institutions which shape and mold us. In a fragmented, repressive society such as ours, it is difficult to perceive the inseparable links between repression and imperialism without a form of political "gestalt" which looks under the surface of liberal rhetoric and uncovers the essential unitary nature of a social system we have been trained to see as a collection of discrete, unrelated events and processes.

Most of us consider ourselves members of a huge, amorphous "middle class" that includes all but a marginal residue of the very poor and the very rich. This "declassification" is rooted in the myths of Equal Opportunity and the Great American Melting Pot which our schools and corporate propaganda inculcate in us. This propaganda has been quite successful; it has resulted in a widespread "false consciousness" that ignores the reality of class conflict and replaces it with the ideology of "pluralism," the concept of political scientists who presuppose a basic congruence of interest between social groups in this country. This congruence, based on a common acceptance of the "rules of the game," emphasizes the stability and "equilibrium" of the social system. In crude form, it states that all contending groups — business and labor, black and white, rich and poor — all must recognize that although each may desire a larger slice of the national pie, it is against the rules to grab the knife and demand the whole pie.

The pluralists, riding the wave of several decades of "false consciousness," are increasingly being shaken by the upheavals and tremors caused by the growing crisis of the system of monopoly capitalism. Trapped by their ideology, they fail to see that the basic "stability" of the system is founded on repression at home and imperialism abroad, and that the revolts they attribute to such causes as "the generation gap" and "communist agitation" are in actuality based on the development of revolutionary consciousness among those who have been subjected to the domestic and foreign repression of the American Empire.

We will return to the concept of consciousness and its revolutionary implications. At this point, our development of a political "gestalt" turns to an analysis of the imperialist nature of American foreign policy, the emergence in the 20th century of the American Empire. Although scholars such as R. W. Alstyne have asserted that "The concept of an American empire and the main outlines of its future growth were complete by 1800,"[2] I have chosen the issuance of the Open Door Notes by Secretary of State John Hay in 1899-1900 as a starting point because by this time the British had relinquished their role as the dominant imperial power to the United States, and conscious imperialism and massive foreign intervention were most directly articulated and legitimized by the Hay notes.

During the decade preceding the Hay notes, the United States had recovered from severe domestic economic depression and had begun the subjugation of Latin America as an economic dependency. The Spanish-American War had loosed a flood of desire for foreign expansion and intervention which turned to the Orient. Hay, in warning the world community that American business intended to grab the lion's share of trade in the Orient, especially the burgeoning market in China, set forth in his notes what historian William A. Williams has called "a classic theory of non-colonial imperial expansion."[3] As we completed our internal expansion and came to consider ourselves a Great Power, our foreign policy became characterized by rapacity, ethnocentrism, xenophobia and Christian "missionaryism."

Leading up to Hay's pronouncements was a campaign by leading politicians, capitalists and ministers seeking not only to open the door to the Orient, but to wrench it off its hinges. Senator Albert J. Beveridge, in April, 1897, put the imperialist ethic in classic summation: "American factories are making more than the American people can use; American soil is producing more than they can consume. Fate has written our policy for us; the trade of the world must and shall be ours."[4]

Lest it be thought that the flowering of imperialism was nurtured solely by reactionaries who shared the outlook of Standard Oil, it should be noted that leading domestic reformers such as Senator La Follette joined the imperialist movement with fervor. Putting his reformist missionary zeal at the service of capital, La Follette hailed American acquisition of the Philippines as allowing America "to conquer (its) rightful share of that great market now opening (in China) for the world's commerce."[5] Imperialism was given his Progressive sanction in the same statement, because "it has made men free." That imperialism stems from the basic drives of monopoly capital was clearly understood by Woodrow Wilson: "Our industries have expanded to such a point that they will burst their jackets if they cannot find a free outlet to the markets of the world. . . . Our domestic markets no longer suffice. We need foreign markets."[6] Wilson also, in a moment of candor, once stated that "The masters of the government of the United States are the combined capitalists and manufacturers of the U. S." [7]

Imperialism, of course, does not begin and end at the doors of the Custom House. It permeates the whole society, and as the American Empire has grown and expanded, the structural unity of all of our social institutions in the service of imperialism has grown stronger. Although every American president in this century has asserted what Wilson said above, the links between domestic capitalism and an aggressive, Cold War foreign policy based on paranoid anti-communism and domestic militarism were most clearly stated in 1944 by Charles E. Wilson, then executive vice-president of the War Production Board. In a speech to corporate and military leaders at a meeting of the Army Ordnance Association, Wilson (later president of the General Electric Company) said that the end of the war must signal an alliance of the large corporations, the military establishment and the executive branch of the government. Outlining a Permanent War Economy that would be "a continuing program and not the creature of an emergency," he said that "the burden is on all of us to integrate our respective activities — political, military and industrial — because we are in world politics to stay, like it or not."[8]

In the two-thirds of a century since Hay's firing of the starting pistol, our capitalist traders have spread out around the globe and taken with them, as protection, a Praetorian Guard of soldiers, planes, tanks and ships. More than a million and a half Americans, civilian and military, serve in the branch offices of the American Empire and those of us living in the home office spend much of our energy in their support. The magnitude of the American Empire has become staggering: as of 1967, there was $60 billion in direct U. S. investment abroad, and the output of American-owned production facilities abroad totaled $120 billion.[9] This made the American Empire the third largest economy in the world, exceeded only by our domestic economy and that of the Soviet Union. Some 4,200 American corporations are now in control of over 14,000 foreign businesses.[10]

Documentation is hardly needed for the assertion that the Permanent War Economy envisioned by Wilson has become a fact. It consumes more than half of the federal budget and employs, directly or indirectly, more than ten percent of the work force. The impact of the "military-industrial complex," as we now call it, extends into every local, state and federal office, as President Eisenhower ruefully noted in his Farewell Address. To protect our foreign investment, we have spread the cloak of the "Free World" wide enough to cover every dictatorship and authoritarian government which will allow American capital to extract profit from the soil and sweat of its people. We have provided the ruling classes of these countries with some $32 billion in arms in the last quarter-century, arms whose functions are the perpetuation of the rule of a privileged elite. Although Congress every year salves the liberal conscience with a meager dose of foreign aid, much of this "aid" is military and most of it (about 85 percent) is actually spent in the United States. The essential nature of American imperialism has recently been best exemplified by a study, initially entitled "Pax Americana," conducted for the Department of Defense by Boeing Aircraft, which was designed, according to the *New York Times*, to show how America can "maintain world hegemony in the future."[11] In spite of pressure from Senate doves, this study remains classified.

Imperialism not only exploits our foreign subjects, but it also, and necessarily, exploits and represses all of us and our basic social institutions. It is this linkage which is essential to our political "gestalt." Our major attention will focus on the educational system, although the family and the state, as basic components of the institutional triumvirate which monopoly capital most depends on, will also be examined. But it is our schools which are the factories in which the raw material, children, are transformed into the finished product, "citizens." This may seem a crude analogy, but it was chosen simply because it is not an analogy but a fact. Schools are factories, and the process involved in turning out mass-produced "citizens" is no different than that by which General Motors turns out cars. The end result is standardization, and the foremen and managers of the schools are as alert to product defect as the engineers in Detroit.

Our schools, from the primary to the graduate level, enroll some 120 million people, more than half the total population. Teachers make up the largest occupational group in the work force, and the vast majority of them are employed by the state and are subject to the constraints placed upon them by the conservative school-board mentality. Although the teaching "profession" absorbs a large number of the children of the working class and provides one of the major avenues of upward mobility in our class-stratified society, the political demands of the system and the status-quo orientation of teacher-training schools insures that most teachers share the values of their conservative, capitalist employers.

That schools are repressive needs little documentation; everyone who has gone through them intuitively recognizes this. Teachers demand order, obedience and docility. The "rules and regulations" would do credit to most prisons. Instruction in the social sciences involves uncritical presentation and acceptance of the capitalist system and current foreign policy. Not every student is fooled, of course, since a good proportion is brighter and more perceptive than its teachers. One high school student, analyzing the content of his textbooks in *Liberation* magazine, wrote that "As might be expected of textbooks written for future managers of the Empire, these reflect all the chauvinistic, anti-communist and counter-revolutionary assumptions which have underpinned American foreign policy for the past twenty years."[12] The point is not that the schools are uniformly successful in producing "good citizens," but that on the whole they attempt to stifle the kind of critical spirit expressed by this young man.

Schools not only serve to repress the instinctive expressiveness of children and indoctrinate them with the virtues of the capitalist system; they also serve the more direct need of maintaining the class basis of this system and channeling students into the American Empire at home and abroad. The process of separating students to serve the varying needs of capitalism is not an openly-acknowledged function of the educational system, but it lies at its heart. Business needs a certain number of operatives and menial workers to fill the factories and mop the floors, and a certain number to become the administrative and intellectual elite, replenishing the upper echelons of the imperialist institutions. It is this function that the schools perform admirably, in spite of the liberal myth of social mobility and equality of opportunity. Upward social and economic mobility do exist, enough to keep alive the Horatio Alger credo, but, as Kenneth Clark has said, ". . . there is concrete evidence which demonstrates beyond reasonable doubt that our public-school system has rejected its role of facilitating social mobility and has become in fact an instrument of social and economic class distinction in American society."[13]

Monopoly capitalism is based on class division, and the schools perpetuate the existing class divisions in American society. The majority of working-class youth, both white and black, ends its education in the secondary schools and becomes absorbed into the factories, menial service occupations and Armed Forces, while the majority of middle-class youth continues on to colleges and universities. Although race and color are primary components of class division, it is their class-linked nature that concerns us here. Black, Puerto Rican, Chicano and Indian children receive inferior education; that hardly needs proof. Working-class white children also receive inferior education. The crucial point is that poor schools are *necessary* as part of the process of ruthlessly weeding out and channeling into manual and menial work those not destined to become part of the capitalist elite. Those who believe in the inherent goodness of the system may balk at this point, but the reality of the educational system in performing this function is beyond dispute. If a child is not exceptionally bright, those who provide "counseling" in the public schools discourage any aspirations to higher education.

The repressive nature of the educational system is less evident in our colleges and universities, but it is obvious in the subordination of higher education by monopoly capital to the training of the elite necessary to staff the American Empire at home and abroad. Our 2,000 colleges and universities, both public and private, are governed by some 50,000 trustees, invested with state-granted power to formulate and execute basic policy. These trustees, most often a self-perpetuating group, are overwhelmingly conservative, white, Anglo-Saxon businessmen, and their values flow from their place at the apex of the capitalist system.

For example, the men who are directors of General Motors also serve as trustees of fourteen colleges and universities, including such elite institutions as Dartmouth, M.I.T. and Duke. This is not to imply that such institutions should be seen as subsidiaries of General Motors, but rather as an indication of the "community of interest" link between corporate power and higher education.

Liberal myth has enshrined the college as the impregnable bastion of reason and rationality. Unlike public primary and secondary schools, colleges shelter a significant minority of liberal and radical critics of the existing social order, which leads to periodic witch-hunts and howls of outrage from legislative super-patriots, corporate donors and conservative alumni. Nevertheless, faculty radicals are disproportionately concentrated in departments which are not vital to the functioning of the American Empire. Most dissident faculty are found in the humanities and social sciences, with a sprinkling in the pure sciences. But departments of business, economics and the applied sciences, in which is trained a majority of the managers and technicians of the American Empire, are distinctly inhospitable to radicals.

It seems probable that the toleration of academic radicals is actually advantageous to the system, since such toleration hardly threatens the recruitment process of the system and allows the perpetuation of the myth of the university as a "marketplace of ideas." In spite of the annoying prick of criticism, the corporations and Armed Forces continue to train an adequate supply of elite personnel in the colleges and universities. For example, there are Reserve Officer Training Corps units on 365 campuses, with a 1968-1969 enrollment of 218,000 students. These programs turn out more than 20,000 commissioned officers each year, more than half of the Navy's line officers and well over half of the Army officers serving in Vietnam.

The ROTC program has been under sporadic attack by student and faculty radicals for years (it was a prime target of students in the 1930's), and during 1969 major outbreaks of student opposition forced several of the prestige universities, most notably Harvard, to reduce ROTC to the status of an extra-curricular activity. This ferment has unsettled the Pentagon officials responsible for ROTC. In April, 1969, the chief of the Army's ROTC division said that "It would be disastrous for the Army if there were no ROTC." He was echoed by the Navy's director of officer education, who added that "We bank on ROTC for our officers. I don't know what we'd do without it." But fears of the demise of ROTC do not really bother the Pentagon; it is still firmly entrenched on the campuses of the major state universities and hundreds of small, conservative colleges as yet untouched by major student protest. In fact, the *New York Times* reported after the Harvard action to remove ROTC from the campus (still permitting the Army to train cadets in its own facilities) that the Army plans to establish new ROTC units at 30 additional schools by 1972.[14] The point here is that the colleges, not only through ROTC but also by virtue of their increasing subsidization by government aid and research funds, remain a crucial institution in the maintenance of the American Empire, a role they have filled for at least a hundred years.

The family is the basic institutional unit of the social system. As such, it is of importance to the American Empire that it perform its functions in the service of the Empire. Through it, the child learns his fundamental values and patterns of behavior. It is our most conservative institution, because it recapitulates and reinforces the patterns of dominance and submission required by every other institution. It is in the family that class position is learned, respect for hierarchical authority instilled and patterns of consumption so necessary to capitalism established. The repressive nature of the family is grounded in the class divisions which capitalism perpetuates. The necessity for children to absorb the "work and consume" ethic of the capitalist system forces parents to treat their children as repressively as they are treated by the system.

The family has its beginning in the private-property contract issued by the state to the husband and wife. At this point the joint accumulation of property and the molding of the family into a unit of consumption begin. The legal system, a product of the necessity of capitalism to preserve and protect existing property relationships, effectively turns the wife into a servant of the husband (who can usually secure a divorce if she refuses to perform the duties of a servant) and the children into the property of the state as well as the parents. The family, an increasingly "closed" system as rapid geographical mobility breaks down extended kinship relations, excludes "others" and fosters ethnic and class prejudice. Property is passed on to children by inheritance. In middle-class families, children learn deference and the necessity to "get along with others," and respect for the authority of teachers, policemen and other agents of the state is instilled. Working-class families have much the same child-rearing patterns, although methods of discipline vary; corporal punishment is more characteristic of the working-class, and the withholding of affection prevalent in the middle-class.

The repressive nature of family structure seems to many an historic continuity unconnected to any particular economic system. It seems probable, however, that the characteristic features of the family in capitalist society, even if molded in the context of pre-capitalist society, necessarily have continued their repressive functions because of the quite specific demands of monopoly capitalism. In a system which demands a work force willing to submit to domination, the family, as the bedrock institution of socialization, cannot deviate significantly from the repressive nature of the system as a whole. In the face of rapid technological change, the crisis of values and deepening global conflict, the family has served capitalism perhaps better than any other institution. We are still, as Sartre said, trying to stuff the live bodies of our children into the dead skins of our ancestors.

If the family serves capitalism by inculcating basic values necessary for the system, the state insures that these values will be placed at the service of the American Empire. The repressive nature of the state is based on two crucial functions: first, it defines our nationality and structures our whole view of ourselves as opposed to "the rest of the world"; and second, it offers all of the other institutions in society the instruments of coercion and force necessary to repress conflict and enforce compliance. The state, most simply, was defined by Max Weber as "a human community that (successfully) claims the *monopoly of the legitimate use of physical force* within a given territory."[15] Weber preceded that definition with the statement that "If no social institutions existed which knew the use of violence, then the concept of 'state' would be eliminated."[16] This is an illuminating insight, which makes the functioning of all other social institutions more clearly visible in their repressive nature.

The state, first of all, by defining nationality, provides legitimacy for the use of force in "defending" that nationality. To protect the American Empire, the state compels military service of males, and jails or exacts forced labor from those who refuse such service. The state enforces the compulsory attendance laws for the educational system. Even the family is dependent on the state's "monopoly of the legitimate use of physical force." Children who run away from home as an act of rebellion are hunted down and returned to their parents by the police forces of the state.

The state, as the servant of monopoly capital in the American Empire, is inhospitable to the demands of the world's poor that this Empire stop exploiting them. Lyndon Johnson put it plainly and aggressively: "There are three billion people in the world and we have only 200 million of them. We are outnumbered 15 to 1. If might did make right, they would sweep over the United States and take what we have. We have what they want."[17] A franker expression of nationalism and xenophobia would be hard to invent. But what Johnson stated in his crude Texas manner is merely the philosophy which undergirds the whole repressive American Way of Life. Imperialism, racism, class conflict: all of these hard-to-swallow concepts are concisely defined between the lines of that quotation.

The repressive nature of the state is an every-day fact of life to those at the bottom of the class ladder. The state thrusts into the front lines of its imperialist wars a disproportionate number of the poor and the black; the state allows the very rich virtual exemption from taxation; the state trains as criminals in its prisons mainly those lawbreakers who are poor and black; the state subsidizes the housing of the middle-class and leaves the poor rotting in slums; the state teaches its children the virtues of "democracy" and representative government and operates so corruptly in the service of class interests that from a third to a half of the eligible voters do not bother to exercize their franchise; the state advertises "freedom of speech and assembly" but prosecutes those who use it effectively to attack domestic repression and imperialism. Increasingly, monopoly capital assists the state in protecting class interests by diminishing the scope of free expression; for example, there are only 45 cities with competing daily newspapers, and the concentration of the mass media into a few corporate hands has been facilitated by the "regulatory" agencies of the state.

The state masks its repression behind the facade of "due process" and the Bill of Rights, but its basic attitude was well stated by Richard Kleindienst, Nixon's Deputy Attorney General, speaking about dissenting students: "If people demonstrated in a manner to interfere with others, they should be rounded up and put in a detention camp."[18]

Let us return at this point to our discussion of consciousness. I have argued that the repressive nature of our domestic social institutions is organically related to the imperialist nature of the capitalist system, which has its current form in the Permanent War Economy, the alliance of politics, militarism and industry outlined twenty-five years ago by Charles Wilson. This analysis is only persuasive to the extent that a "gestalt" apprehension of the organic unity of our social institutions is formed. It is not persuasive if one believes, as does Sidney Hook, that the "welfare state" offers hope for the reform of decaying social institutions and has shown ". . . that democratic political processes could affect the operation of the economic system, abolish some of its worst evils and open a perspective for profound change in the power relations of different classes."[19] Those who agree with Hook have been trapped by the "false consciousness" which is sustained by the illusion of progress and measures progress quantitatively. Although they may believe that Vietnam was a tragic mistake and that we must avoid further military entanglements in the Third World, if they fail to oppose the growing world hegemony of the American Empire in all its forms, they cannot hope to achieve social reconstruction, the rehabilitation of the cities, the salvaging of the physical environment and the eradication of racism at home. All of these social "ills" are a consequence of the inverted priorities forced upon us by the managers of the Permanent War Economy in their quest for an American Empire, and they cannot be cured without the breakup of that Empire.

If "the production of ideas, of conceptions, of consciousness" is, as Marxism postulates, based on "the material intercourse of men," then our consciousness must reflect the crisis of the existing class structure, both at home and abroad. If our politics, law, morality, religion and metaphysics are repressive, this is an indication that the class structure is repressive. If, in our semantic confusion, we describe our society as "free" or "democratic," we have not yet extricated ourselves from the false consciousness imposed on us by those who control the American Empire. Our failure to recognize the direct link between the domestic and the foreign repression of the American Empire constitutes the most terrible fact of our time, that we have become our own oppressors, that, as Herbert Marcuse has said, "the majority of the people is the majority of their masters. . . ."[20]

A full understanding of the historical process which has led us to become, in a real sense, our own oppressors, rests on a comprehension of how social control is exercized in society. Although social control is a function of the relative powerlessness of the individual in a society dominated by powerful and interlocking institutions, there is also the factor of internalization, by which the individual incorporates the repressive demands of these institutions and carries them out unbidden. Social theorists such as C. Wright Mills have asserted that the American Empire is controlled and directed by a "power elite" composed of the corporate, military and political leaders of the Empire.[21] Although the power wielded by these few hundred men is, indeed, massive, it should be kept in mind that we do not feel the daily lash of this power because we have adopted its assumptions and almost automatically and uncritically carry out its demands.

It has been more than two decades since Mills dissected the "power elite." Since that time, its membership has changed considerably through death, retirement and defeat. But the places in the elite, and the power conferred by membership in the elite, have not changed significantly. It is important to avoid considering the men who manage the American Empire as conscious members of a "conspiracy," whose motives and goals are directed at personal profit and power. Desire for such profit and power may motivate men to climb the ladder to the "power elite," but it is the position itself which confers these rewards, and the structure of the American Empire which establishes the positions. Rather than a conscious conspiracy, what we actually have is a "community of interest" in which those who fill the positions of power and those who work for them, directly and indirectly, are in basic agreement. Our social institutions are repressive to the extent that most of us have internalized this structure and have become part of the "community of interest."

Karl Mannheim has written that "Political discussion is, from the very first, more than theoretical argumentation; it is the tearing off of disguises. . . ."[22] Those who control the American Empire have for decades disguised themselves behind the masks of patriotism and public service. The militarization of American Society, our growth into a Garrison State, has been disguised behind the mask of "anti-communism." The growing concentration of corporate power into the hands of an interlocking oligopoly has been disguised behind the mask of "people's capitalism." If our political discourse is to be more than "theoretical argumentation," its primary function must be to tear off the disguises, semantic and ideological, behind which the power of the Empire is concealed.

We have, in the last decade, grown increasingly conscious of the full dimensions of the American Empire and the links it has forged between repressive institutions and imperialism. Losing a war abroad to the forces of revolutionary nationalism has sobered many of us, and has rudely focused our attention on the domestic consequences of imperialism. Watching and experiencing, if only vicariously, the struggle of our oppressed minorities here at home has added to this consciousness. Feeling the repressive weight of our institutions, as they are torn by the conflicting demands of tradition and the accelerating changes in values and technology, has revealed to some of us the necessity of revolution. But our growing consciousness, our awareness of the bond between our ideas and our "material intercourse," does us little good until it is transformed into a commitment to the ultimate goals of the revolutionary struggle.

The consciousness which liberates men from repression and frees them to become the advocates of the oppressed has always been a reality in our history, even when submerged by the waves of "false consciousness." Men such as Denmark Vesey, Big Bill Haywood, Eugene Debs and A. J. Muste, ignored or dismissed in the textbooks written for "future managers of the Empire," have kept alive the revolutionary consciousness which no repressive force can extinguish. The more clearly we see and feel, as they did, the repressive nature of the American Empire, the more conscious we will become of the necessity to bring it to an end.

Notes

[1] Marx and Engels, *The German Ideology*, NY, International Pub., p. 13.

[2] Quoted in Paul Baran and Paul Sweezy, *Monopoly Capital*, New York, Monthly Review Press (1968 edition) pp. 181–182.

[3] William A. Williams, *The Tragedy of American Diplomacy*, N Y, Dell, p. 43.

[4] Quoted in Williams, p. 17.

[5] *Ibid.*, p. 56.

[6] *Ibid.*, p. 52.

[7] Quoted in Eric Mann and Dan Gilbarg, *We Won't Be Used to Put Down the Vietnamese Revolution*, Boston SDS, 1969, p. 24.

[8] *The New York Times*, January 20, 1944, p. 8.

[9] *Business Week*, December 9, 1967, p. 118.

[10] Mira Wilkins, "The Businessman Abroad," *The Annals of the American Academy*, November, 1966, p. 85.

[11] *The New York Times*, February 16, 1968, p. 2.

[12] Bob Goodman, "Textbooks Are Bullshit," *Liberation*, January, 1969, p. 29.

[13] In the Foreward to Patricia Cayo Sexton, *Education and Income: Inequalities of Opportunities in Our Public Schools*, New York, Viking Press, 1961, p. ix.

[14] Quotes and statistics from the *New York Times*, April 19, 1969, p. 19.

[15] Hans Gerth and C. Wright Mills, eds., *From Max Weber: Essays in Sociology*, New York, Oxford University Press, 1946, p. 78.

[16] *Ibid.*

[17] The *New York Times*, November 2, 1966, p. 16.

[18] *The Atlantic*, May, 1969, p. 11.

[19] *New York Times* Book Review, April 20, 1969, p. 8.

[20] H. Marcuse, *An Essay on Liberation*, Boston, Beacon Press, 1969, p. 64.

[21] C. Wright Mills, *The Power Elite*, New York, Oxford UP, 1946.

[22] Karl Mannheim, *Ideology and Utopia*, New York, Harcourt, Brace and World, 1936, p. 39.

RACISM IN THE UNITED STATES
AN INTRODUCTION

Frank Joyce

"There seems to be something in our laws and institutions peculiarly adapted to the Anglo-Saxon American Race, under which they will thrive and prosper, but under which all others wilt and die . . . There is something mysterious about it." Congressman Alexander Duncan, 1845.[1]

Racism was officially discovered by the former Governor of Illinois, the Honorable Otto Kerner, in March of 1968. He was assisted by his colleagues on the National Advisory Commission on Civil Disorders, which included Charles Tex Thornton, President of Litton Industries; Mayor John Lindsay of New York; Roy Wilkins of the NAACP; and Senator Fred Harris of Oklahoma, who served as co-chairman of Hubert Humphrey's presidential election campaign, and others of their ilk.

The startling "discovery" of racism was in keeping with a long tradition in American history begun in 1492 when Christopher Columbus "discovered" America. To think of Columbus discovering America is comparable to thinking of Sitting Bull as discovering Washington. In view of the fact that the nation had successfully ignored, discredited and condemned those blacks (and the very few whites) who had previously labeled the United States racist, the seriousness with which the essentially white ruling class Kerner Commission's charges were taken was itself an interesting reflection of racism. "Social problems" are not taken seriously in the United States until sanctified by that segment of the system which creates them in the first place.

There are those who might argue that the National Advisory Commission's Report represents analytic progress over Congressman Duncan's ingenuous statement in 1845. And if giving the mystery a name is progress, they are right. Unfortunately, the unwillingness and inability of the Kerner Commission to either define or analyze the problem which it correctly identifies makes it the 1960's equivalent of Duncan's statement. If anything, the report mystifies the concept of racism rather than explains it.

Contrary to what one might conclude from reading the Kerner report, racism is not an odorless, tasteless, colorless chemical which somehow got into the water supply. Rather, racism is a natural product of the history, culture, and socio-politico-economic structure of the United States. The following essay is an effort to go beyond both the Kerner Report and the superficial, mechanistic analysis of the past. It is admittedly speculative and tentative in nature. It assumes that recent events, including documents such as the Kerner Report, have created a level of awareness of the objective conditions of black people which make the large scale presentation of empirical data unnecessary.

History

"If there had been as much dissent and disruption in the past as there is now, the Indians would still be here." General Lewis B. Hershey, 1968.[2]

Examples of caste domination can be found before the settling of the New World, and although racism did not begin in the United States, it may have reached its zenith here. The development of the United States has obviously been conducive to the development of racism.

Two "evolutions," although not only two, in the American past have been extremely important in creating the racist behavior and attitudes responsible for the present situation. The first concerns the westward expansion of the nation and its relation to those nonwhite people who were "in the way," and the second involves the United States' system of slavery.

The experience of white "settlers" with the so-called "Indians" is of considerably more significance in the evolution of racism than is generally recognized. The first settlers arrived at Jamestown in 1607, already committed to the racist act of calling the indigenous people "Indians" rather than their self-chosen national names. (And all because Christopher Columbus was lost or stupid or both.) It is as if people insisted on calling an individual named Bob, who had always thought of himself as Bob, Herschel or Elmer. The second racist act in the New World might well be dated from the first death of a native "Indian"; an integral part of the nation's history is its expansion westward from the Atlantic Coast in 1607 all the way to China, and retrenched to Vietnam in 1969.

With the exception of territorial disputes with the remote British, French and Spanish, the only impediments, and hence the only victims of that expansion, have been people of color. Most notably, the "settling of the West" required the systematic reduction of the "Indian" population from more than one million in the late eighteenth century to less than 500,000 by the end of the nineteenth century. Thus, through various methods including starvation, destruction of leadership and national structure, intentional infection with disease, dislocation from the land, and out-and-out massacre, some nations were permanently destroyed and more than half the "Indian" people were eliminated. (When Hitler reduced the Jewish population of Western Europe by more than one third, he was correctly accused of genocide.)

The "settling of the West" did not stop at the Pacific Ocean, but continued on to Hawaii, the Philippines, Samoa (still called American Samoa), Japan, China and ultimately Vietnam. Many of the same generals who fought up to the Pacific also fought in the Pacific campaigns. And although the reasons for expansion changed as the nation became industrialized, the process of expansion is so inexorable that it is plausible to argue that the United States has never had any "foreign policy" whatsoever, at least regarding the Pacific. United States Pacific and Asian involvement is, perhaps more obviously than is usually the case, simply an extension of domestic policy. In this sense, the United States is in Vietnam because it is in California.

The socially accepted justification for expansion and the slaughter that resulted in its wake was, and is still, known as Manifest Destiny. God willed that white people "civilize" the West. In addition to "pioneer" civilians, the vanguard of expansion was the military and the missionaries. The job of the generals (Custer, et al.) was to kill "Indians." The role of the missionaries was to tell the generals (and anyone else who seem concerned) that it was all right to kill "Indians" — that indeed, the only good "Indian" *was* a dead one. According to the missionaries, the "Indians" after all, were uncivilized, unchristian, barbarian and heathen. By and large they did not, in fact, respect private property or land ownership — if only Karl Marx had become popular in time they would undoubtedly have been the first "communist menace."

In short, "Indians" were defined as less than human. There was no reason why the "superior" whites should not take their land, their crops, and their livestock for their own profit since they could obviously make better use of them than could the natives.

The psychological and cultural implications of this experience lie not so much in how whites defined the "Indians," but in how whites defined themselves, or rather in how they were told to define themselves by the ideologues of each succeeding period. By categorizing the "Indians" as inferior and uncivilized, whites automatically defined themselves as superior and civilized. And the definition rested essentially on skin color; that was its most readily identifiable trait. The belief that white equals "civilized" remains and is transmitted through each generation through the rendering of the "history" of the period.

It is essential to note that simultaneous with the destruction of "Indians" was the institutionalization of the notion of "civilization" as the triumph of man over "nature." The fact that the native culture defined civilization as the ability to "co-exist" with the forces of nature undoubtedly contributed to the definition of "Indians" as barbaric and hence to their demise. It is not an accident that trees and buffalo along with "Indians" were casualties of the "winning of the West." Whether for greed and profit, or simply because they were in the way, today we have polluted rivers, lakes, air, and threatened the ecological balance of the nation. This European belief that civilization rested on man's ability to conquer nature, coinciding with industrialization, led naturally to the equation of civilization with technology. Thus, electric carving knives and rocket ships are what make the United States civilized. Those who do not view nature as the enemy, nor strive to control and finally to distort the relationship between man and natural forces, are considered uncivilized, primitive, and "underdeveloped."

The second major, and more important, historical development of white racism concerns, of course, slavery. The United States established and maintained for nearly 250 years the most brutal and dehumanizing slave system the world has ever known. Based exclusively on race, American slavery caused a nation established on the principle that "all men are created equal" to write a constitution defining a slave as "three fifths of a man." The schizophrenia of Thomas Jefferson, the first white liberal (he kept his slaves but felt badly about it), continues to this day.

The slave trade itself was genocidal. On ships with names like "The Good Ship Jesus," which brought the first slaves to the United States in 1619, unknown millions of men, women and children died in passage. Those who survived were subjected to a primitive form of Job Training known as the "Seasoning Process." In order to train them for slavery, every effort was made to systematically destroy the language, awareness of history, religion, culture, customs, and family structure of African people. Those who survived the training were then defined as chattel-objects rather than people — and sold. By 1760, slavery was defined by law as a permanent status from which no slave could be freed as long as he lived except by the whim of his master.

Once again, whites defined an entire group of people as subhuman and inferior on the basis of their skin color. And as with the "Indians," "liberal" European tradition and the Protestant Ethic combined not only to provide the moral justification and rationalization for slavery but also to fundamentally affect its brutal form. In the face of an ideology which talked about human equality and the golden rule, whites had practically no choice but to define slaves and hence blacks as something less than human. Morality obtains only between and among humans. Therefore, if there was slavery, then by definition the slaves must have been less than human. To put it another way, anything which is economically desirable or profitable can somehow be made moral.

Slavery established a number of important traditions in the United States which have yet to be broken. Not the least of these was the blessing and moral authority bestowed by the organized church which, in this case, contributed by defining black people as soul-less — incapable of redemption. Secondly, slavery established the precedent of creating a structure so brutal as to make the ideology of inferiority a self-fulfilling prophecy, such as making people work at backbreaking physical labor for eighteen hours each day and then calling them lazy; sending black children to absurdly inferior schools and calling them stupid and forcing people to survive outside the law and then naming them cr minals.

Most important, however, was the fact that once again in the process of defining "them" (slaves), whites defined themselves. White meant civilized and superior. Non-white meant inferior.

If whites do not know who they are, it is probably because they have since 1607 allowed themselves to be defined by an identity which says who they are *not*. The effort to dehumanize people of color may have tragically resulted in the dehumanization by whites of themselves and each other.

The consequence of these two formative experiences with people of color was to set the nation on an inexorably racist course, one in which the fact of racism has never changed — only its forms. The history of the civil war, reconstruction, the Bureau of Indian Affairs, urbanization and industrialization is the history of the ideological, cultural and structural consolidation of the nation's racist origins.

The balance of this paper seeks a beginning explanation of the culture, structure, and function of racism in the United States.

Definition, Culture and Ideology

Centuries of exploitation and oppression of people of color created an ideology, since transmitted into the culture, to justify, rationalize and explain such behavior. Simply stated, the culture of the United States is, in addition to whatever else it might be, white supremacist. That culture is no less institutionalized, no less self-perpetuating and no less functional than the structure of white privilege itself. Indeed, it may be more so.

To say that the culture is white supremacist, is simply to say that most whites are very carefully taught that people with white skins are better, in all ways that matter, than people without white skins. This is true both for individual whites and collectively for all whites. This has nothing to do with whether one "likes" or "loves" members of the "inferior" group. There is nothing inconsistent about a white supremacist liking a "Negro" or "Negroes" or "not having anything against the colored." People love their pet dogs, cats, monkeys and parrots. They feel genuine sorrow when they get sick and die. They also feel superior to them without ever thinking about it.

Because by definition culture is pervasive, distinctions of class, status, occupation, education, religious persuasion and the like are also irrelevant to assumptions by whites of their own superiority. The form and subtlety of white supremacy may differ but the fact does not; whether white supremacy takes hostile or paternalistic form, it remains white supremacy. There is nothing inconsistent about being a white supremacist and a college graduate, a church-goer, or a liberal. In fact, chances are that it would be more inconsistent to be one of those things and *not* be a white supremacist. According to the September 1968 Harris survey, 44% of those whites interviewed admitted to believing that "most white people have more native intelligence than Negroes" (intellectual superiority). The figure represents an increase from 39% who held the same belief in 1963. In the same survey, 34% said that whites care more for their families than do blacks, an assertion of moral superiority which was held by only 31% of the whites interviewed in 1963.[3]

Nor is this to say that whites are not capable of admitting to exceptions. They do. And the exceptions are very important. For every white who would simply dismiss Thurgood Marshall, Ralph Bunche, Bill Russell, Diana Sands and Bill Cosby as "niggers like all the rest," it is possible to find a white school teacher, factory worker or clerk that would not be ashamed to admit that such people are as clean as, have achieved as much as, and are in general as good as — if not better than — himself. Such attitudes are not surprising in that the Ralph Bunches have been defined as "good" by white standards. The only condition of such an admission of "equality" would be the insistence on the atypical character of such black people and "why aren't the rest like 'them'? "

A significant minority of whites would become hysterical at the mention of such Negro "achievers." Some whites are pathologically, psychotically, or neurotically racist. They assert that people of color are absolutely and irrevocably worthless and a threat to the purity of the white race and hence "mankind." Such whites behave in ways ranging from murder to hate letters to nervous breakdowns and complete personality disintegration when confronted with objective reality in one form or another. Their pathology differs only in degree from the culture of which they are a product.

If the culture and pathology of white supremacy are the simplest ways to understand and define racism, there are other ways to understand its manifestations. Racism makes it impossible for most whites to accept someone as both human and black (or any other color). As has been suggested, most whites believe skin pigment is synonymous with sub- or non-humanity. This attitude is manifested by terms such as nigger or gook, as synonymous for Negro, Black, Oriental or Yellow. The more subtle point can be seen by examining the converse. Many of the best-intentioned whites believe that the highest compliment that can be paid to a black friend or acquaintance is to say, "Why John, I don't even think of you as a Negro." In other words, "I accept your humanity only to the extent that I deny or ignore your color."

This phenomenon was noted in another context by Jean-Paul Sartre in his little-known book *Anti-Semite and Jew:*

There may not be much difference between the anti-semite and the democrat. The former wishes to destroy him as a man and leave nothing in him but the Jew, the pariah, the untouchable; the latter wishes to destroy him as a Jew and leave nothing in him but the man, the abstract and universal subject of the rights of man and the rights of the citizen. Thus there may be detected in the most liberal democrat a tinge of anti-semitism; he is hostile to the Jew to the extent that the latter thinks of himself as a Jew.[4]

This is not to say that racism and prejudice are the same, they are not and the difference is crucial. It is one thing to assume that people are inferior on the basis of their skin color (or some other characteristic). That is prejudice. It is another thing to *desire* that a group of people be inferior and to organize society so as to insure that they will be. That is racism.

In a racist society, prejudice, in its classic form is rampant and inevitable. Its incidence in the United States is phenomenal. The Harris survey mentioned earlier discovered that 50% of the whites interviewed believed that black people smell differently (presumably worse although the study didn't say one way or the other). But if prejudice is unfounded, subjective, stereotypical belief about a group of people, racism is objective fact about them used to justify their continued subjugation.

It is not prejudice but rather empirical fact to say that black people commit a disproportionate share of crimes of violence, have lower reading and I.Q. scores (after they are seven or more years of age), make less money, are more likely to be unemployed, live in poorer neighborhoods, and a host of other true statements. The question is on the one hand, why do such conditions exist, and on the other hand, how do whites feel about that — are they pleased, sad or indifferent? Are whites willing to organize society so that such conditions are no longer true, or do they resist those changes with all their power? Do whites make changes which they say are for the purpose of ending "black inferiority" but which are intended to have the opposite effect, such as "compensatory education," public housing projects, job training, or the welfare program;

or do they make changes in support of black self-determination and liberation?

For the record, it is necessary to deal briefly here with the myth of "Negro Progress." Despite the highly visible advancement of some black people in recent years, it must be understood that the objective situation of most blacks, *relative to whites*, has remained unchanged or deteriorated. Infant and maternal death rates for black infants and mothers have deteriorated in urban areas not only relative to white death rates but also relative to the black rates of the 1940's and '50's.[5] More black children attend segregated and inferior schools today than did in 1960.[6,7]

Black unemployment as a percentage of all unemployment is rising, particularly for black youth.[8] Although poverty is being reduced overall, black poverty as an incidence of all poverty has risen steadily since 1959.[9] Economically and occupationally, black people are joining what is known as the middle class.[10] Yet while the percentage of blacks employed in clerical positions increased from 1.2% in 1940 to 6.3% in 1966, the increase in the percentage of blacks in "household service" went from 22.4% in 1940 to 41.8% in 1966.[11]

The gap in dollar income between whites and blacks has continued to rise since 1959, even when the South was excluded from the data.[12] Again excluding the South, the relative median income position of blacks as compared to whites has remained unchanged since 1953.[13] In fact, the only improvement in relative income position has been in the South.[14]

As a black woman in Atlanta once said, "The food Ralph Bunche eats doesn't fill my stomach."

Finally, the ideology of racism might be defined as, "The natural instinct of whites to oppose the desires and demands of black people no matter what they are or how they are formulated." The ability to control people of color breeds an evergrowing desire to expand that control.

In extreme cases, this response follows the model of what might be called the "Cherokee syndrome." The destruction of the Cherokee nation is particularly significant; it followed the peaceful acquiescence by the Cherokees to every demand and request to relocate put forth by the white man. In an effort to maintain their traditional lands, they maintained schools, had a written constitution, invented a written language, and published parts of the Bible.[15] Yet the efforts to adopt the forms of white society, the efforts of the Cherokees to meet white demands and standards did not prevent the destruction of their nation.

Whatever black people want, whites are against it. In the 1950's the public schools of Prince Edward County and other Southern Districts were closed to prevent their integration. In 1968, the public schools of all New York City were closed to prevent black people in one small part of the system from controlling their own segregated schools.

For years, liberals have been able to obfuscate the fact that the essence of racism is the desire for and fact of control over people of color by defining the question as integration or physical proximity in schools, public accommodations, neighborhoods, and the like. According to such arguments racism consists exclusively of opposition to integration. Nonsense: "integration" is often more racist and more exploitative than opposition to it.

Whites have not only accepted physical proximity when it suited their purposes, they have required it. Were this not the case, every black person in the country would be "pure-blooded." Most are not. In one sense, the society has been racist because it was integrated, not because it wasn't. As Malcolm X said, "There have always been house niggers and field niggers, beginning with slavery." Perhaps the best recent example of racist integration is the United States military, integrated upon order after World War Two. The Korean War, the first war in which the military was integrated, was the first war in the nation's history in which the black casualty rate disproportionately exceeded the white casualty rate. As military integration has progressed through the war in Vietnam, the proportion of black casualties to their percentage in the society and in the army has gotten progressively larger.

In the last decade, token integration in the mass media, middle level industry, etc., enjoyed a significant upsurge after a growing segment of the black population articulated its desire not to integrate. The first public approval through referendum of any open occupancy provisions did not come until two years after the modern cry of "black power" with its initial anti-integration implications.

The fact is, simply to take one common sense example, that opposition to Stokely Carmichael *increased* rather than decreased when he became a "separatist." Those who were only mildly opposed or even supportive of Stokely Carmichael and others in SNCC when they were militant integrationists became hysterical in their opposition when SNCC became militant black power "anti-integrationists."

To put it another way, the fact of racism never changes — only its form changes. The society or an institution within it can be either integrated and racist or segregated and racist. Perhaps this makes growing black skepticism about "integration" understandable. None of this is intended to argue that integration is always racist. Or that its advocates are always white supremacists. In fact, the question for whites is neither integration nor separatism, but rather the continued desire and the ability to control people of color.

Integration is hardly the only euphemism for racism. Ours is a euphemistic, hypocritical society, consequently little or nothing is done in its own name and racism is no exception. Schools are segregated, not to keep blacks separate but to "preserve the neighborhood school." Police are given and exercise excessive power in the ghetto not because blacks must be controlled at all costs, but to stop "crime in the streets." Blacks are never denied jobs because of their skin color, but because they are not "qualified." Housing integration is not resisted because its opponents do not wish to live next door to "niggers," but because black people "lower the property values." Black students, it is argued, fail to learn in ghetto schools not because the schools are inferior, but because the students are inferior by virtue of being "culturally disadvantaged." For every conceivable act of overt discrimination, there exists a euphemism to disguise it.

The "semantics" of racism is reflected in other ways as well, many of them known by now. "Indians" killing whites is a massacre; whites slaughtering "Indians" is a victory. People who insist on calling Muhammad Ali, Cassius Clay, would never think of calling Jack Benny, Benjamin Kubelsky, or Kirk Douglas, Issor Danielovitch. White ethnic groups are "hyphenated Americans," they are referred to as German-Americans, Polish-Americans or Italian-Americans. Such terms connote that the nation is the possession of the immigrant group. "Indians" and Blacks, however, are generally referred to as "American Indians" and "American Negroes," suggesting (quite correctly) that those two groups are the possession of the nation rather than the reverse. The term "American" as a synonym for a resident of the United States is at least ethnocentrism, since America is the name of a continent of scores of nations in addition to the United States. This is all not to mention the derogatory terms applied to people of color. The use of such terms is useful in understanding the spectrum of racism among whites from hostile through paternalistic forms. The spectrum is reflected through the use of terms such as ni~ger, coon and jigaboo through "colored" and "the colored" to Negro, Afro-American and Black. Nor is it to point out, as has Maulana Ron Karenga, that if blacks, reds, browns and yellows are "people of color" then whites are the "colorless."

Analogous to the euphemisms and semantics of racist culture are an elaborate set of collective and individual defense mechanisms. That is, some are designed to "prove" that there is no such thing as racism in the society, others to "prove" that an individual is in no way a racist or even prejudiced. There are naturally hundreds of such mechanisms; a few of the "social" types will serve as examples.

It is not because of racism, discrimination or exploitation that blacks find themselves in ghettoes and "Indians" on reservations. It is because they are a minority — they are only 10%. This is known as the "because blacks are only 10% of the population there is no such thing as racism" position.

Similarly, it has been argued by "academicians," "scholars" and other apologists that there is no problem of race, only a problem of poverty. This is known as the "because there exists in the country poor people who are white, there is no such thing as racism" position.

Still another version more recently proposed is that the United States has no racial problems, only technological ones. Black people (and poor whites) live in poor housing because housing, unlike automobiles and refrigerators, has not yet been "industrialized." This might be called the "because white people can send rockets to the moon and invent hydrogen bombs but not provide decent housing, there is no such thing as racism in the United States" position.

The final example: the Paul Goodman defense mechanism, named after an article by Mr. Goodman, renowned iconoclast, which appeared in the *New York Review of Books* of May 23, 1968.[16] The article, which went unchallenged, stated essentially that the Kerner Report was wrong, there are no white racists in the United States of any consequence and hence the nation is not racist. There are only black racists. White people are merely indifferent and apathetic. This is known as the "because white people are often passive in their acceptance of the racist structure and culture in which they live, and because blacks are active in opposing their continued subjugation, there is no such thing as white racism" position.

Without the ability to transmute the victim into the criminal and the criminal into the victim and to engage in colossal double-think, it is doubtful that either the culture or the structure of white supremacy could have endured as long as they have.

The preceding, however, serves merely to show the depth, tenacity and pervasiveness of racism in the culture. It is something which few whites can escape. Most whites hear about "niggers" and "gooks" from parents, friends or relatives before they ever see a person of color. It is nearly impossible to ride in a taxi, get a haircut, go to a cocktail party, drink at a bar or eat in a restaurant without encountering a barrage of gratuitous racist remarks. The social science curricula are overtly white supremacist even when they do discuss black Crispus Attucks, yet don't discuss white Lyndon Johnson, white Al Capone, white Teddy Roosevelt, white General Custer and white Rev. Josiah Strong.

Few whites are immune from at least the more subtle conditioning of white supremacist culture. Conscious effort is required to maintain a semblance of objectivity in the face of the totality of racism.

Whites who confronted military force at the Democratic Convention in Chicago were quick to compare the use of military force with Prague as indicated by "Chicagoslovakia" and "Chicago-Prague" signs and banners. Apparently it occurred to no one to compare Chicago with Detroit where, following the assassination of Dr. Martin Luther King, 10,000 National Guardsmen were sent into the black community for five days for what the governor called "a precautionary measure of early over-reaction." Nor were comparisons made with Wilmington, Delaware, where, at this writing, National Guard troops have just been withdrawn after nine and one half consecutive months of patrolling the black community.[17] (Perhaps this only confirms the rule that "injustice" is perceivable in direct proportion to its distance from the perceiver.)

Similarly, some whites were outraged at the beatings by police in Chicago. Most of the same whites did not "see," literally or figuratively, the three black people who were killed by police during the Republican National Convention in Miami.[18] Bruised white heads are more important than dead black bodies.

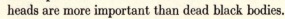

When Biafrans and Nigerians fight a civil war in Africa, that is typical of black primitiveness and savagery. When Germans seek to annihilate Russians, and Yankees try to destroy Confederates, that is at worst an example of *human* weakness and foible. White geographers, who center their maps of the world in Nebraska, make maps of the country's great discoveries, achievements and products; but not of where lynchings took place or "Indians" were massacred.[19]

Ofttimes, racism manifests itself in ways which appear to be contradictory. Support or opposition to the war in Vietnam is a good example. In view of the United States' essentially non-violent response to white communism, including communist "aggression" in Hungary, Czechoslovakia and Berlin, it is at least plausible to argue that there might not even be a war if the citizens of Vietnam (and/or China) were white. Apparently, it is better to be "dead than red" only if you are yellow, red, black or brown instead of white. At least the United States has not seen fit to destroy any white countries in order to save them from the evils of communism. Support for the war appears to be tacitly, if not explicitly, racist.

Yet there is an argument, also based on skin color, which holds that the United States ought to withdraw from Vietnam. This is essentially the position of arch-segregationist Orville Hubbard, Mayor of the all-white Detroit suburb of Dearborn, Michigan. His position, simply stated, is: "Why should we expend good red-blooded American boys and hard earned dollars on those gooks?"

In other words, cultural racism is manifest by omission as well as commission. It appears not only in what whites react to, but in what does not affect them at all.

Finally, a racist society is one in which racism succeeds and anti-racism fails. Historically, anti-racism has failed in the United States, infrequently by defeat, most often by default. One would hardly expect to hear a white politician call for the vigorous enforcement of anti-discrimination law and order, unless perhaps he were seeking black votes. The public is not exactly outraged about bleeding hearts who coddle bigots. The thought of a politician campaigning on a platform of fighting white supremacy in the streets and threatening to run over the first bigot to lie down in front of his or her car seems ludicrous. Some years ago, a white minister in Cleveland, Ohio lay down in front of a bulldozer to try to stop the building of a segregated school. He was run over and killed.

Put another way, the United States is a society in which the rewards for racism — social, financial, political or psychological — appear to be greater than the punishments. Punishment is more likely to be reserved for anti-racists than for racists. Its severity ranges from being ostracized to being murdered in proportion to its perceived threat, although "overkill" is common, as John Brown, James Reeb, Bruce Klunder, William Moore and innumerable black men and women could testify if they were alive.

Bigotry is illegitimate in theory but acceptable in practice; "Equality" and "Humanity" are legitimate in theory but unacceptable in practice.

Racism is not, of course, the only anti-human element in an anti-human capitalist culture. Racism supports and complements other anti-democratic tendencies and is in turn reinforced by them. Xenophobia of all kinds, class bias, materialism, the sanctity of private property and hostility towards nature are also elements of the United States' culture and all are symbiotically related to white supremacy.

Structure

Because culture, by definition, is institutionalized, any attempt to distinguish the culture of white supremacy from its structure is somewhat artificial. It is essential that the distinction be made, however; not to do so is to risk falling victim to "liberal" theories such as the Kerner Report which suggest that all whites are equally responsible for maintaining the subjugation of people of color and that all whites benefit equally from racism.

As in other areas of decision-making in the United States, the crucial decisions which create and sustain the powerlessness of black people are made by very few people.

This is not to say that the masses do not reinforce or support the structure of racism. That they do is indicated by occasions such as the vote on Proposition 14 in California where, by a two-to-one margin, it was voted not to allow black people equal access to housing. Such votes are the natural outgrowth of a racist culture. The fact remains that on a day-to-day basis, a comparatively small number of whites is involved in the domestic exploitation and suppression of black people.

The most common description of the black community suggests that blacks are an internal colony. In addition, it is useful to understand the position of "non-whites"as that of a subjugated caste. Racism cannot be adequately understood through a traditional or classic analysis precisely because blacks are *not* a part of the white class structure. If they were, then there would be no difference between white and black figures for unemployment, poverty, job security, quality of housing, health care, education and the like. The United States does have a class structure. It also has a caste structure, in which some privileges are retained for whites regardless of their class position (such as the right not to be called a "nigger"). Conversely, "non-whites" are accorded certain treatment regardless of their economic position. Neither Martin Luther King, Col. Lemuel Penn, Malcolm X, nor Medger Evers was poor. Nor were many of the Japanese-Americans interred in camps during World War II.

What is common to both colonial and caste descriptions is a permanent state of economic and/or political powerlessness for non-whites as a group.

Most colorless people believe that they do not discriminate against or oppress people of color. In a sense, they are right. Institutionalized, anonymous racism means that many whites do not discriminate in any direct way. They rarely have the opportunity. (As a consequence, most whites also believe that blacks are not discriminated against at all.[20] If anything, they think that blacks oppress *them*.)

Only a small number of whites benefit in a tangible, direct political or economic way from the continued oppression and exploitation of non-whites in the United States. Few whites, after all, can afford domestic help (maids) no matter how low the wages. Not many whites hire labor — cheap or otherwise. There are less and less white politicians who depend on the ghetto vote to retain their electoral position. There are very few Southern plantation owners. Compared to the entire white population, the number of slumlords, loan sharks, and furniture store owners who operate in the ghetto is tiny. Whether individual or institutional, domestic imperialism, like its international big brother, is profitable only to a few.

By far the largest group of whites with a tangible stake in the perpetuation of the colonial-caste position of "non-whites" are those who are hired to administer, contain and control the colony in order to protect the interests of its owners. This group has been labeled by sociologist Lee Rainwater the "dirty workers."[21] Included among their ranks are: employees of the Bureau of Indian

Affairs, ghetto school teachers, welfare workers, policemen, public
prosecutors and judges, apartment managers, members of the
National Guard, bill collectors and the like. Although most dirty
workers are white, for reasons of survival, efficiency and opportun-
ism a growing number of blacks are so employed as well. The
function of the dirty workers, as the appellation implies, is to do
the dirty work. Just as the apparatus of the Departments of State
and Defense operate to subsidize and secure the foreign investment
of Charles Englehard and United Fruit, so, too, the welfare department, poverty program, police department and National Guard
exist in part to protect the slumlord. The labor and taxes of the
many support the profits of the few.

Dirty workers do not necessarily know, wish or intend that their
efforts oppress people of color. Much exploitation and conditioning
of people of color to accept their lot takes place in the name of
"helping." Moreover, racism is such an integral part of the economic, political and social structure, that many, perhaps most,
decisions and actions which adversely affect black people do not
necessarily involve any consciousness of "color" whatsoever. To
say that racism is institutionalized is to say that in carrying out
its day-to-day business, the society adversely affects black people
without anyone thinking about it one way or the other.

In this sense, motives are irrelevant. Racism may be conscious
or unconscious, intended or unintended. The question is: does a
particular act disadvantage black people to the advantage of
whites, or does it disadvantage blacks whether or not whites benefit? Acts which are intended to be racist can, in fact, be anti-racist
in their effect — such as segregating the army and not sending
black soldiers to the front lines because they are "cowards." Conversely, an action may be thought to be anti-racist and produce
racist effects, such as those who supported urban renewal because
they sincerely thought it would provide better housing for black
people.

The fact remains that dirty workers retain a vested economic
and/or political interest in the continued domination and powerlessness of their "clients." As the recent UFT strike in New York
City has shown, such groups are relentless in their opposition to
black self-determination and control over those areas presently
controlled by the dirty workers. Attempts to strengthen and maintain their already formidable political power are also being organized by other dirty worker groups. The police in particular are

already a major force in every city and have just announced plans to form a nationwide "union" to further solidify their growing power.

Despite their power, the dirty workers have failed. The tranquility, stability, and acquiescence of the ghetto in the face of its own exploitation and oppression was irrevocably shattered at least by the 1964 Watts rebellion, if not before.

The response to their failure and the ensuing crisis in ghetto control since 1964 is revealing in terms of the structure of institutional and systematic racism. The first reaction was to summon reinforcements.

Chief among these was the Office of Economic Opportunity or the poverty program. Functioning as a pacification program, OEO rested on solidly middle class theories and assumptions. Essentially it argued that black people are handicapped by their lack of job skills, their inability to speak the language properly, and their unfamiliarity with rudimentary skills such as taking job interviews and punching time clocks. The poverty program sought to help the handicapped. Whatever its success in ending "poverty," by the time of Newark and Detroit in the summer of 1967, it was clear that it too, like the dirty workers, had failed to restore stability and tranquility to the cities.

The summer of 1967 produced the unprecedented (at least for the North) direct intervention of the corporate ruling class itself. *Fortune Magazine* and the *Wall Street Journal* were alarmed. The Urban Coalition and the National Alliance of Businessmen were formed. Faced with continuing disruption, it suddenly became necessary to give black people "a sense of power" and "a stake in society."

At the same time, the police arms race encouraged by the police industrial complex began in earnest.[22] The size of National Guard units, previously ordered demobilized, was increased, and special "riot" training was made mandatory. The culture of racism made any other response by local government impossible. As an example, in Detroit, after the rebellion of 1967, liberal Mayor Jerome Cavanaugh argued that the poverty program had been a success in Detroit because arrest statistics showed that people involved in the poverty program tended not to be arrested during the Detroit rebellion. (Presumably this meant that they did not get involved in the rebellion as a result of their stake in the poverty program, rather than that they were more skillful at evading arrest.)

Cavanaugh did not take the next logical step to ask for a greater city commitment to the poverty program as a future riot preventative. To do so would have been political suicide since it would have meant "rewarding the rioters." Instead, Cavanaugh asked city council approval of a multi-million dollar bond issue with authorization for the purchase of more than one million dollars in armaments, including Stoner machine guns, armored personnel carriers, M-1 rifles, and an "air force" consisting of one plane and one helicopter; with the exception of the "air force," all requests were approved.

Faced with paralysis in local and federal government, the only segment of the society capable of responding to the ghetto was of course, big business. The nature of the response has been to shift emphasis from the French model of colonialism, with its reliance on dirty workers and military force, to the British model, leaning toward "native" self-administration of the colony. Business response might also be described as neo-colonial, since it allows greater political independence while tightening economic control.

On the caste model of white control, the business response can be seen as an effort to maintain the caste system through the restructuring of the class structure of the subservient caste. Thus the creation of a real black bourgeoisie through "black capitalism" serves to intensify competition within the black community for scarce resources, returning the ghetto to a state of paralysis through social darwinism. Class struggle within the black community either renders caste unity impotent and passive, hence not threatening to general stability, or it destroys such unity altogether, at least in the short run.

Whichever interpretation one prefers, it is clear that, as was the case following the Civil War, the new reconstruction is intended to serve, at best, as an alteration in the form of colonial-caste, racist control — not as its elimination.

To pacify the ghetto, that is, to "solve the Negro problem," is hardly to end racism. For proof, one need only turn to the "pacified" (until recently) "Indians."

If the contradiction between Capital and Labor was not resolved by the struggles of the 30's despite accommodation to the labor movement, the concessions to "black power" will not resolve the contradiction of racism. Under the present structure, a reduction in domestic racism would probably necessitate an increase in racial hostilities abroad.

The history of "social change" in the United States is the history of "the more things change, the more they remain the same." Present efforts are no exception in their deceptiveness. As the next section seeks to make clear, United States society, as it is presently structured, is incapable of ending racism.

Function

Just as racism is only one element of an anti-human culture, the structure of white supremacy, whatever its form, is only one part of an exploitative, anti-human system of social organization. Racism in any multi-racial capitalist society is inevitable and functional. To understand its function purely in terms of control of people of color is insufficient. Racism functions to support the existing class structure as well as the caste structure. It is the cement of ruling class corporate power at home and abroad. Put another way, racism is not just "institutional," it is also systematic.

That is, racism not only separates whites from blacks, it also serves to distort relations between whites in a multiplicity of ways. Racism solidifies natural enemies, submerges natural antagonisms and separates natural allies.

Most obviously and simply stated, caste consciousness serves as a substitute for class consciousness. Struggle by white workers against blacks prevents struggle by white workers against the bosses. Poor and working class whites have been told time and time again in hundreds of different ways that everytime they move against powerful whites they risk losing their caste privilege. The threat is carried through frequently enough to make it plausible.

For people without economic security or status in the society, even the illusion of control over someone is attractive. Cicero, Illinois would not be so attractive if even Ralph Bunche could live there, let alone some ordinary colored. Fifty cents more an hour hardly seems worth it if one would have to have a "nigger" as a foreman. Even a strike doesn't seem like such a good idea if it means that "they" will be brought in to work. Welfare workers, school teachers and policemen who do not control their own institutions can derive some satisfaction out of controlling those of black people. Students and white collar workers can be smug in their moral superiority over the "rednecks" because their racism takes a more paternalistic form.

The conflict between caste and class is not a simple one. It will not be resolved through mechanistic calls for unity between white and black workers. The historical fact is that white-black coalitions for economic demands do not necessarily alter either basic economic or racial structures of the society. Indeed, such coalitions may reinforce the basic structure. Serious investigation is needed of the probability that whites have entered into coalitions with blacks for economic and work standards improvement, only on the *condition* that they retain their caste privilege. This has been particularly true in the trade union movement. There is nothing inconsistent about whites striking *with* blacks at the factory and *at* blacks who approach "their" neighborhoods or whose children seek to attend "their" schools. If coalition for economic demands ended racism, then presumably there would be no reason for young blacks to create organizations like the Dodge Revolutionary Union Movement (DRUM) within the U.A.W. organized plants, around demands for black foremen, equal apportionment of dangerous and degrading jobs and the like.

The delicate relationship between class and caste makes racism an irrevocable contradiction in United States society. The white power structure cannot "free" the black community without upsetting the structure of the white community.

As the "enlightened, Yankee" segment of the establishment is learning, it is dangerous to even appear to "allow" things to blacks which most whites do not have for themselves. As the Urban Coalition seeks to redefine its relationship to the black community its relationship is deteriorating with the white. Sometimes this takes the form of Wallace-ite, backlash hostility to blacks and concessions made to them. Such a response is somewhat understandable in view of the fact that working class whites are being asked to pay for the concessions. It is their growing taxes which pay for the welfare and poverty programs. And although they grossly overestimate the numbers of people on, and the benefits of welfare, and the amount spent to fight poverty, they are right when they resent the Kerner Commission for expecting them to pay a disproportionate share to solve a problem which they did not create.

Another less clear manifestation of the same contradiction is reflected in the growing militancy of the labor force which is striking in unprecedented numbers. Faced with worsening in their objective situation caused by inflation, speed-ups and the like, workers are undoubtedly spurred in part by the ironic misperception that "the blacks are getting theirs, why shouldn't we get ours."

"The difference between most whites and most blacks is that whites are economically compensated for their powerlessness at a higher rate than are blacks."[23] If many whites appear genuinely puzzled at black demands for self-determination, power and community control, perhaps the puzzlement *is* genuine. Whites cannot understand black demands for things which are alien or unattainable for themselves as whites. If whites have learned to accept their own impotence in the face of external control of decision making and acquiescence in their own exploitation, "why shouldn't they (black people) do it the same way we did."

Conclusion

Perhaps they will. If not, the present possibility of overt fascism in the United States becomes more likely. The fact that racism is for most whites misguided false consciousness and that whites are victimized as well as non-whites in no way lessens the opposition to demands for self-determination by people of color. White material affluence, however small one's share of it, does "co-exist" with domestic and foreign imperialism. Overwhelming evidence suggests that most whites continue to believe that their interest lies with the suppression of black, red, brown and yellow people rather than with their liberation. Those who are part of the growing, post-Kerner Report concern about "racism" remain more committed to the system which inevitably creates it than to its elimination.

Notes

[1] Thomas F. Gossett, *Race: The History of an Idea in America* (New York, 1965), p. 235.

[2] As appeared in the *Chicago Daily News*, May 13, 1968.

[3] As appeared in the *Boston Globe*, September 16, 1968.

[4] Jean-Paul Sartre, *Anti-Semite and Jew* (New York, 1948), pp. 56–57.

[5] "Mortality of White and Non-White Infants in Major U.S. Cities," *Health, Education and Welfare Indicators January 1966*, United States Department of Health, Education and Welfare.

[6] *Racial Isolation in the Public Schools 1967*, United States Commission on Civil Rights.

[7] James S. Coleman, *Equality of Educational Opportunity*, Department of Health, Education and Welfare.

[8] *Social and Economic Conditions of Negroes October 1967*, United States Department of Labor, Bureau of Labor Statistics, United States Department of Commerce, Bureau of the Census.

[9] *Report of the National Commission on Urban Problems*, Mimeo Edition, Part I, pp. 1–18.

[10] Computed from data published in *Fortune*, January, 1968, p. 144.

[11] Ibid.

[12] Ibid.

[13] Ibid.

[14] Ibid.

[15] Gossett, op. cit., pp. 232, 237.

[16] Paul Goodman, "Reflections on Spite, Guilt and Violence," *New York Review of Books*, May 23, 1968.

[17] *New York Times*, January 22, 1969. See also *National Guardian*, January 15, 1969.

[18] John Boone and William Farmar, *New South*, Vol. 23, No. 4. Published by Southern Regional Council, Inc. pp. 28–37. According to the report, John Austin, 29, and Moses Cannon, 39, were shot in the back by Miami police. Ejester Cleveland was standing on his front porch when police sprayed his building with bullets because of a "sniper."

[19] Marc B. Anderson, "Putting It My Way But Nicely or Ethnocentrism In Geography," unpublished manuscript.

[20] According to the Gallup Poll, published in the Detroit Free Press July 22, 1967, only 99 out of 100 whites do not believe that blacks are treated "badly." Seventy-five percent said they believe that "Negroes are treated the same as whites."

[21] Lee Rainwater, "The Revolt of Dirty-Workers," *Transaction*, November 1967.

[22] An article in the Detroit News, January 1, 1969 by Phil Thomas, AP business writer reports for example Bnagor Punta, a large arms maker specializing in police equipment, reports an increase in sales from $12.8 in 1966 to $16.5 in 1967. See also, *Repression in America* published by People Against Racism, 212 McKerchey Building, Detroit, Michigan 48201.

[23] William Strickland, unpublished manuscript.

WORKERS BATTLE AUTOMATION

CHARLES DENBY

Let the Workers' Voices be Heard

Working as a production worker, and as the editor of a workers' paper, *News and Letters*, I have been in the battle against Automation since it started ten years ago.

Automation was introduced to the mass production industries, first in the coal mines, then in the auto, steel, electrical, and rubber industries. It is in white collar offices as well.

The intellectual — be he scientist, engineer or writer — may think Automation means the elimination of heavy labor. The production worker sees it as the elimination of the laborer.

Not being in a factory, the intellectual may think that the worker in Automation is being turned into a technician. The production worker, however, knows this simple truth: when he is not thrown into unemployment, he is subjected to the inhuman speed of the machine.

No doubt Automation is a "scientific achievement," but this "scientific achievement" has no life outside of production. In the mine, mill or factory, Automation has not reduced the drudgery of labor. The very opposite is the truth. The factory clock is now geared to the pace of the monster machine. It makes no difference whether it is the company foreman or the union steward who makes the worker get out the production set by time-study.

The auto worker, the steel worker, the miner — all workers who battle against Automation know its life-and-death meaning — its speedup, its inhuman way of work, its death by overwork, its unemployment, its permanently depressed areas, its ghost towns.

No matter which industry I take to show the real relations under

Automation, the story is the same: the production workers struggle against Automation, both in and out of the shop. Their trade union leaders line up with the company for what they call "progress."

Take the 1949–50 miners' strike. Part of the time it was an authorized strike led by John L. Lewis. However, he enthusiastically endorsed the use of "the automatic coal miner" as "progress." He ordered the men back to work, but they refused to return to work until their demands for changing the conditions of labor were met.

Or, take the year 1954, when an executive at Ford first coined the word, *Automation* to describe *what* the workers were wildcatting against. Walter Reuther refused to support the men. He told them that they "must not fight progress."

Neither Reuther nor Lewis bothered to ask the workers how *they* saw Automation from the production line.

These battles against Automation reached a certain climax in the 1959 steel strike which David McDonald was supposed to have won. In fact, however, the conditions of work to which the men returned were no different than the ones against which they struck. None of the local grievances had been taken up. The demand for a shorter workweek never reached the bargaining table. Two deaths occurred the very first month after the men returned to work at the Great Lakes Steel Co. in Ecorse, Michigan. Thereupon a wildcat erupted against the new union contract.

It is time to expose the lie behind the fancy talk of "every worker an engineer." To the production worker, this type of talk is as phony as the talk about "prosperity." Profits may rise, but not the money in workers' pockets, and even less the groceries they can buy with it. Production statistics may rise, but the army of the unemployed does not decrease.

If Automation is here to stay, so is the permanent army of unemployed. Whatever Automation means to management, labor bureaucrat, or engineer, to the production worker it means a return to sweatshop conditions, increased speedup and gearing the man to the machine, instead of the machine to the man. The union contract assures management increased productivity by robbing the workers of control over the conditions of labor.

The past ten years have revealed an unending series of crises throughout the world. The basis of it is in production. Here it is High Noon.

If the struggle for freedom does not begin there, it will not be a total freedom. The machines might dig coal, assemble autos, roll steel, but the crises that they bring in their wake can be resolved only by human beings. The millions of miners, auto and steel workers who have lost their means of livelihood, as well as those who are still working the monster machines, will find their stories here. In whatever industry the workmen work they will find that the experience of others add up to a new way of meeting the chaos in production.

It is time the workers' voices were heard.

In the Auto Shops

I have been an auto worker since 1926. I have lived through the terrible Depression of 1929–1939. I have seen the C.I.O. leap into life, and I know what a great promise it held for us who built it. I have also seen the unions we built taken over by the bureaucrats, especially since 1950, and turned against us. I am suffering in my bones and heart from the torments brought by Automation, and I know this can't go on — somehow, some way, we must change it.

This isn't only my story, it is the story of hundreds of workers I know, and the millions I don't know personally but whom I know because their experiences with Automation, their lives and needs and thoughts, are like ours.

Time Study on Your Back

Automation was introduced in Chrysler in 1956. Ford had introduced it in 1954, and I can remember the workers striking there, but Chrysler brought it in only after Ford and GM had already automated production.

They have the time-study man sitting there and he's figuring every angle. We used to see the time-study man once a year. Now you see him forty times a day. He's standing there all the time. I've actually caught these guys standing behind a worker with his stop watch in his hand and his hand behind his back, clocking the guy. I always walk over and let the worker know he's standing there. Most of the time they say, "We see him standing there. We just don't care. We can't work any harder or faster." I know they can't.

They have production set so high that they know you can't do it. But they can keep you working every second of the day and that's what they're interested in. Keeping you on the job sixty minutes every hour. If you stop for just a moment to talk to someone the foreman walks up and asks you, "What's the matter? the job broke down?"

Before Automation, if you had a set quota and if you got that many jobs within the hour nothing was said. If you got your quota you had a few minutes every hour to rest. The way it is now the time-study times the job to as many given pieces you could possibly do in an hour, to the last second.

Let me make it a little more concrete. We were timed on this job at one hundred and twenty jobs an hour, "on a flowing line." For the first time in my life I couldn't seem to figure out what that superintendent was talking about. I soon got what he meant. He kept saying he wanted one hundred and twenty jobs to the minute of the hour so that the line keeps moving with no stops. He said, "We would have to stop the machine if you didn't work this way." That's where the speed-up of these machines that feed production lines comes in. To work this way is almost humanly impossible. If it was some light job, one that you could do easily — perhaps; but even so, to do it in that manner! — but a heavy job to boot, it's murder! You're just standing there, grinding your life away.

What it actually means is that you have to have a movement in your body and a coordination with that machine just like the movement of a watch.

A Fraction of a Man

When you're on a job, you like to feel good about it. You like to feel, "This is the job I work on," and be proud about what you're doing. The way we're forced to work you can't feel good about anything you do.

When the foreman first told me I was so many tenths and so many thousandths of a man I thought he was a nut. I argued with him. I told him a man is a whole human being. You can't split a man into fractions. But that's just what they're doing to us.

On one job, the foreman said that time study showed we had to get nine and one-tenth jobs an hour. He said it took so many man hours, and so many one-tenth man hours to get production. That's why the men had to be divided into tenths. They split us up into fractions. We're not even whole men any more.

A man's body has to be trained to work like the machine. The machine tells the body how to work. We work two hours, then have a rest period. Every man has to be able to go to the washroom at the end of those two hours. You're supposed to train yourself, I guess. We have two washrooms. Approximately three hundred and fifty men all are supposed to use the washrooms in twelve minutes.

The other day they put me on the worst line in the shop. I asked the foreman why I had to work here and he said that it had come to the point that they had to rotate the guys from the stationary jobs onto the line. They started that because you can't take too much of that line. One Monday morning at least one-third of the guys called in sick. They said they were still too tired from the previous Friday's work on that line to come in.

They start the line with a buzzer sounding, then as every job is supposed to be finished they sound it again, and brother you got to jump back or you are likely to get seriously injured.

They set that machine so fast. I turned around and saw a water fountain a few feet behind me. I wanted a swallow of that water so bad. I thought maybe I could beat the machine. I worked fast in between the buzzers so that I could run back and get just a swallow, but every time I laid my welding torch down the buzzer went off. That swallow of water was so close but it was like being on a desert. I never did get it.

One worker told me it seems like the only thing his body is geared for is to come into this shop and work on these machines. He said each night he promised himself he would not come back but each morning he gets up, more tired than when he went to bed. He comes into work and it seems like his muscles would only begin to loosen up after he has been on the job for a half hour.

We Don't Use the Machine; The Machine Uses Us

Automation is the machine, we know that, but it is also making the man a machine too. The machine can't function without the man. Someone has to be able to feed it, stop it, etc. If they don't, the machine will break down. We get quite a bit of repairs. I'd say twenty-five per cent repairs, and another ten per cent that you might as well say is scrap. One worker I know feels they'll always need the man. He says, "Those machines have to be watched constantly because if nobody watches, everything goes wrong." If the machine breaks down the men suffer the consequences because they send them home and then when the machine is fixed one way or another they have to make up the production.

You take the machine I work, it has to be watched. There's no way of knowing how many men this machine replaces. The men who watch the machine actually don't have too hard a day's work. There's the electrician, the repair man and the machinist, and the machine has an electronic brain.

The work that the machine puts out pushes the people ahead of it. Just these three men have good jobs; they're skilled. They take their time. Nobody comes around there to holler at them. They get paid for what they know.

It's the poor men who are in front — as long as that machine is pushing out like that, those men are slaving and sweating. There are approximately sixteen jigs with three men on a jig, each group is to get thirty-seven jobs an hour. They have no time to play.

What alienates a production worker is that he is driven to do work that is separated from his thinking. This along with the terrific pace we have to work, makes a worker doubly tired at the end of a day.

Some years ago, when workers had something to say about how fast they would work and the amount of help they felt they needed if the company wanted more production, the relations among production workers were humanly close.

They could help each other with their work. They worked in a way which would make it easy for every one in a group. Today Automation does not allow anyone to help another worker. Some of the machines are so large you can't even see another worker except the ones right beside you. We are degraded to a cog in the machine. We don't use the machine. It uses us.

The Loneliness of It

The loneliness that is brought about by these monster machines is terrific. Every worker feels it. When you work one of these machines you have no one to talk to. Before, there used to be eight or ten guys doing the same job.

One worker went so far as to say he liked to work the "merry-go-round." "Even though it's the worst job, you're working next to someone. It makes it different. You forget the strain and pressure you're under when you're talking. Sometimes I forget the time and the day goes by."

The worst punishment they give prisoners in jail is solitary confinement. But at work every day Automation forces you into solitary confinement.

I can understand why the English workers struck for "loneliness pay" when they first met up with Automation.

When you work by yourself on these machines you're fighting in your own mind and every minute you look up to see what time it is. One of these days something will explode because you can fight in your own mind just so long; and you know if you're doing it so is every other guy there.

To Break Our Spirits

If we could work the machines slower the way we want to, things would be different. At this speed, everybody's jamming everything down the next man's throat. A worker told the foreman the other day that the machine hadn't put out one good job yet on the shift so far. The foreman says, "Run 'em."

The man said, "Why? The inspectors will stop them." Sure enough, the inspectors stopped them. The man said, "Didn't I tell you?" The foreman turned around and said, "It's easier to work up there and fix up the complete frame instead of piling up the sections here."

What kind of a fool do they think the worker is? Don't we know it's easier to fix up in the section than to tear up a complete frame? As a result, a man works himself to death ten and twelve hours a day.

Also, the machines break down very often. They may not stay down too long, but sometimes they're down for as long as two hours. One day, for example, the machine was down for an hour and forty-five minutes, but they still got over one thousand jobs, which is more than the assemblers could do the old way. They've got fewer assemblers and they get more production because the men have to jump all day long.

I hate to think of my friends and family on the road doing sixty-five miles an hour in a car like that. I worry, is it one of the cars I worked on. I see things go by that are bad, but I can't stop to do anything about them. They make them too fast. I'm told they won't even operate the Plymouth plant unless they can get off a minimum of ninety-nine cars every hour.

A worker said, "We build something like a car a minute. The same thing we throw out in a minute — that's all we have time to do, throw it out — takes us three years of hard labor to pay for."

"We Don't Have Concentration Camps, Yet"

They schedule overtime whenever they want, but they won't call any men back to work or schedule extra shifts. They don't even give us any choice or notice about overtime anymore. They come around a few minutes before quitting time and say "Two hours." And that's it.

I was arguing with the committeeman about having to work ten hours a day. The law says we don't have to work more than eight hours, but now they make us work ten. I said, "How can they force this on us?"

He said, "The company schedules production, and the contract says you've got to work it."

I asked him, "What will stop them from working us twelve hours, and fourteen hours, or as long as they want, whenever they want?"

He just walked away. He couldn't answer. One man who protested against this got five days off. It got everybody scared, and nobody dares to say a word.

As one of the men puts it: "Automation is just a loophole for concentration. We don't have concentration camps here yet, where the man is forced to work under a gun. They don't have a gun on us, but they force us to work by saying, 'If you don't do as we say, starve on the street.' "

The only difference between this kind of working and living, and being in a cell block, is that we have more room to move about in. But they're just waiting. When they take your car, and your house, and your little bit of money, it's the same as being in jail. You can't move around anyway.

"I keep asking myself, will I ever be able to collect my social security when I'm sixty-five? Will I be able to live till sixty-five working in the factory? I doubt it. That Automation machine is killing me. Those men in Washington must be having a good time laughing to themselves knowing how many workers won't be around to collect."

Death by Automation

When you hear about Automation being a man-killer, that's not just a figure of speech. That's what the wildcat strike at Great Lakes Steel was all about.

After the 116 day strike was supposedly won by the men, the steel companies put on a new drive to put automatic processing equipment on the mill floor. From the strain of overwork, a crane operator fell from his scaffold and was killed. When the men went to his funeral they learned of three other operators who had died in the same week from the strain of the crackdown and speedup. That's what made the men mad. That's why they walked out.

As in the steel mills, so in the auto shops, as the speed from Automation becomes more intense, safety conditions are thrown to the wind by the company. I can remember when they first brought those machines into our department. I don't know how many workers were hurt that first day: crushed hands, lost fingers.

There are signs all over the department to work safely. Inside of a couple of hours workers wrote under these signs: "These machines are not safe to do it with."

February 10th of this year [1960] an auto worker got off the bus at the plant gate and fell dead on the pavement. He died of a heart attack. Workers said that he had repeatedly complained to the foreman that it was impossible to keep up with the pace set by time-study and the machine. His complaints didn't mean a thing to management. The union simply shrugged its shoulders.

On Wednesday, December 30th of last year there was a combined wildcat and lockout in one of Chrysler's assembly departments. It resulted from a worker being seriously injured on the frame job.

Chrysler's mad rush for production and more production, with workers bound to the inhuman pace of Automation, is very dangerous to the lives of the men on the frame job. Workers have been severely injured by the cross bars flying out from the frame before it can be welded. Minor injuries are a daily occurrence.

On this last Wednesday in 1959, a bar flew out and struck a worker across his back and head knocking him unconscious.

After the unconscious man was rushed to the hospital on a stretcher, the foreman yelled for another worker to come and work the same job. The worker refused, saying, "You're crazy as hell! I wouldn't work there for double pay." This never happens when the machine is running at a normal pace.

To the production worker in auto, Automation means physical strain, mental strain, fatigue, heart attacks — death by Automation.

"If This Is Progress"

If this type of Automation — machines that put millions out of work and destroy those that remain — if this is progress, said a friend of mine, Joe, that is the kind of progress he's against and anyone else would be if he had to be a slave to a machine.

It isn't progressive, but destructive to the worker who has to work it. It destroys the relations between husband and wife. Many workers cannot have regular sexual relations with their wives because they are so tired they go to sleep as soon as they get home from work. It also disrupts the parent and child relationship, indeed the whole family. Just recently I received the following letter from a steelworker's wife in Pittsburgh:

"There are so many people out of work here it is really shameful to see all the man-power going to waste. If we get out of work I guess we will have to leave here, because there is nothing for anyone.

"You know it is really sad to see boys and girls come out of school and there isn't anything for them to do but sit around and get into trouble or leave town."

Chained To The Machine

The newest machine they have added to their collection now, chains the worker to the machine. They put it in during this year's model changeover. A maintenance man told us about it.

He said, "A man has to be handcuffed with heavy leather straps and the cable — I'm sure that cable is what used to hold up the old welding guns — it's steel cable that runs from the leather cuff up his arms to under his armpits and comes over his shoulders from behind. They say the breaking point of this machine is ten thousandths of a second.

"It works by electric eyes. The worker puts the metal to be cut in the machine. As soon as the metal gets into the machine — no buttons need to be touched — the machine comes down and cuts. This machine works so fast, it isn't humanly possible for the worker to get his hands back out of the way before it cuts. They put these cuffs around the worker's wrists and at the point where the machine breaks and comes down, his hands are automatically jerked out of the way to keep him from getting them cut off."

He went on to tell us that there was such a commotion about this machine that they couldn't get anybody to start it off. So the supervisor put the cuffs on the foreman. It takes two workers to work the machine because the one who is handcuffed to it doesn't have room to turn around. He only drops the metal into the machine. After they ran two or three pieces the foreman begged them to turn him loose because he was forced to go to the rest room.

After hearing this, one worker said, "This sounds worse than the chain gangs in the South." Nobody believes it when you tell them about it.

Detroit Is Auto; Detroit Is Rubber; Detroit Is Unemployment

Detroit is auto. Detroit is also rubber. One rubber worker I know told me: "I was working in the process development department in rubber. A tire is built on a tire building machine — and in our production a tire is built on a merry-go-round, it looks like a carousel which has ten tire building machines on it. And these machines move around just like an assembly line, and each man does a particular operation as the tire building machine moves around. For each merry-go-round they had fifteen men working, that was ten on the merry-go-round itself and five supplying the material for it.

"They started a project for putting in an automated unit to replace the merry-go-round. This is a unit which has four tire building machines on it and revolves on a turret. All a man has to do is press a button on that machine and it will build a tire completely by itself. All the hand labor will be gone. I told the engineer who was working on this, 'You know that's going to put half the men in that department out of work.' He says, 'No.' So I said, 'Okay, figure it out.' He thought about it and said, 'You know, you're right.' This engineer saw only the building of the machine, he didn't see its relation to the human being.

"From my experience and in my estimation in that particular factory, before the sixties are over, that factory will be run with ten per cent of the manpower. In other words, where they now have six thousand men, it will be run with six hundred."

Detroit has been put on the depressed areas list. At the very same time the "Big Three" in auto — G.M., Ford, Chrysler — have revealed that their executives have been given enormous rewards in bonuses and dividends. There has been an absolute drop of thirteen per cent in auto employment. The 200,000 jobless in Michigan have joined the national army of unemployed to boost it to five million.

These are the official figures and everyone knows that many more than that walk the streets in search of jobs they cannot find, and by now are not entitled to collect any unemployment insurance. By the time the elections are over and they have stopped using this fact as a football, the Detroit worker has nothing to look forward to but more unemployment.

When I went back to work at Chrysler after the 1956 model changeover, they had introduced Automation as their "forward look." I was shocked at how many workers were missing. There used to be over 12,000 workers in my plant. Today there are fewer than 2,000. A worker with twenty years seniority told me that this was the first time he felt sad at being called back to work. He predicted then that our plants would become ghost plants with skeleton crews. They have become that.

Ford used to employ 80,000 at the River Rouge plant in Dearborn, and another 40,000 at the Highland Park plant. Today there are fewer than 40,000 at River Rouge and only a couple of thousand at Highland Park. The major operation there is tractors. Due to the depression in the farm areas tractor production has dropped fifty per cent.

This year when we were laid off for model changeover we were wondering just how many new machines they would bring. They laid us off "indefinitely" and we knew that meant new machines and more unemployment. When I was called back I found that the whole fifth floor was covered with new machines. The steward said that at least one third of the workers will not be back. They say they will cut back to 1942 seniority.

At one point in 1959 no less than seventeen per cent of the total labor force in Michigan was unemployed. 1960 is moving in the same direction of great unemployment and hardship. 1961 promises to plunge the country into a depression.

I have never seen so many men and youngsters, especially Negro men, pushing ice cream wagons and selling magazines, rags and junk as I do now. I know the reason they're doing it. They're out of work and don't have anything to live on. That's how it was when we sold apples on every street corner during the Depression.

Wherever Automation moves in workers are thrown out, and unemployment leaps. I can't help feeling as if we are headed towards slave labor here as they have in Russia and China. Where are they going to send the millions of unemployed we have here?

Talk with Office Worker and Engineer

When I heard about one of the office departments at Ford laying off one hundred and fifty girls and replacing them with some sort of brain, which only two girls work, one sitting at either end of the machine unable to talk to each other even, I felt it would be important to get a white collar worker's story into this story on Automation. Here is one from Los Angeles:

Mental Machines?

I've been thinking about Automation. I work with computers and so if I said anything it would be on them. I'm not a production worker. I've read in the paper many workers' reactions to Automation and how they feel about working with the machine in the auto industry. I get certain feelings from working with a machine that is automated and I must say it's just about the same I think as in a factory.

The Automation that I deal with is not an automation of what man would perform manually. It's an automation of what man would perform mentally. The machine is one that does not think exactly, but does a sort of mental process for you.

Automation does an action over and over again. That's what makes it Automation. The machine can handle an operation an unlimited number of times. My particular machine does some mathematics, and computation and makes up pay checks.

There is a pace to be kept and it's a tremendous pace on these computers, because the thing that is stressed — and I imagine stressed wherever you work with automated machines — is the enormous cost of the machine.

The man who is running the company is always stressing that this machine is costing quite a bit and we have got to get the work right away. If you make any mistakes at all they are going to write you up; three times and you are out. They have such a system where I work.

Mistake Time

Any minute, or whatever amount of time you waste by making a mistake, they log against you. There is no joking about it. I mean everybody knows that there is a log kept of how much mistake time you have. The mistakes can be so small. There is a row of switches that you have to lower or raise. If you lower or raise one by mistake you might waste three or four hours, and sometimes it can multiply because what follows after your mistake is also wrong. I mean five or six people have done things that have cost as much as ten hours time and this can mean five hundred dollars an hour worth of rent. I don't care what the cost is, of course, but the point of all this is that they keep pushing this at you.

You always hear about this log in which they "log" this time. They call it eighty-one time: that means personnel error and they charge it to somebody. You always hear, "How much eighty-one time have you got?"

This is just half of it. The other half is that when the machine is going it's doing things at fantastic speeds, but between jobs when you take one job off and put the next job on — this is where they're losing money and where they really push you. So you're pushed physically at that time. It's not only a race to go faster, it's a mental strain too because you have to go fast and you know it.

I feel that from working this type of machine that you have all the strain except the back-breaking strain that you can get from Automation in the factory. It develops a tenseness in me. When I get home it takes me two hours to be able to talk to people or do anything. I can't get to sleep and I get home in the middle of the night. They've got the whole thing built up to the degree that you don't dare make mistakes, and yet you've got to go fast. I imagine that this is also the essence of what Automation is to the production worker. There's nothing I like about Automation.

This is the story of a college youth with a very high I.Q. who was chosen to work an automated machine in an office. He didn't know how many workers it replaced but there are statistics which show that office workers too suffer from what they call "technological unemployment."

Taped Electronic Controls

I asked an engineer who knows some of the problems of working men to give me an explanation of what Automation consists of, as he sees it. This is what he said:

Automation as a system is not just an automatic machine. We have had automatic machines for years, automatic screw machines, machines which turn out any one of a number of various sizes and shapes of bolts, screws or small parts without anyone in constant attendance at the machine.

Automation is something quite different. It is in effect a whole series of automatic machines linked together to produce either a finished or semi-finished product which has gone through an assembly process as its various parts come together in the automation complex. In many cases the automation process is controlled by a recorded tape which contains the "program" telling the machines what to do next. Since many of these machines are capable of many different kinds of operations, the taped electronic controls are a necessary part of the machine function. Actually they take the place of the man who used to be the machine operator.

It is this feature of the automation process which makes it so objectionable to the men on the production line. Since there are still men who must work on these automated production lines, feeding it parts or raw materials or removing the finished parts, these men are forced to work at the rate predetermined by the machine, the machine becoming the master of the man.

The number of men assigned to any one process is usually determined on the basis of a smoothly functioning machine under ideal conditions. Any Detroit production line worker can tell you that this condition rarely exists. The machines have their faults, break down, or some one part of it refuses to function properly. Some machines have been known to produce as much as 40% scrap. If a machine completes only fifteen out of the seventeen welds it is supposed to, or drills only part of the required number of holes, or leaves a few nuts or bolts out of the assembly, then the product must undergo repair or be delivered to the consumer in an incomplete condition.

The workers can tell you how many of these badly made products are "passed" by foremen who are more anxious to set production records than they are to assure the quality of the products. Thus, while a machine may be set to perform certain functions, it cannot think or use judgment without the use of men to control it.

Their Scientists, Their Time-Study Men

I knew before the engineer told me that they design and build those machines that way in order to prevent the worker knowing anything about them. They don't want to use his own judgment on anything.

Before Automation, when a major change was made and a new machine was introduced, they had to rely on the workers' knowledge and experience to get it working properly. We had to get the kinks out of it. For a few weeks we felt like human beings working out the problems together and getting things organized and moving smoothly. Then, the engineers, the time-study, the foremen and superintendents kept out of our way and off our backs. They needed us to get the production flowing. Only after that did they use the old crack-down and speed-up.

Now, all they need is a man to watch it. They can't eliminate that, because if nobody watches, the machine breaks down and everything goes wrong. But just watching a machine doesn't mean knowing it. It doesn't take knowledge to operate a machine that way. I would have to build it from the start and know all about how it functions. That way there would be no monotony and every job is a little different and you get to use your head and it takes everybody to work it out.

Automation hasn't been designed to get everybody's knowledge behind it. It's been designed to get rid of the men and to push those who are left. They don't want us to use our heads while we're working, they just want to push us.

As a steelworker said, management can threaten its pushers that the job can run without them. But they don't want us running the job. They impose their own pattern and they have their scientists and their time-study men and their control engineers and their pushers to make sure that the machines get built so that we have to work the way they want us to.

He told me that as he sees it in the mill, really to run the job without the pattern the company imposes, really to run it for yourself, you would have to have the full confidence of your fellow-worker and he would have yours and you would work together without tension. You would get up in the morning and want to go to work. It's quite a problem to get up in the morning to go on a job when you know you'll have somebody nag you several hours of the day through no fault of your own. He'll just come along and find something wrong. That's the way they work it.

Workers' Control of Production

The road to the new society can begin in no other way than by changing the conditions of labor, which means, in the first place, control of production.

Workers' control of production means workers themselves decide what they produce, how much they produce, the conditions under which they work. They decide all questions. Once the majority of workers decide what is best for all of them, then all work according to that decision. There are no "favorites," no company men. The labor fakers who are trying to say that control of production would mean that the lazy would get away with murder don't know the first thing about workers and the cooperative spirit between them, once they work, not for the capitalists, but for themselves. When we first organized the C.I.O. even the leaders spoke of the need for a change in society. Now they know nothing, not even how to control the inhuman speed of the line.

Even the trade union leadership should be able to control the speed of the line. The early C.I.O. did it. We had some say on the job then. With World War II, when the C.I.O. leaders began to out-plan the capitalist planners they changed completely.

The Labor Leaders Get Brainwashed

It all began in 1947–49 when management raised a hue and cry about the "low labor productivity" of the older workers and the newly-returned war veterans. The government called conferences on productivity. The trade union leaders attended those conferences as they had attended government conferences during the war when they shackled us with the no-strike pledge.

It should be added that the labor bureaucrats were not the only "patriots." The communists outdid them in this type of patriotism, earning the hatred of the workers.

To me it seems that, just as out of the shotgun wedding of science and the government against the foreign enemy, the A-bomb was born, so out of the union of science and industry against the working people in this country, Automation was born. And just as the war transformed the labor leaders into labor bureaucrats, so Automation brainwashed them.

Along with the government and the companies, the labor bureaucrats began identifying Automation with "progress" without once asking how Automation would be used. Big Business was very happy to see that both the government and the union leaders had forgotten all about the "Full Employment Act" Congress enacted in 1946 when the workers made it clear that they had not fought a world war to return home to face another Depression. Automation moved from the drafting boards to application in the factories.

No torture chambers were needed to brainwash the labor bureaucrats. They are so busy putting blinders on to avoid seeing "local grievances" and concrete demands of workers that they become all too willing victims of abstractions about "progress" which help maintain the capitalist system.

Reuther talks about the need for re-training workers to meet "the challenge of Automation." I've been re-trained. I'm working on an Automation machine. What kind of re-training is that? I have never worked under such brutal conditions before. He certainly can't mean re-training to become the kind of technicians that do nothing but push buttons and get good pay doing it. There are very few of these jobs and less will be needed as we get fully automated.

It would be far better if Reuther, and other AFL-CIO leaders, and Hoffa too, got away from the high but empty summit type of talk and came in the plant — to work. Altogether too many years have gone by since they have had any taste of what any work is like, much less production work under Automation. If they really worked in the plant they couldn't possibly be brainwashed. Resistance comes naturally when you have to operate those monster machines. But when you sit in your ivory tower at Solidarity House and walk out of it only to confer with management here or the government in Washington, brainwashing comes naturally.

At union election time, Reuther comes out with big programs

on what to do with the millions of workers thrown into unemployment by Automation, on "profit sharing," on the shorter work week. But he drops these on the way to the bargaining table.

By the time he leaves the negotiation table and waves a contract at the workers, he has signed away the workers' rights to any say over conditions of labor. These just become "local grievances that can easily be settled locally." When the locals strike for these grievances, the International steps in once again — to order the workers back to work in accordance with the national contract. As local grievances pile up, each day, each week, each month, every year, they are filed away "until contract time." At contract time, however, they become "local grievances." The run-around the union leadership gives the men is no different from what they get from the company.

The Wildcat and Organization Building

As against the brainwashing the union bureaucracy got both at the war time conferences with the government, and at the post-war Automation conferences with government and industry, the workers came up with their wartime invention: *the wildcat.* Just as there was no other way for workers to act during the war when the bureaucracy had us shackled to the no-strike pledge, so there is no other way for the workers to act as the bureaucracy keeps shackling us with union contracts that do the boss's production for him.

The wildcats have not yet created what the *sitdowns* did in the 1930's — a new organization like the early C.I.O. to meet the challenge of the times. But one thing is sure: they have unmistakably shown what workers are against. They are against the present union leadership.

In 1955, a "first" happened in the history of the U.A.W. — the men wildcatted against the contract before it was brought up for approval. In 1956 John L. Lewis was complaining about the 170 wildcats that had taken place from January to May 1956 and warned the delegates at the UMW convention that if they dared to keep this up, they would find the International "breathing down your necks."

All sorts of organizations are beginning to emerge. Whether they have been organized from the top, as the Negro American Labor

Council was, or emerged from below but were taken over and squashed like the Unemployed Councils; whether it is white workers wildcatting, as at Great Lakes Steel in Ecorse, Michigan, or Negro student youth sitting down at segregated lunch counters in South U.S.A., we can see that ever greater numbers of people feel that the old organizations are doing nothing. Therefore they are creating new ones to do something.

In each case the something they do points also to a new philosophy, a way of looking at life, a way of living. Take the question of wildcats again. It was an action and an attitude. Automation is not an abstraction. It is a reality. Toward this fact of life, two opposed class attitudes stand out:

1. On the part of the management, the attitude is: the machine can almost run by itself, and the men are expendable.

2. On the part of the workers, the attitude is: this machine is a man-killer. Half of the men it throws out of work, and those it keeps at work it sweats so mercilessly that it would seem, that, far from running by electricity, it runs on the nervous system of the men themselves.

The Unemployed, the Retired Worker and the Shorter Workday

The one burning issue outside the plant that affects us as well is unemployment. Several times during the three postwar recessions, the unemployed workers began to organize. They asked the union leadership to meet in the union hall. At first they were refused. A worker is of no use to these labor bureaucrats if he does not pay dues. An unemployed worker cannot pay dues, so he is just not counted. He doesn't even get notices of union meetings, even though the contract affects him as well.

The unemployed therefore began to organize outside of union halls. They no sooner began to have mass attendance that the labor bureaucracy moved in to stifle their voice. They began to let them use the union halls, and even organized a national conference. Only instead of listening to what the unemployed, or, for that matter, the rank and file employed workers had to say, they began talking at them and getting all sorts of Senators to talk to them. No wonder the unemployment conference in Washington on April 8, 1959 was a stillbirth.

But the fact was that the unemployed at the conference wore

those 30/40 buttons as prominently as the workers. So for that matter did the retired workers. Now that election time has come around they are hearing as many promises as the unemployed did last year and will again this year. Promises are easy to make, but to do anything requires mass action.

I repeat: no matter what specific slogan is used, no matter whether you are in the plant, or out of it, the burning issues are: 1. Shortening of the Working Day with no reduction in pay, 2. Workers' Control of Production, and 3. Health and Retirement Benefits as well as Guaranteed Annual Wage.

KNOWLEDGE AND POWER

Intellectuals and the Welfare-Warfare State

Noam Chomsky

"War is the health of the State," wrote Randolph Bourne in a classic essay as America entered the first World War:

"It automatically sets in motion throughout society those irresistible forces for uniformity, for passionate cooperation with the Government in coercing into obedience the minority groups and individuals which lack the larger herd sense . . . Other values such as artistic creation, knowledge, reason, beauty, the enhancement of life, are instantly and almost unanimously sacrificed, and the significant classes who have constituted themselves the amateur agents of the State are engaged not only in sacrificing these values for themselves but in coercing all other persons into sacrificing them."

And at the service of society's "significant classes" were the intelligentsia, "trained up in the pragmatic dispensation, immensely ready for the executive ordering of events, pitifully unprepared for the intellectual interpretation or the idealistic focussing of ends." They are:

". . . lined up in service of the war-technique. There seems to have been a peculiar congeniality between the war and these men. It is as if the war and they had been waiting for each other."[1]

Bourne emphasizes the ideological consequences of national mobilization: the "irresistible forces for uniformity" that induce obedience to the State and subservience to the needs of the "significant classes." To this we may add the material benefits of mobilization for war, particularly evident in World War II and the

172

Cold War as government intervention in the economy brought the depression to a close and guaranteed the "healthy functioning" of an economy geared, quite extensively, to the social goals of destruction and waste. Events have verified Bourne's prediction that the mobilization for war would bring the intelligentsia to a position of power and influence "in the service of the war technique." His remarks may be compared to those of James Thomson, East Asian specialist at the Department of State and the White House between 1961 and 1966:

". . . the increased commitment to Vietnam was also fueled by a new breed of military strategists and academic social scientists (some of whom had entered the new Administration) who had developed theories of counterguerrilla warfare and were eager to see them put to the test. To some, "counterinsurgency" seemed a new panacea for coping with the world's instability . . . There is a result of our Vietnam policy which holds potential danger for the future of American foreign policy: *the rise of a new breed of American ideologues who see Vietnam as the ultimate test of their doctrine* . . . In a sense, these men are our counterpart to the visionaries of communism's radical left: they are technocracy's own Maoists. They do not govern Washington today — but their doctrine rides high."[2] (his italics).

To this observation we can conjoin another, regarding a parallel phenomenon that has been the subject of wide discussion in recent years:

"Power in economic life has over time passed from its ancient association with land to association with capital and then on, in recent times, to the composite of knowledge and skills which comprises the technostructure . . . [that is, the group that] embraces all who bring specialized knowledge, talent or experience to group decision-making [in government and corporation]."[3]

The role of the technical intelligentsia in decision-making is predominant in those parts of the economy that are "in the service of the war technique" (or such substitutes as the space race) and that are closely linked to government, which underwrites their security and growth. It is little wonder, then, that the technical intelligentsia is, typically, committed to what Barrington Moore calls "the predatory solution of token reform at home and counterrevolutionary imperialism abroad."[4] Elsewhere, Moore offers the following summary of the "predominant voice of America at home and abroad" — an ideology that expresses the needs of the American socio-economic elite, that is propounded with various gradations of subtlety by many American intellectuals, and that gains substantial adherence on the part of the majority that has obtained "some share in the affluent society":

"You may protest in words as much as you like. There is but one condition attached to the freedom we would very much like to encourage: your protests may be as loud as possible so long as they remain ineffective. Though we regret your sufferings very much and would like to do something about them — indeed we have studied them very carefully and have already spoken to your rulers and immediate superiors about these matters — any attempt by you to remove your oppressors by force is a threat to civilized society and the democratic process. Such threats we cannot and shall not tolerate. As you resort to force, we will, if need be, wipe you from the face of the earth by the measured response that rains down flame from the skies."[5]

A society in which this is the predominant voice can be maintained only through some form of national mobilization, which may range in its extent from, at the minimum, a commitment of substantial resources to a credible threat of force and violence. Given the realities of international politics, this commitment can be maintained in the United States only by a form of national psychosis of the sort given voice for example, by the present Secretary of Defense, who sees us "locked in a real war, joined in mortal combat on the battlefield, each contender maneuvering for advantage"[6] — a war against an enemy who appears in many guises: Kremlin bureaucrat, Asian peasant, Latin American student, and, no doubt, "urban guerrilla" at home. Far saner voices can be heard expressing a perception that is not totally dissimilar.[7] Perhaps success can be attained in the national endeavor announced by this predominant voice. In Moore's informed judgment, the system "has considerable flexibility and room for maneuver, including strategic retreat."[8] In any event, this much is fairly sure. Success can be achieved only at the cost of severe demoralization which will make life as meaningless for those who share in the affluent society as it is hopeless for the peasant in Guatemala. Perhaps "war is the health of the state" — but only in the sense in which an economy is "healthy" when a rising GNP includes the cost of napalm and missiles and riot-control devices, jails and detention camps, placing a man on the moon, and so on.

Even in this sense of "health," it is not war that is the health of the state in the modern era, but rather permanent preparation for war. Full-scale war means that the game is lost. Even a "limited war" can be harmful, not only to the economy,[9] as the stock market and the complaints of aerospace executives indicate, but also to the long-range commitment to the use of force. Probably what success the peace movement has had in limiting the attack on Vietnam came not from its present power, but rather from the danger that the "predominant voice" that Moore correctly hears might be challenged in a more general and far-reaching way. Better to nip dissent in the bud while it is still focussed on the specific atrocity of Vietnam, and deflect a movement that might, if it grows, begin to raise serious questions about American society and its international role. Thus we now hear of the mistake of bombing North Vietnam (which caused moral outrage and thus threatened the stability of the body politic)[10] and of using conscripts to fight a colonial war; and we hear proposals for a volunteer army at "market prices" so that resistance will be cooled when Vietnam is re-enacted elsewhere.

I would like to elaborate on both of Bourne's points: the function of preparation for war in guaranteeing the health of the state, and the opportunities that this condition provides for "the new breed of American ideologues" — adding some historical perspective and some comments on what intellectuals might hope to do to counter these tendencies.

The intellectual has, traditionally, been caught between the conflicting demands of truth and power. He would like to see himself as the man who seeks to discern the truth, to tell the truth as he sees it, to act — collectively where he can, alone where he must — to oppose injustice and oppression, to help bring a better social order into being. If he chooses this path he can expect to be a lonely creature, disregarded or reviled. If, on the other hand, he brings his talents to the service of power, he can achieve prestige and affluence. He may also succeed in persuading himself — perhaps, on occasion, with justice — that he can humanize the exercise of power by the "significant classes." He may hope to join with them or even replace them in the role of social management, in the ultimate interest of efficiency and freedom. The intellectual who aspires to this role may use the rhetoric of revolutionary socialism or of welfare-state social engineering in pursuit of his vision of a "meritocracy" in which knowledge and technical ability confer power. He may represent himself as part of a "revolutionary vanguard" leading the way to a new society or as a technical expert applying "piece-meal technology" to the management of a society that can meet its problems without fundamental changes. For some, the choice may depend on little more than an assessment of the relative strength of competing social forces. It comes as no surprise, then, that quite commonly the roles shift; the student radical becomes the counter-insurgency expert. His claims must, in either case, be viewed with suspicion: he is propounding the self-serving ideology of a "meritocratic elite" which, in Marx's phrase (applied, in this case, to the bourgeoisie), defines "the *special* conditions of its emancipation [as] the *general* conditions through which alone modern society can be saved . . ." Failure to present a reasoned justification will simply confirm these suspicions.

Long ago, Kropotkin observed that "the modern radical is a centralizer, a State partisan, a Jacobin to the core, and the Socialist walks in his footsteps."[11] To a large extent he is correct in thus echoing the warning of Bakunin that "scientific socialism" might in practice be distorted into "the despotic domination of the laboring masses by a new aristocracy, small in number, composed of real or pretended experts,"[12] the "red bureaucracy" that would prove to be "the most vile and terrible lie that our century has created."[13] Western critics have been quick to point out how the Bolshevik leadership took on the role outlined in the anarchist critique [14] — as was in fact sensed by Rosa Luxemburg,[15] barely a few months before her murder by the troops of the German socialist government exactly half a century ago.

Rosa Luxemburg's critique of Bolshevism was sympathetic and fraternal, but incisive, and full of meaning for today's radical intellectuals. Fourteen years earlier, in her *Leninism or Marxism*,[16] she had criticized Leninist organizational principles, arguing that *"nothing will more surely enslave a young labor movement to an intellectual elite hungry for power than this bureaucratic straitjacket, which will immobolize the movement and turn it into an automaton manipulated by a Central Committee"* (her italics). These dangerous tendencies towards authoritarian centralization she saw, with great accuracy, in the earliest stages of the Bolshevik revolution. She examined the conditions that led the Bolshevik leadership to terror and dictatorship of "a little leading minority in the name of the class," a dictatorship that stifled "the growing political training of the mass of the people" instead of contributing to it; and she warned against making a virtue of necessity and turning authoritarian practice into a style of rule by the new elite. Democratic institutions have their defects:

"But the remedy which Trotsky and Lenin[17] have found, the elimination of democracy as such, is worse than the disease it is supposed to cure; for it stops up the very living source from which alone can come the correction of all the innate shortcomings of social institutions. That source is the active, untrammeled, energetic political life of the broadest masses of the people."

Unless the whole mass of the people take part in the determination of all aspects of economic and social life, unless the new society grows out of their creative experience and spontaneous action, it will be merely a new form of repression. "Socialism will be decreed from behind a few official desks by a dozen intellectuals," whereas in fact it "demands a complete spiritual transformation in the masses degraded by centuries of bourgeois class rule," a transformation which can take place only within institutions that extend the freedoms of bourgeois society. There is no explicit recipe for socialism: "Only experience is capable of correcting and opening new ways. Only unobstructed, effervescing life falls into a thousand new forms and improvisations, brings to light creative force, itself corrects all mistaken attempts."

The role of the intellectuals and radical activists, then, must be to assess and evaluate, to attempt to persuade, to organize, but not to seize power and rule. "Historically, the errors committed by a truly revolutionary movement are infinitely more fruitful than the infallibility of the cleverest Central Committee."[18]

These remarks are a useful guide for the radical intellectual. They also provide a refreshing antidote to the dogmatism so typical of discourse on the left, with its arid certainties and religious fervor regarding matters that are barely understood — the self-destructive left-wing counterpart to the smug superficiality of the defenders of the status quo who can perceive their own ideological commitments no more than a fish can perceive that it swims in the sea.

It would be useful, though beyond the bounds of this discussion, to review the interplay between radical intellectuals and technical intelligentsia on the one hand and mass, popular-based organiza-

tions on the other, in revolutionary and post-revolutionary situations. Such an investigation might consider on the one extreme
the Bolshevik experience and the ideology of the liberal technocracy, which are united in the belief that mass organizations and
popular politics must be submerged.[19] At the other extreme, it
might deal with the anarchist revolution in Spain in 1936–7 — and
the response to it by liberal and Communist intellectuals.[20] Equally
relevant would be the evolving relationship between the Communist Party and popular organizations (workers councils and
commune governments) in Yugoslavia today,[21] and the love-hate
relationship between party cadres and peasant associations that
provides the dramatic tension for William Hinton's brilliant account of a moment in the Chinese revolution.[22] It could draw from
the experience of the National Liberation Front as described, say,
by Douglas Pike in his *Vietcong*[23] and more other objective sources,[24]
and from many documentary accounts of developments in Cuba.
One should not exaggerate the relevance of these cases to the
problems of an advanced industrial society, but I think there is no
doubt that a great deal can nevertheless be learned from them, not
only about the feasibility of other forms of social organization[25] but
also about the problems that arise as intellectuals and activists
attempt to relate to mass politics.

It is worth mention that the post-World War I remnants of the
non-Bolshevik left re-echoed and sharpened the critique of the
"revolutionary vanguard" of activist intellectuals. The Dutch
Marxist Anton Pannekoek[26] describes "the aim of the Communist
Party — which it called world-revolution — " in this way: "to
bring to power, by means of the fighting force of the workers, a
layer of leaders who then establish planned production by means
of State Power." Continuing:

"The social ideals growing up in the minds of the intellectual class now
that it feels its increasing importance in the process of production: a well-
ordered organization of production for use under the direction of technical
and scientific experts — are hardly different [from those of the Bolshevik
leadership]. So the Communist Party considers this class its natural allies
which it has to draw into its circle. By an able theoretical propaganda
it tries to detach the intelligentsia from the spiritual influences of the
declining bourgeoisie and of private capitalism, and to win them for the
revolution that will put them into their proper place as a new leading
and ruling class . . . they will intervene and slide themselves in as leaders
of the revolution, nominally to give their aid by taking part in the fight,

in reality to deflect the action in the direction of their party aims. Whether or not the beaten bourgeoisie will then rally with them to save of capitalism what can be saved, in any case their intervention comes down to cheating the workers, leading them off from the road to freedom . . . The Communist Party, though it may lose ground among the workers, tries to form with the socialists and the intellectual class a united front, ready at the first major crisis of capitalism to take in its hands the power over and against the workers . . . Thus the fighting working class, basing itself upon Marxism, will find Lenin's philosophical work a stumbling-block in its way, as the theory of a class that tries to perpetuate its serfdom."[27]

And in the post-war Western welfare state, the technically trained intelligentsia also aspire to positions of control in the emerging state-capitalist societies in which a powerful state is linked in complex ways to a network of corporations that are on their way to becoming international institutions. They look forward to "a well-ordered production for use under the direction of technical scientific experts" in what they describe as the "post-industrial technetronic society" in which "plutocratic pre-eminence comes under a sustained challenge from the political leadership which itself is increasingly permeated by individuals possessing special skills and intellectual talents," a society in which "knowledge becomes a tool of power, and the effective mobilization of talent an important way for acquiring power."[28]

Bourne's critical words on the treachery of the intellectuals thus fall within a broader analytic framework. Furthermore, his perception of the ideological role of the mobilization for war has been proven accurate by events. When Bourne wrote, the United States was already the world's major industrial society — in the 1890's, its industrial production already equalled that of the United Kingdom, France, and Germany combined.[29] The war of course greatly enhanced its position of economic superiority. From World War II, the United States emerged as the world-dominant power, and so it has remained. The national mobilization for war permitted the exercise of means to escape from the economic stagnation of the 1930's, and provided some important insights into economics. As Chandler puts it:

"World War II taught other lessons. The government spent far more than the most enthusiastic New Dealer had ever proposed. Most of the output of the expenditures was destroyed or left on the battlefields of Europe and Asia. But the resulting increased demand sent the nation into a period of prosperity the like of which had never before been seen. Moreover, the supplying of huge armies and navies fighting the most massive war of all time required a tight, centralized control of the national economy. This effort brought corporate managers to Washington to carry out one of the most complex pieces of economic planning in history. That experience lessened the ideological fears over the government's role in stabilizing the economy."[30]

Apparently, the lesson was learned very well. It has been pointed out, accurately, that in the post-war world "the armaments industry has provided a sort of automatic stabilizer for the whole economy";[31] and enlightened corporate managers, far from fearing government intervention in the economy, view "the New Economics as a technique for increasing corporate viability."[32]

The ensuing Cold War carried further the depoliticization of American society and created a psychological environment in which the government was able to intervene, in part through fiscal policies, public works and public services, but very largely through "defense" spending, as "a coordinator of last resort" when "managers are unable to maintain a high level of aggregate demand" (Chandler, ibid). The Cold War has also guaranteed the financial resources as well as the psychological environment for the government to undertake an extensive commitment to the project of constructing an integrated world economy dominated by American capital — "no idealistic pipe dream," according to George Ball, "but a hard-headed prediction; it is a role into which we are being pushed by the imperatives of our own technology."[33] The major instrument is the multinational corporation, described by Ball as follows:

"In its modern form, the multinational corporation, or one with world-wide operations and markets, is a distinctly American development. Through such corporations it has become possible for the first time to use the world's resources with maximum efficiency . . . But there must be greater unification of the world economy to give full play to the benefits of multinational corporations."[34]

The multinational corporation itself is the beneficiary of the mobilization of resources by the government, and its activities are backed, ultimately, by American military force. Simultaneously, there is a process of increased centralization of control in the domestic economy, as also in political life, with the decline of parliamentary institutions — a decline that is, in fact, noticeable throughout the Western industrial societies.[35]

The "unification of the world economy" by American-based international corporations obviously poses serious threats to freedom. The Brazilian political economist Helio Jaguaribe, no radical, puts it as follows:

"Increasing dependence on alien developed countries, particularly the United States, together with increasing internal poverty and unrest, would leave the Latin American peoples with the choice between permanent foreign domination and internal revolution. This alternative is already visible in the Caribbean area, where the countries have lost their individual viability and are not being allowed, by the combined action of their own internal oligarchies and the external intervention of the United States, to form a larger autonomous community. What is happening today in the Caribbean is likely to happen in less than two decades in the major Latin American countries if they do not achieve minimal conditions of autonomous self-sustained development."[36]

It is no secret that the same concerns arise in Asia, and even in Western Europe, where national capital is incapable of competing with state-supported American enterprise, the system that Nieburg describes as "a government-subsidized private profit system."[37]

Economic domination carries with it as well the threat of cultural subjugation — not a threat, but a positive virtue, from the point of view of the colonial administrator or, often, the American political scientist delighted with the opportunity to preside over the "modernization" of some helpless society. An example, extreme perhaps, is the statement of an American diplomat in Laos:

"For this country, it is necessary, in order to achieve any progress, to level everything. It is necessary to reduce the inhabitants to zero, to disencumber them of their traditional culture which blocks everything."[38]

At another level, the same phenomenon can be observed in Latin America. Claude Julien comments:

"The revolt of Latin American students is not directed only against dictatorial regimes that are corrupt and inefficient — nor only against the exploitation by the foreigner of the economic and human resources of their country — but also against the cultural colonization that touches them at the deepest level of their being. And this is perhaps why their revolt is more virulent than that of the worker or peasant organizations that experience primarily economic colonization."[39]

The classic case in the American empire is the Philippines, where the effects have been disastrous.

The long-range threat is to national independence and cultural vitality, as well as to successful, balanced economic development.[40] The factors interweave. Domestic ruling elites develop a vested interest in American dominance and even in American imperial ventures — a fact illustrated clearly in the Far East, where the Korean war and now the Vietnam war have substantially contributed to the "health" of the states that are gradually being "unified" in the American system. At times the results verge on the grotesque: thus Japan produces the plastic containers used to ship home corpses of American soldiers, and "the successor companies to I. G. Farben, the firm which produced Zyklon B for the gas chambers of the German extermination camps, . . . have now set up an industrial plant in South Vietnam for the production of toxic chemicals and gases for the US expeditionary force."[41] The ordinary reality is grim enough, without such examples.

Each year in the Economic Survey of Asia and the Pacific published by the *New York Times* we read such items as this:

"*Thais see Peace as a Mixed Blessing:* . . . [It is an] unarguable fact that an end to the fighting [in Vietnam] would pose a grave threat to Thailand's economy. *The Investor*, the new monthly magazine of the Thai Board of Investment, put the case candidly in the cover story of its first issue, published in December. 'The economic development of Thailand has become so inextricably linked with the war,' the magazine said, 'that whatever decisions the United States makes about its future role in Southeast Asia cannot fail to have far reaching implications here.' 'An abrupt termination of the American war effort in Southeast Asia,' the magazine went on to say, 'would be quite painful economically.' . . . If, however, as many people think, an American pullout from Vietnam actually results in an even bigger United States military presence here, the Thais will be faced with the even more difficult choice between a continued boom and further deterioration of their traditional society."[42]

The impact is severe, and cumulative: it is added to the devastating heritage of the colonial era, nicely summarized, for example, in the testimony of the director of the U.S. AID Mission in the Philippines before a House sub-committee on April 25, 1967:

"Agriculture . . . is a product of almost studied neglect — inadequate transportation, limited irrigation, insufficient farm credit programs, price policies aimed at cheap food for urban areas which discourage farm production, high rate of tenancy, absentee land ownership, poorly organized markets and high interest rates. The average farmer (with a family of six) in Central Luzon makes about 800 pesos from his farming operation. His condition has not changed in the last fifty years [to be more precise, since the Spanish occupation]. Perhaps even more critical than the actual condition of the rural inhabitant . . . is the ever increasing gap between urban and rural living . . . In the past ten years the rich have become richer and the poor have become poorer."[43]

Conceivably new technical advances — e.g. "miracle rice" — may help. One certainly hopes so, but the advance euphoria seems questionable:

"The new high-yielding varieties, developed partly by Ford- and Rocke-feller-financed organizations, require scientific management, two to three times the cash inputs previously needed, and extensive water control . . . [If self-sufficiency is reached], the market price of the commodity will drop considerably in the Philippines. This means that only the most efficient farming units will be able to survive the competition. And such efficiency will lie with the large, mechanized, tenantless, agro-business farms. This technological fact, coupled with a loophole in the Land Reform Code that allows a landlord to throw his tenants off the land and retain it himself if he farms the area, might destroy whatever attempts are made at land reform in the Philippines . . . [President Marcos] is very much aware of a little-publicized report issued in 1965, which clearly proves the feudal, and therefore explosive, nature of Philippine rural society. The report reveals that only eighteen years ago, less than half of 1 percent of the population owned 42 percent of the agricultural land. Two hundred and twenty-one of the largest landholders — the Catholic Church being the largest — held over 9 percent of the farm area. In 1958, nearly 50 percent of the farmers were tenants and an additional 20 percent were farm laborers. Thus 70 percent of those employed in agriculture were landless . . . In 1903, the tenancy rate for the entire country was 18 percent excluding farm laborers. By 1948 this figure had climbed to 37 percent. In 1961, it was over 50 percent. There is no evidence that this trend has at all changed in the last eight years. It may even be outpacing the miniscule efforts at land reform . . . Will the Congress in Manila, composed of the very same rural banking elite, ever vote the necessary funds to finance the Agricultural Credit Administration, the Land Bank and Coopera-tives?"[44]

The report might have gone on to indicate that this situation is, largely, a consequence of American colonial policy, and it also might have ventured a prediction as to the fate of those driven off the land under "rationalization" in a country that has been described as an American vegetable garden.

Similar reports are coming from India: "Though it is clear that the Indian farmer wants to exploit the new technology, it is less clear that he has been able to do so to any dramatic degree in the paddy fields."[45] The same report cites another problem, namely:

"State governments in India have been eliminating taxes on the incomes of the more prosperous farmers at a time when those incomes have been rising steadily. Politicians are convinced that it would be suicidal for any party to press for the restoration of these taxes. But without some mechanism for diverting a portion of the new income in rural areas to development, growth will inevitably lag."

Again, this situation is a legacy of colonialism. It can be met only by social reconstruction of a sort which, throughout the world, will now be resisted by American influence and direct application of force, the latter applied, where possible, through the medium of the American-trained and -equipped native armies. Brazil is merely the most recent and most obvious example. There, the military elite preaches this ideology:

"Accepting the principle of 'total war against subversion,' the doctrine of national security considers that the 'underdeveloped countries must aid the leading State of the Christian world to defend civilization by furnishing it with primary materials.' "[46]

In such ways, it becomes possible, to return to George Ball's formulation, "to use the world's resources with maximum efficiency" with "greater unification of the world economy." In such ways we strive to realize the prediction outlined long ago by Brooks Adams: "Our geographical position, our wealth, and our energy pre-eminently fit us to enter upon the development of Eastern Asia [but why only there?] and to reduce it to part of our own economic system."[47] Our own economic system, meanwhile, is heavily dependent on government-induced production. Increasingly, it is becoming a "government-subsidized private profit system" with a deep involvement of the technical intelligentsia. The system is tolerated by public opinion, which is tortured by chimeras and stupefied by the mass media.

That a situation such as this is fraught with perils is obvious. From the point of view of the liberal technocrat the solution to the problem lies in strengthening the federal government (the "radical centralizer" goes further, insisting that all power be vested in the central state authorities and the "vanguard party"). Only thus can the military-industrial complex be tamed and controlled:

"The filter-down process of pump-priming the civilian economy by fostering ever-greater economic concentration and income inequality must be replaced by a frank acceptance of federal responsibility to control the tide of economic bigness, and to plan the conservation and growth of all sectors of the economy and the society."[48]

The hope lies in skilled managers such as Robert McNamara, who "has been the unflinching hero of the campaign to reform and control the Contract State."[49] It is probably correct to suppose that the technostructure offers no greater hope than McNamara, who has clearly explained his own views regarding social organization:

"Vital decision-making, in policy matters as well as in business, must remain at the top. This is partly — though not completely — what the top is for."

Ultimate control must be vested in the hands of management, which is, "in the end, the most creative of all the arts — for its medium is human talent itself." This is apparently a divine imperative:

"God is clearly democratic. He distributes brain power universally. But He quite justifiably expects us to do something efficient and constructive with that priceless gift. That is what management is all about."[50]

This is a relatively pure form of the vision of the technocratic elite.

We can arrive at a more considered judgment regarding the likely role of a strengthened federal authority in a state capitalist society by examining the past record. The federal government has continuously accelerated the arms race and the centralization of the domestic and international economy, not only by subsidizing research and development, but also by investment which is turned over to private capital and by direct purchase.[51] A plausible forecast is suggested by Letwin's observation that in the past, "businessmen invented, advocated, or at least rapidly recognized the usefulness of each main measure of [government intervention]" since they could thus "put government to positive use as a means for imposing the social arrangements that suited their own economic interests" (op. cit.). McNamara's capitulation on the ABM system, in the face of his clear understanding of its irrationality (except as a subsidy to the electronics industry) indicates rather dramatically what the more humane Forces among the technical intelligentsia can hope to achieve solely by "working from within."

As we move into the Nixon period, there is every reason to suppose that even the feeble gestures of the McNamara's will be restrained. In a series of articles in the *Washington Post* (December, 1968), Bernard Nossiter quotes the president of North American Rockwell: "All of Mr. Nixon's statements on weapons and space are very positive. I think he has perhaps a little more awareness of these things than some people we've seen in the White House." The present prospect, Nossiter concludes from his study, is this:

". . . powerful industrial giants eagerly pressing for more military business, Pentagon defense planners eager to get on with new weapons production, Congressmen whose districts profit directly from the anticipated contracts, and millions of Americans from the blue collar aircraft worker to the university physicist drawing their pay checks from the production of arms. About to take over the White House is a new President whose campaign left little doubt of his inclination to support the ABM and other costly arms spending while tightening up on expenditures for civilian purposes. This is the military-industrial complex of 1969."

Of course, any competent economist can sketch other methods by which government-induced production can serve to keep the economy functioning.

"But capitalist reality is more intractable than planners' pens and paper. For one thing too much *productive* expenditure by the state is ruled out. Seen from the individual capitalist's corner, such expenditure would be a straight invasion of his preserve by an immensely more powerful and materially resourceful competitor; as such it needs to be fought off."[52]

Furthermore, in a society in which a "vigorous appetite for income and wealth" is extolled as the highest good (see note 50), it is difficult — subversive of the prevailing ideology, in fact — to mobilize popular support for use of resources for the public welfare or to meet human needs, however desperate they may be. The point is explained clearly by Samuel F. Downer, financial vice president for LTV aerospace, who is quoted by Nossiter (*op. cit.*) in explanation of why "the post-war world must be bolstered with military orders":

"It's basic. Its selling appeal is defense of the home. This is one of the greatest appeals the politicians have to adjusting the system. If you're

President and you need a central factor in the economy, and you need to sell this factor, you can't sell Harlem and Watts but you can sell self-preservation, a new environment. We're going to increase defense budgets as long as those Russians are ahead of us. The American people understand this."

Similarly, the American people "understand" the necessity for the grotesquerie of the space race, which is quite susceptible to Madison Avenue techniques and thus, along with the science-technology race in general, serves as "a transfigured, transmuted and theoretical substitute for an infinite strategic arms race; it is a continuation of the race by other means."[53] It is fashionable to decry such analyses — or even references to the "military-industrial complex" — as "unsophisticated." It is interesting, therefore, to note that those who manipulate the process and stand directly to gain by it are much less coy about the matter.

There are some perceptive analysts — J. K. Galbraith is the best example — who argue that the concern for growth and profits-maximization has become only one of several motives for management and technostructure, that it is supplemented, perhaps dominated, by identification with and adaptation to the needs of the organization, the corporation, which serves as a basic planning unit for the economy.[54] Perhaps this is true, but the consequences of this shift of motivation may nevertheless be slight, since the corporation as planning unit is geared to production of consumer goods[55] — the consumer, often, being the national state — rather than satisfaction of social needs, and to the extension of its dominion in the organized international economy.

In his famous address on the military-industrial complex, President Eisenhower warned that: "The prospect of domination of the nation's scholars by Federal employment, project allocations, and the power of money is ever present — and is gravely to be regarded." In fact, the government has long been the "employer of last resort" — in fact, the dominant employer — for the engineering profession, and there is little doubt that the world would be a better place without a good deal of the technology that is being developed.

The facts are clearly perceived and rightly deplored by many very able critics. H. L. Neiburg, in the work cited, explains the background for the "science-technology race" as follows:

"Built into this equation and secondary to it is the need to maintain a healthy economy. Fear of stagnation, the habit of massive wartime spending, the vested interests embracing virtually all groups, pork-barrel politics — all are aspects of what has become deliberate government policy to invest in the 'research and development' empire as an economic stimulant and a public works project."

He shows how government contracts have become "an escape route" from the "stagnating civilian economy," with the "contemporary dedication to science" and the "popular faith in the mystique of innovation" serving as "a cover for the emergence of an industrial research-and-development and systems-engineering management cult with unparalleled private economic and public decision-making power."

"For almost three decades the nation's resources have been commanded by military needs, and political and economic power have been consolidated behind defense priorities . . . The surviving myths of private enterprise insulate the industrial giants from social control, distorting the national reading of realities at home and abroad, concealing the galloping pace of corporate mergers and economic concentration, protecting the quasi-public status of narrow private interests . . . In addition to claims of security, national prestige, and prosperity, the sacred name of science is hailed as a surrogate consensus, an alibi to soften, defer, and deflect the growing divisions of American society . . . The science-technology race provided an avenue of substitute pump-priming which maintained personal income without increasing civilian goods, further aggravating inequities in the structure of purchasing power which commands and organizes national resources."

In his analysis of these developments, and in his passionate denunciation of their perverse and inhuman character, Nieburg is acting in the highest tradition of the critical intellectual. He is unrealistic, however, when he suggests that enlightened bureaucrats — McNamara, for example — can use the undeniable power of the federal government to ameliorate the situation in any fundamental way by working from within; just as the scientists who rightly fear a nuclear catastrophe are deluding themselves if they believe that private lectures to government bureaucrats on the irrationality of an arms or space race will succeed in changing national priorities. Similarly, it may be true, in the abstract, that "the techniques of economic stimulation and stabilization are simply neutral administrative tools capable of distributing national income either more or less equitably, improving the relative bargaining position of either unions or employers, and increasing or decreasing the importance of the public sector of the economy."[56] But in the real world, as the same author points out, these "neutral administrative tools" are applied "within the context of a consensus whose limits are defined by the business community . . . " The tax reforms of the "new economics" benefit the rich.[57] Urban renewal, the war on poverty, expenditures for science and education, turn out, in large measure, to be a subsidy to the already privileged.

There are a number of ways in which the intellectual who is aware of these facts can hope to change them. He might, for example, try to "humanize" the meritocratic or corporate elite or the government bureaucrats closely allied to them, a plan that has seemed plausible to many scientists and social scientists. He might try to contribute to the formation of a new or revitalized reformist political party, operating within the framework of conventional politics.[58] He can try to ally himself with — to help create — a mass movement committed to far more radical social change. He can act as an individual in resistance to the demands placed on him, or the temptations offered to him, by a society that affords him privilege and affluence if he will accept the limits "defined by the business community" and the technical intelligentsia allied to it. He can try to organize large-scale resistance by the technical intelligentsia to the nightmare they are helping to create, and to find ways in which their skills can be put to a constructive social use, perhaps in cooperation with a popular movement that searches for new social forms.

The importance of collective action — obvious enough in itself — becomes still more clear when the question is approached in more general terms. In a society of isolated and competitive individuals, there are few opportunities for effective action against repressive institutions or deep-seated social forces. The point is underscored, in a different but related connection, in some pertinent remarks by Galbraith on the management of demand, which, he observes:

". . . is in all respects an admirably subtle arrangement in social design. It works not on the individual but on the mass. Any individual can contract out from its influence. This being so, no case for individual compulsion in the purchase of any product can be established. To all who object there is a natural answer: You are at liberty to leave! Yet there is slight danger that enough people will ever assert their individuality to impair the management of mass behavior."[59]

The real threat that has been posed by organized resistance in the past few years has been to the "management of mass behavior." There are circumstances when one can assert his own individuality only by being prepared to act collectively. He can thus overcome the social fragmentation that prevents him from coming to recognize his real interests, and can learn how to defend these interests. It is quite possible that the society will tolerate individuals who "contract out," but only insofar as they do not organize to do so collectively, thus impairing "the management of mass behavior" that is a crucial feature of a society designed along the lines that appeal to the liberal technocrats (cf. the remarks by McNamara cited above) or to the radical centralizers of whom the Bolshevik ideologists have been the most prominent examples.

In small but important ways such tasks as those suggested above are being undertaken — for example, by the students and junior faculty who have formed a Committee of Concerned Asian Scholars to try to reconstruct Asian studies on a basis that is both more objective and more humane, and in this way strike at one of the underpinnings of the aggressive ideology that supports the national commitment to repression, social management on a global scale, and ultimately, destruction; or by the groups of scientists and engineers who are just now beginning to organize in opposition to the demands of the military-industrial-academic complex, a development of very great potential; or by those who, recognizing that university teaching and research are, in large measure, conditioned by the demands of the privileged, are seeking to construct alternative programs of study and action, of teaching and research, that will be more compelling on intellectual and moral grounds, will change the character of the university by changing not their formal structures — a relatively insignificant matter — but what is actually done by students and faculty in the university, and will reorient the lives of those who pass through it; or, outside the university, by those who are resisting the war machine directly or who are working to create alternative social institutions that might, ultimately, serve as the cells of a very different society; or those who are trying to organize, and to learn, in communities or factories; or those who attempt to construct a political movement that will integrate such efforts on a national, in fact international scale. Other examples might be mentioned. I see no reason why there should be conflict between such efforts as these. We cannot know which will prove successful, or how far they can advance, or how experience may cause them to develop, or, in detail, what vision of a new society might grow out of thought and action directed to these ends. We can predict that the elitist and authoritarian tendencies to which intellectuals are all too prone will subvert such efforts unless they are vigorously combatted. We can predict that only mass participation in planning, decision-making, and reconstruction of social institutions — "the active, untrammeled, energetic political life of the broadest masses of the people" — will create the "spiritual transformation in the masses" that is a prerequisite for any advance in social evolution and that will solve the myriad problems of social reconstruction in a decent and humane fashion. (See above, p. 43.) We can also predict that if such efforts become effective and significant in scale, they will meet with repression and force. Whether or not they can withstand such force will be determined by the strength and cohesiveness they have developed, as part of a general, integrated movement with a strong base of popular support in many social strata, support by people whose ideals and hopes are given form by this movement and the social forms it tries to bring to reality.

It has always been taken for granted by radical thinkers, and quite rightly so, that effective political action that threatens entrenched social interests will lead to "confrontation" and repression. It is, correspondingly, a sign of intellectual bankruptcy for the left to seek to construct "confrontations"; it is a clear indication that the efforts to organize significant social action have failed. Impatience, horror at evident atrocities, may impel one to seek an immediate confrontation with authority. This can be extremely valuable in one of two ways: by posing a threat to the interests of those who are implementing specific policies; by bringing to the consciousness of others a reality that is much too easy to forget. But the search for confrontations can also be a kind of self-indulgence that may abort a movement for social change and condemn it to irrelevance and disaster. A confrontation that grows out of effective politics may be unavoidable, but one who takes his own rhetoric seriously will seek to delay a confrontation until he can hope to emerge successful, either in the narrower senses noted above or in the far more important sense of bringing about, through this success, some substantive change in institutions. Particularly objectionable is the idea of designing confrontations so as to manipulate the unwitting participants into accepting a point of view that does not grow out of meaningful experience, out of real understanding. This is not only a testimony to political irrelevance, but also, precisely because it is manipulative and coercive, a proper tactic only for a movement that aims to maintain an elitist and authoritarian form of organization.

The opposite danger is "cooptation," again, a real problem. Even the most radical program cannot escape this danger. Consider the idea of workers' councils. Attempts at implementation have frequently led not to a radically new form of management by producers, but to administration of welfare programs or even improved factory discipline.[60] This possibility is recognized by those concerned with more efficient "industrial management" as a potential benefit, from their point of view, of council organization. Thus in his introduction to Sturmthal's study, John T. Dunlop, a Harvard economist who has won a considerable reputation in industrial arbitration, writes:

"There is keen interest in the plant level, in the relations among the worker, his supervisor, and labor representative, in both the advanced and the newly developing countries. Governments, managers, and labor organizations everywhere are concerned with ways of eliciting improved effort and performance; they are exploring new ways of training and supervising a workforce, and they seek new procedures to develop discipline and to settle complaints or dissipate protest. The range of experience with workers' councils provides a record of general interest to those shaping or modifying industrial relations and economic institutions.

What can be said of workers' councils is true, *a fortiori*, of any other attempt at radical reconstruction of existing institutions. In fact, some have even argued that Marxism as a social movement served primarily to "socialize" the proletariat and integrate it more effectively into the industrial society.[61] Those who oppose a plan merely on grounds of the possibility (even likelihood) of cooptation merely signal that they are opposed to everything imaginable.

To an unprecedented extent, the university has become the gathering-place for intellectuals and technical intelligentsia, attracting not only scientists and scholars, but even writers and artists and political activists. The causes and consequences can be argued, but the fact is fairly clear. The Port Huron statement of SDS expressed the hope that the university can become "a potential base and agency in the movement for social change"; by permitting "the political life to be an adjunct to the academic one, and action to be informed by reason," it can contribute to the emergence of a genuine new left which will be "a left with real intellectual skills, committed to deliberativeness, honesty, and reflection as working tools."[62]. Many in the New Left now think of such ideas as part of their "liberal past," to be abandoned in the light of the new consciousness that has since been achieved. I disagree with this judgment. The left badly needs understanding of present society, its long-range tendencies, the possibilities for alternative forms of social organization, and a reasoned analysis of how social change can come about. Objective scholarship can contribute to this understanding. We do not know, for a fact, that the universities will not permit honest social inquiry over a broad range, scholarship that will, as many of us believe, lead to radical conclusions if conducted seriously and in an open-minded and independent way. We do not know because the attempt has barely been made. The major obstacle, so far, has been the unwillingness of students to undertake the serious work required and the general fears of the faculty that its guild structure may be threatened. It is convenient, perhaps, but mistaken to pretend that the problem, up to now at least, has been the unwillingness of trustees and administrators to tolerate such attempts. Cases of repression can be found, and they are deplorable, but they do not constitute the heart of the problem. I think that the movement has been ridden by certain fantasies on this score. Consider, for example, the argument of one well-informed activist that the goal of university agitation should be to build "anti-imperialist struggles in which the University administration is a clear enemy."[63] This is much too easy. In fact, whatever the organizational chart may seem to show, the universities — at least, the "elite" universities — are relatively decentralized institutions in which most important decisions as to teaching and research are taken by the faculty, usually at the departmental level. Only when a serious and committed attempt to create alternatives within the university has been blocked by administrative fiat (or by trustee intervention) will such judgments be appropriate. For the moment, such cases are exceptions. The great problem has been, as noted, the failure to make the attempt in a serious way. It would not be a great surprise to discover, when such an attempt is made, that it is blocked — though I would be inclined to speculate that the faculty will prove more of a barrier than trustees and administration. Here too is a case where confrontations may take place as a result of effective, principled, and meaningful action. They should not be sought, nor should they necessarily be avoided at the proper time.

To mention just one case, if the attempt to organize scientists to find meaningful alternatives to the subversion of their disciplines proves successful, it is fair to suppose that this action will become an "illegal conspiracy," precisely because it threatens "the health of the state," in the manner indicated earlier. At that point the organizers of such a movement will find themselves faced with the necessity for resistance. They will have to devise forms of action to combat such repression, if in fact their politics threatens entrenched social forces to the extent that repression is undertaken.

The opportunities for intellectuals to take part in a genuine movement for social change are many and varied, and I think that certain general principles are clear. They must be willing to face facts and refrain from erecting convenient fantasies.[64] They must be willing to undertake the hard and serious intellectual work that s required for a real contribution to understanding. They must avoid the temptation to join a repressive elite and must help create the mass politics that will counteract — and ultimately control and replace — the strong tendencies towards centralization and authoritarianism that are deeply-rooted but not inescapable. They must be prepared to face repression and to act in defense of the values they profess. In an advanced industrial society many possibilities exist for active popular participation in the control of major institutions and the reconstruction of social life. The rule of a technocratic meritocracy, allied or subordinated to a corporate elite, does not appear inevitable, though it is not unlikely. So little is understood that no forecast can be given more than a minimal degree of credence. To some extent, we can create the future rather than merely observing the flow of events. Given the stakes, it would be criminal to let real opportunities pass unexplored.

Notes

[1] The quotes are from various essays collected in *War and the Intellectuals*, Carl Resek ed., Harper, 1964.

[2] In *No More Vietnams?*, R. Pfeffer, ed., Harper, 1968. The phrase "technocracy's own Bolsheviks" would perhaps be more apt, given the actual role of Mao in opposing the party bureaucracy and in the conflict of "red" and "expert," particularly in the past few years. There is a substantial literature on the latter topic. See, for example, Benjamin Schwartz, "The Reign of Virtue: Some Broad Perspectives on Leader and Party in the Cultural Revolution," *The China Quarterly*, July, 1968. He stresses Mao's opposition to the "technocratic element" and his attempt to realize "the concept of the masses

as active and total participants in the whole political process" under the guidance of an "ethical elite" that acts as a "moralising agency" in the society, "transform[ing] the people below them through the power of example, education and proper policy." I return to this matter briefly below.

³ John K. Galbraith, *The New Industrial State*, Houghton-Mifflin, 1967.

⁴ "Revolution in America?", *New York Review of Books*, Jan. 30, 1969.

⁵ "Thoughts on Violence and Democracy," *Proceedings of the Academy of Political Science*, vol. 29, no. 1, 1968: *Urban Riots: Violence and Social Change*.

⁶ Melvin Laird, *A House Divided: America's Strategy Gap*, Henry Regnery, 1962. Not surprisingly, he concludes that: "Step one of a military strategy of initiative should be the credible announcement of our determination to strike first if necessary to protect our vital interests." Only in this way can we exercise our "moral responsibility to use our power constructively to prevent Communism from destroying the heritage of our world civilization." See *I. F. Stone's Weekly*, Dec. 30, 1968, for additional quotations from this amazing document. Compare *N. Y. Times* military expert Hanson Baldwin, who urges that in the post-Vietnam era we be prepared to "escalate technologically rather than with manpower" when we find it difficult to "bolster governments under attack and secure them against creeping Communism": "Such escalation might involve the use of exotic new conventional weapons, or the utilization under carefully restricted conditions, where targets and geography are favorable, of small nuclear devices for *defensive* purposes." (*New York Times Magazine*, June 9, 1968). Particularly interesting is the concept of "defensive purposes" — as we bolster a weak government against creeping Communism. As far as I know, this is the only country where the Minister of War has spoken in favor of a possible preventive war and the leading military expert of the press has advocated first use of nuclear weapons.

⁷ For some discussion, see my *American Power and the New Mandarins*, Pantheon, 1969, particularly Chapter 3, "The Logic of Withdrawal."

⁸ "Revolution in America?"

⁹ In a number of respects. For example, a war that demands a shift of government spending to boots and bullets fails to benefit the technologically advanced segments of the economy, a fact that has been noted by many. Cf., e.g., Michael Kidron, *Western Capitalism since the War*, Weidenfeld and Nicolson, 1968, who comments on "the technologically-regressive impact of the Vietnam war with its reversion to *relatively* labor-intensive products ..."

¹⁰ For a remarkably cynical example, see the comments of Ithiel Pool in *No More Vietnams?* — and for his own interpretation of these remarks, *The New York Review of Books*, letters, Feb. 16, 1969.

¹¹ *The State: its historic role*, 1896.

¹² *State and Anarchy*, cited by Daniel Guérin, *Jeunesse du socialisme libertaire*, Marcel Rivière, Paris, 1959.

¹³ Letter to Herzen and Ogareff, 1866; cited by Guérin, *ibid.*

¹⁴ See, for example, the informative essay by Daniel Bell, "Two Roads from Marx" reprinted in *End of Ideology*, Free Press, 1960.

¹⁵ *The Russian Revolution*, written in prison, 1918.

¹⁶ Reprinted in English translation together with *The Russian Revolution*, Ann Arbor, 1961, Bertram Wolfe, ed.

¹⁷ In 1918, she of course makes no mention of the functionary who later

became dictator of the Russian state, realizing these fears to an extreme that no one anticipated.

[18] The closing words of *Leninism or Marxism.*

[19] In the latter connection, see Michael Rogin's excellent critique of "The Pluralist Defense of Modern Industrial Society" in contemporary liberal sociology: *The Intellectuals and McCarthy: the Radical Specter*, MIT Press, Cambridge, 1967.

[20] For some discussion of both the events and the response see my *American Power and the New Mandarins*, Chapter 1, "Objectivity and liberal scholarship."

[21] A concise and useful review is presented in George Zaninovich, *The Development of Socialist Yugoslavia*, Johns Hopkins, 1968.

[22] *Fanshen*, Monthly Review Press, 1966 — a book that would have appeared many years before had it not been for the scandalous behavior of U.S. customs officials and the Senate Internal Security Committee, who released Hinton's impounded notes only after a lengthy and costly legal battle.

[23] MIT Press, 1966. As a work of propaganda, this book is of course tainted from the start. But it gains a certain credibility from the fact that it presents a remarkably powerful argument-against-interest, apparently without the author understanding this.

[24] For example, the eye-witness accounts of journalist Katsuichi Honda published in the *Asahi Shimbun* in 1967 and translated into English: *The National Liberation Front*, in the series *Vietnam — a Voice from the Villages*, c/o Room 506, Shinwa Building, Sakuraga-oka-4, Shibuya-ku, Tokyo.

[25] In this connection, an example of major importance is provided by the Palestinian (later Israeli) Kibbutzim. For analysis and discussion, see Haim Darin-Drabkin, *The Other Society*, Gollancz, 1962. The significance of these cooperative forms has largely been missed by the left for two reaons: first, the social and economic success of the Kibbutzim seems unimportant to the "radical centralizers" who see the move towards socialism as a matter of acquisition of power by a revolutionary vanguard (in the name of . . . , etc.); and second, the matter is complicated by a factor that is irrelevant to the question of the Kibbutz as a social form, namely, the problems of national conflict in the Middle East (it is useful — though again basically irrelevant to the Kibbutz as a social form to recall that until 1947 the left-wing of the Kibbutz movement, a substantial segment, was opposed to the idea of a Jewish State, correctly, in my opinion).

[26] One of the "infantile ultra-leftists" discussed by Lenin in his pamphlet of 1920. For a comparison of Lenin's views before and after the acquisition of state power, see Robert Daniels, "The State and Revolution: A Case Study in the Genesis and Transformation of Communist Ideology," *American Slavic and East European Review*, Feb. 1953. He emphasizes Lenin's "intellectual deviation" to the left "during the year of revolution, 1917." Arthur Rosenberg's *History of Bolshevism* (1932, reprinted by Russell and Russell, 1965), which remains, to my mind, the outstanding study of this topic, presents a more sympathetic view, recognizing Lenin's political realism while pointing out the basically authoritarian character of his thought. For more on this subject, see Daniels, *The Conscience of the Revolution*, Harvard, 1960, and a

useful collection by Helmut Gruber, *International Communism in the era of Lenin*, Cornell, 1967: and other sources too numerous to mention.

[27] *Lenin as Philosopher*, 1938. The date is important for understanding the specific references.

[28] Zbigniew Brzezinski, "America in the Technetronic Age," *Encounter*, Jan. 1968. A number of citations with similar content are given in Leonard S. Silk, "Business Power, Today and Tomorrow," *Daedalus*, Winter, 1969, *Perspective on Business*. Silk, chairman of the editorial board of *Business Week*, takes a rather skeptical view of the prospects for transfer of corporate power to a "bureaucracy of technicians," expecting rather that, useful as the technostructure may be, business will maintain its socially dominent role. The only question of this sort seriously at issue, in this study of the American Academy of Arts and Sciences, is the relative power of owners, management, and technostructure in control of the corporation. Popular control of economic institutions is of course not discussed.

[29] Alfred D. Chandler, Jr., "The role of business in the United States: a historical survey," *Daedalus, op.cit.*

[30] *Ibid*. The experience prompted the following remark by Paul Samuelson: "It has been said that the last war was the chemist's war and that this one is the physicist's. It might equally be said that this is an economist's war." *New Republic*, Sept. 11, 1944. Cited in Robert Lekachman, *The Age of Keynes*, Random House, 1966. Perhaps we might regard the Vietnam war as another "economist's war," given the role of professional economists in helping maintain domestic stability so that the war might be fought more successfully.

[31] Jerome Wiesner, cited in H. L. Nieburg, *In the Name of Science*, Quadrangle, 1966. As Nieburg notes, "as the arms race has slackened [temporarily, as we now know], . . . space and science programs become a new instrument by which the government seeks to maintain a high level of economic activity."

[32] B. Joseph Monsen, "The American Business View," *Daedalus, op.cit.* For important observations on these matters see Galbraith, *op.cit.*

[33] Quoted by John J. Powers, Jr., President of Charles Pfizer and Co., in an address delivered to a Conference of the Manufacturing Chemists Association, Inc., Nov. 21, 1967. Reprinted in the *Newsletter* of the North American Congress on Latin America, (NACLA) vol. II, no. 7.

[34] *N.Y. Times*, May 6, 1967. Cited in a perceptive article by Paul Mattick, "The American Economy," *International Socialist Journal*, February, 1968.

[35] For some discussion, see Kidron, *op.cit.*

[36] "A Brazilian View," *How Latin America Views the American Investor*, Raymond Vernon, ed., 1966.

[37] Nieburg, *op.cit.* It might be more accurate to say that European capital finds its interest, in a narrow sense, best served by taking the role of junior partner in the American world system.

[38] Quoted by Jacques Decornoy in *Le Monde hebdomadaire*, 11–17 July, 1968. The series from which this is taken presents one of the very few detailed eye-witness accounts of the Laotian guerrillas, the Pathet-Lao, and their attempts at "nation building" and development. Decornoy observes, in this connection, that "the Americans accuse the North Vietnamese of intervening militarily in the country. But it is they who speak of reducing Laos to zero, while the Pathet-Lao exalts the national culture and national independence."

[39] *L'Empire Américain*, Grasset, Paris, 1968.

[40] On this matter, see André Gunder Frank, *Capitalism and Underdevelopment in Latin America*, Monthly Review Press, 1967, and many other studies.

[41] Documents of the World Conference on Vietnam, Stockholm, July, 1967, Bertil Svahnström, ed.

[42] *N.Y. Times*, Bangkok, Jan. 17, 1969. The writer is a bit naive in suggesting that the choice lies with the Thai. For some discussion of past "choices" for the Thai see my *American Power and the New Mandarins*, Chapter 1.

[43] Cited by Hernando Abaya, *The Untold Philippine Story*, Quezon City, 1967.

[44] *Far East Economic Review*. Reprinted in *Atlas*, February, 1969.

[45] *N.Y. Times Economic Survey*, Jan. 17, 1969.

[46] Marcel Niedergang, in *Le Monde hebdomadaire*, 12–18 of December, 1968. Quotes are from the professors of the military college, who have constructed "a manichean vision of the world": the Communist East against the Christian West" in a manner that would delight John Foster Dulles, Dean Rusk, Melvin Laird, and other luminaries.

[47] Cited by Akira Iriye, *Across the Pacific*, Harcourt, Brace and World, 1967.

[48] Nieburg, *op.cit.*

[49] *Ibid.*

[50] Speech at Millsaps College, Jackson, Mississippi, Feb. 24, 1967. Others offer different justifications for managerial authority. For example, historian William Letwin explains that "no community can do without managers," those whose role is to make "arbitrary decisions within a private firm," for "the function of making ultimate arbitrary choices in production cannot be eliminated" ("The Past and Future of the American Businessman," *Daedalus*, *op.cit.*). Letwin, who finds it "reassuring . . . that today's managers show the same vigorous appetite for income and wealth that spurred yesterday's businessmen to bold progress," fails to point out that on his theory of management, the manager can be replaced by a random number table.

[51] "In the United States at the end of the fifties more than nine-tenths of final demand for aircraft and parts was on government, overwhelmingly military, account; as was nearly three-fifths of the demand for non-ferrous metals; over half the demand for chemicals and electronic goods; over one-third of the demand for communication equipment and scientific instruments: and so on down a list of 18 major industries, one-tenth or more of whose final demand stemmed from government procurement." Kidron, *op.cit.* He also quotes an OECD report of 1963 noting that "the direct transfer to the civilian sector of products and techniques developed for military and space purposes is very small . . . [and] that the possibilities of such direct transfer will tend to diminish."

[52] Kidron, *ibid.*

[53] Nieburg, *op.cit.*

[54] A major thesis of his *New Industrial State*. A parallel analysis in the political realm is provided by Richard Barnet, with his investigation of the role of the National Security Bureaucracy in foreign policy. See his contribution to *No More Vietnams?*, and his *Intervention and Revolution*, New American Library, 1968. Without denying the relevance of his analysis, it is proper to add that the goals of this "organization" coincide with those of the great

corporations, by and large. Even in earlier stages of imperialism it was not unknown for the flag and the gun to precede, rather than follow, the pound, the franc, or the dollar.

[55] As Galbraith notes: "Goods are what the industrial system supplies." Thus "management of demand" performs this service; "it provides, in the aggregate, a relentless propaganda on behalf of goods in general" and thus helps "develop the kind of man the goals of the industrial system require — one that reliably spends his income and works reliably because he is always in need of more."

[56] Lekachman, *op.cit.*

[57] "Like 1964's tax harvest, much of 1965's improvements would be realized by prosperous corporations and wealthy individuals." (*Ibid.*) The regressive character of American tax structure is often overlooked. See Gabriel Kolko, *Wealth and Power in America: An Analysis of Social Class and Income Distribution*, Praeger, 1962. The current report of The Council of Economic Advisers to Congress notes that: "As a share of income, higher taxes are paid by households in the lower income classes than by those with incomes between $6,000 and $15,000. This reflects the heavy tax burden on low-income families from state and local taxes. Federal taxes also contribute to this burden through the Social Security payroll tax." The devices for tax avoidance in higher brackets have been discussed at length, the oil-depletion allowance being only the most notorious example.

[58] For a reasoned analysis, see Michael Harrington, *Toward a Democratic Left*, Macmillan, 1968. See also the review by Christopher Lasch in the *New York Review of Books*, July 11, 1968.

[59] *Op.cit.*

[60] See the contribution to this volume by Paul Mattick. For an informative survey, strongly biased against radical hopes, see Adolf Sturmthal, *Workers' Councils*, Harvard University Press, 1964.

[61] See, for example, Adam Ulam, *The Unfinished Revolution*, Random House, 1960. He suggests that "a vigorous growth of capitalism helps the growth of Marxist socialism among the workers; but, also, a speedy extinction by Marxism of syndicalist and anarchistic feelings among the workers can be a contributing factor to the flourishing development of capitalism! The lesson of Marxism has been absorbed by the worker: he works more efficiently since he accepts the inevitability of industrial labor and its appurtenances; his class hostility does not find expression in sabotage of the industrial and political system that he expects to inherit." In short, the revolutionary movement can contribute, in striking opposition to its goals, to the creation of a "race of patient and disciplined workers" (Ulam, quoting Arthur Redford).

[62] Parts of this statement are reprinted in *The New Student Left*, M. Cohen and D. Hale, ed., revised edition, Beacon Press, 1967.

[63] *New Left Notes*, Dec. 11, 1968. It is difficult for me to believe that the author, who knows Harvard well, really thinks of Nathan Pusey as the representative of imperialism on the Harvard campus.

[64] Recall George Orwell's painfully accurate characterization: "Particularly on the Left, political thought is a sort of masturbation fantasy in which the world of fact hardly matters."

COLUMBIA: AN EXPLANATION

or

Applesauce, Epicycles, and the Joplin Proviso

STEVE HALLIWELL

In Archibald Macleish's play *JB* the hero Job, trying desperately to understand his plight, says in frustration of an explanation "you put God in, you get God out." This same frustrating fact, it seems, holds true for all explanations: your outcome is determined by what you include at the start. Any set of presuppositions, no matter how ridiculous they may sound, will make an explanation possible if they cover enough eventualities. It is possible, for example, to explain everything from why it rains to why governments fall in terms of the activities of little blue devils if you grant the little fellows sufficient powers in your presuppositions (some American political theory approaches this level of sophistication, but the little devils are usually red).

It is hard, as a result, to decide between competing explanations. No "objective" standards exist, so it becomes essential to decide what kind of presuppositions you find most acceptable. That's easy enough on abstract questions — most of us choose scientific laws over supernatural forces. But in relation to our own lives, there are no laws to fall back on; the presuppositions for these problems are basically what we believe about ourselves and others. In America, it is hard to know what we can believe in. So choosing explanations — choosing between presuppositions, actually — becomes like bobbing for apples: every explanation is out there floating around in the soup of experience, each one as self-contained, internally consistent and externally appealing as the next. Seeking meaning in our lives, we snap at them with a certain desperation but when we finally sink our teeth in one or another, we are likely to discover it is full of worms. The whole apple, the whole truth, is hard to find.

Philosophy offers us several ways out of this dilemma. One solution adopted by many young people is abdication: there is no truth, no reality, they declare, and they will no longer bite at apples they know are all wormy. They slip away into a pedestrian form of existential despair, blowing grass and listening to rock while struggling to get through college so they qualify for a place in somebody else's reality. This solution can also be called, to follow through on the metaphor, the "applesauce" solution, since it means that a person draws out of the soup whatever fragment of reality or partial explanation seems to fit the moment. An individual develops not an identity but a multi-faceted "image," each facet defined by an appropriate set of values, social affectations and emotional responses. Thus a person has a family image, a student image, a sexual image, a car-driving image, etc., depending on where he finds himself. Polishing the rough edges of his image and developing new facets is the individual's life work, for his image is his most valuable piece of property. The clinical name for this condition is schizophrenia, but we all know it better as The American Dream. Existing this way is not easy: it is not only hard to get up in the morning but hard to justify being alive. Many can't — there were 1000 suicides and 9000 attempts among American college students this year.

There is another way, more rigorous philosophically, for choosing between explanations: the simplicity criterion. In this solution, when two explanations seem equally capable of explaining any event, we choose the one which employs the simplest presuppositions. The rejection of epicycles and acceptance of the heliocentric theory for explaining the movement of heavenly bodies occurred, we are told, because the epicycles were getting very complicated as man's knowledge of the stars grew while heliocentrism, an appallingly simple alternative, worked equally well.

The simplicity criterion could be applied in choosing between explanations of the Columbia revolt — Columbia is the topic of this essay — but would have to be changed somewhat since the Columbia revolt is a case of human behavior. It is all right to accept Galileo's dictum "the earth moves" when explaining something as impersonal as celestial bodies, but the simplest possible formula for explaining intentional activity is Janis Joplin's statement: "you know you've got it baby if it makes you feel good." Historical explanations, in other words, have to capture the sense that human beings were making the events happen. The common element between the historical actor and the historian is their humanness; an explanation "clicks" when the events of a given moment in history have a recognizably human element.

Opponents of the Columbia revolt dislike simple explanations. The reason is obvious: the first simple explanation that comes to mind — if we ignore the "little red devils" thesis — is that a great many people believed the radicals were right and joined them. That is a very dangerous explanation to accept, for to concede that radical politics were relevant to a large number of people would be to admit that the revolt was essentially a battle between two conflicting political views of the university. That admission explodes the liberal myth that the university is above politics — the "value-free university" as Grayson Kirk used to call it before the lid blew off — and makes it painfully clear that the administration "won" — that is, that Columbia serves the same masters it did before the revolt — because it had the power to call the police and crush the opposition by force. Victories like that administrators can do without, for such events make clear to people a simple truth: with power over property goes power over the machinery of state, in particular the repressive machinery, no matter what the will of the people might be. And truths, especially simple ones, are very dangerous — people get all stirred up when they think they know the truth. Better to keep things complex, then there's plenty of "dialogue" and everybody stays inert. Applesauce, anyone?

Archibald Cox and his Fact-Finding Commission are the proponents of the complex explanation par excellence. In their Report,[1] the Cox Commission finds a zillion and a half things wrong at Columbia that made people unnerved, disgruntled, distraught and so on. As might be expected, no two problems seem to have any relation to each other or to any broader problem. Faculty members are bothered because pay scales are becoming noncompetitive and the central administration seems distant; students are bothered because the faculty is hard to approach, the administration alternatively ignores or belittles them, and their dormitory rooms are like ratty prison cells; community people are annoyed because some administrators were discourteous when describing their feelings about the community.

The Commission also touches upon issues of broader social concern as a source of discontent but these are played down because they are only tangential in the university context — after all, what do political problems like the war in Vietnam and racism have to do with the university? But the Report does present its version of the student's moral dilemma:

When students see work being done at a university on the application of science to spreading death and destruction in Vietnam, but little evidence of similar work on eliminating poverty and racial injustice, they are naturally concerned about the decision-making process (p. 21).

(NOTE TO THE READER: If this statement does not strike a sympathetic cord in your experience as a human being, if you have not found yourself using this ethical balance sheet in your own moral searchings — the "kill a little there, save a little here" approach, then you are just not appreciating the complexities of life. No matter what your instincts tell you, the duty of all men is to raise the "save a little here" side.)

The radical students are also given a place in the Cox analysis, but one safely removed from any contact with reality. In Cox's version of the revolt, the SDS leadership comes off sounding like a bunch of lunatics that would have trouble flagging down a cab much less shutting down a university. The Report isolates out a group of "hard core revolutionists" (not revolutionaries, for that would give the idea of revolution an ounce of credibility) whose single aim in life is "to subvert and destroy the university as a corrupt pillar of an evil society" (58). If the description of the radicals' goal sounds more like Martin Luther than the libertarian New Left, we must not be surprised for the Commission needs that language to explain why the mass of students joined the revolt. For the rest of the SDS chapter, the explanation is twofold. 1. They were stuck on the idea of "participatory democracy" which as Cox explains "stresses the right of an individual to take part directly in all the decisions which affect his life." This is a bad thing to Cox because this concept "can hardly bear the weight of today's complex society without some modification." (56). 2. They were overexposed to their deranged leadership who in spite of their small numbers — "We cannot estimate the number of hard core revolutionists but we are convinced that it was tiny," (58) adds J. Edgar Cox — plant disruption and violence in the minds of others.

For the rest of the students involved the problem, as one might suspect by now, lies in an insufficient respect for the complexity of things. Today's students feel alienated, we are told, and fall prey to a "romantic reaction against complexity, rationality and restraint":

In politics, the appeal of rigid doctrine with simple explanations becomes irresistible. A simplistic demonology purportedly describing the "Establishment" that controls "the system" comes to explain all the hardships and injustices resulting from the complex cross-currents of a technological society and the selfishness and blundering awkwardness of man (8–9).

Mr. Cox and his colleagues, it seems, have begun to spin epicycles. It is time to look for a simple explanation with the Joplin proviso that the analysis start from and recognize the importance of felt human needs.

We return to the simple explanation offered at the beginning: many people thought the radicals were right and joined them. However, even to make that statement we are presuming all sorts of things that fly in the face of established insanity in America. Some of these things are: 1. radicals can say things that are intelligible to other people (whether their arguments are persuasive will be considered later); 2. it is possible to decide what is right and what is wrong; 3. there is a relationship between thought and action.

To the reader, these presuppositions may sound innocuous or self-apparent, but we must all have a healthy respect for the degree to which these basic ideas are denied in our daily experience. Take (1) above: if for example a person's view of the New Left were shaped solely by what he read in the *New York Times* — and this is true for many people — the closest thing to an intelligible statement by a young radical he would know would be something to the effect "Yeah, my parents don't like what I'm doing, but they still give me money." The imminent death of the New Left has been celebrated in the *Times* with increasing frequency over the last few years.

Point (2) is implicitly denied by America's liberal mystique. It is all right to have opinions — in fact, it is considered our duty to have opinions — but not too strongly. To say that what you believe is "right" is seen as somehow undemocratic or even totalitarian since there are people with other views and in a democracy, we are all "equal." That means that no one can be "right" because that makes him "better" than everyone else. There are no laws against thinking you are right but through socialization we are all taught to be both advocates of viewpoints and referees to insure that the views we express in no way intrude on the "rights" of another to believe what he does. Any statement no matter how outrageously principled, just and true it might be — "I think black people are the same as everyone else" — has to be hedged. In social ritual we perform this responsibility by adding "Of course, that's just *my* opinion."

Liberalism in America has been transformed from an aggressive attempt to extend justice to an apology for the existing sordid state of affairs. You are no better than anyone else, everyone is equally perverse, so mind your own business and don't get in anyone's way. Respect authority because if you don't, we'll all be slitting each other's throats. Cox and friends tell us to have more respect for the "selfishness and blundering awkwardness of man"; so be selfish and if you feel a little awkward at times, don't worry about it: that's life. Liberalism has projected the little white picket fence and shotgun of the American Dream into a definition of human nature.

If liberalism is disturbed by point (2), it is absolutely terrified by (3). Everyone who joined the lunatic "revolutionists" did so out of "romantic reaction" or for "student power" (even though Cox has to admit "student power" was never an issue of the revolt) but never, never because they were acting on what they believed was true. The very idea of acting upon beliefs subverts the ingrained idea of democratic "rights" in America. We are taught to treat freedom of speech etc. as some kind of gift from the government that will be taken away if we get uppity; the notion that a government is legitimate only if it acts upon the expressed beliefs of the people is shoved under the rug. When young people act upon their beliefs, they become very dangerous; by affirming that principle for themselves, they threaten to expose its failure in the society.[2]

These questions out of the way, we can move to the substantive problems of the revolt. If the students were not dupes of the lunatic fringe, then what was it about the radical critique that brought people into motion behind the demands? What is the substance of this "simplistic demonology" that made the radicals such a vital element on the campus? Why was it, as the Report indicates in several places, that SDS researchers were able to reveal facts about the university that embarrassed and discredited administrators who had lied to cover over these facts?

Much of the success of the revolt rested on months of intensive research and propaganda about Columbia's role in the American power structure. This research, contrary to anything Cox and company may think, is anything but simple: doing power structure research is like studying the behavior of several thousand rats conditioned to act as if driven by greed and lust for power while running in a maze hidden behind a wall of dummy corporations, holding companies, social clubs, foundations and — last but not least — educational institutions. It is a giant step from the simple truth that control over capital resources means control over a society to an understanding of exactly how the machinery of control operates and what course of development it will follow.

But the simple truth stands: power over capital means power over people. And in America, that power is increasingly concentrated in the hands of very few people. Call them the "Establishment" if you wish, but most radicals refer to this group as "the ruling class." Analysis and documentation of their role is available;[3] in this essay, it is important only to indicate the extent of that concentration.

By the end of 1964, the 20 largest manufacturers in the country controlled 25% of total corporate assets and 32% of profits after taxes. In 1965, the top 200 companies controlled 55.4% of total manufacturing assets. In 1963, 112 industries had over 50% of their production controlled by the top four companies in that industry and in 29 of these industries, the four largest firms controlled over 75% of production. The five largest banks in each of the cities listed below had the following percentages of all local deposits as of June 1960: Boston, 90.5%; Cleveland, 97.9%; New Orleans, 99.3%; San Francisco, 91.9%. The trend toward concentration continues: at the present rate, it is estimated that by 1975 the top 200 firms will control 66% of all manufacturing assets.[4]

Since the ruling class rules through its power over capital,[5] it follows that the goal of the ruling class is to maximize profits, regardless of social consequences. This is by no means a novel idea. Old Adam Smith, hailed as the father of laissez-faire capitalism, had his wits about him when he said:

The consideration of his own private profit, is the sole motive which determines the owner of any capital to employ it either in agriculture, in manufactures, or in some particular branch of the wholesale or retail trade. The different quantities of productive labor which it may put into motion, and the different values which it may add to the annual produce of the land and labor of the society, according as it is employed in one or other of those different ways, never enter into his thoughts.[6]

To achieve their goal in modern society, the ruling class must have a section of the working population skilled in advanced technology. Technology means increased productivity, which in any rational economy would mean greater social wealth and less human labor. Under capitalism, however, technology means bigger profits and greater attention to instruments of social control. Technicians are needed, specialists who can develop and administer the systems that will make the society run as smoothly as the massive corporate conglomerates that sit on top of it. The universities have become the training ground.

Universities are factories: they have production schedules, cost analyses, and priorities dictated by return on capital investments. They must produce skilled technicians in every field from biophysics to human resources management. Every specialist that rolls off the assembly line must be as carefully codified as the field in which he works. Those who will practice law must know the intricacies of corporate structure, for corporation law is where the money is; those who will teach must know how to ram a standardized curriculum down the child's throat so the child can "make it" on the standardized criteria for college acceptance; those who will run the ship of state must assimilate the current orthodoxy on the nature of our enemies and allies. Education as the transmission of technique: "twenty years of schooling and they put you on the day shift," as Dylan says.

There are a few exceptions: out in the wilderness, there remain a few places where undergraduates ponder basics and exercise the freedoms that a large endowment fund makes possible. But since the Renaissance man would have trouble filling out a job application, most of these students have to be completely retooled in a multiversity on the graduate level before they can venture out into the real world.

What does all this mean? It means that professors bury themselves in their research, administrators are very busy with business, and students, packed into crummy little dormitories, feel very alienated — all for very good reasons in the context of capitalism.

Columbia was a particularly likely place for a revolt against all this because so much of the business of Columbia is business. The

Trustees perched on high plan priorities for the university from the vantage point of some of the biggest corporations in the American Empire. Among those represented: Lockheed Aircraft and General Dynamics, corporations that split between them 10% ($3.6 billion) of all military contracts, Allied Chemical, AT&T, CBS, Standard Oil of New Jersey (Esso), Consolidated Edison, Shell Oil, Tishman Realty and General Foods. Banks are there as well: Chase Manhattan, First National City, Chemical New York, Manufacturer's Hanover Trust, Irving Trust and Banker's Trust. For those unfamiliar with power structures, the corporations listed above are not each represented by a different person: rather, each trustee has a little string of directorships, sort of like a pedigree, that qualify him for serving on this august body. This is the phenomenon of the interlocking directorates and is one important way in which the ruling class consolidates and coordinates its interests; by this mechanism, the tendency for capitalists with large holdings to try to destroy each other is tempered — everyone gets a share of each of the pies and the ruling class moves in ways that are in the common interests of all of them. Grayson Kirk, for example, is a director of Socony Mobil Oil, Con Ed, IBM, and two financial institutions. He also sits on the boards of the Asia Foundation and the Institute of International Education, two foundations that received funds covertly from the CIA, and the Institute for Defense Analysis (IDA).[7]

With all this stuff going on, random selection alone would guarantee that at some point people would get hip that their own misery is somehow tied to the tramping of corporate elites across their chests: add a little human intelligence and you have a very unstable environment. And since Columbia is a capitalist venture, like capitalism it must expand to survive; as a result, new aggravating elements arise frequently. Columbia's physical expansion into the neighboring vicinity met with hostility because the residents — largely black, Spanish-American, and poor white pensioners — had the fundamentally correct perception that Columbia has no more use for them than they for Columbia. From within the university, it was clear to students that poor people were being evicted to meet the needs of mammoth corporations and government agencies. In one all too typical move, Columbia bought a single room occupancy hotel, redid the inside, and turned it into the Institute for Space Studies with armed guards at the door.

In the year or so before the revolt, the campaigns against Dow Chemical, the CIA and military recruiters across the country took root at Columbia in the form of a prolonged campaign against IDA. Servicing the empire was not a special feature at Columbia a few days out of the year, but a full-time occupation. Government contracts alone account for $58 million or 46% of Columbia's total budget; 25% of that is for secret research. IDA is in itself small potatoes: it is a twelve-university think tank operation for the Department of Defense and actually only involves three Columbia professors, one trustee (William A. M. Burden, who is chairman of its board), and ex-President Kirk. But IDA captures the essence of the university's total involvement with the ruling class: research is done on everything from bombing trucks at night (on the Ho Chi Minh trail, perhaps?) to putting down ghetto insurrections.

Mark Rudd was much quoted in the mass media when he said a few months ago that "the issues were manufactured" in the Columbia revolt. It was as if he had let the cat out of the bag, but anyone should be able to see that the two substantive demands in the revolt — the gym in the park and IDA — were simply cases of much broader problems. The analysis behind the demands explained why these issues were important, but there had to be something specific to focus on.

And make no mistake: the powers that be understood from the start that the revolt was about something fundamental. If by some fluke the administration had awoken one morning to find 1000 students occupying buildings just because those two issues rubbed them wrong, probably they would have given in, made some minor adjustments and the "value-free university" would have gone its merry way, the family reunited once again. But it was clear that the revolt was aimed at the relationship of the university to capitalism and the demands were no more than the vehicle of that challenge.

For the first three days, the people with power stayed quiet, hoping that enough articles in the *New York Times* and the thing would go away (the recently deceased Arthur Hayes Sulzburger, publisher of the *Times* for years, sat on Columbia's board). Any mention of the Trustees was brushed off on the grounds that it would take three days under University statutes to call a meeting.[8] But after three days, any semblance of legitimate authority had disintegrated and the basic questions of power were on the table. All illusions that there is any power in the university among

students and faculty were stripped away by the continued intransi-
gence of the administration as the campus moved more and more
behind the rebels; the faculty reinforced this fact of life every time
it came to the students with a compromise solution and had to
admit that it had no power to enforce its settlement. These poor
souls stood trapped between their students whose goals they accepted and an administration capable of calling in the police at
any moment; the more they tried to negotiate between principles
and police, the more convinced students became that it was
essential to hold on to their one lever of power, the buildings.[9]

SDS had argued that power over the university comes from the
outside world of corporate capital; as it became clear that no one
on campus had the power to grant the demands of the revolt,
students' attention turned naturally to power relations in the outside world. Students looked to both the maneuverings of the city
administration and the trustees, their adversaries in the conflict,
and that of their allies — the surrounding community, black
organizations, other campuses, and the broad-based anti-war
movement in New York City. There was suddenly real significance
to a basic principle of the radical student movement that the
campus can change society only if it relates to "off-campus" groups
moving around issues that are important to them. The dynamic
of the strike was taking people through the basic questions that
lead to radical consciousness.

When a student revolt takes place around truly radical demands, this progression in thought is inevitable. That is to say,
if the demands of students confront the present distribution of
power in America (as opposed to challenging the authority of
administrators over purely internal questions), then the evolution
of the struggle necessarily leads people to recognize that the
fundamental issue is power in the society. Police clubs alone do
not a radical make; there has to be a clear tie to problems affecting
the whole society.

The workings of this progression is important to any understanding of Columbia and the student movement, so an example
is in order. The gym is a good one because SDS paid it little
attention before the revolt, so the radical content of the issue
emerged in the course of the revolt.

Many people had been bothered by the gym because it was such
an arrogant move by Columbia against the black community.
Columbia sits in its haughtiness on the top of the fortress-like

cliffs of Morningside Park; below, stretching eastward is the gray jumble of Harlem. When construction of the gym began in the park, it symbolized that Columbia could not be happy with its empire on the Heights but had to move on Harlem as well. The plan for the building didn't help either: it called for neighborhood residents to enter the gym by a rear door at the bottom of the hill while Columbia students entered from the Heights. Black state and city officials and solid liberals like Thomas Hoving had condemned the incursion into the park. Demonstrations at the start of construction had led to the arrest of community people and students. The case against the gym enjoyed widespread support.

But when the gym became a demand of the revolt, it became an issue that had to be resolved; as attempts at resolution were put forward, the radical content came clear. The faculty suggested that gym construction be suspended and representatives of Harlem be consulted on the future of the project. But who represents Harlem? The Mayor, it was suggested, would appoint a committee of representatives. The students knew whose side the Mayor was on and knew what the decision of his kind of representatives would be: Fanon's description of the relation of colonial masters and their "native" administrators to the colonized people suddenly took on real meaning to students. Even an opinion poll could not break through the colony/mother country relationship: "Free elections of the masters by the slaves does not eliminate the masters or the slaves" (Marcuse, *One Dimensional Man*).

And Harlem's masters, the students realized, were our masters as well. The unity of interests of Harlem's oppressors and Columbia's trustees and administrators was clear on the gym issue. It was a tremendous insight: white students realized that fighting racism was not just a matter of helping blacks. The "institutionalized racism" of which the radicals talked was a fact of life for everyone, for Columbia needs racism in order to be the kind of place it is. The university is racist at its roots, all universities are racist at their roots, because to be meshed into power in America is to be racist.

It is hard to know if an insight that comes out of struggle can be communicated in words. People might read the above argument and think the students were saying something about the *views* of people in the institution ("anyone who doesn't agree with us is a racist") but that is wrong: the students were talking about an essential aspect of the *institution* and how it defines our roles for us, no matter what views we hold. It was as if people had been going to classes, reading books and worrying about their lives when suddenly they discovered that all of this was going on aboard a high-speed train hurtling along the rails of American Racism. No matter what was said or done on the train, the speed and direction was unchanged. And as Eldridge Cleaver says: "Either you're part of the problem or part of the solution." Only one thing to do — stop the train.

This new understanding of the gym question was a radical understanding, for it related our efforts to the power that defines the institutions in which we live. The same radicalizing logic was evident in other aspects of the revolt. It was clear, for example, that the only way to understand the administration's actions was to see that they wanted to defeat the revolt: ground they yielded was yielded to minimize their losses; their interest in the debates in the buildings was defined by their desire to split the rebels (particularly the blacks and whites). The faculty, in its attempts at mediation, showed that even honest attempts at "conflict resolution" could only lead to undercutting the insurgent movement and strengthen the hand of the administration. Refusing to act as an organized political force, the faculty remained to the end "part of the problem."

It was positively exhilarating to be at Columbia during the revolt. The stark geometry of sprawling plazas and imperial architecture was offset by red flags from rooftops and milling crowds that filled the campus. Trimmed hedges and lawns gave way to people with something more important on their minds than preserving the ornate decorum of the campus. Everywhere people were arguing about issues fundamental to themselves and their society, so fundamental in fact that they had never before in their lives stopped long enough to think that anything could be said about them. Faculty members were talking to students, not at them. The machine had been stopped in its tracks and people were coming out of their little compartments to look around. In the buildings, what Cox calls "romantic reaction" was creating new communities. Collective action against common oppressors broke down the inbred isolation of the individual; human creativity was expressed and acted upon by people united by their common goals. The potential for a society based on a communitarian ethic — communism, if you will — was being directly experienced by the people in the buildings.

The quality of the experience at Columbia during the revolt is not of the variety that produces groovy young college deans, idea men for aggressive young corporations and "whiz kids" for the federal bureaucracies. The Columbia revolt taught many people that change will not come from within the many institutions through which power expresses itself today; we will have to work out our own alternatives, defining them through a constant attack on the institutional power that we know must be ended. Some people will doubt that this is the legacy of the Columbia revolt and point to the failure of the revolt to reignite in the fall. But this simplistic, straight-line theory of history — shared by too many radicals — does not do justice to the changes of consciousness that a revolt like Columbia produces. People will not mechanistically repeat actions that led them to an awareness of the scope of the problems that confront all of us. Some, it is true, will retreat in fear. But most will carry the lessons learned at Columbia into other parts of the society where in other forms and around other issues, the human need for meaning in our lives and community among people will lead to attacks that carry the message learned at Columbia. If there were private corners left in America, avenues of escape for the individual, we would have to worry that our revolt would become some historical curiosity to be analyzed in ways we know all too well: were New Left radicals subject to early childhood trauma? how many square meters of living space do students need to prevent alienation? how many committees should students sit on to overcome their "feeling of powerlessness?" and make them "goal-oriented"?

But a continuing rise in insurgencies in all the institutions of our society — schools, hospitals, labor unions, corporations, and even the federal bureaucracies — is as inevitable as the trend toward concentration among the corporate interests that define those institutions. It is only as the insurgency among the poor and oppressed of this country and the rest of the world grows and the battle breaks out on the many institutional fronts of America that the harvest of the Columbia revolt and the rest of the student movement will be reaped.

Notes

[1] *Crisis at Columbia: Report of the Fact-Finding Commission Appointed to Investigate the Disturbances at Columbia University in April and May 1968.* New York, 1968.

² For the philosophically inclined, it should be noted that analytic philosophy has been trying for the past twenty years to establish whether in fact there is any relation between thought and action. There will probably be a tentative verdict as soon as there is some agreement on the meaning of these two words; until then we will all have to carry on in our benighted ways, hoping for the best.

³ G. William Domhoff's *Who Rules America?* and Gabriel Kolko's *Weatlh and Power in America* are a good place to start. For a study of the power structure at Columbia, there is an excellent booklet published by the North American Congress on Latin America (NACLA) called "Who Rules Columbia?" It is available for one dollar from NACLA, Box 57 Cathedral Park Station, New York, N.Y. 10025. Material on Columbia and its Board of Trustees in this essay is drawn from that publication.

⁴ The figures cited are drawn from a speech by Lawrence Chait of the advertising firm of the same name. The speech, entitled "Four Vital Ingredients of the Coming Revolution in Consumer Marketing 1970–2000," was presented to the Adcraft Club of Detroit in May 1968. If the figures are untrue — he cites testimony from members of the Federal Trade Commission and the Senate Anti-Trust Committee, as well as the Federal Reserve Bulletin — then at least we — radicals and capitalists alike — are laboring under a common set of illusions. The speech is available from Lawrence G. Chait and Co., Inc., 641 Lexington Avenue, New York, N.Y. 10022.

⁵ One argument by apologists for this situation holds that there is a growing tendency toward "democratization" of corporate power as more people become stockholders — the National Advertising Council and the USIA are gross enough to call it "people's capitalism." This is bunk — Domhoff cites figures that show 76% of all corporate stocks in the personal sector was held by 1% of the adult population in 1953. There is no reason why these people would have allowed the expansion of stock ownership to cut into their relative share even if by some miracle the capital was accumulated elsewhere to do it.

⁶ Adam Smith, *Wealth of Nations*, Vol. I, pp. 289–290. Homewood, Illinois, 1963.

⁷ In one of the Cox Commission's finer epicycles, the authors try to deal with "the often fine line between university activities and the private consultation and research of individual professors" (93) in regard to the Electronics Research Laboratory (ERL), an institution that grew out of the Department of Electrical Engineering in the '50's to handle contracts for missle tracking systems from the Department of Defense. The good gentlemen are disturbed that they cannot determine whether members of Columbia's faculty were "acting as individuals or for the Department" (92) when ERL was founded. ERL was formally disaffiliated from the University in 1967 and renamed the Riverside Research Institute (the name Columbia Research Laboratory was suggested but found wanting); one of its trustees is John R. Dunning, Dean of the School of Engineering. Dunning, an advisor to the Defense Department, Army and National Science Foundation, sits on the boards of three private corporations that handle military contracts; one of them, the City Investing Corporation, manufactures spray defoliant systems for chemical warfare. So much for Mr. Cox's "fine line."

⁸ Jerry L. Avorn *et al, Up Against the Ivy Wall* (New York, 1969), p. 143.

Jerry Avorn and the editors of the *Columbia Daily Spectator* have done a good job of chronicling events in this account of the revolt. The book's major failing is its typically journalistic emphasis on personalities which gives the account too strong a sense that the revolt was shaped by decisions made in small meetings.

[9] The arrogance of administrators toward the "university community" is incredible. At one point in the strike at New York University this fall over the firing of John Hatchett, head of the black student center, one administrator was asked by a striker how effective the strike would have to be to make the administration change their mind. Smiling faintly he replied, "Try 90% for two weeks."

REVOLUTIONARY CHANGE
AND THE
URBAN ENVIRONMENT

Michael Appleby

Introduction

If one thing has become clear in the 1960's, it is that our major cities have become a primary locus of radical action opportunities and offer the greatest potential for eventual revolutionary change. Both of the critical ingredients for radical social change are present or are developing in American urban areas: the conditions which demand change and the people who could carry it out. There are large concentrations of students who appear to be the most overtly radicalized segments of our population, and there are large numbers of the poor whose living conditions and stymied hopes for relief make them potential agents of revolutionary change. The apparent fate of our large cities is the clearest example of an unwillingness if not the inability of our society to meet the needs of all its people. The so-called urban crisis demonstrates the consequences of a political economy which is far more responsive to private interests than it is to the more generalized public interests.

The net results of such a political system are well known. Giant highways slice through those areas of the city which offer the least articulate, organized resistance. The highway system illustrates the way in which conflicts between private gain and the public good are typically resolved in the American political economy. While the highway system is paid for by all the people, its benefits largely accrue to certain segments of the population. A growing network of highways is built in response to powerful highway construction and automobile industry lobbies and in the urban context it is often constructed at the expense of the poor, the minority, and the unorganized neighborhoods.

The American political economy is not unresponsive. The rapid growth of the highway system has occasioned a rising wave of protest, and the outgoing Democratic administration has revised the federal regulations dealing with public hearings on proposed highway construction so that affected neighborhoods could be more adequately consulted, the social costs could be computed, and alternate locations considered. However, the operation of a political system where private interests dominate public goals is illustrated by the experience of these innovative regulations. Here, the Department of Transportation was immediately inundated with protests from highway construction and automobile lobbies and their constituents across the country. By contrast, the support for the new regulations was pitifully weak. Few community groups who would benefit from such regulations knew of them, or of the importance of supporting them. It is likely that under a Nixon administration, highway regulations which are responsive to neighborhoods through which the roads must pass will not apply for very long. This is especially true in view of the present Secretary of Transportation, who is a strong proponent of massive highway construction.

Urban Renewal is another example of a program which was theoretically conceived in the public interest, and has worked to the benefit of special groups and the more affluent classes. It was intended to strengthen the central city tax base which was severely affected by the exodus of business and industry to the suburbs. It was to do this by providing publicly financed sites for redevelopment in an effort to induce profitable commercial activity to come back into the central city. At the same time, renewal was to contribute to the 1949 Housing Act goal of "a decent home and suitable living environment for every American family."

It has now become clear that Urban Renewal has not achieved its promise. Indeed, a great deal of activity has ensued, but it is unclear in most cases whether the expense of acquiring the land, clearing it, maintaining it in a vacant state (frequently for extended periods) and promoting its redevelopment (often by offering prospective developers considerable tax incentives) have been offset by sufficient increases in tax income. What is quite clear, however, is the impact of renewal upon the low-income populations of the central cities. Over 80 percent of those relocated have been poor; two-thirds of these have been black. In many cities renewal has become synonymous with "Negro removal." Even where renewal sites do not serve this function they also do not, indeed they cannot, meet the needs of the low-income populations who are displaced. Low-income housing has rarely been incorporated into renewal strategies, and where it is, it must be a function of a separate federally-supported program. Nevertheless, providing for the people who bear the greatest social cost of renewal conflicts with the priority of bringing the middle class back into the core city. The conflict reduces to the fact that there is only so much space available and given the possible counter effects of including the poor (especially the black poor) in middle-class projects, it is the interests of the poor which are sacrificed. Thus, in Boston, where one of the most forceful, talented renewal administrators created a program which involved up to $300 million in public funds (federal, state and city) and a great deal more in institutional investment ($193 million) and private expenditure ($400 million),[1] the result for the low-income population was a 12–15% reduction in the available low-cost housing supply (for families earning less than $3,000 per year) and considerable dislocation of their neighborhoods.[2] Renewal, if anything, has worsened the plight of the poor in our cities.

Other major public programs intended to benefit the poor have also had little success in easing the lot of the urban poor. For example, public housing programs have been so heavily compromised by private housing interests, that the low-income housing needs of the poor are still unmet almost 35 years after the inception of the program. In most cities, waiting lists of eligible applicants outnumber the annual number of vacant units by four or five to one. The program has instead created a set of public institutions whose bureaucratic arbitrariness and petty regulations demean the individual fortunate enough to obtain a unit. The public housing tenant holds his unit more at the sufferance of his public landlord than he would if he had a private landlord. (Leases are on a month-to-month basis to facilitate rapid eviction.)

Public welfare programs exhibit similar defects. In response to economy minded conservatives, welfare programs have become a maze of bureaucratic regulations designed to enforce stringent eligibility standards. Such standards lead to numerous incursions into the private lives of welfare recipients and work to undercut an individual's sense of self worth. The invasions of privacy, arbitrariness of the rules (and their application), the erosion of a recipient's integrity, and the low levels of benefits actually provided, have all contributed to the present unpopularity of the welfare system among those it is supposed to benefit. The attacks on welfare offices in the recent riots, the necessity of protecting welfare workers from their clients in some areas, and the rapid growth of welfare action groups across the country are the consequences of a system which puts economy considerations before human welfare. What was once thought to be a solution to the problem of poverty within an affluent society has become an oppressive institution in its own right.

Wherever one looks, public programs have done little to remove the causes of poverty, and have, in some cases, exacerbated existing problems. Unemployment Insurance in many states is dominated by business interests, and is operated in such a way as to protect the employer and not the employee. The war on poverty has been limited by the level of resources committed to it; has had its most controversial community action program drastically reduced; and is in the process of losing its accepted programs to other, more conservative, federal agencies.

The highly-praised Model Cities Program has, to date, produced very little in the way of concrete improvements in poor neighborhoods. The Model Cities Program was designed to avoid the serious problems associated with urban renewal, and to encourage local residents to participate in the formulation of programs to meet neighborhood residents. Yet, it too has had to operate with far too little to appreciably affect the conditions of the poor. One important achievement of both the Model Cities and Poverty programs is that they have succeeded in creating expectations among the poor that indeed something will come out of all of this activity. This may be the reason why the Nixon administration may continue the Poverty Program and emphasize existing Model Cities programs. Here, as with all other affirmative public actions, there must be heavy political costs if the action is not taken.

Finally associated with higher expectations of the poor, there is also a greater awareness of how legal, political and economic systems as determined by private interests, discriminate against the poor as a group. For example, the biased character of the law has become apparent through the experience of the Legal Services programs. Consumer law is found to be written to protect the merchant, not the consumer; property law is found to assert the interest of the landlord, not the tenant; regulations of public institutions protect the service-giver, not the recipient, and redress for arbitrary and often illegal treatment is hard won in the courts. A direct consequence of the increased awareness of the sources of the many daily injustices of poverty and minority status has been an increased militancy among the poor. Welfare programs are under national attack by recipient organizations. Legal challenges to arbitrary practices in public housing projects accompany increased tenant organization. Highways are increasingly under attack and in some cases have been stopped. Renewal in many areas has become so controversial that it has dropped out of public policy-maker's lexicon; Model Cities programs and housing rehabilitation policies are preferred. Of course, some of the opposition is a direct result of the public scarcities created by the Vietnam war. Nevertheless, most issues arise out of the way in which these programs have been designed and thus exist independently of the simple fact of war.

Another source of urban financial problems which limits the ability of the central city to meet the needs of the poor can be found in the political divisions between suburb and city. This is the same old financial crisis which prompted the urban renewal strategy. The exodus of the middle-class and tax-producing activities continues; the financial squeeze on the city worsens. Without substantial federal aid, municipal finances might have collapsed long ago. The movement toward block grants with fewer restrictions upon their use is encouraging, but may become a serious threat to the large cities if they are administered through often unfriendly state governments, as the Nixon administration apparently intends to do. The important point here is that many features of the present urban condition are likely to continue substantially unaffected for some time to come. A corollary to this is that opportunities for radical organizing and action will also continue to develop. The central city with its high concentrations of the poor and the attendent critical issues is a strategic locus for radical action.

Perhaps, the most important ingredient in the sense of crisis in our cities is the growing racial polarization. The series of riots which have affected nearly every major city have elicited some positive attempts to eliminate numerous forms of racism in employment, housing and education, but have also led to a hardening of resistance among lower- and lower-middle class whites and an increased emphasis upon repressive means of maintaining law and order. The possibility of civil war in our cities is abundantly clear to those willing to see. Response to the black demands for jobs, decent housing, a relevant education, equal treatment with respect to standard municipal services and community resources may be stymied by the quasi-violent attitude of surrounding white communities and the political mood of the nation.

Thus, the emergence of white gangs whose ostensible purpose is to provide security in their own neighborhoods (Chicago, Newark), and are instead a source of retaliatory violence against black communities is a frightening development. We may well be in the early stages of an evolutionary process of conflict where the end point would be civil war or genocide. The experience of other countries' attempts to resolve communal violence is not very encouraging. When in India of the early 1900's it was suggested that the country be divided into Hindu and Muslim states, the speakers were dismissed as unhinged visionaries. Yet in the space of thirty-five years, the scale of communal violence rose to the point where the choice was becoming either the formation of separate nation states or widespread slaughter. While the resources for co-optation are substantially greater here than in India, the question here is less that of economic ability than it is political understanding and willingness to work out cooperative non-violent solutions. Unless bridges are built and passions turned into radically constructive paths, the growing racial confrontation may have little relevance to revolutionary goals and may ultimately pose the same choice as that faced by India in 1947: separation or genocide. In any case, the nation's cities will be the arenas in which either the battles will be fought or the bridges will be built.

While the discussion so far has presented nothing new, my intent here is to sketch out a strategy for making the best use of these opportunities for change. The purpose of the foregoing was to outline some of the features of the urban context within which the Left must work if change is to come about. At the outset I should make it clear that I believe if revolutionary change is to come in this country, it will occur along the lines of the "Pluralistic Revolution" described by the Habers in "Getting Along with a Little Help from My Friends" in this volume. This model holds that:

"The revolutionary situation, if it does occur, will be created slowly, without a single decisive struggle and transfer of power: by mobilizing small enclaves of radicalism in a variety of social locations, by changing people's consciousness, by creating alternative ways of living, by extending people's definitions of the possible. . . . The role of the radical is to create programs which lead people beyond their subjective experience of discontent toward a radical analysis of society and into struggles for root changes. Such struggles will not be successful until there is enough strength on the Left to change the whole system at once. But the escalating confrontation with power around a variety of issues in a variety of social locations is seen as a major tool for drawing isolated problems into radical focus, and for radicalizing new constituencies."

What I want to do here is propose a strategy for establishing the radical enclaves discussed by the Habers and indirectly referred to by Howard Zinn in his paper also contained in this volume.

The New Left has employed confrontation tactics on specific issues to force change if possible and to create radical consciousness among those affected. Confrontation politics has not, however, been instrumental in developing a community power basis. For this purpose, New Left organizers have employed more traditional community organization techniques to develop neighborhood constituencies. Single or small groups of organizers or project groups establish themselves in a lower- or working-class community, seek out salient issues, and begin to organize around them. The trouble is that, as the Habers indicate, this work is extremely emotionally demanding, is usually only possible on subsistence pay, and is therefore rarely possible for radicals who enter the family-rearing phase of their lives. Moreover, people simply burn out and/or drop out to have families and develop careers. Moreover, community projects have been, by and large, transitory events in a neighborhood's life. Many different faces come and go during a project; there is little chance to develop a sense of permanency in the neighborhood, or to become a natural part of the community landscape. A further problem is that the neighborhood really belongs to someone else; few of the organizers plan to be there over a long period of time. Organizers will remain with the community until they must go on to other things. This approach has been almost impossible in many black communities which increasingly resist outsiders who come in to organize them. This is true in varying degrees for most ethnic communities. The challenge to the New Left is, I believe, to organize its own community. I do not mean by this to organize the middle-class of America, but rather to organize a community of radicals.

However, another serious set of problems faces New Left community organizers. The Habers present the dilemma facing New Left activists as they move out of student life and into full-time organizing. Few post-full time activists satisfy their radicalism through their careers; yet there is a deep-felt need to feel politically effective; jobs are expected to be radically relevant. Among professionals there is a common feeling of having opted for the material benefits of middle-class status. A sense of having given up the resistance is often associated with the perception of the emptiness or irrelevance of most career patterns.

Only a few professions offer the possibility of work which can be immediately useful to the movement. For example, there are far more lawyers than there are positions for them in the movement. Commercial practices on the side are a necessity in any case. Only recently radicals have begun appearing in the medical profession. There the initial task would be to challenge the entire structure of the profession. The activities of city planners, social workers, community organizers can be relevant to the movement although in almost every case some outside work or association is necessary to support the movement work. The point here is that there are few positions in the movement which can support the professional on a full-time paid basis.

The Habers describe three options open to someone who intends to maintain an active role in the movement. The first is simply to continue as a full-time organizer. This option requires dogged perseverance, willingness to exist on subsistence wages, and the postponement of taking on family obligations or a professional career. All of this involves a substantial risk of "burning out" in the fairly short run. A second option is to act as a "weekend radical," regard radical activity as an avocation, and reserve the bulk of one's time and energy to meet family and career commitments. This is an unsatisfactory alternative because a part-time activist usually must remain relatively marginal to movement activity. The third option the Habers propose, that of the "avocational radical," is feasible for a small minority of those who wish to continue movement work while at the same time taking on families and developing some other professional competence. This kind of role is open only to those movement activists who for some reason have acquired a national reputation, and are able to continue in movement affairs by writing articles, giving lectures, providing consultant services to both radical groups and more establishment organizations which seek to effect social change. While such roles can be emotionally satisfying and provide a living, they are available to relatively few talented individuals. The central question is how can a person take on the responsibilities of middle adult life and remain active in or relevant to the movement? What is needed is a strategy which relates to the following goals:

— The creation of a community power base of the New Left;
— Reduction of the isolation of radicals;
— Reduction of the danger of "burning out" radicals through community work and lengthy deferment of other life goals;
— The creation of radical alternatives to present institutions;
— The establishment of a context within which families can be reared, careers pursued, and movement activity can be simultaneously pursued;
— The provision of sufficient flexibility that a wide variety of personal goals, age groups, and differing relationships to the movement can be accommodated;
— The construction of a revolutionary society.

The accomplishment of these goals requires a strategy which will permit the performance of many different functions and activities at once. For some time now there has been considerable talk of the necessity of creating alternative institutions. Free universities and free stores have been attempted but like many community projects have largely been transitory events in the life of their neighborhoods. What was needed was a resource base which could sustain the experiments so they could be given a real try. Moreover, as already indicated, New Left community projects have attempted to organize other people's neighborhoods, and therefore in addition to their transitory character, have largely failed to leave lasting organizational structures and continuing community leadership behind when the activists have gone elsewhere.

A Mass Strategy For Community Action

What I want to propose in the next few pages is a strategy for dealing with both the personal dilemmas of movement activists and the general problems encountered in running community projects and establishing alternate institutions. The two sets of problems come together and indicate the broad outlines of a strategy. I would propose that the emphasis upon organizing community projects in working-class and black communities be shifted to the organization of our *own* communities. I would further propose an alternate strategy to that of sending small numbers of organizers into a neighborhood and then proceeding to build some sort of radical organization there. I would propose that a mass strategy of organization be employed in several locations across the country. The strategy would involve encouraging or recruiting large numbers (in the hundreds or thousands) of radicals at all stages in their life development to settle in one distinct area in each of several major cities. Via word of mouth and New Left publications it would become known that any radical who is moving into, say, Boston or San Francisco, and wishes to participate in the creation of a radical community and alternate institutions should plan to locate in a designated neighborhood.

Proximity of large numbers of radicals in a particular geographical area and a distinct political unit is an essential element of this strategy for a variety of reasons. First, we need to live close together if we are to establish the kinds of communal relations which would serve as a basis for the creation of radical institutions. Secondly, settling in a small political unit of a larger city is important if there is to be a chance of winning a measure of political influence in the immediate area. Thus, if for example a block of 500 to 1500 votes could be assured to a particular candidate, seats on the city council could be won, schools could be influenced, etc. However, if a radical community were located in a political unit the size of municipal Boston (630,000±) it would be swallowed up and could not hope to exercise the same kind of influence as in a much smaller community.

A third set of advantages would derive from economies of scale which would be possible when a sizeable community of radicals existed. Many forms of economic power can be employed where large numbers of people are involved. Cooperative economic institutions could be established with a fair chance of survival. Buying cooperatives, cooperative laundries, markets, etc., could be initiated. Economies of scale in community services would also be possible where sizeable numbers of radicals were present. Cooperative day-care centers could release the women of the community to apply their talents outside the home. If local schools proved intractable, community schools could be organized and financed *by* the community. Boycotts of exploitative merchants of the products of an offending firm or country could be employed with greater effectiveness. Moreover, a radical community of some size could provide a private market for the services of radical professionals, and in this way relieve some of their need to develop commercial practices. Thus, if several doctors were part of the community they could open a free clinic for the community. Lawyers might support movement work through their community practice. A great number of economic advantages would be derived from the massing of radicals in a single area. The radical community could also win political benefits from its size. If, for example, the community could obtain control of the municipal government, experiments in the reorganization of municipal services and local political processes could be undertaken. Unequal standards of municipal services (garbage collection, street cleaning, police-fire protection) could be done away with; methods of policing the community could be reorganized; new community service institutions could be established. In short, given political power in a small municipality, considerable social change could be accomplished. Whether or not truly radical change would be possible short of a revolutionary situation is unclear. However, the use of municipal powers for implementation of radical goals is an intriguing possibility.

How Can This Be Done? Why Should It Be Done?

To this point, the discussion has had the character of a fantasy; there has been no discussion of the mechanics of employing such a strategy, nor of the problems associated with it. The basic requirements of the mass strategy are three: a sizeable number of radicals, proximity of their location, and their degree of commitment to the community/commune/cooperative/corporation (etc.).

While the three are clearly interrelated, proximity which involves the choice of neighborhood to settle in involves the most clear-cut issues. What follows are criteria for the location of a radical community.

Location In A Large Urban Center

The community should be formed in a large city because, as sketched in the first part of the paper, there are many issues, problems, and communities to which a community of radicals might relate. Location in a large city would be critical because the wide range of interests, abilities, and skills which would exist in such a community would require an equally large range of opportunities for radical involvement.

Some members of the community might want to organize welfare recipients; others might become involved in organizing a grape boycott; others might work with the black community; still others could work on building community institutions or developing community political strength. Involvement in issues outside the community, however, would be necessary if it were to remain relevant to on-going opportunities for change in the rest of the urban area. There would be a danger of the community turning inward on itself, were not such opportunities for action present. Involvement both in community work and in other areas of the city would be necessary to maximize the community's contribution to the movement for revolutionary change.

A Small Political Unit

A municipality of not more than 100,000 to 150,000 population would be an ideal choice because, as already noted, of the possibility of influencing the operation of that political unit. In light of the almost inexhaustible supply of issues and scenes of involvement, the smaller the municipality, the better.

A Mixed Community — A Declining Neighborhood

In choosing the location for a radical community, tightly-knit ethnic communities and black communities should be avoided (although for different reasons). Black communities are struggling to organize themselves, and the establishment of a radical commune/community within their boundaries would complicate their efforts and would likely lead to undesirable conflict. It would be counter-revolutionary to fight for neighborhood turf with a black community. The incursion of a large number of outsiders into any urban neighborhood will bring forth considerable resistance. Just as black communities would be avoided for ideological reasons, tightly-knit ethnic communities would be avoided for practical reasons. For example, in some heavily Italian-Irish working-class neighborhoods, attempts to set up a community would likely be met with open, violent warfare, which could destroy the early stages of a radical community. It would seem that a mixed (ethnic and class) area which is in a process of gradual decline would be preferable on several accounts. First, there would be a lower level of organized resistance; the housing market would be more open and capable of accepting sizeable numbers of entrants; and finally, community institutions would likely be in need of leadership, and amenable to influence. In any case, the establishment of the community would involve a struggle, first for the turf and second for power within the institutional structure of the area. In summary, the area should be able to receive large numbers of families (in terms of housing) and should not be socially or politically well-organized. Given this set of requirements, the choice would probably fall upon an aging community near or bordering, but not within, the inner city. The point here is to choose your area and your struggle carefully.

The two most serious problems with the strategy are first, the task of assembling large numbers of radicals in one area, and secondly, the imperative of agreeing on a common framework or goal which is specific enough to elicit the involvement of radicals yet flexible enough to allow and encourage everyone to do his own thing. Obviously, the two tasks are closely interrelated. For example, in order to draw large numbers of radicals into one area, a clear goal for the proposed community, one which would permit a variety of activities within it, would have to be offered.

Whatever the goal of the community was, it would have to appear sufficiently worth doing to warrant a first-priority emphasis in the life of a radical. Important consequences would follow from a decision to participate. For example, people would have to agree to move into the designated area and perhaps put up with local services and schools inferior to those found elsewhere in a metropolitan region. Some form of income sharing might be required and, obviously, the location would also affect a person's job selection by determining commuting time to possible job locations. Moreover, a person might have to face the resistance of the original residents. Finally, personal requirements are many and further complicate problems of recruitment. For these reasons, the community would have to offer something quite tangible if it were to induce the requisite numbers of radicals to settle in the area.

In an article of this length, it is not possible to propose in detail what the organizational focus of the community should be, except to indicate that the Community Development Corporation concept seems to offer a sufficiently flexible framework and the potential for creating a resource base to be worth close scrutiny. One possible approach would be for a small group to put together a Community Development Corporation with an initial set of activities, and then put out an invitation throughout the New Left for all those committed to building a radical enclave. Also, as radicals came into the area they could become members of the corporation and enter the community. Hopefully, some income-producing activities could be established before the community became very large and before much demand for financing new activities was generated.

In any case, the most serious problem confronting both the initiation of a radical community, and its maintenance and later growth would be the political fragmentation endemic to the Left. There would be many visions of how the community should work, what it should do, what its goals should be, what radicals should commit themselves to, and how they should organize their lives, etc. The key to whether the community will split up into many warring factions will be the flexibility of organizational framework, the tolerance of many different activities within and outside the area, and the willingness of community members to compromise. In sum, a commitment to making the community work which goes beyond specific ideological points will be necessary (and, clearly, will be difficult to obtain).

Difficult and controversial choices will have to be made as long as resources, time and energy remain limited. Choices involving the direction of the community and the use of its resources should be made on a community-wide democratic basis. However, issues of life style or the activities of community members should be left to the individual or families concerned. Differing patterns of communal living may emerge, but should not be controlled. The same is true for how community members should divide their time between community projects and issues in the larger urban area. Perhaps, the only requirement would be a sharing of income on some minimal level according to ability to contribute. The purpose of the corporate framework would be to lay the basis for a community where the wide expression of and experimentation with radical values would be possible. Any tendency toward restriction of options for radical activity would diminish both the usefulness and the strength of such radical enclaves. A minimum of organization can be seen as a virtue in light of the potential for the fractionation of a radical community. The difficulty will be to devise an organizational strategy sufficiently loose to permit all variety of radical expression yet specific enough to win substantial personal commitments from large numbers of radicals. To conclude this argument, I want to consider how this approach relates to the set of goals for movement community strategy outlined above.

Creation Of A Community Power Base

A radical community would constitute a power base in itself and hopefully, through demonstration effects, contribute to the formation of similar institutions and power bases in other communities. The existence of a radical community which was able to devise solutions to a number of critical urban problems would be an important radicalizing influence on other communities facing similar problems.

Reduction Of The Isolation Of Radicals

The gathering of radicals in itself would relieve the sense of isolation in unfriendly communities. Communal family groups, the encouragement of other radicals, associations in radical activities, and the creation and defense of the community would serve to reinforce a radical's commitment to the movement.

Reduction Of The "Burning Out" Of Radicals

The wide choice of radical activities characterized by the communities described here would permit a person to move out of full-time, highly demanding activities into other work and still contribute to the movement. Moreover, the reinforcement of the community would also reduce the possibility of dropping out of the movement due to sheer exhaustion of the will to fight for change.

Construction Of Radical Institutions

The community could bring together the resources necessary to create and maintain radical institutions, and could provide that such institutions were more than transitory events.

Provide A Context Within Which Radicals Can Raise Families And Remain Relevant

The community, by providing a locus of activity for radicals in the family-rearing phase of their lives, could deflect many of the forces which draw them away from the movement. While full-time organizing might not be possible, involvement in creating institutions to serve families with children, participation in attempts to create radical forms of education, etc., would be highly relevant both to the movement and to radicals in this stage of their life cycle. Such communities could be seen as a kind of urban kibbutz, where child-rearing and productive functions are carried on within a community cooperative context. At the same time, much of the activity could also focus on issues in the larger urban area.

Sufficient Flexibility To Accommodate Differing Personal Goals

It is unclear whether a community corporation could be so structured as to avoid crippling forms of factionalism in the community. This is one area where a good deal of thinking is required. Hopefully, this fairly general argument will contribute to the development of organizational strategies to deal with political divisions within the community. The purpose of this essay is to lay out the overall strategy of mass community organization; detailing the specific organization of the corporate, kibbutz, etc. framework of radical action will have to come later.

The Construction Of A Revolutionary Society

Successful radical communities will themselves constitute simple building blocks out of which a revolutionary society can be fashioned. Moreover, to the extent to which they can devise working solutions to problems of housing, public services, and family rearing in urban life, they can become an important influence on other urban communities which are beset by the same kinds of problems. The demonstration of successful radical solutions to urban problems can have a profound effect on the course of events in other areas of the city. The demonstration effect of radical communities is one of the strongest justifications for the strategy, in that the net effect is to create a new sense of what is possible among low-income groups whose major problem is often the disbelief in efficacy of acting in their own behalf.

While it might be argued that communities of radicals in the existing political economy cannot be all that radical, and it is indeed unclear how far such communities will be able to go in making radical values real, it is, however, clear that they can serve as resource bases for a variety of organizing activities, and the source of attempts to create radical institutions and life styles. Communities of radicals may not be the same as radical communities, but they can accommodate many who otherwise might not remain in the movement. Their contribution to the struggle for a revolutionary society may ultimately be unclear, but at this point no strategy appears certain to contribute to that goal. And it is worth trying to integrate our personal lives with the requirements of the movement.

Notes

[1] Nancy Arnone, *Redevelopment in Boston: A Study of the Politics and the Administration of Political Change*, Ph.D. Thesis, Department of Political Science, MIT, 1965, p. 59.

[2] Boston Redevelopment Authority.

III

THE MOVEMENT

A MEDITATION

DANIEL BERRIGAN

Every page that deals, as this one tries to, with the news about today, finds itself fairly buried before it is born. Last week's omelette. This week is still in the egg shells. I sit here, breaking eggs to make an Easter, to feed the living as I hope, good news for bad.

Some 10 or 12 of us (the number is still uncertain) will, if all goes well (ill?) take our religious bodies during this week to a draft center in or near Baltimore. There we shall, of purpose and forethought, remove the 1–A files, sprinkle them in the public street with home-made napalm, and set them afire. For which act we shall, beyond doubt, be placed behind bars for some portion of our natural lives, in consequence of our inability to live and die content in the plagued city, to say "peace, peace" when there is no peace, to keep the poor poor, the homeless, the thirsty and hungry homeless, thirsty and hungry.

Our apologies, good friends, for the fracture of good order, the burning of paper instead of children, the angering of the orderlies in the front parlor of the charnel house. We could not, so help us God, do otherwise. For we are sick at heart, our hearts give us no rest for thinking of the Land of Burning Children. And for thinking of that other Child, of whom the poet Luke speaks. The infant was taken up in the arms of an old man, whose tongue grew resonant and vatic at the touch of that beauty. And the old man spoke; this child is set for the fall and rise of many in Israel, a sign that is spoken against.

Small consolation; a child born to make trouble, and to die for it, the First Jew (not the last) to be subject of a "definitive solution." He sets up the cross and dies on it; in the Rose Garden of the executive mansion, on the D. C. Mall, in the courtyard of the Pentagon. We see the sign, we read the direction: you must bear with us, for his sake. Or if you will not, the consequences are our own.

For it will be easy, after all, to discredit us. Our record is bad; trouble makers in church and state, a priest married despite his vows, two convicted felons. We have jail records, we have been turbulent, uncharitable, we have failed in love for the brethren, have yielded to fear and despair and pride, often in our lives. Forgive us.

We are no more, when the truth is told, than ignorant beset men, jockeying against all chance, at the hour of death, for a place at the right hand of the dying one.

We act against the law at a time of the Poor People's March, at a time moreover when the government is announcing ever more massive paramilitary means to confront disorder in the cities. It is announced that a computerized center is being built in the Pentagon at a cost of some seven millions of dollars, to offer instant response to outbreaks anywhere in the land; that moreover, the government takes so serious a view of civil disorder, that federal troops, with war experience in Vietnam, will have first responsibility to quell the civil disorder.

The implications of all this must strike horror in the mind of any thinking man. The war in Vietnam is more and more literally brought home to us. Its inmost meaning strikes the American ghettoes; in servitude to the affluent. We must resist and protest this crime.

Finally, we stretch out our hands to our brothers throughout the world. We who are priests, to our fellow priests. All of us who act against the law, turn to the poor of the world, to the Vietnamese, to the victims, to the soldiers who kill and die, for the wrong reasons, for no reason at all, because they were so ordered — by the authorities of that public order which is in effect a massive institutionalized disorder.

We say: killing is disorder, life and gentleness and community and unselfishness is the only order we recognize. For the sake of that order, we risk our liberty, our good name. The time is past when good men can remain silent, when obedience can segregate men from public risk, when the poor can die without defense.

We ask our fellow Christians to consider in their hearts a question which has tortured us, night and day, since the war began.

How many must die before our voices are heard, how many must be tortured, dislocated, starved, maddened? How long must the world's resources be raped in the service of legalized murder? When, at what point, will you say no to this war?

We have chosen to say, with the gift of our liberty, if necessary our lives: the violence stops here, the death stops here, the suppression of the truth stops here, this war stops here.

We wish also to place in question, by this act, all suppositions about normal times, about longings for an untroubled life in a somnolent church, about a neat timetable of ecclesiastical renewal which, in respect to the needs of men, amounts to another form of time serving.

Redeem the times! The times are inexpressibly evil. Christians pay conscious, indeed religious tribute, to Caesar and Mars; by the approval of overkill tactics, by brinkmanship, by nuclear liturgies, by racism, by support of genocide. They embrace their society with all their heart, and abandon the cross. They pay lip service to Christ and military service to the powers of death.

And yet, and yet, the times are inexhaustibly good, solaced by the courage and hope of many. The truth rules, Christ is not forsaken. In a time of death, some men — the resisters, those who work hardily for social change, those who preach and embrace the unpalatable truth — such men overcome death, their lives are bathed in the light of the resurrection, the truth has set them free. In the jaws of death, of contumely, of good and ill report, they proclaim their love of the brethren.

We think of such men, in the world, in our nation, in the churches; and the stone in our breast is dissolved; we take heart once more.

A WOMAN IS A SOMETIME *THING*

or

Cornering Capitalism by Removing 51% of its Commodities

A COLLECTIVE EFFORT[1]

EVELYN GOLDFIELD, SUE MUNAKER,

NAOMI WEISSTEIN

When Mrs. Victoria Woodhull called a meeting at Steinway Hall, at the turn of the century, and proclaimed that she was for free love, the shit really hit the fan. " . . . newspapers hounded her, cautious feminists snubbed her, and the sisters fell on hard times, financially and emotionally."[2] But, the feminist movement became solvent once again: ignoring Mrs. Woodhull's radical interest in women's dignity, the women moved to concerns more easily acceptable to men, concerns seen as more respectable — like the abolishment of child labor and the gaining of social welfare — and more conservative demands — such as the vote. Finally they won. But what did they win for themselves — the right to vote, which forty-eight years later has yielded them a sprinkling of legislators who are indistinguishable from their male counterparts.

In 1910, Pamela Benjamin was caught smoking in the gazebo behind the juniper trees. She got a severe scolding and no supper that night.

That's all changed. Now there's a slim cigarette made just for women. New Virginia Slims.

Regular or Menthol

You've come a long way.

You've come a long Way, Baby, To Get Where You Got To Today: You Have a Cigarette Of Your Own Now, Baby. You've Come a Long, Long, Way.[3]

What went wrong with the women's movement? Where did the feminist struggle of the 1800's and 1900's fail? Why has there been no movement since 1920 for women's rights?

While fighting for the abolition of slavery, many women became aware of their own lack of freedom. In 1848 the first national radical women's meeting was held. Of vital concern in their "Declaration of Sentiments" were discussions of women's role in society: love, marriage, work.[4] While they felt the right to vote was key to their emancipation, it was only one of many projected struggles. Their position was principled and based on the Declaration of Independence: all women are human beings; thus, they have all the rights of human dignity and political equality. Although ignored or ridiculed, trivialized and belittled, they continued to struggle.

By the turn of the century middle class women whose *sole* concern was the vote dominated the movement. Many were political conservatives; others felt that stands against women's political, economic and social inferiority would alienate potential suffragists. The powerful Southern chapter, organized some years later, was opposed to voting rights for Black women. Suffragist leadership abandoned arguments of principle for arguments of expediency. Black and immigrant men's votes were becoming of consequence and this frightened good up-standing, decent, white Americans. The suffragists eventually won the vote by convincing the male leadership of America that if all women could vote, the vote of the white, middle class, Protestant women would out-number blacks and immigrants of both sexes. The women got their vote[5] and the status quo was maintained.

After obtaining the vote, there was nothing left. The suffragist movement became the League of Women Voters; middle class women were pre-occupied with being participant citizens. Their daughters flocked to the Bohemianism of Greenwich Village in the '20's or to the "liberated" life styles of the flappers.

What remained in American thinking concerning women's rights by the 1940's could be found in the union struggles and in the politics of the "old" Left. Although women's active participation in labor organizations dates from 1823, union leadership and control has always been concentrated in the hands of men. This is still true even in those industries dominated by women. The "woman question" like the Negro question was raised by the Communists and socialists in a formalized manner. But because little action was taken for or by women, unionism and the Left vaguely kept alive the notion that somehow society was unjust to women.

Because of the demands of its war economy, World War II legitimated work for all women. Rosie the Riveter symbolized the breadth of work women were allowed to perform for the first time. When the war ended, middle class women were told to return home to become "real women" again. Working class women who remained in the factories were pushed to the bottom of the labor force, where they continued their struggles, primarily for bread and butter, in isolation.

With the collapse of the "old" Left in the 1950's, and the ethos of privatism which succeeded it, the importance of the family became paramount. The woman question was buried. As soldiers returned from World War II and then the Korean War, girls were taught through the media, in school, by the churches and their families that the one route to happiness for a woman was to snare a "successful" husband, be a creative and loving wife, mistress, mother.

Yes, Virginia, we've come a long, long way.

"Somethins Happenin' But You Don't Know What It Is, Do You Mr. Jones?"   Bob Dylan

The college generation of the early 1960's barely remembers World War II; a world without television, satellites, cold war, racial strife, automation. We can vaguely remember small businesses, cities without suburbs, superhighways. It is hard to imagine that air travel was not always a daily reality. For us, the breadlines and massive unemployment of the depression are faraway legends. Yet, for our parents, the depression was a reality of youth, a major war and the McCarthy era were realities of adulthood. We were raised by people who had to struggle to survive and who instilled in us the ethics of "private survival." We were bequeathed a personal morality: be kind to others; don't be prejudiced; don't use the word "nigger"; be fair; don't take what is not yours; be generous with what you have. On the other hand: don't be a sucker; remember it's a rough world and if you don't look out for yourself, nobody else will. Worth is measured in terms of status, wealth. You want to "make it" or if you are a woman, you must marry a guy who will "make it." Don't get too involved with saving the world; remember: take care of *number one.*

We called our parents cynics, hypocrites, privatistic and timid. Reared in the comforts that their struggles brought us, we felt that their world reeked with internal contradictions. What good did it do to be kind to your fellows if "making it" demanded that you squeeze someone else out of first place? Did a split level home and a two car garage really bring happiness? Were our parents really happy? Why were their friends respectably drinking their lives away? We learned that America was, in fact, much worse than our parents told us; it was a racist society, a vicious imperialist power, a totally rigged democracy. What did their Sunday school sermons about prejudice mean in the face of ghetto rebellions? When they told us to love other children, did they also include the millions of communist or black children in the world? At what age did we have to stop loving others and learn to stick with our "own kind"? When they taught us to pity, did they want us also to pity the boring, drab, empty lives of the vast majority of the middle class Americans whom we were supposed to imitate? They taught us decency, but their notion of decency was vacuous. We needed to develop a stern analysis of their "dog-eat-dog" reality and a program for how to change it.

The early New Left movement was predicated on the understanding that an incredible disparity existed in America, and in the world: a disparity between the enormous abundance and freedom that modern technology made possible and the terrible deprivation and coercion that people actually faced. It called upon young people to reject the image of the "bullet-headed, swivel-hipped, button-down, make-out artists" of the fifties.[6] It talked about people "making it" *collectively:* controlling their own lives, so that those lives could become human again. It talked about people determining their own destinies, collectively fashioning a new world rather than having them be determined by the rational economics of a competitive profit system.

The Only Position For Women In The Movement Is Prone.
                                              Stokely Carmichael

By and by, and much later than we should have, women discovered, to our surprise and dismay, that despite the New Left change in head shape, hip action and buttons — most of all buttons — that the position of women was no less foul, no less repressive, no less unliberated, than it had ever been. We realised that while we may have been radical on many issues, as women, we accepted the status quo. Although we wanted to be revolutionaries, we also wanted to be feminine. (Feminine: intuitive, creative, cuddly, non-castrating, warm, loving, sweet, submissive, unobtrusive, quiet, cheerful, rhythmic, sensuous, good smelling, intellectually supportive, serving, gracious, charitable, unpredictable, etc., etc.) We were still the movement secretaries and the shit-workers; we served the food, prepared the mailings and made the best posters; we were the earth mothers and the sex-objects for the movement men. We were the free movement "chicks" — free to screw any man who demanded it, or if we chose not to — free to be called hung-up, middle class and up-tight. We were free to keep quiet at meetings — or if we chose not to, we were free to speak in men's terms. If a woman dared conceive an idea that was not in the current, limited, ideological system, she was ignored or ridiculed. The work done by women organizers (the status role for movement activists) was often considered of secondary importance in the overall effort. We found ourselves unable to influence the direction and scope of projects. We were dependent on the male elite for direction and recognition. We were free, finally, to marry and raise liberated babies and clean liberated diapers and prepare liberated dinners for our ass-hunting husbands, or "guys we were living with."

What's This, a Movement For Pink Power?

New Left men have had one of two extreme reactions to the emergence of the woman's movement. One is ridicule: we are not politically correct; we are easily co-optable and no threat to capitalism. "Why aren't you 'chicks' working to end the draft, organize the poor, support the working class?" "You want Pussy Power?" — they jeer with lascivious grins. The other reaction begins with deep concern and understanding and quickly evolves into heavy political abstractions about why a woman's movement is useful and necessary and quickly degenerates into condescending advice about how we ought to run our movement. What men just can't dig is that we, females, are going to define our movement, that male advice is paternalistic — no less so than when given by a white to a black. If men have a task, it is not to tell us how to deal with our oppression; it is to understand and fight the individual and systematic manifestations of male chauvinism.

In 1968, one hundred and twenty years after the suffragists held their first national meeting, radical women gathered in sisterly compassion at Lake Villa, Illinois, to learn about our history and to determine our destinies. Large groups of women were able to overcome societal pressures and lies; they freely discussed their marriages, being single, having orgasms and the political implications of such revolutionary discussions.[7]

The suffragist movement nearly sank under the weight of radical notions like "free love" and an end to marriage and the family; it managed to keep afloat only at the expense of throwing overboard any fundamental change, any revolutionary notion of how to alter the degrading position of women in society. But Mrs. Woodhull was right: if we are ever going to know what a free human being is, what it means to be really liberated, to realize the potential that we, all of us, every human being has, we are going to have to talk about love, marriage, the family, work and play. We are going to have to talk about true human dignity and freedom and make clear to a society and to a Left movement, both of whose rhetoric has little relation to reality, just what the denials of those rights mean.

The Use Of The Media

In *The Graduate:* Old man of 50ish to Benjamin Braddock, *"Plastics!"*

People who hold the power have the ultimate power to define. In America — not the free-enterprise capitalism we learn about — but the neo-capitalism, monopoly capitalistic system which exists — the power to define is held by big business. Everyone knows that the vast amount of wealth and resources of this country is centered in a small number of male controlled mammoth corporations, banks and financial institutions. But we are less aware of the enormous power these corporations hold and of the effects of that power on our daily lives. We do not see clearly what *their* concepts: competition, efficiency, profit, national interest, consumerism, do to our minds and souls. We do not have the ability to define for ourselves what we really *need* for existence and happiness, because they make those definitions for us.

In order for a corporation to maintain its wealth and power, it must expand its markets, not only abroad but at home. Thus, we are constantly bombarded with "new" products which it is our duty, as Americans, to consume. No matter if these products don't fulfill the real needs of our society. No matter if they are wasteful and not really new at all like this year's fashions or the latest in planned obsolescence, Americans must be cajoled, intimidated and coerced into buying them. Business engages in mass propaganda campaigns to convince us that fulfillment, status, identity, our very destinies lie in our constant consumption of their "plastics."

We are all children of Coca-Cola;[8] even those of us on the fringes of society, who have consciously attempted to reject the constant, insistent messages of the mainstream mass media. The men who control the media, tell us not only what we want and need, but what a man is and what a woman is, how to achieve happiness, and, on various conscious and sub-conscious levels, we have believed them. The male and female images which pervade our movement media and make up our movement stereotypes testify strongly to our subliminal acceptance of the "man."

The Ads

Half-man, Half-beast, All Male or What Sort Of Girl Reads Cosmopolitan?

"An alligator is like a woman, the wise man said,
the best are soft, supple, and non-belligerent."

In the course of selling a purse, the ad has defined womanhood. But, just who is it that digs the soft, supple, non-belligerent female? The answer is simple, men, of course. By implication, men also dig women who dig soft, supple, non-belligerent alligator purses.

"Woman exists for man" is the message of the woman's magazine. *Cosmopolitan, Glamour, Mademoiselle, Ladies Home Journal, Woman's Day*, and the rest are handbooks on how to make oneself, one's home, one's life, attractive to men. The beauty and glamour programs set forth directly and indirectly on their pages, require incredible amounts of a woman's time, energy, cash, resourcefulness, and ingenuity. But, they are well worth it because life for a *girl* — even if she is 50 — is hell if she doesn't know all of the feminine wiles and tricks. Disgusting as these magazines may be, they serve an important function as self-defense manuals for females who are forced to spend their days either catching a man or keeping one. Huge quantities of effort are needed to attain the "unique you" within the confines of a rigid conformity. The art is to attain an elusive image, to be the mysterious woman who is constantly dissolving into next season's fashions, next year's *new look*.

Whether sporting the latest fashions in *Mademoiselle* or sprawling naked across the pages of *Playboy*, the woman's body is seen in terms of its sexual functions, i.e. attracting men, enticing men, turning men on. Yet, the sexuality is dismally one-sided; it is defined only in its relationship to men. What is conspicuously absent is the notion of the woman as sexual subject, whose body yearns to receive pleasure as well as give it, who wishes to be enticed as well as to be enticing. The female is the universal sex object. In a leading woman's magazine, an adveriesment for a breast reducing operation appears. The operation left one with lovely, firm, hand-size breasts. The fact that it also removed all sensory organs was casually mentioned, a trivial price to pay for beauty. An extreme case? Perhaps, but what about a girdle? It may make one look "sexy" but it feels miserable. The sexually aggressive female who emerges in some of the "hipper" magazines is aggressive only in what she'll do to catch a man; her sexuality remains essentially passive, based upon self-denial. What pleases a man is still the final criterion for her behavior.

The objectification of woman's sexuality has been enormously useful to the advertising industry. Both men and women have been conditioned to look at pretty, young women. A female model adds a touch of spice, of zest to an ad for a non-sexual product like toothpaste, a car, an airline. Glamour girls appear on the covers of *Playboy, Cosmopolitan, Science and Mechanics, Popular Photography* and *Silver Screen*. Studies show that male models or movie stars don't sell magazines as well. Of course, "serious" magazines like *Time* or *Fortune* usually sport men but not models, "important" men with names, status, identities, power. Women on the other hand, are merely decorations, usually nameless, the universal sex symbol made flesh. The use of sex to sell products plays around with the sexual hang-ups of everyone in this society. But, for females, it reinforces the idea that their worth consists in being pretty, irrelevant objects.

The sixteen billion dollar a year advertising industry has swollen since the end of World War II, paralleling women's mass exodus from productive labor to the home or to the bottom rung on the labor force. The frustrating, boring, essentially passive and self-denying aspects of females' present roles probably make them "natural" consumers and suckers for ads. Yet, the advertising industry consciously and purposefully plants the idea in women that the road to fulfillment, to happiness, to overcoming obstacles, to catching and keeping a man lies in greater and greater consumption. After all, the business of advertising is to sell and females make up 75% of all private consumer decisions. More important, it is women who consume most of the "wasteful" products of an over-productive economy — with the exception of military waste — the ever-changing cosmetics, the latest in patterned, scented, fancy paper products, decorator extension phones, lovely flowered plastic boxes of margarine, the final word in any of the fifty brands of soap powder.

By glorifying the role of housewife and mother, by setting up unattainable standards of beauty, by defining jobs as glamourous because they require extensive wardrobes, the advertising industry has unleashed an insatiable desire for commodities. At the same time, it has helped to condition women to their secondary status. Women are portrayed in ad after ad, as trivial, stupid, helpless, in dire need of a man. "Behind every smile is a brain," is the copy over a smiling girl at a Hertz-Rent-A-Car table: the ultimate in smug, maculine condescension, a sorry attempt at flattery, which only reinforces the general notion that brains are unusual in women.

Yet, everyone knows that the woman's role is not all joy and roses. Even ads admit that:

Mother, for a while this morning, I thought I wasn't cut out for married life. Hank was late for work and forgot his apricot juice and walked out without kissing me, and when I was all alone I started crying. But then the postman came with the sheets and towels you sent, that look like big bandanna handkerchiefs, and you know what I thought? That those big red and blue handkerchiefs are for girls like me to dry their tears on so they can get busy and do what a housewife has to do. Throw open the windows and start getting the house ready, and the dinner, maybe clean the silver and put new geraniums in the box. Everything to be ready for him when he walks back through the door.[9]

Other ads are even franker in cataloging the trials and harassments of a housewife's daily ordeals. The cure: buy a new hat, take a bubble bath, dry your tears on new expensive bandanna sheets. But never, never, never, let the woman question the validity of her daily existence. The rehearsal of women's problems is merely a device for selling more products. Particularly when advertising labor saving devices, Madison Avenue must be careful not to imply that they might eliminate the need for full time housewives. The following statement appeared in an advertising trade journal:

The housewife being hard pressed is felt a symbol of worthiness and of her love for her family. Therefore advertising which places too great an emphasis on washing her burden away runs the risk of being reacted to negatively because it seems to detract from her personal importance. These women need to be busy keeping house — both because they need to feel they are doing something worthwhile and because they have few psychic resources for occupying themselves in ways other than housekeeper for the family.[10]

But some of the women Madison Avenue must reach already have careers or professions. Others have unquiet feelings, longings for equality with men. Then, let the *Time* magazine researchers have mini-skirts and sheer-sheer blouses; the lady doctors have fashionable wigs for house-calls; the clothes-buyers have pant-suits and boyish hair-cuts. Even let them have their own cigarettes. Just don't let them forget that they are women, that they must be stylish and attractive, that they have come a long way and that's plenty far enough.

Non-ad Media

The non-ad media aren't much better: Ann Landers with her conventional "woman's place is in the home" morality; women's sections of the newspapers devoted to fashion, recipes, gossip, and endless pictures of brides; mother-in-law jokes; cartoons depicting mindless secretaries who can't add; endless portrayals of luscious young "broads" succumbing to fat, old lechers for the price of a mink coat; television's banal situation comedies which celebrate the traditional family roles; Laugh-In's painted women's bodies and subtle, unfunny, dirty jokes about sex; newspaper writers who apparently believe that a young woman and her ideas are best described by her "measurements"; the "hip" and exploitative sex of *Playboy*, and even "hipper" men and women about-town of *Esquire*. The list is endless.

"Please, Madame Binh . . . can't we hurry along?"

No need to call Mrs. Binh a Red to insult her. Just remind the public that she is a woman, show her doing some "trivial woman thing" when she is supposed to be engaged in serious work, and the point is made. No female, no matter how important a figure in world affairs, can escape the media's stereotypes of womanhood.

Movement Media

Women do not fare much better in the Left and movement media. Men run most of the left-wing publications. The few women who hold top positions, if they are concerned about the oppression of their sex, are expected to present the subject only in terms that men can understand and accept as politically relevant. The underground papers are full of "revolutionary" cheese-cake. For example, a recent issue of *Kaleidoscope*, a Chicago underground paper, contains a photograph of a nude woman sporting ammunition belt and rifle. (Will the "hip chick" really fight naked at the barricades?) These papers contain articles praising hippy life because there are so many chicks around to screw and the chicks can help each other take care of the kids. They contain articles which clearly assume that men are the only people worth writing for — articles with phrases like "you and your chick" or "there will be lots of chicks around."

Liberation News Service circulated a cartoon which juxtaposes the verile, aggressive, potent, movement-male — against the fawning, prissy, decadent system-female. The cartoon appeared in various underground and movement papers, including the *Guardian*. When angry women sent in an alternative cartoon and a protesting letter, the *Guardian* refused to print them.[11]

Ramparts, a left-liberal magazine, is not above using sex to boost its circulation. The January, 1968 issue carried a story about "Woman Power" which was filled with more condescending cuteness, more stylish photographs and chatter about clothing, more female stereotypes, more insulting metaphors, "the late afternoon mist clung like a corset to the back-country highway," more political inaccuracies than any article in the establishment press. The article was announced on the *Ramparts* cover by a picture of a woman with two tits and no head. Several months later the cover sported a perky blonde dressed only in flimsy black bra and panties to announce the important political subject of wire-tapping.

After much criticism and pressure from radical women, *Ramparts* finally accepted what was, for that magazine, an unusually accurate, concise and well written article entitled, "Orgasms," which they promptly buried on page 59, under the erudite term, Sexology. In the same issue, December 14–28, a cute, stupid, politically irrelevant story appeared on page 38 entitled "Nixon Girls."

Straighter movement papers are filled with articles praising the heroic struggles of Vietnamese and Latin American female guerilla fighters, but they almost totally ignore the struggle for female liberation at home. While some of them have printed occasional articles on the subject — often written by men, sometimes full of ridicule, sometimes containing admonitions to "go slow," not one

paper that we know of has taken a consistently militant stand on
the subject, nor have many papers actively sought out articles by
militant women.

It might be argued that the media are so bad that they can't
possibly be taken as representing the consciousness of this society.
Like the Hollywood, sunshine and lolly pops formula for love in
previous, less frank decades, one may have good cause to wonder
whether anybody really believes that stuff. We think that nobody
believes it entirely; there is an area of human decency which even
the almighty dollar cannot touch. There is a folk wisdom which
assures that the female can be admired for her personality as well
as for her body. She can be assertive in some ways. If she can't
live life as a blond, it may be ok; she can really be sharp in other
ways: a good cook, a good companion, a nice person. What the
media present us with is the form, the platonic ideal. What is
filtered down to people is the substance: females live for the
approval of men; they are worthwhile to the extent that men find
them worthwhile.

The Search For Fulfillment — Make Up — Make Out — Make It

> "Do you need anybody,
> I just need someone to love,
> Could it be anybody,
> I want somebody to love."[12]

The media not only teach us how to look but also how to
think. We learn to see things in terms of their profit value; everything and everybody must be marketable. We, like business, seek
the "saleable package." Men seek a particular commodity when
shopping for a mate. Their image of what is ideal is in large part
shaped by the kinds of images projected by the media. Since a
woman's value lies in her body, her face, her legs, in sum her sex,
in order to make herself into a saleable package — she must be
"physically attractive." As long as a woman is pleasant to look
at, she remains on the sexual market place. As she grows older she
becomes less saleable. Every wrinkle, every grey hair is a mark of
her decay . . . her depreciation. If she is useless as a beauty
symbol, her true value is lost.

The female learns that she had better catch a man while she is
able, if she wants any kind of love, companionship, respect or
even economic security after her youth and beauty have faded.

We must learn — and learn well — a whole lot of complicated lessons which we can forget only after we have that gold band securely on our left-hand, ring finger. We learn to compete with other women for the most eligible men: to project auras which hint a deep, secret, feminine mysteries, to flirt and charm, to play hard to get, to submit gracefully, to be cute and argumentative at one moment, passive and filled-with-worship at another moment. In short, we learn a whole lot of bull-shit which has nothing to do with who we really are.

And what do we seek: the all man, man. A man who is strong, aggressive, cool, ambitious, successful. A man who is certainly brighter, better, and stronger than we. Yet, because he fell for our tricks and wiles, we can't help suspecting, from time to time, that he and all other men like him, are really fools. A fool who doesn't want to love another human being but instead wants a phony, hollow stereotype who torments him and feeds his ego.

Marriage

Do You Promise To Love, Honor And Obey?

A recent newspaper cartoon depicts two old women speaking of a bride. One says to the other, "She can throw her diary away; she won't need it now." In other words, her life is over. Her beauty, her charm, her activity have fulfilled their goal: she has caught a man. From now on she can live through her husband, his successes and failures will be hers. His ambitions will be hers. Secure in her domesticity, he will be her contact with the outside world; from him she will get her ideas about important matters like politics and social change. His work will determine where they live, what kind of friends they have, their status and social class. Her role will be to back him up, support him, comfort him. After all, a wife is an important asset to a career; they say: behind every successful man is a woman.

> Hard is the fortune of all womankind
> She's always controlled, she's always confined
> Controlled by her parents, until she's a wife
> A slave to her husband, the rest of her life.[13]

Back in the old days, when a certain amount of honesty prevailed in society, marriage was seen for what it was: a property relationship, a relationship of master to his slave, an exploitative relationship. A man married to have someone to serve him, bear and rear his children, manage his household, perpetuate his name and his property. A woman was married because she was forced to, because economic security demanded it, because it was the only upright, honorable thing to do. Conjugal love was a very secondary matter, so secondary that marriages were often arranged by parents, without husband and wife even knowing each other until the wedding day. Romantic love, sexual love, these had nothing to do with marriage.

Nowadays, women are taught that the ultimate love, romantic and sexual, is found only in marriage. Yet, marriage is still the same old property relationship. A woman is still her husband's servant. She cooks his meals, cleans his house, raises his kids in his name, and gains her identity through him. She usually has little or no contact with the outside world; her life is circumscribed. In addition marriage can be physically coercive — one of the defining qualities of a "good" husband is that he doesn't beat his wife.

Even if she has her own career or interest, the home is considered her "proper primary sphere." Her husband may encourage her outside interests and even "help" her around the house. The essential relationship hasn't changed; he is merely a benevolent master. When his career is at stake, she is expected to drop all of her interests in deference to his future. Most important, she has been trained to feel guilty or that she is being selfish if she resents any part of married life. Love is the name given to her isolation, sacrifice, dependence, boredom, loneliness and emptiness.

People do not really expect romantic love to last through marriage. It is part of our folk wisdom that the joys of new love cannot last. We look at the enraptured, excited engaged couple and say, wisely, "Just wait 'til they're married." Yet, people are disturbed that so many marriages, perhaps even their own, are moderately or desperately unhappy, that one out of four end up in divorce. Social commentators blame it on the fast-changing times, bad up-bringing, neurotic-ever-present mothers, "frigid" women who don't give their men enough sex, or passive, absent fathers. No one calls into question the institution of marriage. Most often, those marrieds who are "trying hard" to make it are merely trying to make the best of a difficult situation. The fear of having to search and play the flesh game again is too threatening to most couples.

Yet, is it surprising that a master-servant relationship gives rise to resentment and bitterness rather than feelings of warmth and tenderness? Is it any wonder that when people begin to live together and see each other for the first time not playing the flesh game, that they may not like what they see? Why should a man who works outside of the home all day and a woman who keeps house and communicates with four year olds have anything in common? How can love, which implies warmth, mutuality, understanding, respect, excitement, flourish in an atmosphere infused with dullness, routine, with every element of domination and submission? When all of the romantic nonsense is swept away, marriage is still justified in terms of function and duty; it is the duty of human beings to perpetuate the race; it is the duty of women to bear and raise children.

Having Children

Females are told, "having a child is the most creative thing you can do." Of course, if simply bearing offspring were really creative, then rats, cats, rabbits — not to mention frogs — would be among the most creative things going, since they bear whole litters. Or is raising children into "warm, beautiful, human beings" the creative part? Much of child-raising is not creative at all; the bulk of the job is either custodial or janitorial. Nor is it clear that a child learns best about the world when she or he is totally dependent for warmth, affection and guidance upon one human being — particularly a human being who is permitted to experience life only through the activities of other people, usually children. Why should a child have only two adults as models in the most formative years? Why shouldn't childhood be spent in the company of many other children and a diverse grouping of adults? Why should the task of raising children be the burden of only the female sex?

Private Property Is a Total Concept[14]

If we strip marriage of the property function, what is left — an intimate relationship between two people? Most marriages, we are told, last only because there are children. Why should people be forced to decide at age 20 whom they will love at 45? Why should we be allowed only one intimate relationship? Why always a man and a woman? Why can't there be an intimate relationship between more than two people? Why must there be a legal contract? Why must it last a lifetime? Why does the world have to be divided up into couples who relate to everyone else as couples or else as "unfortunate" singles? Why should each couple live by itself, isolated from other friendships, other intimacies? Marriage is the cultural manifestation of a society based on private property. Married people possess one another and their children — they are each other's private property. The family is a basic consumption unit. It spends money and accumulates property which it passes down to its children, whom it has raised to love property. It teaches the children to need to possess and accumulate property and to marry to continue the cycle.

In the abstract, it is easy to imagine capitalism surviving the breakdown of the family. Single or communal units of consumption could prove even more profitable. Public institutions could inculcate the "proper" selfish values even better than the family does. Yet, a movement to abolish the family in favor of more communal, less property-oriented forms of living threatens the privatistic, anti-social, competitive values that the capitalist system is based upon.

Remaining Single

"I never will marry, I will be no man's wife, I intend to live single, all the days of my life"[15]

Every game has its losers. Every game has those who refuse to play. In short, some females never marry. For such a woman, there is the threat of a life of sheer hell. She faces ridicule and humiliation. If she is a virgin, she is called a dried up old prune. If she has affairs, she is a slut. Affairs are for young girls, not for women over thirty. If she lives with a man she constantly faces the fact that he can leave her any time he wants, anytime she doesn't please him. It will not be so easy for her to get another man. Women over thirty have low market value. Everyone, everyday, subtly or bluntly, points out to her that her life is a failure, that she is unfulfilled, that she has lost out. When is she going to get a man, be respectable, settle down?

She faces loneliness and social ostracism. Her friends have all married and no longer have anything in common with her. She is an embarrassment to her family. People, who have arranged their lives in couples, only invite her to dinner if they can dig up a "date" for her or if some "eligible man" is in town. Out of loneliness, out of desperation, she may marry for convenience — to get people off her back — or she may let men walk all over her, hoping to get one before it is too late.

There are few places where single women can find male companionship merely for fun as well as for marriage prospects. With so much pressure to marry, single women seek out men in the most destructive ways. Young women in their mid-twenties who have skilled jobs such as secretaries, teachers, beauticians, case workers, nurses often spend many hours waiting for men in the humiliating atmosphere of a singles' bar. Some, less honest, will find men friends and go in crowds to similar bars, each hoping that by some magical happening, she will meet the man of her dreams: puff — all of her worries will end.

While the folk wisdom assures us that there is no such thing as the flashing knight in shining armour, there is hardly a girl who does not dream that there is someone special who will be hers, someone who is just a bit of a superman. With movies and TV so dominant in our lives, it is difficult to accept the known, ugly truth instead of the beautiful, romantic myth.

A single woman will often sleep with men who obviously don't respect her to prove that she is "hip," hoping that something of the "real" her will get to him in bed and he will want *her* forever. Why shouldn't she hope that in this way she may have her chance to capture the junior executive?

> "I get by with a little help from my friends,
> With a little help from my friends
> Yes, with a little help from my friends."[16]

Since our society is so harsh on those who never marry, most single women are lonely and desperate. But, the single woman who digs being independent, for whom the prospect of marriage is not only not a panacea, but a horror, there is isolation as well. While she may believe and hope that single women together might provide each other warmth, companionship, community, most of her friends are preoccupied with finding a mate.

If the single woman is fortunate enough to have a good career, she is looked upon as a castrating bitch, too wrapped up in her own life to be able to love. Most single women aren't so lucky. Working class, single women, divorced women with children, women living on welfare, widows on small pensions or social security, these women face severe and horrible economic deprivation as well as social humiliation. If a single female wishes to raise children, she faces total martyrdom since society frowns most extremely on "illegitimate" children and seldom allows her to adopt children. If she does have a child out of wedlock or if her husband deserts her, she is constantly faced with the threat that unless she leads a "model" existence, she will be considered an immoral and unfit mother and that her children will be taken away from her. Unwed mothers have a difficult time finding employment. More subtle and often more important ostracism, such as being the subject of morning coffee clatches in other homes in her town, will often prove deterrent enough. In every way imaginable, the single woman is constantly punished for not having found a husband, or for having found one and lost him.

Denied love, denied self-respect, denied companionship, denied economic security, a single woman often begins to believe that there is something wrong with her, that she is a freak. Few females can look at singleness as a positive state; for most, it is the worst of all possible worlds. The threat of being "single" once again deters many women from leaving husbands who mistreat them or husbands they can't stand. No matter what is wrong with marriage — she thinks, it is infinitely preferable to the single state.

Females have always been isolated from one another. Marriage isolates married women from each other and from single women. Single women who may be very close know that their friendship is predicated on both of them remaining single. Thus, single women are isolated by the nature of a search for a man. Perhaps that is why females have suffered for so many centuries without engaging in collective action to change their situation. If we want to create a revolutionary female movement, we are going to have to find ways of overcoming that isolation.

Sexual Liberation: For Whom And For What?

Today, we are told, women have been sexually liberated. Not very long ago, women were taught not to ever enjoy sex, not even in marriage. Now, in the age of the sex-manual, women are allowed to enjoy sex, encouraged to dig sex even without marriage. So how come so many females still don't like sex? Why do so many young females, hip females, groovy females, consider themselves frigid?

There are many reasons. One of them is that with all the sex talk, sex education, frank discussions and the rest, women are still not taught anything about their own sexuality by other females. Most women don't understand their own bodies, have hardly any idea of what their own genitals are like, even what they look like, and don't have the faintest notion of how to get sexual pleasure. Real honest discussions about such matters are not only taboo, they are unheard of. A woman isn't supposed to be so "crude" as to tell a man how to "turn her on." If she is forward enough to do so, she'll probably turn him off.

Sexual pleasure has been defined by men in accord with what gives the male pleasure. "Sex education" for women is learning how to satisfy a man. She knows what a male orgasm is. But, a whole lot of mystery and mystification surrounds the female orgasm. Freud, and his followers, spun theories about "two kinds of orgasm," the "wrong" kind received by direct clitorial stimulation, and the "right" kind, achieved with the penis inside the women. If she can't get the "right" kind, the kind that gives direct pleasure to the man, then, baby, she is screwed up. But, large numbers of women just can't get the right kind; these women are called frigid. Since they don't like to screw the way the master likes it, they just don't deserve to get any pleasure.

Until recently, no one even bothered to take the trouble to find out what such an important thing as the female orgasm really was. Masters and Johnson[17] studied 7,500 orgasms, achieved by many different techniques and found out that all the orgasms were physiologically the same. Interesting, but even if there were two kinds, why should one be right, the other wrong? Why not do whatever will provide warmth, affection, sensual stimulation and erotic gratification for both partners? Why are we all so hung up?

Because that is not what sex is about in this society. Sex is also using people, conning people, messing over people, conquering people, exploiting people. Many of us who rebel under exploitative relationships, still have fantasies of mutilation, masochistic nightmares which excite us sexually. What we can't stomach in reality, we perpetuate in our dreams. Why? Because we women are taught that sexuality and love are to be dug in a context of cruelty and submission. That men are supposed to fuck us over. That sex means being fucked over.

It is a joke to talk about love in such a dehumanized context. This degraded form of man-woman relationship, master and slave, which is held ideal by our society, deprives all of us of our right to human love and human community. Cruelty, humiliation, domination and abject submission pervade the one area of our society where it is considered "proper" to show dependence, need for others, and intimacy.

These conditions disgust us. We are working to create a society where people don't have to get married in order to have love, respect or security. We want to eliminate marriage as we know it today. We want to have the freedom to love, to choose whom to love and how to love. We want the freedom to love more than one person; to love members of our own sex as well as men. We want people to be free to love in dyads, triads, tribes, packs or swarms, sexually or asexually. We want to liberate society from taboos about homo-sexuality, celibacy, promiscuity, perhaps even eradicate the concepts. We want to liberate love from economic necessity, from coercive, compulsive, exploitative sexuality, from all patterns of dominance and submission.

Work

If a woman doesn't manage to "catch" a man, or if she catches one and loses him, or if the one she caught doesn't make enough money, or if she just can't stand to stay at home all day long, she finds herself on the female job market. It is very different from the male job market, usually separate and totally unequal. Within any given type of work, women's jobs are the lowest paying, have the lowest status, and are often the most boring.

Usually ununionized and supervised by men, female factory workers perform the most unskilled, menial and poorest paying tasks. But factory work is not the only labor available to the unskilled woman. She can be a domestic, cleaning the bathtubs and toilets of the privileged who are raised with the idea that they deserve her services. She can be a salesgirl and work long, hard hours on her feet, her $1.75/hour plus commission dependent on her ability to coerce others into buying junk that she probably wouldn't buy for herself.

Women are welcomed as elementary and high-school teachers, but not as principals or supervisors. The doors of university faculties are virtually closed to us. In hospitals, women are the nurses or aides, not the doctors. In law offices, we are the secretaries and clerks, not the lawyers. In offices everywhere, a male can gauge his success by how many pretty receptionists, secretaries, file clerks he has at his disposal.

The female who makes it in the white man's world, like the black, is token, and has had to struggle against enormous barriers. She has had to prove herself ten times better than her male competition. Like the black, she has had to pay the price of denying her identity. She is forced to identify with men, and unless she has a strong sense of her own oppression, she is likely to thumb her nose at her sisters who didn't "make it."

Like the black, her field of work opportunity is restricted by societal stereotypes. While a black man's job role is defined by white society's notion that he is a dumb, strong, sexy brute,[18] a female's job role is an extension of her role as wife, mother, sex object. How "glamourous" her job is, the ease of her work, the degree of servitude, her status and her salary depend on her looks, her education, her class. As an "extended" wife she can clean people's homes, empty bed pans in a hospital, or serve a boss in a luxurious office. As an "extended" mother, she can be a full-time babysitter for someone else's kids; she can teach kindergarten or she can become a child psychologist. As a sex object, she can become a street-walker, a high-class call girl, a barmaid, an actress, a dancer in a neighborhood honky-tonk, or an exotic fashion model. The "glamourous" jobs are the exception, not the rule. Everyone knows that the black man earns less than anyone else in this society; right? According to the 1964 Department of Labor Statistics, the median annual income for white working women is $426.00 less than that for black working men. The median annual income for black working women is $1611.00 less than for black working men. What really makes a career "glamourous" for a woman is not salary nor interesting work, but the chance to wear beautiful clothes, work in relatively pleasant surroundings, and, most importantly, the chance to meet successful, eligible, single men — so that she can marry and take on the equally glamourous role of "domestic engineer" — or is it domesticated engineer?

We are told that women are bad risks. They do not take their work seriously as men do. All they want is to get married and have babies. They require extensive pregnancy leaves. They take more sick leaves than men because of menstrual discomfort. They are, in general, less responsible. These statements may have statistical validity, but they are also self-fulfilling prophesies.

Since most "women's work" is dull and poor-paying, is it any wonder that a female prefers to leave her job as soon as possible? Is it surprising that she prefers to marry a man who will earn much more money and have much more status than she could ever hope to get on her own? A woman is trained to believe that her ultimate fulfillment must come through a husband and children, not through work. So is it really very surprising that she doesn't feel the same need to be successful in a career that men feel? Society makes it virtually impossible for a woman with small children to work; child-care services eat up almost the total salaries of many working mothers. Working in an office all day and doing housework in the evening is too much for most of us. The professional woman with children manages to solve her dilemma by passing her domestic chores on to a woman with less education and "class"; thus, the oppressed becomes the oppressor.

Finally, a society which resents giving females paid pregnancy leaves, which resents the fact that the woman may need a few more days sick leave a year than the average man, is a society based on profit and efficiency, not one based on human considerations. There have been few, if any, human societies which have not exploited their weaker members. Women are, in general, physically weaker than men, and they were, in the past, subject to debilitating pregnancies. We think that this is the main reason why there are only a handful of cultures where women enjoyed a rough equality with men.

Those who argue that since women have always been treated badly in human society, there must be some good reason for it, might just as well argue that because murder has always existed, it is a good thing. But, some embellish this argument by pointing to the behavior of animals. Female primates are submissive and male primates dominate. Thus, the reasoning goes, these roles are "natural" for human females. Those who argue for doing what comes naturally, however, seldom go so far as to refuse to live in heated buildings, preferring their own body warmth and would be very surprised if they were denied sexual access to females solely on the basis of their lack of physical strength — as it is with the baboons. Given the infinite variation of human culture and behavior, it is ridiculous that humans should live by the limited models provided by animals. Animals are too stupid to change their social conditions. People are not. The biological or historical argument for the natural inferiority of women is really an argument for the inability of human beings to create a just, humane society. Tom Paine wrote that the function of civil society is to redress the inequities of power found in the natural state. If women have been exploited throughout human history, it is because civil society has failed, not because females deserve this exploitation.

Working On Maggie's Farm

Today, in this most technologically developed of societies, it is a crime that people spend their lives at toil, in unending and un-rewarding drudgery, in suffocating boredom, just as it is a crime that people are poor. For the first time in human history, it is possible to think in terms of creative, serious, non-alienating labor for everyone, not for just a privileged elite. What do we mean by such labor? By unalienated labor we mean that people democratically control the conditions under which they work: no more bosses, hierarchies of control, high and low status occupations, no more management and no more managed. We mean that people control the uses to which the products of their labor are put. We want people to decide collectively what to produce and how to produce it so that we don't waste resources on advertising and military equipment. Instead, we want to produce: food for everyone, beautiful, well-made homes for everyone, decent public mass transportation systems, free and good medical care for everyone. In addition to being socially worthwhile, our labor should make full use of our human potential to be intrinsically challenging. Serious and creative work should be the birthright of every human being.

Under capitalism, all of us, men and women, are denied this birthright. The "free" labor market is a series of slots which people have to fit into if they wish to eat. The needs of corporations, not of people, determine what kinds of work are available, how much work is available, how much each type of work pays, what sort of work is most status-packed, the uses to which technology and automation are put. The labor market is highly stratified. Some jobs pay more and provide more status and security than others. Some jobs offer more fulfillment, more control over one's work, more power over the work of others.

As kids we were taught how to make it in America, and as adults we began an unending search for economic security, for status, for a little more power or a little less boredom. We mold ourselves to fit the needs of the "free" labor market, in order to survive. We sell ourselves and our talents.

Some of us sought careers which we thought were outside the money and status rat-race, that would give us a chance to serve humankind or to search for truth. We quickly learned better. Academicians, for example, far from being free scholars searching for truth, far from being educated beings who wanted to put their knowledge at the service of humanity, are, for the most part, merely servants of the state and big business. Social and political theorists use their talents to glorify the ideologies of modern-day capitalism, "free-world" democracy, and anti-communism. They teach their students to become intellectual snobs, to fear the "masses." They preach that all mass movements are inherently authoritarian, that social change must be gradual and piece-meal and managed by the "educated." They hide from their students the history of mass social movements — particularly the woman's movement — and radical traditions of thought. They pretend that all important change came about through the efforts of rulers and other assorted "great *men.*" Scientists offer biological and chemical warfare, bigger and better bombs, petite and specialized riot control weapons to suppress the mass movements that the theorists teach us to fear. Economists put forth schemes to insure that U. S. business will always dominate the economies of other nations. They produce plans which tell corporations how to make enormous profits "developing" the ghettoes. Political scientists design pacification programs to control the impoverished without fundamentally altering their condition. They tell the politicians which foreign military dictator, neutralist government, or pro-western hack to support, to insure that the country stays within the "free world." They tell the foundations which civil rights groups to fund to insure that black power only means black capitalism. Engineers, doctors, researchers of all kinds could be planning exciting, progressive advances for humankind: a cure for the common cold, cancer or muscular dystrophy, liveable cities, an end to air pollution. Instead the task of a good industrial researcher is to plan obsolescence. For example he takes a lightbulb which burns 10,000 kilowatt hours and makes it burn only 1,000 kilowatt hours so that the corporation can make a larger profit.

The university itself, for the faculty, is as competitive, as full of pressure, as full of mindless conformity as any major corporation. For the student it is little more than a place of indoctrination, of training for a more or less high status place in the labor market.

All of us, in whatever field, in whatever social class or caste, are pitted against one another in relentless competition, for each of our successes come at the price of another's failure. The New York teachers won their strike at the expense of black self-determination; we buy cheap grapes at the supermarket at the expense of starving, exploited, Mexican farm workers. Average Americans take luxurious vacations at the expense of Latin peasants. The skilled, white worker maintains his position at the expense of the black. The average man maintains his few privileges at the expense of the woman. Those who lose out are the most oppressed, found in the rubbish heap of this society. They haul its garbage for a few crumbs or sometimes they starve. It is a joke to speak of freely chosen, unalienating labor in such a context.

While such a system is dehumanizing to everyone, it is most dehumanizing to those who, because of caste, are kept from even participating equally in the rat-race. We don't believe that a business executive is more important than a secretary, both jobs are wasteful of human potentiality; most aspects of them are necessary only within a system of profit and exploitation. But the boss and his secretary, the man and the woman, are not in the same boat. The top executive makes one hundred thou, and the secretary makes one hundred; so, the definition of his work as more important, more serious, has teeth. The teeth are more than monetary. The secretary is subordinate to her boss. He controls her. Her work is in fact more alienating as well as less serious by definition. She has been trained to believe that she could never be anything so important as an executive. The fact that females are not considered capable of any work that grants status, respect — and in this society — money and relative power, takes its toll. This toll is not only economic, although the economic deprivations are real and horrible; it is exacted in terms of the dehumanization of an entire caste of people. It creates a sense of inferiority, the cultivation of a mentality which assumes that it is proper to serve and defer to men.

In order to overcome this sense of inferiority, we must fight for equal job opportunities for females. But our goal is not a society where females have an equal chance to become advertising executives, weapons experts, corporation presidents. While struggling for our own equality, we are also struggling to change a system which only provides alienating, boring, dehumanizing and harmful labor.

Strategy

"Your broom is a phallic symbol, you witch."
"On the contrary, my dear fellow, your phallus is a broom symbol."[19]

In her book, *The Second Sex*, Simone De Beauvoir talks about woman historically having been defined only in relation to man. In this essay we talk about women being the property of men, only having legitimate identity through men, and only working in the New Left on issues which men define as relevant. Oppressed people gain great power when they have gained consciousness of their oppression. But they gain their greatest power when they begin to demand changes to humanize their society in such a way as to affect their personal situation.

There is a radical movement for female liberation; it is still small but is growing rapidly, gaining momentum. For many of us, it is the most exciting and important thing that has happened in the Left. It is great to groove on other females, to take each other seriously, to argue about what concerns us deeply, to freely and seriously talk about sex, about love, about our lives and the myriad subtle and blatant ways that we are messed over. It is mind-blowing to feel sisterhood, to work together to rid ourselves of the mental rubbish, the false myths and stereotypes, the competitiveness, the unreal and alien categories that we inherited, that were forced upon us by the masculinely defined world. It is groovy to know that many females care about the same things, have lived through similar experiences, that our problems don't result from personal hang-ups, but from a screwed up society. It is exciting to know that together we can confront this society, that we can struggle together, support each other, sustain each other. Together we can study the history of our sex: the history of Amazons, witches, suffragists, female revolutionaries, all women. We can rescue that history from oblivion and consciously use it to help us make history.

How will we struggle? What will we fight against? What will we fight for? We need to develop strategies which allow us to get at the roots of our oppression, which allow us to attack the ideas, mythologies, folk-wisdom which keep females down. We need to attack each and every institution in this society which contributes to the oppression and subjugation of our sex: the schools, universities, corporations, advertising, the mass media, the church, marriage, singles' bars, labor unions, cosmetics firms, Wall Street, beauty parlors, welfare departments, homes for unwed mothers, women's prisons, the A.M.A., public and private "service" agencies, and the rest.

Each attack, each struggle for reform must be made in the context of a thorough, radical, and passionate analysis of women's oppression. The analysis must aim at exposing, clarifying, making vivid the many ways that society humiliates, oppresses, and exploits us because we are female. An ADC (Aid to Dependent Children) mother who receives welfare gets hostile and punitive treatment not only because she is poor but because she is female. She is a woman who may have made the mistake of enjoying sex and having babies as a result. It matters not to the welfare department that having children and loving them is the only fulfillment she may receive in life. The welfare recipient is interrogated: which of your children are illegitimate; does your husband ever come home; are you sleeping with another man regularly? They make demands of her: work at any menial task to earn any meagre salary; send your young child to a vague somewhere while you work.

At present, our movement is composed primarily of the daughters of the white middle class. Yet many of us come from lower middle class and working class backgrounds. Our commonality does not come from our "middle class" origins but from our radical rejection of the middle class values of this society. From our discussions about our differing backgrounds we have come to understand that females form a caste. All women in every social and economic class are given an inferior rank in that class simply because we are female.

The oppression of females, like the oppression of blacks, is not simply a form of social or economic class oppression and cannot be resolved by class struggle alone. Women must fight explicitly for their liberation — to break the caste system. That is the only way liberation will come about. Nevertheless, each of us is a member of a social and economic class and we suffer from the hardships and enjoy the privileges of that class. The form, degree, and even the content of our oppression as women depends to a large extent upon what class we belong to.

We recognize that the upper class woman, in spite of her economic independence, her servants, her luxury is still oppressed as a woman. She must conform to a stringent set of dictates concerning proper, refined, cultured, lady-like behavior. Yet we also recognize that the upper class woman contributes to the security of her class position by actively setting the standards and norms of feminity to which all women are supposed to aspire. Thus, she is our oppressor.

In America, the illusion of a "middle class" society is maintained by the pretense that we all participate in a common middle class culture. This culture, far from being democratic, is defined by the ruling elites. It is a culture of consumption and status, based on the premise that people derive a sense of worth and dignity by emulating the consumption behavior of those in the classes above them. Fashion trends, for example, are set by the upper class woman with her personal dress designer, exclusive beauty salon, private showings of haute couture from Paris and Rome. Even the long hair and the sandals of the "beats" and the bell-bottoms and love-beads of the hippies became the general fashion trends after they were seized by the upper classes as the "in" thing. Only the upper class is "free" to emulate the rebels; it has no higher class to imitate.

A struggle for women's liberation is both a class and a caste struggle because we are a movement from the bottom fighting at once domination by men and by the ruling class. We do not expect upper class women, in mass, to wage war against their class privileges. Our base must be among middle and working class women. On the surface it seems that the ADC mother (mother receiving welfare payments entitled, "Aid to Dependent Children") struggling to attain the most elemental necessities for herself and her children, and the suburban housewife, fed up with the comforts and the boredom of her life have little in common. The woman on welfare is constantly humiliated and punished for not having a man to support her. The suburban housewife has fulfilled her destiny and is expected to like it; furthermore, she is supposed to believe that she is a proper lady because she has a male provider. A woman has to make a deal in this society; that deal is marriage. There is social and economic punishment for the crime of not "hooking" a man. "The only difference between 'upright decent women' and mothers on ADC is that 'upright decent women' made a better deal for the same thing."[20] The same beliefs about the role of womanhood oppress them both.

We must destroy the images set by wealthy, glamourous, women and define anyone with a stake in perpetuating those images as our enemies. We must aim, like any revolutionary movement, at building a truly democratic culture which comes from ordinary women themselves and whose values are fundamentally opposed to the values of the ruling class.

Working class and lower class women are the most fundamentally oppressed women in our society in whatever role they assume — as wife, mother, worker. Yet in the absence of a revolutionary feminist movement, these women may see the solution to their problems as individually or even collectively attaining the comforts, security, and privileges of middle class women. Middle class women who understand the oppressive nature of their own situations are in an excellent position to "reject" the best that America has to offer its females. Yet, a solely middle class based feminist movement would end up only making things better for middle class women. We must be aware of the class content of our demands. For example, a demand for legalized abortion is not enough. We must demand free and safe abortions for all women. If legal abortions cost $600, the poor woman will still be forced to resort to knitting needles or shady practitioners. We must also demand that women have a free choice whether or not to have an abortion, so that the "social planners" who wish to limit the number of poor or illegitimate children who are born do not require abortions for lower class, black or unmarried pregnant females. Demands for an end to job discrimination must be accompanied by demands for free and good childcare facilities so that working class women's wages are not eaten up by the costs of child care. We must not demand equal access to the professions without also attacking the professions, demanding they serve the poor rather than lead, abuse or ignore them. We must develop our understanding of the differences in the oppression and exploitation of women of different classes and of Black, Latin, and Indian women as well as white women.

In our fight we must confront many bread and butter issues. We will attack unequal pay, restrictive labor laws, welfare abuse, job discrimination — all in the context of women's liberation. Many women are now involved in struggles which are in fact struggles for women's liberation although they are not self-consciously defined that way, such as welfare battles, insurgent union organizing of women. We will seek to develop alliances with these women so that we can learn from each other and fight together. Women must have economic independence if they are to be at all free from the enslavement of men. But simple demands for economic equality are not enough; we will not be satisfied with incorporation into the male rat race. If we only demand more bread and butter they will develop a machine which produces thousands and thousands of tons of plastic bread and butter. Then they will make us eat it.

We have to attack that "plastic" and we must attack it in a way that is real, in a way that speaks to the terrible quality of women's lives, that projects an alternative, a vision and moves females to fight for it. We cannot simply throw away our make-up and brassieres and proclaim ourselves liberated. Everyone knows, or should know, that liberation is never simple or easy.

In 1969, Darien-born, blonde, blue-eyed, pretty, perky, mini-

skirted, Mrs. Virginia Slim was caught in her newly decorated den, talking on her pink, princess phone, arranging an abortion for herself. Although she was 34 years old, married, protestant, with 2½ children, her husband reported her to the local judge who severely punished her by sentencing her to ten years in prison . . . you've come a long way, baby . . .

We do not think we have come very far at all.

We demand liberation from the necessity to be desirable and attractive to men. We demand new and cooperative forms for the pursuit of community and affection so that we do not have to spend our younger years in the wasteful, lonely and competitive pursuit of males. We demand detailed and honest reports of the harmful aspects of birth control pills. We demand effective, easily accessible, harmless and non-obnoxious methods of birth control. We demand that the same sort of methods be developed for men. We demand that new forms of living arrangements be explored: child raising communes, all women communes, mixed communes.

We are going to attack, mess up, foul, destroy the media and all other degrading institutions: no more beauty contests, no more playboy clubs, no more first lady, Miss America, Miss Clairol, Junior Miss, misfit, mystification, *Seventeen, Life, Time,* the *New Yorker,* brides' magazines, Faye Dunaway, Tuesday Weld, Marlon Brando, Jean-Paul Belmondo, *True Romances,* hair spray, fire engine red lipstick, My Sin perfume, false eyelashes, false breasts, mother and daughter dresses, avocado-colored kitchen accessories, fieldcrest patterned towels "that look like big red and blue bandannas," home economics courses, beauticians schools, secretarial schools, help-wanted women, no more Norman Mailer and Andy Warhol, Stokely Carmichael, *Ramparts,* no more feminine mystiques, no more abuse, no more shit.

We refuse to have our most private behavior, our most human and personal needs made degenerate and twisted by the dictates of a market society which must also convince men of its myths — that they be tough, "male," and monstrous and, lately, stylishly dressed.

Unless we can combat the complex of ideas, attitudes, social patterns, functions and expectations which keep people tied into the capitalist system, we cannot hope to build a popular, revolutionary socialist movement. We do not present women's liberation as the final crucial key in the struggle to take humanity out of the darkness in which it lives, nor do we claim that we will find the perfect tactic which will bring capitalism to its knees. We want our revolution to be in the context of a total revolution: we cannot be free while others are not. But we say to those others that they will not be free while we are not, and we will not work with any movement which does not treat us with dignity, respect and justice. The question of female liberation is not separate from political questions; it gets to the essence of all political questions. If a movement does not speak to all forms of oppression, especially when oppression hits at the very essence of human existence, then that movement cannot be truly socialistic.

The "new" society proposed by the New Left will not be truly new unless there is an end to male supremacy and chauvinism, as there must be an end to racism, imperialism, paternalism, capitalism. The conclusion is inescapable: we are going to fight for our own liberation, and develop and define a powerful ideology which tells us just what that liberation means, because our struggle is not going to end up like all the others: a new cigarette, perhaps, or a whole wardrobe of mini-skirts.

Notes

[1] We apologize to our sisters throughout the country for being so presumptuous as to speak for them, and regret that time did not permit circulation of the paper to allow for full discussion. We take total responsibility for all of the ideas stated here. But our thinking could not have progressed without the Chicago Writing Group which besides ourselves includes Heather Booth, Amy Kessleman. and Fran Rominsky and with discussions with our sisters from across the country.

[2] O'Neill, William L. "Feminism as a Radical Ideology," ed. Alfred F. Young. *Dissent: Explorations in the History of American Radicalism*, Northern Illinois Press, Dekalb, Ill., 1968, pp. 275–300.

[3] Jingle from a commercial television appeal, announcing Virginia Slim cigarettes, the cigarettes for women only!

[4] Kraditor, Aileen, *The Ideas of the Woman Suffrage Movement, 1890–1920*, Columbia University Press, N.Y., 1965, p. 1.

[5] *Ibid.*

[6] Carl Oglesby, Students for a Democratic Society, Nov. 1965 at Washington anti-war march.

[7] Held November 27–30, 1968, the conference of 150 radical women was aided by a grant from the Institute for Policy Studies.

[8] Jean-Luc Godard, commenting on his film *Masculine-Feminine*.

[9] Fieldcrest, 1966.

[10] Rainwater, Lee, *Working Man's Wife.*

[11] The alternative and letter appeared in the *Voice of the Women's Liberation Movement*, a newsletter produced in Chicago.

[12] Beatles Album — *Sergeant Pepper's Lonely Hearts Club Band*, "Do You Need Someone To Love?"

[13] American folk ballad.

[14] According to *May Day*, No. 10, a weekly periodical, this was the postage meter slogan of a private school, founded by a John Bircher, which is dedicated to teaching "the libertarian philosophy of individualism."

[15] American folk ballad.

[16] *Op. cit.*, Beatles.

[17] W. H. Masters & V. E. Johnson, *Human Sexual Response*, Little, Brown & Co., Boston, 1960, p. 15.

[18] Cleaver, Eldridge, *Soul on Ice*, McGraw-Hill Co., N.Y., 1968.

[19] New York Witch replying to a heckler in a guerilla theater demonstration in which the women's liberation witches' group (Women's International Terrorist Conspiracy from Hell), hexed Wall Street, all male bars, and other oppressive institutions.

[20] Mike Royko, in his column in the *Chicago Daily News*, in response to a housewife who counterposed "upright decent women" to mothers on ADC.

EVOLUTION OF THE ERAP ORGANIZERS

Richard Rothstein

As this is written, in January 1969, feelings of uncertainty and depression are common to many New Left activists. The mass anti-war sentiment which the movement created was never translatable into mass radical organization; though there were many local and national attempts. Anti-racist, anti-imperialist, even socialist consciousness has become the cultural definition of the country's most important intellectual communities. Yet there is no indication that these communities are about to transform themselves from a subculture to a revolutionary movement.

The regular appearance of new radical books and journals, rather than new projects and organizations, describes our situation. This book is an example. We are a cultural phenomenon, not a political threat.

The single most obvious exception to all this is the militant activities of organizers working on college campuses and in high schools. Yet there is little evidence that college radicalism has produced any long term organizational results. Graduates become part of the new culture, but not of the New Left. Additionally, much of the campus ferment is initiated and led by black students in support of racial demands. That the New Left owes undivided commitment to such struggles is undeniable; but the motion can be misleading if it encourages a belief in the growth of a radical white movement.

These university and high school incidents are numerous but isolated. Unconnected to each other except by the news media (underground included) and by cultural trend, the campus rebellions threaten only the deans and chancellors directly involved. If a radical strategy exists here, it is deeply implicit.

Faced with this situation, much of the New Left has become frustrated. It has also become more verbally revolutionary. As the verbal stakes get higher, so too does the commitment to militant (and sometimes romantic) ideologies. The New Left today is beset with the kind of factionalism that the 1930's Left produced.

Much of the openness and experimentalism that the New Left attempted in the early 1960's is now hidden. The factions, making few attempts to put their prescriptions to work, produce little concrete evidence of their worth. Where radical organizers are at work, they are generally out of touch with others to whom their experience should be communicated.

Yet many of the revolutionary conclusions of the New Left today were formulated in large part as a result of very public direct tests of earlier, more moderate, strategic and analytic hypotheses. In its early years, Students for a Democratic Society had clear, relatively moderate notions of how militarism and racism could be ended in American society. SDS attempted to put these ideas into practice, in part with its community organizing program, ERAP (Economic Research and Action Project). As the goals of the ERAP projects were found to be impossible to achieve, a new view of American society and strategies of change began to take form. This new view has contributed immeasurably to the present ideological stance of the New Left.

In this connection, a history of the ERAP projects may be useful today. This history does not imply criticism of any of the ideas or strategies of the present New Left factions. If anything, it tends to support desperation and militancy. But the fact that so much of our knowledge of American society and radical strategy is the result of conclusions from experimental tests of earlier ideas may suggest something. It may suggest that tactical errors may not be harmful to a young movement, that doubt may carry many of the benefits presently attributed to certainty, and that many factional battles in the movement could be solved by *encouraging* opponents to put their ideas into practice so their chances of success might be tested.

SDS established ERAP two days after the 1963 "March on Washington for Jobs and Freedom." We had a clear notion of how indigenous democratic organizations of the poor and the enemployed would contribute to social change in America and in the world.

SDS still believed in the possibility of change within the framework of America's formally representative political institutions. ERAP's goal was to stir those institutions, to create currents in American political life which would reverse the corruption of established liberal and trade union forces. It was believed that these forces, under pressure from ERAP and other "new insurgencies," would demand that resources be transferred from the cold war arms race to the creation of a decentralized, democratic, interracial welfare state at home.

Those of us involved in ERAP no longer focus on the arms expenditures of what we then regarded as an "equal blame" cold war — Vietnam and the Dominican Republic unmasked for us an obviously aggressive economic imperialism. We are now enemies of welfare state capitalism, with little faith or desire that the liberal-labor forces within this system be strengthened vis-a-vis their corporatist and reactionary allies. We view those forces — and the social "reforms" they espouse — as being incompatible with a non-interventionist world policy and as no more than a manipulative fraud perpetrated upon the dignity and humanity of the American people.

We owe these conclusions in large measure to four years of ERAP experience. In a healthy pragmatic style we tested an optimistic hypothesis about the limits of American pluralism. If ERAP failed, it was only because we were unable to conceptualize and test our subsequent hypotheses about America and the building of a movement to revolutionize it.

Community organizing was never valued in itself by SDS or its early leadership. Nevertheless many false debates occur between proponents of SDS and those of Saul Alinsky. Social workers, ministers and students have debated this issue in many forums in recent years. Alinsky-trained community organizers usually fault New Left organizers for raising false expectations in communities, for not subordinating personal political whims to winning victories that bring real change to local people, and for being undemocratic in not choosing issues around which a majority of a community can be mobilized. SDS answers by pointing out that since Alinsky's Industrial Areas Foundation enters a community only when sponsored by the local business and religious leadership, IAF organizers are not really democratic either.

While the charges are true, the debate is false. The purposes of ERAP and the IAF were so radically different, that an argument about comparative technique is misleading. The IAF attempts to create community change, ERAP was testing a technique for influencing national and international change. While substantive local improvements are goals in themselves for IAF community organizers, they are measured by SDS organizers in terms of their contribution to the building of political momentum. Local improvements can be won in areas of housing, merchandising, racial discrimination, administrative arbitrariness. Yet housing can be improved only within the limits of present mortgage, tax, and urban renewal structures. These limits are relatively narrow, and can be expanded only by changes in national policy, demanded by a national political movement. IAF technique is superior if change within the present limits is desired. The power of any urban community or small town, however, is relatively marginal in the creation of a movement to curtail American imperialism or to guarantee decent housing for all. It was to experiment with that marginality that ERAP was created.

The hypothesis of "new insurgencies" on which ERAP was originally based was set out in *America and the New Era*, a document adopted as policy by the 1963 SDS national convention.

This document assumed many of the arguments of two earlier 1963 statements. One, *The Triple Revolution*, was issued that winter by a coalition of liberals and radicals, including some leaders of SDS. It argued that three distinct contemporary crises were actually interrelated. The first was the "cybernation revolution" which promised drastic unemployment and vast leisure time. Second was the "weaponry revolution" which threatened to obliterate the world after wasting billions of dollars. And third was the "human rights revolution," encompassing both third-world liberation movements and the domestic civil rights struggle. The statement argued that funds could become available for construction of equalitarian societies at home and abroad only by a curtailment of the arms race; and only by a recognition of the new opportunities presented by automation could America meet the demands of the civil rights movement. Equal opportunity was meaningless in a shrinking job market; the racial problem could not be dealt with unless obsolete economic organization was replaced.

The second analysis was summarized by the Nyack Conference, held only a few days after SDS' adoption of *America and the New Era*. Ray Brown, an economist then working for the Federal Reserve System, predicted that even if new job opportunities were increased at twice the 1963 rate, by 1970 unemployment would be about 13% — and astronomically higher for the young and non-white. "None of the present or proposed (Kennedy Administration) programs," Brown warned, "amounts to more than economic tokenism."[1]

America and the New Era added to these analyses a condemnation of the "corporatist" make-up of the Kennedy Administration and of the anti-democratic, managerial solutions which it proposed. SDS described the "dilemma of labor and liberal forces" as a tendency to identify with this managerialism and a consequent loss of the American populist tradition:

Organized liberalism, however, must take at least part of the credit for America's political statemate. A style of politics which emphasizes cocktail parties and seminars rather than protest marches, local reform movements, and independent bases of power, cannot achieve leverage with respect to an establishment-oriented administration and a fundamentally reactionary Congressional oligarchy.

SDS felt that within these liberal organizations (below the "middle levels of leadership" there were still people who would support more militant action and more far-reaching solutions than those proposed by the liberal leadership in alliance with Kennedy. In part, some rank and file sentiment would be crystalized by the obviously worsening economic crisis.

But just as important, the populist impulse in labor and organizations of liberalism can be reinforced by the emergence of new popular movements . . . It . . . seems likely that popular upsurge in many communities . . . could provide a stimulus which would move labor to become an important center of power and leadership . . . a democratic insurgency could also provide for many middle class people a revived and inspiring vision that might stir them out of privatism.

Consequently, one of the chief goals of ERAP was to galvanize the quiescent populists in the ranks of labor and liberalism. The organization of the poor was, at least in part, a political public relations maneuver designed to speak to the imagination of stable America. The first two actions of JOIN (Jobs or Income Now), the original ERAP project in Chicago, were to sell apples, a symbol of Depression unemployment. JOIN members, recruited at an Unemployment Compensation Center, sold apples first in Chicago's

Loop, the center of white collar lower middle class employment; and second, outside a Pete Seeger concert where JOIN could be expected to reach the membership of most of the liberal organizations we were trying to inspire.

Joe Chabot, the first ERAP organizer in Chicago, spent much of his time speaking to trade unionists and other liberals about JOIN's activity — fund raising was a chief motive, but the political purpose was not overlooked. A JOIN advisory committee, made up largely of church action and leftist trade union staff, was put together. The chief achievement was the commitment of the United Packinghouse Workers Union to set up a recruiting office next to a South Side Unemployment Compensation Center while Chabot established an office next to a North Side Center.

Richard Flacks, writing the prospectus for the Chicago ERAP project, expressed this purpose by proposing that

leafleting and sales of apples at plant gates on pay-day will be an effective way of reminding employed workers of threats to their own job security, of arousing interest in JOIN, and of raising money. This effort will be considerably enhanced if local union leaders and shop stewards visibly assist the JOIN workers.

Flacks went on to argue that the JOIN advisory committee

can become a kind of representative body of those forces and groups within the city which can be mobilized for effective political action. Thus the members of this group, although acting as individuals, become centers of initiative within their own organizations and institutions. In this way, a city-wide political movement for full employment and a better Chicago may develop. . . . JOIN by itself cannot mobilize sufficient power to achieve social change; only a new alignment of forces in Chicago can bring this about.

Flacks was overly optimistic about the power of JOIN's example to create success for solitary leftists who had been struggling for years to fire their labor unions with a new commitment to popular struggle. Rank and file assistance for plant-gate apple sales never materialized; and the JOIN advisory committee was disbanded after one year — partly because of lack of interest, but partly also because the new Vietnam peace movement was beginning to absorb some of the advisory committee members' energies.

Nonetheless, "speaking truth to liberals" remained a key part of the ERAP organizers' program. JOIN organizers never turned down speaking engagements before liberal or church organizations (fund raising was again a key, but not sole, rationale), and made frequent attempts to involve liberals in JOIN's program — collecting clothing in the suburbs for a JOIN Christmas party, inviting the Fellowship of Reconciliation membership to do a door-to-door survey with JOIN members, accepting the most inefficient part-time volunteer arrangements from students who did not yet have a campus movement with which they could become active.

In many cases the students who did short term tours of duty on ERAP staffs returned to their campuses to lead university reform and Vietnam protest movements. They were, as a result of their contact with ERAP, reinforced in their radical impulses. The democratic, "participatory" tone of all ERAP projects has, in this respect, contributed to the emergence of a new popular movement (SNCC veterans returning to campus were, in the same fashion, much more important). But with respect to the labor movement and liberal membership organizations, no such success could be claimed. Before too long, the attitude of most ERAP organizers toward the organizations of labor and the liberal middle class changed from one of hope to one of the deepest hostility and contempt.[2]

In addition to a missionary effort to liberal-labor forces, the achievement of social change was a second goal of early ERAP. *America and the New ERA* emphasized that

by concentrating attention on domestic problems, and by demanding the concentration of resources on their solution, the poor and dispossessed of the United States (and every other country) could force a cessation of the arms race. The objective meaning of their demands for goods and social services would be to make continued support for massive military programs untenable.

"The creation of a series of short run social reforms" was one of the priorities to be used by ERAP director Rennie Davis in choosing localities for projects, according to a resolution of the December 1963 SDS National Council.

When it soon became obvious that full employment could not become such a *short range* reform achieved by ERAP, a new conception of organizing projects began to develop. At first, ERAP organizers defensively described this approach as GROIN — "garbage removal or income now." But by the end of 1964, the

GROIN approach was unanimous: even the Chicago project changed its name from J.O.I.N. to "JOIN — Community Union" and moved its office from next to the Unemployment Center to the poorest of the Chicago North Side neighborhoods.

The issues shifted from national full employment to more local issues: welfare administration, housing conditions, local city housekeeping issues. The original rationale for the shift was soon lost, however, as ERAP found local political structures to be so rigid that not even petty reforms, completely unthreatening to the national economic structure and distribution of resources, could be won. A documentary film, *The Troublemakers*, details the tragic story of the Newark ERAP project's inability even to win a traffic light at a dangerous intersection. Although ERAP projects developed a facility for winning specific welfare (public aid) grievance cases and for forcing, by rent strike, an occasional landlord to fix up, in all ten ERAP projects only two concessions were gained from the "power structure." In Cleveland, a free lunch program was granted to the children of aid recipients who attended public school; and in Newark, a locally elected war on poverty board was able to appropriate funds for a recreation center.

ERAP organizers soon began to look at local issues as an opportunity for bitter political education rather than for substantive reform which would begin to chip away at the defense budget and reinforce the ERAP organization with a reputation for success. Rennie Davis, in proposing a program for JOIN in October, 1964, stated that an essential ingredient was a demand which would probably be denied by local officials, but which those officials clearly could meet if they so desired. Such a demand "will involve people in experiences which develop a new understanding of the society which denies them opportunities and rights; and which will open possibilities for more insurgent activity in the future."

JOIN adopted the suggestion. It took an informal survey of its community and established that a day care center and a public spot-labor hiring agency were the two most cited needs. JOIN proposed these to the local War on Poverty Office and picketed that office in their behalf. Neither was granted.

The third area of ERAP objectives concerned our relationship to the civil rights movement in which we had all worked. For it had become clear, as a result of the experiences of some SDS leaders within the Northern Student Movement, that the role of white radicals could no longer be one of organizers in black communities

and in black organizations. The fact that most ERAP projects
were eventually placed in such communities was not originally
intended: the site of the Newark project, for example, was believed
to have been inhabited much more by working class whites than
was in fact the case by 1964.

In the long run, ERAP's purpose grew out of a concern that the
objectives of the civil rights movement would be frustrated by
working class white reaction. In part, therefore, our goal was to
form organizations in white communities which could counter the
"backlash." But also in part, SDS had concluded that the job of
white radicals was to provide the civil rights movement with white
allies who would reinforce the power of black demands. And what
better allies are there than those organized around their own needs
and demands, a functional and not merely charitable alliance?
The dream of a new interracial Populism was hard to resist.

In a paper written in the spring of 1964, *An Interracial Movement
of the Poor?*, Tom Hayden and Carl Wittman surveyed the civil
rights movement's lack of substantive achievement and the backlash mood developing in the white community. Hayden and Wittman categorized four types of then current civil rights demands:
demands to eliminate segregation (which have less appeal to lower
class blacks than would demands for improvement of present facilities); demands which assert symbolic Negro dignity but neither
achieve change nor alienate whites very much; demands which
are specifically racial, do not achieve very much, and potentially
alienate large numbers of whites (such as a demand to replace
white workers in particular jobs with black workers); and finally,
demands for political and economic changes of substantial benefit
to black and white poor alike.

Hayden and Wittman clearly favored the fourth type, and
argued for the organization of poor whites as well as blacks to make
such demands:

The alternative to an interracial movement is more likely to be fascism
than freedom. We are not convinced that violent conflict between
Negroes and lower-class whites will force the American establishment to
even make significant concessions, much less dissolve itself. The establishment might merely ignore the trouble and leave it to the local police, or it
might use troops to enforce order. In either case, poor Negroes and poor
whites will continue to struggle against each other instead of against the
power structure that properly deserves their malice.

The feared violence was not, of course, the then unpredicted mass violence of the black community against ghetto institutions, but rather the then common violence of working class whites against Negroes moving into new communities or attending previously all-white schools. The mass organization of whites around issues of their own oppression, ERAP hoped, would help blunt that violence.

It was also hoped that ERAP's organization of poor whites would influence the program of the activist civil rights movement (particularly SNCC, NSM, and to some extent CORE). It seemed clear to SDS that the civil rights movement was erring in not focussing on economic issues. The March on Washington for Jobs and Freedom made the connection between racial oppression and national economic crisis explicit. But the targets of SNCC, for example, still remained primarily symbolic: the integration of lunch counters, movie theaters, and so on.

ERAP hoped to urge its radical economic analysis of American problems on the civil rights movement in two forms: first, by focussing attention on economic targets and by organizing the poor around economic issues: unemployment, housing, welfare, poverty. But secondly, it was felt that the organization of the white poor would of itself be a step forward in the movement's radical consciousness: an interracial movement of the poor, in which whites too were demanding decent homes and incomes, could not help but demonstrate that civil rights acts which merely outlawed segregated accommodations missed the essential point. Rent strikers' demands could not be met by non-economic integrationist concessions.

It seems clear in retrospect that ERAP played a significant (though not sole, by any means) role in the subsequent redirection of the civil rights movements. In particular, ERAP's emphasis on urban organization around issues of poverty played a part in influencing the program development of CORE and SNCC since 1963. Much more important, of course, was the civil rights movements' own dynamic which, inspired by its own failures, created an economically oriented black power movement which swept over and past whatever marginal influence ERAP might have had. But ERAP's role was complementary and, in this respect, should be considered a success.

Not nearly so successful was ERAP's attempt to produce massive white allies in the struggle against white reaction. We clearly demonstrated that racism could be overcome by poor whites genuinely in motion around their own demands. JOIN in Chicago worked closely with black community groups elsewhere in the city, and the indigenous JOIN leadership, while Southern, was clearly committed to the abolition of racism as a political goal. JOIN rent strikes were coordinated with rent strikes in black communities; coordinated demonstrations of black and white welfare recipients occurred more than once at public aid offices.

But the desperately slow pace with which JOIN grew, the inability of ERAP ultimately to commit itself to more than a few white communities, and a national war economy which temporarily reserved poverty for the black masses, made the promises of white allies we had made earlier seem very unreal.

By the winter of 1965, ERAP organizers found themselves at a difficult juncture. The three major original purposes of ERAP — the inspiration of mass protest from the ranks of labor and liberalism; the achievement of specific, though minor, concessions to social reform; and the addition of significant numbers of poor whites to the ranks of the movement for Negro freedom — had been abandoned by most ERAP organizers. (JOIN's contribution of poor whites to the Chicago civil rights movement was in no sense numerically "significant.")

Whether ERAP was justified in concluding after so short a trial that the ranks of labor and liberalism could not be galvanized by the power of our example, and that the "power structure" was totally inflexible and unresponsive to demands from below is a question that must remain unanswered. Certainly these are conclusions now shared by most of the New Left.

More significant is: what new hypotheses replaced the old in the minds of ERAP organizers, and how did these organizers set out to test their new theories against political reality?

The question is difficult, because the shift from old premises to new was barely conscious or discussed. But by the winter of 1965, if you asked most ERAP organizers what they were attempting, they would simply have answered, "to build a movement."

There would have been little ideological disagreement about this movement's goals. SDS people were convinced that their movement must be one that could end racist exploitation and imperialism, collectivize economic decision making, and democratize and decentralize every political, economic, and social institution in America.

These goals, however, were long run — and quite appropriately not a problem of concern to ERAP organizers. The short run problems of beginning to build a movement which could some day have the power and skill to organize society in a humane, collective, decentralized and democratic fashion were much more difficult.

Not only were the alternative short run tactics and organizational emphases numerous; they were often in direct conflict with each other. The need to develop indigenous independent leaders, the need to awaken the country's (or the community's) sense of crisis by emphasizing dramatic confrontation, the need to polarize the community's attitudes in conflict, the need to create paradigmatic participatory democratic community institutions which illustrate to residents the radical vision: each of these needs seemed urgent to organizers, yet none could be initiated without destroying opportunities for the others.

This mutual exclusiveness of tactics was not merely a problem of limited time and energy. For each choice of tactics necessarily limited the future options of the organizing project. For example, a decision to emphasize the dramatic housing crisis to the city by a series of dramatic rent strikes and building take-overs might require fairly close direction by the SDS organizers. If publicity were important to the goal, timing might be crucial: the second rent strike in the series might need to be announced some days before the building tenants would be inclined to call it on their own. Not only would such a situation present an agonizing moral problem to the organizers; it was also the case that to choose to create the crisis (in the hope that by doing so official action on housing would be forthcoming) would also give the organizers a deserved reputation for heavy-handedness in the neighborhood. Future opportunities to encourage the development of indigenous leadership would be foreclosed.

Because ERAP organizers had no experience or standards with which to make such decisions, the ERAP structure dissolved in the spring of 1965. The rationale for dissolution was that the required decisions (whether a given project should attempt to emphasize rent strikes or leadership training classes, community newspapers or democratic day-care centers, community issues or the war in Vietnam) depended too much on specific local information which organizers from other projects could not hope to have. In fact, however, nobody had any experience in making such decisions even within a project. This situation was so demoralizing that no two ERAP organizing staffs sat down to evaluate and discuss their work after March, 1965.

It was probably true that a national organization of half a dozen local organizing staffs could not be a forum for working out such difficult problems of movement building. Those local ERAP staffs which continued to survive began to hope for the creation of regional unions of organizers (including ERAP organizers, campus leaders, Latin American and black community organizers, professional union insurgent leaders, etc.) which could assist individual projects in making such decisions. In a few ERAP projects, staff was assigned to work on the development of regional groups. In Chicago, a regional "union of organizers" met for a year. But nowhere did a regional organization develop rapidly enough to assume the burdens that ERAP workers needed assigned to it. A new framework within which organizing priorities could be set, attempted and evaluated was never developed. In the three and a half years after the disbanding of ERAP, projects foundered and disappeared. Some, at best, achieved unanticipated success.

One characteristic of projects in these three and a half years has been a regular re-evaluation and shifting of direction. JOIN, to use the example already given, engaged in a rent strike campaign which had the potential of creating dramatic crisis or new institutions of local democratic control (tenant councils) through tenant-landlord collective bargaining agreements. But instead of seeing the implementation of these agreements (where achieved) completed, and instead of nurturing the tenant councils into genuine democratic bodies, JOIN organizers adopted new organizing priorities soon after the rent-strike movement had begun. They began to emphasize ideological training for the handful of potential leaders in JOIN, the creation of a newspaper to increase community consciousness of conflict, and the development of democratic block clubs. The rent strike campaign was abandoned.

Around any given activity, there was also uncertainty about organizing goals. Was welfare grievance activity undertaken to maximize the number of grievances actually won for public aid recipients in order to expose (and, in part, obligate) these recipients to a radical, inter-racial, anti-war organization? Or was its purpose to develop a core of recipient leadership which was skilled in the administration of a democratic group or in the processing of grievances for other recipients? Since the development of such an indigenous leadership group could only proceed very slowly, it was in conflict with the first alternative which permitted staff organizers themselves to handle a large number of grievances rapidly and efficiently. A third purpose might be to dramatize actual conflict at welfare offices — getting in public fights with caseworkers, belittling the offices' authority, picketing and screaming in front of public aid headquarters. Such tactics, through newspaper publicity or the impact it made on recipients who were present, might prepare fertile ground for future organizing and consciousness; but it too might sometimes conflict with the efficient handling of grievances or the quiet development of indigenous recipient leadership.

Beacuse ERAP organizers were generally unclear about the meaning of these alternatives, they often shifted their emphasis from one to another, and then back again. The result was too often a failure to accomplish any of the possible movement-building purposes; if one was accomplished, it was usually inadvertent.

Lack of clarity about tactical alternatives was only one reason for the constant shift of direction on the part of community organizing projects. Another was frustration. If rent strike and tenant organizing was difficult and frustrating, it was always possible to develop a political rationale for abandoning it. It was decided, for example, that the ideological training of potential leadership was more essential at this time to the building of a movement than was the development of conflict-stimulated tenant councils.

A convincing political analysis could always be made for such a shift — complete with demonstrating how the shift remedied historical errors of the Left since the nineteenth century. But soon, frustration with the new direction would give birth to another equally cogent political rationale. And yet another direction would be embarked upon.

If organizing staffs had continued to be responsible to a larger group of radicals, such shifts would have been much more difficult. If the JOIN staff had been responsible to the radical movement in Chicago (or earlier, to ERAP) for the development of tenant councils in uptown Chicago, a change in that responsibility would have required a more detached and delayed debate with the Chicago movement (or ERAP). But in the absence of such an organizational context political programs could change as quickly and as irresponsibly as the whims of the organizers. And since the success of any program, whether leadership training or rent strike develop-

ment or massive welfare grievance victories, takes longer than the
development of an organizer's frustration, often no program was
given a chance to succeed.

The isolation of individual organizing projects also led to the
erosion of ERAP's earlier commitment to experimental organizing
and the pragmatic development of theory. In isolation, each
project came to develop an exaggerated sense of its own importance. Not feeling itself to be part of an experimental tactically
variegated movement, each project acted as though it bore the
burden of history on its shoulders alone. Even when the perception of new political imperatives was not simply the product of
frustration, such perception had to result in new directions, leaving
unfinished business behind. A project could not decide that a given
task was important, without itself dropping everything else to
effect that new imperative. Thus, if JOIN was involved in the
training of welfare recipient leadership, and reasonably decided
that it was politically important to focus public attention on the
arbitrariness of caseworkers, it could not propose that a different
organizing project assume responsibility for attention-getting welfare demonstrations while JOIN continued to experiment quietly
with creating indigenous leadership. In the absence of any multi-
project structure, a division of political labor was inconceivable.
Any project had to sacrifice its ongoing activities to whatever
seemed the highest priority of the moment.

How could a project experiment with factory organizing, or consumer organizing, or draft resistance organizing, or even with
leadership training in such a context? Experiments produce new
information for a movement and its organizers. Experiments do
not necessarily produce mass movements. But in the absence of a
broader structure, with the burden of movement building borne
subjectively by each project, experiments could not be risked.
Each organizer judged his own worth and value by the extent to
which he built a section of that movement. If a project experi-
mented with working class draft resistance, and failed, to whom
could the organizers give the benefit of their experience? In the
absence of a mandate from a larger group, political experiments
are much too risky — not only to the future of the movement but
to the organizers' self esteem.[3]

The ERAP structure was established to test particular hypotheses about American society. Its conclusions after a very short
period of testing are now commonplace in the movement — that

established liberal-labor forces are not likely to activate their now passive memberships for mass radical action; that the local and national governing classes in America are too rigid to respond to grass roots demands for reform, even if these reforms are rational for the maintenance of the long term power of those classes; and that a meaningful alliance between lower class whites and blacks is a long way off.

When these hypotheses were abandoned, the ERAP structure suffered a similar fate. This was as it should have been, for the ERAP structure could not have dealt with the new problems that organizers committed to building a long term revolutionary movement faced.

Ultimately, the most important contribution of ERAP may be the hundreds of student volunteers who passed through the projects as organizers, some for long and some for short periods of time. Many of these students returned to campuses and led the Vietnam peace movements and student power struggles that occurred in the years immediately after ERAP. Others remained in ERAP projects until they collapsed, leaving indigenous community based welfare action or poverty council groups in the ghettoes where ERAP organizers worked. But many others moved on to other communities, to attempt to experiment with tactics that didn't really have a chance in the political atmosphere of the original organizing projects. Some have attempted factory organizing, high school teaching and organizing, lower middle class consumer organizing, electoral action, draft resistance, servicemen's anti-war activity, community Vietnam protest, community schools, trade union activity, or street gang work. Recruits from the student community have joined the original ERAP organizers in many of these new organizing experiments. Yet the new experiments are unconnected; tactical hypotheses are barely formed or explicit; no organized means of sharing the resultant knowledge exist. The student movement to whom many of these organizers held an original allegiance is becoming more dogmatic, factionalized and committed to jargon, less tolerant of organizers who wish to experiment in ways that deviate from the untested assumptions of the factions.

The opportunities for participation in local organizing projects of all kinds is as great now in the New Left as it has ever been. Whether the New Left can collectivize this variety of experience in such a manner that we learn from the old and not fear to try the new — this is at least one of the tasks facing us today.

Notes

[1] The Nyack Conference led directly to the establishment of an organizing project among unemployed Hazard (Ky.) coal miners, a project which affiliated with ERAP when it was created some months later.

[2] In one respect, ERAP projects and rhetoric had a very deep impact on labor and liberal organizations. It is certainly true that the liberal-labor programs of community development and "community action projects" which began in 1964–65 were influenced very heavily by SDS and ERAP. The rhetoric of participatory democracy (in ERAP, "let the people decide") transformed the War on Poverty in its middle stages, the Citizens Crusade Against Poverty, the Peace Corps, and the curricula of some of the major academic social work schools. In 1966 and 1967, ERAP organizers were quoted and used by VISTA, for example, for highly paid consultant work. ERAP organizers did this work both for the money and for the opportunity to reach VISTA volunteers who often, unlike their superiors, took the rhetoric seriously. Some later joined ERAP staffs or similar New Left projects after leaving VISTA.

Thus, one of the lasting results of ERAP might have been to provide liberalism with a more sophisticated rhetoric of co-optation. This may not be an insignificant or negative achievement. One of the dangers for establishments involved in the careless use of democratic rhetoric is that the ruled sometimes take the rhetoric seriously. The New Left itself probably owes its origins in the early 1960's as much to this phenomenon as to any other.

Nonetheless, the provision to liberalism of a new rhetoric of co-optation was never a conscious goal of ERAP organizers. The use of ERAP rhetoric by the United Auto Workers elite in the Citizens Crusade Against Poverty is a far cry from the mobilization of the UAW rank and file to mass protest.

[3] One crucial problem encountered by ERAP projects with which this article has not dealt is the problem of personality conflicts on organizing staffs. It goes without saying that in many cases, the problems of ERAP projects in choosing goals and tactics were reflective of personality conflicts.

GETTING BY WITH A LITTLE HELP
FROM OUR FRIENDS

BARBARA AND ALAN HABER

The Radicals in the Professions Conference was a response to an essentially personal crisis that is widespread among people in the movement: the crisis of remaining radical beyond the college or graduate school years, or beyond the two year initiation period into the movement.

This is not to say that the crisis is politically insignificant. The New Left has mobilized a large number of people over the past five years. But the work of building a radical movement that can be successful is far from done. It cannot be done only by students serving two year hitches, or by a hundred or so "thirty year men" struggling on in organizational bureaucracies or urban ghettos.

The personal crisis and the needs of the movement intersect. The movement is the focus of moral reference for post-college radicals, and must therefore be a part of their personal "salvation." And the movement has a large number of unspecified tasks to do over the next decade. So far it has not been able to use its available pool of people to do those tasks. The result has been an under-effective politics and a growing number of movement people in private crisis: moving into establishment positions and cynicism; trying to do isolated and peripheral acts of radicalism inside or outside of professions; or clinging to the ghetto with a diminishing sense of political meaningfulness.

But while it is clear that the problems of the movement and the crisis of the individuals are connected, it is not yet clear whether a solution can be found that encompasses both. The Radicals in the Professions Conference was the first collective attempt to seek such a solution.

The official focus of the conference was of course political. Partly this focus is a ritual of legitimization. Partly it indicates a recognition that the personal hangups cannot be solved in non-political terms. Partly, but only partly, it reflects the honest priority of the participants in the conference. Yet, if the conference is measured in terms of political accomplishment — new analysis, new strategy, new organization, new program — then its success must be judged as minimal. Most of the participants, however, seemed to think the conference was a good, even an excellent one. What the conference did was to expose the common need of the participants, to change it from a private, half-admitted thing to a shared, articulated experience. Its most important accomplishments were that it created an embryonic sense of comradeship, established a minimal form of ongoing communication, raised the level of commitment, and reduced the sense of isolation.

The people who came to the conference were of many kinds and many histories: radicals who work in professions or plan to; non-professionals who are no longer sure what to do outside of mainstream institutions; people whose career choice was made on non-political grounds and whose growing political concerns create a schism between work and self; people who chose professions because they thought they could be politically effective within them and are now at various stages of struggle or disillusionment. There were doctors, lawyers, social workers, teachers, planners, clergymen, journalists, intellectuals and movement organizers. Most of them were in their late twenties or early thirties: trained but not yet established.

But regardless of background, most of the participants expressed a common set of questions and mood of frustration: "It's hard to be radical for long — nothing happens. How shall we live? Where is the revolution? How do we measure and aid its coming?" They were people who had, by themselves or in groups, been seeking answers for a long time, but had not found any; people who felt to some degree that they were failing and who were anxious not to fail; people young enough to change but perhaps too rooted or uncertain to change by themselves. There was a deeply felt need to be politically effective. And among the bona fide professionals, at least, there was a great deal of guilt: for having "opted in"; for wearing a suit; for having given up some of the badges of opposition; for making a living; for having had too little success as radicals-within-professions.

The sense of crisis that people brought to the conference comes out of real conditions of their lives. On the one hand, many of us can no longer tolerate psychologically the demands of orthodox jobs or the training they require. Radical consciousness has produced a painful awareness of the personal emptiness and social evil of most traditional career patterns — even those not directly involved in making and administering policy for government, the military and industry. The movement has created a generation of people who expect their work to be what most jobs in our society are not: radically relevant; personally challenging and expressive; free from bureaucratic control; open to spontaneous innovation.

On the other hand, once we recognize the unviability of an orthodox career line, we are left in the cold. The alternatives which have been created by the movement, and by radical generations before us are too narrow, too limited and too unsuccessful. There are three action alternatives open: we can take establishment jobs and seek other outlets for our human and political needs; we can "drop out" and work for the movement; or we can try to transform our professional roles from ones supportive of the status quo to ones that use their location to undermine it.

The first alternative, to take a non-political job and become avocational radicals, we have learned is a dead end. Politics cannot be sustained if they are not expressed in what we spend most of our time on. We cannot be radicals on weekends and evenings if all day, five days a week, we function as hacks or cynics or apologists. We will be either constantly at war with our jobs or constantly at war with ourselves. Which means that either we get fired or our politics change and we learn to "fit in."

But the second alternative is even more problematic. Working directly for the movement has great psychological attractiveness: it is uncompromising; seen as legitimate by those whose opinions we most value; provides a maximum of camaraderie; is encumbered by a minimum of formality and financial potentiality. But it has not worked. For most of the people that the movement has reached and changed, the movement has created too limited a range of jobs, using too limited a range of skills, and provided too limited a range of personal satisfaction and financial support. If we work for the movement — as now defined — we can be organizers, usually in an urban ghetto or low wage job setting; we can work in an organizational office; or we can be "principled amateurs" or freelance intellectuals and charismatic leaders. Only a tiny fraction of those who have been active in the New Left are able to remain in these roles for more than a few years.

Organizing simply burns people out. Working in ghettos requires a dogged perseverance and a faith in its political effectiveness that few people have been able to sustain. It also requires
skills and preferences that few of us have or seem to be able to get
on-the-job, while it does not use many of the skills and preferences
that we do have. People working for the movement in ghettos
shove the discontents and questions under the rug for as long as
possible, then crack and leave.

Office work, on the other hand, is menial and boring. It is the
movement work that most resembles the stereotype of the bureaucratic box, which is after all what most of us are rebelling against.
For a time comradeship and power compensate, but when friends
disperse and power is lost then bureaucrats depart.

The third movement role is perhaps the most satisfying — at
least for some. It comes closest to the personal ideal that many of
us share with artists and hippies: it is autonomous, yet responsive
to a group of comrades; it is self-defined and therefore matches
personal inclination as perfectly as any job ever can; it can change
as the sense of political need or personal preference changes; it
allows peripheral participation in office and organizing work which
means that it avoids identification with middle-classness. It provides a kind of financial and status gain that is most rewarding to
movement people, and at the same time most morally acceptable:
income remains low, life style bohemian, but there are paid travel,
royalties from books and articles, opportunities to teach and to
speak, entry into the rooms of the powerful of the Left and Right.
Most people in the movement would probably choose this over all
lives. But most have come slowly and painfully to realize that
they do not have the qualities to make a go of it. "Principled
amateurism is the luxury of the brilliant," one conference participant put it. The principled amateur life in the movement, as the
life of the artist, is a viable possibility only for those with extraordinary talent, intelligence, self-confidence, sense of opportunity,
autonomy, and self-mythologizing ability. In addition, it is open
only to those who are able to get personal satisfaction from leadership, writing, being a public representative, and travelling.

The combined effect of these three role possibilities within the
movement is to create a model of the radical life that most radicals
cannot emulate. People at the conference were in essentially that
position. They had been part of the movement often as avocational
radicals while pursuing student or post-graduate work, and now

when long term vocation has become an issue they could not fit in. They were struggling with the third "career alternative": to enter some kind of professional role, something that they could feel would be personally viable, and to seek to transform that work and relate it to the movement, make it into a political vocation.

The struggle is complicated by the fact that people who cannot find a role within movement possibilities often feel worthless, bitter, defensive; and those who do function in movement roles often have a self-righteous arrogance toward other radicals.

The point that must be insisted upon, and which often has not been, is that people caught in the bind between the limited jobs of the movement and orthodox careers are often as dedicated and as "radical" as those who are more successful at "making it" within the movement.

As discussion progressed, two major barriers to the solution of this vocational bind became evident. The first was the problem of language, of the moral connotation of words which has developed on the Left. We lack a vocabulary in which to define our problems and our position in the movement. The vocabulary we have is too narrow, seems continually to put us outside the movement, to force a division and antagonism between our political commitments and our personal needs. The second problem was one of analysis and strategy. It is simply not clear what to do, what constitutes radical politics over the long run, what is relevant. Movement political thinking is too abstract or underdeveloped as a guide for action and life choice, and our own thinking is still too personal and pragmatic to produce a more adequate view of strategy within which we can direct our work.

The Problem Of Language

The movement is the source of our moral and political vocabulary. But the experience of the movement — the post 1960, mostly student, mostly white, New Left — has been too limited to provide us with an adequate vocabulary: the struggle out of the middle class and into political opposition has been defined and circumscribed through programmatic focus on issues of poverty, material deprivation, and by identification with "third world" guerrilla revolutionaries, in the hills or the ghetto.

The white movement has been a student movement of people with few personal, private responsibilities, no families, no children; people for whom subsistence living constitutes no lasting sacrifice; people who have no expertise outside of the movement role situation, but who would be able to attain it easily at any time in the future; people whose participation in politics has been mobile and episodic; people who are very young. The language created by this movement has been the language of political conversion and of young people breaking loose from society.

The people at the conference represented the first generation of New Radicals faced with the problem of creating a language that will define terms in which to grow older and persevere without returning to the slots that have been reserved for us. The current language of the movement keeps us from solutions because it limits the terms of issues, deals with situations not like our own, often sets up false definitions, associations, cleavages.

1. In movement vernacular, "middle class" is a broadly inclusive epithet. It defines everybody who earns more than subsistence and works within "the system." Professionals are automatically termed middle class. Social location and income are assumed to determine absolutely a life style that is careerist, acquisitive, status climbing, and consumption-oriented. And it is assumed to determine a political style that is reformist, compromised, liberal. This vocabulary prejudices the efforts of radicals working in professions to create new definitions of life style, professional goals and values within social locations traditionally identified as middle class; who are trying to demonstrate that radical work can go on in professions and that an ongoing functional participation in a radical movement can be maintained by people working in established institutions.

The experiment may prove that being a professional makes no sense for a radical; but it is an important experiment and should not be precluded or impeded by a biased vocabulary.

2. The movement has created a definition of "ideal political man" which serves the binding function of myth in the radical community. For "political man" choices are based on a calculation of political utility — he puts himself where he is needed; he gets his rewards only from the movement; he is pure of all material and personal needs that cannot be met by the movement. While nobody would take this ideal type literally, it plays a crucial role in defining the expectations, obligations, commitments and terms of comradeship that make political activity existentially meaningful.

The problem with the current notion of ideal political man is that although it seems to work as a means of unifying personal rebellion and political opposition for young people just entering the movement, it creates dysfunction among the older people in the movement. After the initial conversion period the myth ceases to correspond to the experience of people. As personal limitation, inclination, passion, and talent reassert themselves, and as the practical problems of living on thirty dollars a week intensify, radicals find that they are forced to explain natural behavior and worries as though they were exceptions, departures, aberrations.

The movement has no language to give legitimacy to the problems of people preparing realistically for the long haul. The myth of the ideal political man places growing numbers of radicals outside of the movement and hence outside of the political community. It creates radical "push outs" just as the school system does. People who are unable to approximate the ideal type see themselves, and are seen, as backing down from an earlier commitment; becoming less radical, less part of "the movement."

3. The movement definition of "political work" is narrow. Political work is work that fulfills a strategic purpose. Yet the definition of "strategic" is a crude one. The movement does not have a broad systematic view of tasks necessary to a movement of radical change. In the absence of strategy, work priorities tend to be justified either by a direct confrontation with a key part of the power structure, or by a highly militant style expressive of opposition.

Nobody disputes the importance of direct political confrontation or symbolic opposition, though the substitution of style for strategy is problematic. But direct confrontation is not a sufficient basis for justifying radical work. The movement needs, and movement people are doing, many jobs whose value is not primarily that they produce direct confrontation: they are creating models of good practice; analysing the social reality; procuring information; providing service to the movement; reaching at various levels potential constituencies. Much of this work goes on outside of organization. It is sometimes contained within the practice of a profession itself, and often it involves a great deal of individual rather than collective effort.

The problem is that the language of the movement tends to denigrate such efforts; to see their practitioners as "second-class radicals." This implicit stratification undercuts the sense of comradeship which is the basic cohesive force of the movement.

4. The movement has a narrow purist view of "motivation," a view which equates the desire to work in a profession with the orthodox careerist motivation. There is no doubt that "professional careerism" is a weapon of the status quo to confuse and co-opt opposition.

Middle class children are taught to value "success": wealth, security, status, order, propriety, and carefully selected forms of achievement. And they are taught to fear the opposite. Anxiety over success-concerns is a bulwark against radical consciousness and action. Most whites in the New Left were raised to hold these aspirations. It is valid that we be suspicious of our own motivations in pursuing professions.

But "middle class aspirations" are not the only reasons why people want to teach, practice medicine, do intellectual work, be artists. There are "good" reasons for wanting to develop a particular skill, or practice a particular craft. And even if the initial selection of a career and acquisition of skills was "contaminated" there is no reason to assume that motivation cannot be transformed and that skills once acquired cannot be put to important social use.

The response of the movement to the idea of profession, or craft, or specialized skill, is too often to regard it simply as an opting for privatistic gain and fulfilment, and as an abandonment of radical commitment.

There is little recognition that decent motives toward professions exist and that the attempt by radicals in professions to invent and act out modes of practice that are infused with radical purpose is both valid and valuable.

The effect of this response is to inhibit communication with people practicing in a profession and to undermine the process of giving political definition to professional work.

5. The word "poverty" also creates a problem for radicals in professions. The experience of the movement is one of voluntary and involuntary poverty. Money is an important distinction between those in the movement and those who are greedy or have been bought. Radicals who earn more than subsistence share material identity with the ambitious and have sold out. And because they do not share the state of poverty they are outside the psychological community that the mystique about poverty has created in the movement. Poverty is thus a de facto prerequisite to full status in the radical community.

It has become difficult to talk about money in the movement. The mystique of poverty creates a defensiveness and withdrawal among those who are not poor and who are reluctant to be poor, and a self-righteousness and suspicion among those who are poor. There is no easy solution to the very real problem of allocation of available resources. But it would be unfortunate if viable solutions were to be blocked because we are unable to demystify the political sanctity of poverty.

The language problem creates a psychological oppression that makes it difficult to see our way through the vocational bind. There is no easy way to get rid of this obstruction to problem solving. Language is rooted in experience. Until our experience and the work we do becomes more central and relevant to the movement, language will remain a problem for us.

The psychological oppression that the movement has inadvertently created is not the central problem facing radicals. But it is the major obstruction to finding creative solutions to what is the central problem: namely how to function effectively as a radical over a long haul. "Self-fulfilment" of individual radicals is not the goal the movement must strive for: finding ways to use people to create a movement of radical social change is. That will mean, inevitably, that as radicals we will often have to do things we are not good at, and do not enjoy. It means that we ourselves cannot be our final worry. The tension between self and community is inherent in our politics. We are part of a community of political purpose to which we have major obligations.

But it is fruitless to ask people to focus their lives on obligations that they cannot fulfil well, that do not give them self-fulfilment. And it is a delusion to expect that abstract political discipline will substitute for existential satisfaction in the long run. Political strategy and the demands of the community upon the individual must be the guide toward individual choices. But the present stalemate of so many radicals demonstrates that one element in any strategy and any set of community demands has to be an acceptance of individual needs and idiosyncracies. When a political movement tries to objectify its members, to deal with only a part of them, or a mythical version of them, then the members become fragmented, cracked.

The Problem Of Strategy

Beyond breaking down the irrational barriers to problem solving, what is most needed is an overall picture of how the political changes we seek might come about. We can give political meaning to personal choices only if we have a sense of the political context in which we are operating. Actions, however exciting, innovative, creative or expressive, are important politically only when they are carried out with a view to some broader strategic purpose, only when they are designed to lead to something, to make possible further acts. What the important acts are and what leads to what are questions of strategy.

By the second day of the conference, participants were beginning to shift from subjective concerns to these more political questions. How will the revolution happen, if it is to happen at all? Where is it important to be? What is it important to do? How do you choose among options? The difficulty in dealing with these questions is simply that the movement does not have a commonly understood and accepted strategy, and that people working in professions for radical change have done little strategic analysis of their work. Thus there were really no criteria in terms of which to talk concretely about political vocation in the professions.

The conference was not structured to deal with strategy, hence assumptions about strategy tended to remain implicit in suggestions for action projects, rather than becoming the explicit basis of deciding on action projects.

In the conference discussion, underlying program proposals and occasionally stated explicitly there seemed to be three rough models of strategy that operated:

Model One: The "New Working Class." Teachers, technicians, certain professionals are seen as having key roles in maintaining the economy. They are an exploited class, alienated from the end product of their labour, their skills perverted. They are key because their skills give them the power to stop the economy, and because the objective conditions of their work create the precondition for subjective radical consciousness. They will form the basis of a revolutionary party (as the old working class was to do in the classical Marxist revolution).

Professionals should work within key professions to organize political unions making radical demands that cannot be met within the existing structure of society. The character of these demands — for control of the work situation — will coalesce these unions into a revolutionary party. The criteria for choosing key professions remain unclear: which professions actually do have essential, irreplaceable economic functions and which are irrelevant; are the only "essential" functions directly economic? But the role of the radical professional is clear: to organize an opposition union and raise demands that cannot be met without a massive political upheaval.

Model Two: Economic Crisis. The revolution will occur through an inevitable breakdown of the economy. Key agents of change will be the underclass and majority sections of the working class who suffer deprivation and exploition or who are caught in the squeeze and are no longer able to maintain an on-going role in the collapsing system.

Political education is the central job of the radical. Either through rigorous ideological education, or through a more open-ended process of learning-through-doing, the role of the radical is to organize self-conscious political cadres by raising radical consciousness among those whom economic theory predicts will be the victims of the collapse of capitalism.

Intellectuals and professionals can have central vanguard roles, but only insofar as they locate themselves within the under- and working-classes as organizers and educators. Otherwise they are fellow travellers having supportive roles: providing services, funds, protection, acting as buffers, neutralizing attacks on the movement. In these support roles, the tempo of need is set from the outside, by the core movement. The professional is to be in readiness when needed. His politics have no strategic importance in directing the main line of his professional work.

Both of these models assume that "the revolution" will be the product of some kind of "class struggle" led by a self-conscious, unified political movement of total opposition. Their strategy is to organize in the key areas that intersect the key contradictions of the political economy, to exacerbate those contradictions until they lead to a general economic and social crisis in which a massive shift of psychological allegiance takes place from the old order to the new. On the basis of this shift of allegiance, a revolution in political power will be achieved.

Both models focus theoretically on two problems:

1. Identifying the key areas for organization and the key agents of change: e.g. the black ghetto, the white underclass, the industrial working class, the new working class.

2. Identifying the key issues or contradictions to exacerbate: e.g. poverty, exploitation, imperialism, alienation.

Once a transfer of power is accomplished, institutional transformations in all social locations will be brought into being through democratic decision. Reformist, experimental, communitarian, utopian efforts at institutional change, innovation prior to the revolution are bound to fail. At best their gains will be peripheral and more likely their struggles will lead to a narrowing definition of objectives, co-optation and abandonment of the central radical task of building political opposition.

Model Three: Pluralistic Revolution. This view stands in contrast to the class struggle models. It sees no present basis for class revolution: the adaptive, co-optive, ameliorative, manipulative, repressive powers of the system are too great. Nor does it see economic breakdown in the international capitalist system as inevitable or even likely. The revolutionary situation, if it does occur, will be created slowly, without a single decisive struggle and transfer of power: by mobilizing small enclaves of radicalism in a variety of social locations, by changing people's consciousness, by creating alternative ways of living, by extending people's definitions of the possible. This model is characterized by agnosticism about the precise criteria for choosing social location, the form the revolution may ultimately take, and the constituencies who could form the basis for a revolution.

Disaffection will be on issues of quality of life and work as well as economic deprivation and political disenfranchisement. Life-style issues, even when accompanied by affluence, are seen to be legitimate concerns of a radical movement. The role of the radical is to create programs which lead people beyond their subjective experience of discontent toward a radical analysis of society and into struggles for root changes. Such struggles will not be successful until there is enough strength on the Left to change the whole system at once. But the escalating confrontation with power around a variety of issues in a variety of social locations is seen as the major tool for drawing isolated problems into radical focus, and for radicalizing new constituencies. Eventually a number of disparate segments of the movement will have to coalesce. But how and when that will happen is not foreseeable.

Within this view the range of jobs for radicals is wide and partially undefined. Certain central tasks are accepted: direct organizing and office work for the movement. Beyond that is a large area of possibility in terms of what profession a radical should choose, and what strategy he should develop within that profession.

The problem is not to decide definitively among these three models or any other alternative. None of the models is sufficiently developed and rooted in the present empirical reality to provide an adequate or convincing basis on which to decide the priority of tasks or the relative importance of different professions and social locations.

The problem is how to make tentative choices, how to build a bridge between models, to allow diversity while doubt persists, to amass new experience and analysis that could make tighter theoretical formulations possible.

This requires a commitment to experiment: not meaning every-one-go-do-his-thing. An experiment is a controlled venture: with clarity about intended political purpose; based on stated assumptions; testing hypotheses; having explicit criteria of evaluation; arriving through experience at confirmation or disconfirmation of theory; making results public to comrades; seeking criticisms and help, eventually limiting the possibilities and building theory.

There is already too much unanalysed, unshared experience. Projects are carried out without evaluation. Work proceeds on impulse, vague formulations, romantically hopeful projections of the improbable. A non-cumulative, atheoretical, astrategic pragmatism is perpetuated. We are basing too much hope that we will stumble into a revolution, that our intuition will be sufficient to show us the way to a decent world.

A Radical In A Profession

The failures of the movement — to develop a convincing line of action and to be sensitive to human need — are real and do interfere with the solution to our problem. But they are not decisive failings. It is too easy and too common for individuals to use these failings as a dodge for their own unwillingness to confront, in a tough-minded way, the consequences of their abstract political commitment. Radicals who are in professions are often unwilling to make any significant commitment to the movement or make any concrete effort to change their lives to accord with their politics. Movement suspicion is not entirely unfounded: there are enough examples of former activists trading on a "left wing analysis" and cloaking fairly standard careers with the aura of movement idealism.

One of the important accomplishments of the conference was that people began to lay out the rudiments of an orientation for radicals working in professions: guidelines of how to function, how to see your work, how to define the meaning of political vocation in the professions. This orientation did not rest on preconceptions about strategy but was seen more simply as a kind of operational expression of what it means to be a radical.

The first principle of orientation for a radical who chooses to work in a profession is that he is different. He must reject and separate himself psychologically from the commonly held social definition of his work. He must substitute an agenda of his own: a set of short- and long-run objectives that derive from a tentative view of strategy and that are pursued as political experiments.

This view has several implications:

1. The movement must be seen as a utility — which helps us define what we do, and without which our work loses political relevance. This means we must pay our dues. The dues include financial support. And they include support both of action programs and of the "radical wing" in emerging social conflicts. Thus we have to anticipate the possibility of helping deserters, risking jail, supporting rebellions, and other highly illegitimate, nonprofessional things. If our personal aspirations or professional work precludes our doing things that are not safe or respectable, then we are kidding ourselves about our politics.

2. A radical cannot have an orientation toward professional "success." If we function as radicals, high status and respect and rewards in the professional establishment are foreclosed. We must expect job instability, the likelihood of getting fired periodically, the danger of increasing difficulty in finding jobs.

3. A radical cannot see his loyalty as being to the profession or institution in which he works. Our loyalty is to our political comrades and to the political aims for which we are organizing. Obviously this presents a moral difficulty because others will assume we have traditional loyalties; and we will, in fact, be playing a two-faced game, knowing that we will "betray" them

when difficult issues arise. But then, that is what being a radical is about and the question is whether you betray your professional colleagues or your political comrades.

A corollary of political loyalty is that we can criticize movement policy and actions among "the brothers and the sisters," but not to outsiders. We are not intellectuals above it all who say the truth to whomever will listen or asks: we are partisans who support the movement against the outside world, whatever our private criticisms might be.

4. Radicals cannot accept without reservation the code of ethics and responsibility of their professions. Ethics are not abstract ideals. They are sanctifications of certain types of social relations, purposes and loyalties. Conventional ethics entrap us into support of things which we do not support politically and into loyalties which conflict with our own values and politics. We must develop both a critique of established ethics and a counter code which squares with our values. This means, for example, that we should have no "ethical" scruples about providing "cover" to movement people; using politics as a criterion in giving recommendations, references, jobs; that we will make professional resources such as equipment, supplies, travel funds, expense accounts, available to movement people under the guise of professional expense; that we might not respect the confidential status of documents, meetings or privileged information if their contents would be valuable to the movement. Again, this presents moral problems, which require, at least, that we must be honest about our politics and values, so that people do not expect us to automatically conform to "accepted standards."

5. Radicals must break the link between expertise and authority. In our movement and our professional work we must break down the notion that "experts" and "specialists" are best equipped to make political decisions, a notion that is sponsored by the establishment and is antithetical to democratic participation. We must relinquish that private view of ourselves as "superior" to our comrades and constituencies which leads us to act as though we have much to teach and nothing to learn.

6. There is no such thing as an isolated or secret radical. Action is strategic only if it is part of a broader design, only if it is planned in concert with others with whom we are politically interdependent, only if it contributes to what others are trying to do. We must participate in groups that make strategy decisions. We must

strive to develop our own work in a way which supports others. We must maintain relationships with the movement outside of our professions.

7. Radicals in the professions must avoid provincialism. Intra-professional issues are generally important only as they lead to consciousness or action on issues of national policy, power and institutional change. Without that perspective, the organizer is more likely to be professionalized than the profession organized. Even more centrally, we must keep in focus that the primary struggle for radical change at this point involves blacks and poor whites and students. Our work may not always parallel these movements, but it must not conflict with them and we must stay close enough to these movements so that local and national coalition can eventually be forged.

These "rules of orientation" are beginning formulations. Some of them are certainly problematic and require refinement. But the basic point is: which side are we on? If we fail to define and make explicit our opposition orientation, we will fall easily into accepting establishment ethics, norms of practice, and procedures of change — all of which function to support the status quo we are trying to destroy.

Areas Of Strategic Emphasis

Given a general radical orientation, the problem remains of how radicals can actually work in professions in the absence of a widely shared conviction about strategy. In general people at the conference talked about four kinds of strategic emphasis which work in the professions could serve:

1. To organize political struggle against the power structure of the profession or institution in which we work.
2. To try to transform the way in which the profession is practiced and its content.
3. To fight the social control functions of the profession or institution.
4. To recruit more people into the movement.

What the confreres were not able to do was to analyse the conditions, if any, under which each of these makes sense, what the limits of their value are, and the dangers they pose. The answers to these questions await further experiment and debate on overall strategy. One of the jobs of radicals in professions is to help develop such analysis based on their own experiences.

But the value of outlining various kinds of tasks is that it suggests that a strategic view of work may include a wider variety of functions than is now usually accepted within the movement.

1. Organizing political struggle is the most widely recognized function of radicals in professions. This means setting up independent political unions or organizing causes within professional groups to develop and fight for a set of radical demands within the profession or institution: control of work situation; shift in political role; change in standards of membership and recruitment, etc.

2. Transforming the practice and content of the profession is one of the most problematic functions of radicals. It often involves creating "counter institutions" to serve as models or creating a small space within the system in which to practice more or less as we wish. The political value of such work tends to be underrated in the movement. This is because so often counter institutions become a substitute for direct challenge. But they have also the possibility of aiding direct challenge. The creating and acting out of models is an important way of re-forming sensibility and creating the consciousness that confrontation is necessary.

There are people in the movement who are gifted at creating such models. Their skills should not be rejected. The failure to make use of the imaginative aspect of political consciousness has often split radical movements into two parts: one narrowly political, the other irrelevantly utopian. A task that the New Left faces is to create a strategy that can keep the two parts together so that image retains political meaning and politics retain human imagination.

3. Fighting the social control function of the profession is one of the goals of a radical union. But it may also be a function for small groups in under-organized professions to play, at least in the short range. Radicals in professions may see their job as organizing groups to block the effectiveness of "cooling out operations," such as riot control; practicing in a way that directly defies authority and professional standards, such as refusing to grade.

Such acts, if militant enough, carry a high penalty of job loss. They also may interfere with long range organizing efforts. But, then again, they may serve as models of behavior that spark organizing. Here the special value of professionals acting to "stop the machine" is that they usually don't, and hence may break into the circle of safety of middle class America. In planning activities the movement should consider making concrete demands of such interference on groups of professionals. Meanwhile one of the jobs of professionals might be to develop analysis of what social control functions the profession plays and how these could be undermined.

4. The initial recruitment of people into the movement is a function many professionals are well placed to do. Recruitment is never an end in itself independent of other strategic goals; but it may be worth emphasizing in some cases, even to the sacrifice of direct confrontation or interferences. Many professionals, particularly teachers, have as one of their chief political assets an opportunity for intensive communication with potential constituencies. Recruitment is not the same as direct confrontation with power. While direct confrontation may be a means of recruitment, it is not the focus of recruitment campaigns. Nor is it the only important element in recruitment. More than any other facet of political work, recruitment of people requires "dramatic" skills: the radical organizer's job is to live out his politics, to embody an alternative. Again, there is a special "talent" or inclination that the movement often fails to see as legitimate; a certain emphasis of action that is often underrated.

A Feeling Of Isolation

There should be no illusion that the political functions one can undertake as a radical in a profession are easy. One problem that people at the conference spoke about with concern was the "time bind," particularly for people in "fee-for-service" professions but to some extent for all professionals. Professional practice takes up time. There are basic things you must do in order to survive: for example, a lawyer cannot earn a living if he does only movement work. In addition, much of the obligation work of an in-the-system job drains energy and produces inertia. But when practical demands of profession come first, the political work is shoved onto a sideline and often it drifts out of the picture altogether.

Perhaps a more substantive problem that was identified is that it is very hard to practice differently. It is difficult to define new standards of effectiveness, to invent and implement new ways of doing things. Most things that we try fail — and often not because of the oppressive power structure, but simply because they are difficult and original and most of us have limited capacity. Self-confidence is difficult to maintain and it is easy to slide into the standards of the establishment out of sheer demoralization.

The most pervasive problem expressed was the feeling of isolation from the mainstream of the movement. Many people described difficulty in finding emotional sustenance for political activism. They felt they were going dry, losing perspective. Political argument was becoming formalistic; conviction was floating away. Taking risks and being a marginal man was losing its reason. Signs of middle age stodginess were overcoming them. The movement people were remote physically and psychologically. Without adequate sources of spiritual support the dangers of co-optation are imminent. Professionals have access to many rewards. Under the best of circumstances, these may lead to abandoning the tough requirements of the political role.

The themes of isolation and co-optation dominated the professionals conference. In a sense they were the real issue: now to stay sane and how to stay honest, while trying to be effective. On the last day, especially, solutions began to be suggested — concrete things that people could do if they were serious in wanting to "change their lives": things which did not depend on perfecting theory, agreeing on strategy, winning political victories, or building new organizational superstructures.

What is needed is a network of comradeship that can serve as a reference group outside of the professions for radicals working within established institutions. Such a network would help break the barriers of isolation and create pressure against copping out. It would form groups in which people might plan their political agendas and evaluate their work and it would give people facing risk material and spiritual support.

Basically the problem must be met where people live. One workshop began to build a picture of a "commune" designed to help radicals sustain themselves and attain effectiveness.

The idea is simple: we must be close to our friends and we must help each other survive, stay honest, be effective. Our professional colleagues and random neighbors cannot be our reference group. Nor are mechanistic alternatives such as news-letters sufficient.

Structurally the commune means that people live within walking distance of each other and take on certain explicit obligations to each other.

The commune is seen not as a utopian ideal, but as an instrument preserving individuality and privacy while fulfilling certain politically significant functions. Beyond fulfillment of those functions members would decide how much or how little they wanted to link themselves to the commune.

The following functions were seen as essential:

1. The commune helps people define and evaluate their work: weekly meetings describe, criticize, evaluate what members are doing politically.

2. The community would take on some kind of joint political activity to insure that participation in politics extended beyond a professional work setting. This could be centered around the neighborhood, the war, etc.

3. The commune takes on clear responsibilities to provide services for the radical movement as a whole: such as helping with education and research; acting as a center of hospitality for movement travellers.

4. The commune has economic responsibilities: professionals make money, and as radicals they have an obligation to support the movement. Professionals tend to escalate their standard of living until they fear economic risk and can no longer function as radicals. What we need is a formal means of getting our money to the movement before we get used to spending it and become corrupted.

The community might meet its financial obligations to the movement through a "tithe" whereby, for example, ten per cent of all income over $4000 per family would be put into a fund that would periodically be allocated to action organizations or movement projects.

The community might also protect its own members through a "community strike fund" or "war chest" that would be a cushion against economic risk as well as a tangible sign of group support for risk-taking as a necessary part of political activity.

5. The commune would establish a collective child care arrangement that would give responsibility for children to both men and women. This is a practical necessity to allow all members of the commune to participate equally in political life, and other non-domestic activities.

6. Beyond these basic functions the commune might seek ways

to create more desirable alternatives to individualistic consuming patterns: for example cooperative buying; sharing capital goods, such as cars, washing machines, tools.

It should be stressed that the purpose of the commune is not to create a counter community into which radicals can retreat, or on which they can lavish their attention. Rather it is to create a communal life style that is supportive of increased political activity outside of the community. Certainly a commune is no panacea for the problems of radicals in professions or out. But it may be a necessary framework within which to develop ways to bridge the gap between personal need and political effectiveness.

If we do get by, it will be with a little help from our friends.

THOUGHTS ON THE MOVEMENT

John McDermott

Terry was eighteen and a draftee. I met him and three of his buddies atop a machine gun bunker north of the "Iron Triangle" and it was there that we talked. Characteristically for a Movement writer, I had spent my time so far in Vietnam talking only to officers. They knew the same colleges I did, the same books, the same music. It was easier to talk to them and anyway they know more about the war. Finally, however, I determined to talk to some ordinary soldiers. I am glad I did. They taught me very little about the war but an enormous amount about our Movement.

Like most young combat troops I came to meet, Terry and his friends were at first more anxious to hear my views on things than to give their own, but eventually they talked a great deal about their own lives and about the war, and about the draft, Berkeley and the Movement. Terry was by far the most articulate of the four and as we talked on and on through the night, pausing only to watch some strafing helicopters to the south, to listen to outgoing howitzer rounds or to scrutinize the wire barrier thirty meters away, his role as accepted spokesman for the others became more marked. My admiration grew apace.

He had gotten married immediately on receipt of his induction notice. This is a common reaction among young draftees trying to retain at least some link to a familiar civilian world. For Terry, the well-being of his frightened seventeen-year-old wife placed a heavy burden on his already busy and dangerous life as a combat infantryman. Most U.S. casualties in Vietnam are inflicted on the infantry battalions which, almost alone among American units, venture outside the mammoth fortified camps that now scar the Vietnamese countryside. Terry was generally aware that these

310

battalions, which total only 75,000 men at one time, were taking 85,000 casualties a year. More pointedly, in his own platoon only 17 of the original 35 GI's were left after five months of combat. Out on patrols and other operations for three days of every five, battling the ever-present mines, mortars and snipers, Terry had very few "interesting experiences" with which to reassure his young wife, and even less time to write about them. Yet he understood that his daily letters were essential to allay the impotent terror she felt and thus he assumed the burden of making sure that every day — even in his absence — a letter of his would be mailed the girl, full of reassurance and affection and topped off with a fund of stories — entirely made up — of the dull rounds of his placid army life.

Of all the soldiers I met Terry was most unusual for his character and intelligence. But in one respect he was typical of the others. His life was dominated by his immediate problems and those of his family, just as it had been before he came into the Army. Then as now it was enough merely to try to do his job and take care of his family. Staying alive in Vietnam was a new problem but not fundamentally different from the others. He had neither the time nor the inclination to reflect on the difficulties presented him by an incomprehensible fate (he called it "bad luck" and "the breaks"). Handling them was a full time job; he didn't always succeed in it.

What significance has the Movement got for people like Terry? Not just soldiers, though them too, but for all the people of this country whose names don't count in the *Times* ads and whose energy and attention are largely dominated by the demands of their daily lives?

Just before being shipped off to Asia, the Movement, in the person of some university peace demonstrators, approached Terry and his buddies in Oakland. The GI's were so disgusted with the "draft-dodgers" that they wanted to beat them up but were satisfied merely to push them around and curse at them. People who "weren't willing to fight for their country" were not worth trouble with the MP's.

The four suspected I was anti-war, deducing their conclusion from the fact that (a) I was a professor, (b) they hadn't heard of *Viet-Report* and, especially, (c) I had long hair. (Every unit I stayed with in Vietnam coyly offered me the free services of its barber.) When my passionate disagreement about the demonstrators confirmed their conjecture, their friendliness was undiminished. In their eyes the fact that I was in Vietnam and, for the moment anyway, at a forward defense post apparently entitled me to have any opinion I wanted about anything at all. They turned out to be anxious to talk about the war and our discussion soon ranged freely over the whole Vietnam controversy but came back again and again to the draft.

They were very much aware of the inequities of the draft. They knew all the connections between being less well off than others, doing less well in school, marrying earlier, getting poorer jobs, earning less and having fewer opportunities for training and advancement later. They realized that others were making it at home while they chanced death or mutilation in Vietnam — and yet they bore no anger for the lucky ones. Their anger was reserved for the "draft-dodgers."

Under the pressure of counter-arguments Terry made a very curious distinction. You had to accept the principle that it was right "to fight for your country." Terry couldn't understand people who didn't accept that; there had to be something wrong with them. But once you accepted the principle, he thought it was all right to weasel on the consequences. In fact, he admired those who did so and got away with it. Only stupid guys voluntarily went into the Army. You tried anything you could to get out of it: trick knees, "going queer," playing at being crazy, influence, anything. But you had to accept the principle of fighting for your country and if "the breaks" went against you, you went to Vietnam and fought — no questions asked and no complaints.

I tried a different tack; it was a dirty war and the Saigon Government a gang of cut-throats. They agreed with enthusiasm, rivalling one another with stories illustrating the point. They thought worse of LBJ than I did and seemed content that the real reason for the war was that somebody was getting rich on it. They weren't sure exactly and didn't seem to care.

For most of eight hours we went 'round these same points, but they wouldn't budge. Terry understood the alternatives just as clearly as I did. Draft-card burners showed more guts than "2-S Hawks"; the war was bad for America and for Vietnam. Still, he didn't like "draft-dodgers" and "demonstrators" and you had to fight for your country. Terry seemed aware of the contradiction he was caught in. He accepted a principle whose consequences he knew were evil. Being an intelligent and reasonable man he found ways to mitigate the consequences: he called them fate. But the principle — and the contradiction — stood undisturbed. Why? Why couldn't he bring himself to oppose a war and a draft system of which he himself was a conscious victim?

Intellectually, Terry had a far closer grasp of the war's evil than a majority of Movement people. Morally, his courage in facing the life dealt him was not less than that of David Mitchell or Dennis Mora. If he couldn't break with the war system, we can't expect his friends and comrades to do so either, and that's the point. The roots of Terry's inability to oppose the war can't be found in his personal inadequacies. We have to look for them instead in the net of social relationships which bind him into a passive acceptance of his fate.

An upper middle class boy is nurtured by his family and school experiences to think himself capable of dealing with the decisive components of his life. Terry isn't. A privileged boy gains sufficient confidence in himself, in his social place and in his judgment of events so that he comes to assume a competence to control his own destiny. Within a university environment which, for all its faults, exaggerates this competence, and within a social world made up of others like himself, it is not strange to find students of average intelligence and character able to pierce the veils which surround government behavior and with courage enough to oppose it.

By contrast the family experiences of lower middle class and blue collar boys are proverbially authoritarian. Their school experiences emphasize the value of "staying in line" and out of trouble. The likelihood of early marriage, uncertain job prospects, the great certainty of being drafted and the pressure of like-situated friends all combine to teach them the same lesson. Thus, even gifted boys like Terry bend before a social system whose oppressiveness they early learn they cannot effectively control.

These are matters of common knowledge even for college freshmen but not, apparently, for our Movement. Terry cannot accept principles of behavior, however noble sounding, which do not have sanction from the authorities which dominate his life. That is the path to certain trouble and all his life he's been taught to avoid such trouble. He knows, for example, he has not been properly trained to deal with political questions, and he knows he and his buddies haven't the skills and resources for political organization. His own limited experience leaves him believing that politics must be either a racket or nonsense; a racket he can't master, or non-sense with which he wisely had better have nothing to do. Thus, for boys like Terry, not to have anything to do with the Movement is a sign of intelligence and good sense. And, when Movement people preach politics at him, like rich men urging paupers to grow rich, he has a perfectly natural and commendable reaction to them; he wants to beat them up.

There is no place for Terry in the Movement and it isn't his fault. That's the point which must be driven home for when we realize that then we'll realize how much the Movement is still a preserve for the children of the over-privileged and a vehicle for their social vision and social ambitions. Rhetorically, the Move-ment is democratic and humane but socially, and therefore funda-mentally, it remains the preserve of the few.

This conclusion may appear at first strange and unfounded. If anything has characterized the Movement it has been its resistance to manipulation and standardization, the central thrusts of our national life. Under slogans such as "participatory democracy" or, more crudely and colorfully, "Do Not Bend, Fold, Spindle, or Mutilate," the Movement has tried to assert the primacy of people and their wishes against the needs of an increasingly rational and mechanical system. Noble words, however, are belied by ignoble deeds. From the fact that the Movement has no place for Terry we must see that its noble demands have only the *intention* to be an *avant-garde* political program for the whole country. In their *social character* they consist so far merely of a defense of the tra-ditional life style and values of the old professional middle class.

The narrow class character of the Movement asserts itself in other ways. The high status assigned the "organizer" has manage-rial overtones in spite of the disclaimer on manipulation. The propensity for organizing only the poor and the black smacks of the settlement house missionary mentality of the Progressive Era among the young ladies of the best families. Currently the writing of Regis Debray is all the rage because it suggests that small bands of revolutionary intellectuals, largely unrelated to mass organiza-tion and effective political analysis, can carry off a successful revolution. In context this must be seen as a flimsy attempt to make a virtue out of our social isolation. Most convincing of all perhaps is the Movement's dogged defense of its peculiar life-style against the needs of its politics. The virtues of a revolutionary are more akin to those of the soldier than of the hippy, but a hippy life style for all remains near, if not quite at the center of the Movement's working political vision.

There is no doubt at all that, squarely faced with a choice, the Movement would opt enthusiastically for the "masses" and against any variant of elitism. It remains the only organized group in the country which would do so, but how can we put flesh on these thin bones? How can the Movement relate itself to people like Terry and become a vehicle for his aspirations?

In the first place, it has to learn that without a privileged place for him, the Movement has no right to its rhetoric. Where Terry actually is, is the home, good or bad, of democracy. The task before the Movement is not to create an ideal democracy for those who "know where its at." The task is to take people like Terry, the real life Terry with all his inadequacies, distractions and prejudices, and shove him down the road which leads to political power.

Secondly, we have to learn that achieving political power is not a matter of "building consciousness." Terry has all the consciousness he needs. He knows exactly how bad things are because he is the one on the receiving end of this society's injustice, the best vantage point for building consciousness. What Terry needs are direct and familiar ways out of the trap he knows he's in, ways that he understands, ways that are neither nonsense nor a racket. In his eyes, electoral politics is the biggest racket; demonstrations the worst nonsense.

Thirdly, strategies which emphasize "creative disorder" and other scattered forays against established authority are of no use to Terry. The view that the creation of social disorder and chaos will lead unjust authorities to make improvements is not very compelling to anybody. But, for Terry, whose life is a continuous struggle, frequently unsuccessful, to maintain a creative order among family, job, mortgage and other responsibilities, any disorder, creative or Debrayan, can only be seen as a threat to the thin fabric of his life.

This last fact gives us a clue as to how the Movement can be of use to Terry. The everyday life of ordinary Americans has been struck disordering blows by the political and economic history of the years since World War II. Families already hard-pressed to meet the exigencies of daily life have been forced to adjust to an enormous number and variety of corrosive changes. Television and the schools have created alien and often dismaying social models which their children ape. The intricacies of specialized training and the draft system leave them unable to assist their grown children except by inadequate finances and excessive fatuous advice. New consuming, residence and working patterns disrupt the old harmony of family, neighborhood and civic life, and the disruption is confirmed and deepened by an alien culture purveyed through incomprehensible and uncontrollable mass media. Lurking nearby are recurring racial and international crises whose threat is sharpened rather than obscured by the murkiness of their origins. Most important of all, the fundamental impulse of all these disordering novelties stems not from the inner needs of people's lives and aspiration but from the evermore insistent demands of an industrial-political-military system bent on creating the same disorders on a world-wide scale.

The distorted and fear-ridden politics of post-World War II America is a projection of the distortion and fear which afflict ordinary Americans as they try to bring life-serving harmony to their daily activities. Even Terry's seeming mindless clinging to a vague patriotic slogan is evidence of this. It is an attempt to impose harmony and value over chaotic circumstances which threaten his family, his future and his very life itself.

It is at the level of fundamental social relationships, rather than in electoral "racketeering" or Debrayan fantasy that the Movement must locate its fundamental tasks. Social organizing among the Terrys of our country rather than political missionary work among the totally poor should be the main, though not the exclusive thrust of our work. We have got to help manipulate social environments so that individuals can learn to be free. Schools must be forced into educating children in how to deal with their neighborhoods, not just the national job-market. High schools should prepare boys and girls to deal with city councils, school boards, police chiefs and draft boards, not just college entrance exams. Neighborhoods have to be recreated and the fundamental services they can perform for families, such as child supervision, mutual self-help and broader social recreation, must be brought into life. People's job lives have to be re-understood and the values of comradeship and craftsmanship re-asserted against the boss's "efficiency." A new people's culture has to be developed, aimed at enhancing the values of life and work and at diminishing the effects of the acquisitive, exploitative and largely sterile culture of the national elite.

For a start we should examine organizations like the VFW, volunteer fire departments, church bowling leagues, the Boy Scouts, PTA's and Rotaries. For all their seeming fecklessness they enter into the real life of our people and provide essential relationships and irreplaceable services for them. Even the American Legion, with its rich fraternal, social, civic, athletic and young people's programs, has ten times more day to day value in the life of our people now than the Movement itself. Can't we do better than the Legion?

No more important or difficult tasks face the Movement than these: to close the immense gap between itself and the direct and immediate concerns of our people, to learn in all their concrete detail the social problems which beset them, to trace out their sources, to play a creative role in developing new ways to contend with them, and to fuse these ways into the democratic folk tradition which still persists so strongly among our people.

A Movement which saw these things included among its primary tasks could lay claim to representing the fundamental aspirations of our people. Its voice would be the voice of the American people and the power of its politics irresistible.

FROM "RESISTANCE"
TO STUDENT-WORKER ALLIANCE

Hilary Putnam

The New England Resistance — Fall 1967 to Fall 1968

I became involved with the New England Resistance at its inception on October 16, 1967 and remained a very active supporter until the fall of 1968. During the nine months of the 1967–1968 academic year I witnessed the Resistance undergo phenomenal growth. Hundreds of men turned in their draft cards at large and small "turn-ins" — nearly 300 on April 3rd alone — and thousands of people came to mass meetings called by the Resistance, and participated in demonstrations against the war in Vietnam and against racism sponsored by the Resistance. During the late spring of 1968 there were several spectacular "sanctuaries"[1] which produced a mood of great excitement and optimism in Resistance circles. Yet, when I returned to Boston in the fall of 1968 after a summer's absence I discovered that the Resistance had all but ceased to exist as a functioning organization in the Boston area. Since then, in company with a number of other ex-Resistance people, I have rethought my whole attitude towards the politics of mass draft-card turn-ins. In the space available to me here, I want to try to analyze the reasons for the failure of the New England Resistance, and draw the lessons from that failure that the student (and faculty) anti-imperialist movement needs to learn.

A number of organizational factors obviously played a role in the abrupt decline of the New England Resistance, but those organizational factors were not an accident. Rather, I shall try to show that they arose from the way in which the group was formed, from the politics of the mass draft-card turn-in itself.

The Resistance[2] is governed by a self-selected steering committee of about a dozen people. Allowing the steering committee to select itself was thought to be democratic and "informal"; in practice, very power-hungry individuals gravitated to the steering committee, as well as some very selfless and willing workers. On the other hand, potentially very good workers were not in the steering committee because they were a little shy to put themselves on it. At Monday night dinners the steering committee would report to a larger group of fifty or sixty (sometimes even more would show up), and would conduct "discussions"; but this was always done in a very missionary spirit. It quickly became clear that the steering committee was the actual decision making body of the Resistance, and that a group of about four people (known as "the cabal") within the steering committee was the actual governing body of the steering committee.

This unfortunate state of affairs is an example of the way in which anarchist ideas (which were very prevalent in the Resistance) served to frustrate rather than produce participatory democracy. True democracy requires serious agreement on interests and ideas; a willingness to engage in collective struggle; and the deliberate practice of criticism and self criticism so that the ideas of the group will be evaluated in the light of how they fare in practice, so that the basis of unity of the group will grow and constantly be made explicit to the satisfaction of all members of the group, and so that the effectiveness of the group will constantly increase as its understanding and experience grows. It is especially important that every member of the group understand and accept the ideas on the basis of which the group works; that no one simply "go along" without really agreeing.

This kind of democracy does exist in sections of the movement — for example, in the Cambridge Peace and Freedom Party, with which I am now working, and in the Student Worker Alliance forces in S.D.S. But, in my experience at least, anarchists, for all of their talk about "community," are never able to attain it. To begin with, anarchists, and people influenced by anarchist ideas, tend to be more interested in emotion than in reason. I do not mean that all Resistance people were or are anarchists, by any means; but anarchist ideas of "organization" were very prevalent in the Resistance, and one effect of this was to reinforce an anti-intellectual bias which many Resistance people brought with them from the hippy wing of the student community. The fact is that there was never a serious attempt to articulate a set of ideas on which Resistance people were supposed to agree (except, perhaps, some rhetoric about not letting oneself be "channelled" by the Selective Service System, and about the system and the institutions being "illegitimate"). Certainly there was no attempt to articulate a strategy for *winning* anything, or a set of assumptions upon which such a strategy might be based.

The result of all this was, as I already remarked, that the Resistance became extremely undemocratic — in fact, elitist. The great majority of the people who turned in their draft cards — the "resisters" — never came to a steering committee meeting, since they were obviously not wanted. This accounts for the situation I discovered when I returned to Boston in the fall of 1968; the resisters had dropped entirely away from the organization, which was reduced from what it had momentarily been after April 3rd, a spirited group of over three hundred people, to a dozen or so — in fact, the steering committee had become the Resistance!

The Perspective of Moral Witness

Why were mass draft-card turn-ins organized in the first place? Partly, of course, there was a feeling of desperation; one simply had to do *something* to help stop the war in Vietnam. Partly, there were far-fetched ideas of "clogging the machinery." But, mainly, I think, two ideas were operative. First, there was the idea of putting pressure on the ruling class. If young, educated, elite young men voluntarily chose prison over both the draft and Canada, that would upset the parents of these young men, and other people of their parents' generation, and thereby produce a moral indignation that might help end the war. And second, there was the idea of setting a moral example to the people. "Your draft card is another man's death warrant," David Harris[3] says in his speeches — i.e., wars in general continue because ordinary men are not moral enough; the moral example of their betters may one day change this sorry state of affairs.

The Perspective of Student-Worker Alliance

There are only two ways of proceeding in any struggle; one can rely on the people or one can rely on the ruling class. If one wants to defeat the ruling class, then the second way is a loser. Moral witness is one form of this losing tactic of relying on the ruling class. It is an appeal to the ruling class; an appeal which might be couched in some such words as these: "Gee Dad, I'm terribly angry at what you're doing in Vietnam." (Silence.) "Gee, Dad, I think you're a rotten imperialist." (Silence.) "Gee, Dad, if you don't answer me, I'll wreck my whole life. *I'll go to jail.*"

Of course, the resisters were not, in general, sons of the real ruling class — the men who actually own a controlling interest in the giant corporations that dominate this country are a very small group. And the resisters were, of course, right to be furious about the war, and genuinely willing to sacrifice to stop the war. Opposition to the tactic of mass draft-card turn-ins is by no means denigration of the sincerity of the resisters or the justice of their cause. But what I mean to suggest by the above one-sided dialogue is that however just the resisters' cause, and however sincere their belief, their tactic was fundamentally misguided. For it sought to display anger to people like their parents, people who identify with the ruling class even if they are not actually part of it. And the ruling class does not stop killing and oppressing because nice people get angry with it; it stops killing and oppressing only when people who are oppressed and people who are at any rate not exploiting unite and use their power to *make* the ruling class stop.

This idea is the basis of a perspective for the student movement: the perspective of "Student-Worker Alliance." This perspective was first put forward in S.D.S. by forces friendly to the Progressive Labor Party,[4] and there has been a violent attempt inside S.D.S. to red-bait student-worker alliance people as "wooden, mechanical Marxists" (vision of a horde of robots, all under iron P.L. discipline), and simultaneously, if inconsistently, to split student-worker alliance people, the great majority of whom do not belong to P.L., from P.L. by attacking various other positions of P.L. In spite of this, the strength of the student-worker alliance position has grown at each S.D.S. National Council and National Convention until at the recent National Council at Ann Arbor about half of the uncommitted delegates were won over to the position in the six days of the N.C., bringing about the passage of one resolution with clear worker-student politics (the resolution on racism), and forcing high-level ideological debate for the first time in the history of the organization. I want to discuss this perspective here because it seems to me to represent a very healthy development in the student movement, and a needed contrast to the perspective of moral witness just mentioned.

As the expression "student-worker alliance" clearly indicates, the perspective is one which calls for a movement based on an alliance between working people and students. But this does *not* mean that one is calling for students to go out and organize workers (by the way, this is a common misunderstanding of the student-worker alliance position). In order to avoid this and other misunderstandings, I want to discuss the perspective under several separate headings.

1. The importance of the working class.

Today many illusions are current about the "well being" of the American working class, many of them fostered by Marcuse and other New Left theorists. Students frequently claim that all workers live in the suburbs, own two cars and a color television set, and that the main problem of the working class is over-consumption! For convenience, let us divide the wage workers of the country into two groups: the basic industrial working class (production, transportation, and communication), and the secondary working class (secretaries, clerical workers, teachers, social workers, etc.). The secondary working class includes much of the so-called middle class (e.g., teachers, social workers), but it also includes some very ill paid workers: recent income studies show that the position of white collar workers is rapidly worsening, in fact, relative to blue collar workers. The basic working class includes some highly paid workers, for example, tool and die makers; but its average wage is much lower than the typical student realizes. *The average weekly wage of a member of the basic industrial working class* (nearly 50% of the work force) *is under $90 dollars a week.* In addition, members of the basic industrial working class are the victims of the worst housing crisis in the country's history: skyrocketting rents in many cities, skyrocketting property taxes, and rotting dwellings. Also, over the last five years real wages have been declining while taxes and surtaxes for the war are piling up. Workers are very unhappy about the conditions in their schools — the vicious and rigid "tracking" system is an especial grievance, which most of the Left knows nothing about, and about many other conditions. Yes, workers are still exploited. Yes, workers are still oppressed.

The failure to understand that workers are materially and not just "spiritually" oppressed is accompanied by a failure to see black people as a part of the working class (as 98% of them are) and to see their material oppression not as mere spitefulness on the basis of skin pigmentation but as super-oppression and super-exploitation of a section of the working class. (The profitability — to the ruling class — of this super-exploitation is often overlooked: 22 billion dollars in wage differentials alone, not even to count the profits made on super-high prices, super-high rents, etc., from the black communities.) Since black workers are not seen as workers but just as blacks by many students (a subtle form of racism), and since these students are anyway contemptuous of workers (an attitude in many ways similar to racism, though directed at fellow whites), these students tend to be unaware that black workers are leading wildcat strikes all over the country, and that in case after case they have triggered the white workers to join them, in spite of the racism which is prevalent.

The fact that workers are the most savagely oppressed part of the population — materially *and* in so-called "spiritual" (i.e., non-economic) ways — means that they have the *need* for social revolution. The fact that they are organized, present in force at the point of production, have a fighting history, and are a very large part of the population means that they have the *power* to make a social revolution. Anyone who is serious about wanting to see social change in this country, social change made by oppressed people in their own interest, has to aim at building a mass radical movement based on the working class.

2. The importance of the student movement.

While the industrial working class must be the driving force in any serious mass radical movement in this country, even the industrial working class cannot bring about social revolution by itself; it will require an alliance of the industrial working class with "secondary" working class people, with middle class people, with farmers — an alliance, as we said before, of people who are oppressed and people who are at least not exploiting — to do that. What is the role of students in such an alliance? What is the role of students in social change?

The important thing about students is *not* that they are in college. The important thing about students is what happens to them *after* they leave college. Fifty percent of all college students do not even finish college. Of those that do finish college, fifty percent become teachers and social workers. These figures indicate that on a national level, college is a training ground primarily for "middle class" and secondary working class jobs; what is the social role of these jobs?

A teacher can side either with the ruling class or with the people. He can join a racist walk-out, like the A.F.T. walk-out in New York, and support a racist on the School Committee, like Louise Day Hicks in Boston. Or he can strike *with* the people for smaller classes, more guidance counselors, better conditions for teachers and students (which is how the A.F.T. originally got built in New York).

Similar observations apply to social workers. A social worker can be a racist, or a fighter for winter clothing and other essentials for her "cases."

What these facts suggest is that the student movement should be viewed as a swing movement. It does have considerable power; and it can use that power to aid either side in the class struggle. Our aim, then, must be to make sure that students link up with the people. We must foster attitudes and styles of political work that will bring students to appreciate the fact that people are oppressed, to see their own present and future oppression as linked to the oppression of working people, of black people, of Vietnamese people, of people all over the world, and that will help students to retain these attitudes of solidarity with oppressed people even after they cease to be students. The ideas that "pot is the revolution," or that Student Power is the revolution, or that hippy dress is the revolution must be fought — because these ideas in fact build an elitist and anti-working class student movement. Such a movement may call itself "revolutionary"; but its "revolution" will always turn out to be mere middle class protest and such "revolutionaries" in fact hurt the chances of social change for the better in America. Middle class protest is not a bad thing when it links up with working class protest; but *mere* middle class protest (petty bourgeois protest) is a bad thing because it ultimately links up with ruling class protest; protest *against* the people, and for special privileges.

3. A strategy for the student movement.

The over-all strategy of the student movement should then be this: to build a student movement which consciously links up with the struggles of working people and the struggles of all oppressed people. That movement should lead students to see themselves in perspective; as people who are being ideologically and technically moulded to serve the interests of a ruling class, and to aid in the oppression of people. It should not say to students "your courses are *meaningless*"; it should lead them to see that their courses are very meaningful — they have a *wrong* meaning, a *bad* meaning, because they are all designed to turn out teachers, social workers, etc., with certain kinds of attitudes. Students should not fight for the right to take Yoga courses, but for courses which will help them really serve the people — courses in the history of black struggles taught by radical black organizers, courses in the history of working class struggles taught by radicals ("official" history covers the doings of Presidents and Kings very well — it only leaves out one thing: the people), courses in Marxist philosophy and economics, radical critique courses in literature, etc. It should not say to students: "you are being *channelled*" — i.e., authority in the abstract is bad; it should lead them to see that they are being channelled to oppress people, and to serve a ruling class. Even under socialism there will be "channelling" — i.e., mechanisms of authority and social responsibility (*pace* our anarchist "friends"; *their* contribution to "democracy" in the movement has already been described in these pages). The point is that under socialism people will be "channelled" to help people, to advance the material and cultural level of people's lives, and in ways that have been collectively and democratically decided upon. It should not say to students that their real needs are to smoke pot, enjoy "liberated" sex (i.e., use one another as sex objects in a fashion not different from that advocated by *Playboy*), and do no work; it should lead them to see that unless they develop a fighting spirit and a sense of solidarity with oppressed people they are going to lead miserable lives. The life of a school teacher, for example, is generally a miserable one; only a struggle can make it less miserable, and the only struggle that will have a chance to win is one that joins teachers together with working class parents, white, brown, and black. The life of a social worker is similarly a miserable one, and the same lesson applies.

Let us now consider some of the tactics that flow from this overall strategy.

(a) Choice of Issues.

I have already suggested a number of issues *not* to choose. A special word may be in order about Student Power as a demand. This demand is bad not only because it fosters a kind of petty bourgeois elitism, but because it is a loser. The ruling class does not share power. Boards with "student representatives" will *always* turn out to have no real power. In addition, they will always get co-opted; if one struggles for a year to get such a board set up, the very next year one finds oneself struggling against that very board, when the "student representatives" on it decide not to abolish ROTC, or to punish student radicals.

This is not to say that one cannot win real concessions within the university; it is to say that one should fight for the specific things one wants the university do do, and not for "structural reforms" which always turn out to be meaningless.

On the other hand, there are many issues one should choose; all the familiar anti-imperialist issues (R.O.T.C., military, C.I.A. and Dow recruitment on campus, military research on campus, etc.) are excellent. Certain less familiar issues are also excellent, and flow naturally from the perspective of student-worker alliance. It is important that students join picket lines when there are labor disputes in college towns; not to organize the workers, but to show support, and also to gain experience in talking to working people, and in raising such issues as the Vietnam war and racism with working people. Above all, students need to learn the experiences of working people in this society if they are to be good allies of working people, and to combat their own anti-working class prejudices. And it is even more important that students support the struggles of workers on their own campuses; college workers in cafeterias, laundries, etc., are miserably paid, company unionized, etc. One most important way in which students can concretely link up with working class communities is by fighting university expansion; when the Columbia students centered on this issue they received massive community support. In the fall of 1968 the Columbia S.D.S. made the serious mistake of shifting its focus from Columbia's expansion in the community to the demand for amnesty for demonstrators (which is a good demand, but which should never be allowed to obscure the original issue). In addition, it treated the issue of university expansion in a fundamentally silly way; it "liberated" tenement buildings for a few hours (complete with red and black flags, Resistance speeches, etc.), to the fury of the tenement people, instead of mapping out a real strategy to fight the expansion. Result: support for Columbia S.D.S. among the community *and* among the student body has evaporated. The other most important way of linking up with the community is by fighting for special admission[5] for black (and if possible, for white working class) students. Black people are excluded from the "middle class" jobs we have been discussing — teacher and social worker — by being excluded from universities. Fighting for "proportional representation" of black people in the colleges, and in the middle class jobs we have been discussing is very important, not only to correct a historic injustice, but to show black people that we are prepared to give up our own unjust privileges (like an 11% better chance at admission to college), unjust privileges whereby we benefit from the racism fostered in this society. Only if we are prepared to give up these unjust privileges will the blacks have any reason to accept us whites as allies; and it is not enough to say "we will give them up after the revolution." We must give them up *now*. Even being prepared to accept special admission of black students as just is not enough; unless we are prepared to *fight* for special admission of working class students and especially black students, black people should not want us as allies.

One further remark about fighting racism; one does not fight racism successfully by just telling white students that the black demands are just; that only builds a missionary, fundamentally liberal type of support that evaporates in a serious crisis. (Which is not to say that the demands aren't just, or that it isn't important to say so.) To fight racism successfully — and this is the hardest and most important problem facing the whole radical movement — one must convince *white* students that the black demands are in *their* interest. And in fact they are; for around the struggle for those demands one can build the kind of united radical movement that alone can combat the oppression of whites as well as blacks. Racism has as a principle function to divide the people and to keep white people from accepting black leadership, from following the militant initiatives of the blacks. If we refuse to be divided, and if we follow the impressive lead taken by black students on many campuses in militant struggle for their rights, we can build a movement that will be tremendously effective, just as white workers can build a movement that will astonish the whole world if they learn to unite with blacks and to follow the highly advanced struggles that the blacks have already initiated in this country. That this is not mere theory can be seen from the example of San Francisco State where white students have supported the demands of black and third world students on just these grounds and the result has been the longest and most intense student strike on a white campus in American history.

An absolutely crucial factor in the San Francisco State strike has been the support of black ghettos and third world barrios; only this support has stayed Reagan and the trustees from even more reliance on armed force than has already been displayed. (And what has been displayed — and successfully resisted — is fantastic: hundreds of riot police, detectives, helicopters, etc.) Columbia — in the spring of 1968 — and San Francisco State show that alliance with the community *can* be built on these issues of university expansion and special admissions, and that a tremendously effective fighting student movement can grow from such an alliance.

(b) Presentation of Issues.

Choice of good issues is not enough; equally important is how one presents them. Frequently it is overlooked that *talking* is a "tactic," and as important as any we have. Some student radical "leaders" publish articles proudly listing their latest "disruption" — as if "disruption" were helpful by itself. Militant tactics are sometimes successful — e.g., Columbia and S.F. State — but only when a mass base has been built. About three years of discussion on the issues of the gym and the war had taken place at Columbia before the sit-ins, and at S.F. State there was likewise a long history of agitation and education. And even when militant tactics have been preceded by base building, they will fail if they are not successfully *explained* and defended to the people one wants to win over. To think that going to Washington D.C. and breaking windows is advancing the revolution is to delude oneself; it *hurts* the revolution, because it only alienates people. And it alienates them for good reason; they are *right* to be alienated; for they see that the window breaker is not supported by a mass base in Washington, and is not struggling around a demand that his tactic contributes to winning. He is just expressing his individual anger, not unlike the person who engages in acts of moral witness, whom we discussed before.

Talking is important, then. We want to *win people over* — win them over on the basis of ideas. We want to build a base, so that we can fight with a real chance of winning, and we want to accompany each of our struggles with constant explanation so that the struggle itself can be used to bring more people in, and bring them in on a good basis. I hate talk of "radicalizing" people and "politicizing" people; what this talk usually comes down to is leading someone into a situation in which he will get clubbed on the head by a cop so that he will "join the movement" — never mind on what basis, or with what ideas!

Let us take the case of anti-imperialist struggles. The fight to abolish R.O.T.C. is extremely important; unlike the Selective Service System, R.O.T.C. is wholly on campus, and it supplies 85% of all second lieutenants for the Vietnam war. But on what basis should one demand the abolition of R.O.T.C.? If one demands the abolition of R.O.T.C. on the basis that it has "no place in a university," one only fosters liberal illusions about the university. If one demands the abolition of R.O.T.C. because R.O.T.C. "channels" people, and the army is "authoritarian," one is fighting authority in the abstract. If a fight against R.O.T.C. is to have any chance of winning it must be on the only sound basis — that R.O.T.C. should be abolished because it provides the officers that America needs and uses to suppress the Vietnamese people, and to put down popular revolutions all over the world. This is a hard case — one has to have one's facts ready about the Vietnam war, about popular revolutions, about what has been going on in Latin America and all over the world. One has to convince students that there is a right to revolution, and that there is no right to suppresss legitimate popular revolutions. One has to convince students that America is playing a reactionary counter-revolutionary role. But this is not impossible. At Harvard hundreds of students have been won over by these arguments — not just by leafleting, but by speeches, discussions, and, most important, by students "canvassing" — going night after night to dormitories, and talking, talking, talking about the R.O.T.C. issue. Militant action — a sit-in at Paine Hall — played an important part; but without the enormous attention to political work, to *talking*, and to talking about the real issues, the militant action would only have led to students being expelled. R.O.T.C. has not yet been abolished at Harvard; but perhaps as many as two thousand students have now been convinced that the demand is just and the issue is important, and convinced for the right reasons.

Why is this an illustration of student-worker politics? Because saying that R.O.T.C. should be abolished because of what R.O.T.C. *does* is telling students that their struggle against R.O.T.C. is linked with the struggle of oppressed people, workers and farmers — in this case Vietnamese. Telling them that R.O.T.C. should be abolished for ivory tower reasons, or for pacifist reasons, on the other hand, fosters anti-working class sentiments which are too

prevalent already. It would be easy to get agreement that
R.O.T.C. should be abolished from many students on the basis of
university purity and pacifism; but the harder case is the one that
builds a movement.

(c) Fighting Anti-working Class Attitudes.

Part of what the student-worker alliance perspective means is
that one chooses good issues — issues that link up the concerns
of students with the oppression of working people, farmers, etc.,
at home and abroad, and that build community support for student
actions and student support for community actions. But another
part of what it means is a conscious effort to combat the anti-
working class attitudes of students that we have been mentioning.
These attitudes must be brought out into the open, faced, and
discussed. A particularly good way to do this is the device of the
"work-in." Last summer 350 members of S.D.S. around the
country took jobs in factories for the summer. Their aim was
(I repeat) not to "organize" the workers but to learn from the
workers — learn their experiences, and gain experience themselves
in raising issues with working people. I believe that the "work-in"
should be repeated and extended.

Organizing Inside The Army

The individual resister is a man who has to be supported, whatever one thinks of the mass draft-card turn-in. He sees that the
war is wrong, and he is trying to fight it. His refusal to enter the
army is abstractly just: no one should have to fight imperialist
wars. So one supports him in any way one can against the police,
the courts, the whole repressive apparatus. But one is left with
the question: if turning in one's draft card is the wrong tactic,
what is the correct thing to do?

This question frequently arises in counseling situations. Here,
I think, the position is clear; one should not attempt to dictate
to an individual what action he should take. The counselor should
help the person he is counseling become completely clear on his
own problem and, most important, on the nature of the war. But
he must not attempt to decide whether the person he is counseling
should go to Canada, or refuse induction, or enter the army. To
dissuade people from entering the army is to betray a fundamental
lack of trust in them; I believe that men in the army who under-

stand why the war is wrong will not kill Vietnamese and that they will do a great deal of good in the army. The counselor must make it clear that he will support whatever decision the person he is counseling arrives at.

While we support people who go to Canada, and people who refuse induction, I think that we have to recognize that the politically most useful thing for someone to do, if he is faced with the draft, is to accept induction with the intention of talking about the war inside the army.

To see why this is so, let us return to the draft-card turn-in again. This was a tactic of deliberately placing oneself in jeopardy. It was also a tactic limited to middle class students.

Why was it so limited? Partly, of course, because of the aspect of deliberately placing oneself in jeopardy. Jail is a familiar risk for working class youth — much more so than for middle class youth. A middle class youth may deceive himself that he is "refusing to be channelled" by going to jail; a working class youth is perfectly aware that he is doing no such thing, that jail is just another channel (the least pleasant one), and that there is no such thing as "refusing to be channelled" in this society. A middle class youth may think that one wins political fights by going to jail (by appealing to the conscience of the ruling class); a working class youth knows that you sometimes risk jail, but you never demand to go there.

But there are other reasons. Working class people are more savagely victimized than middle class people (it is difficult to get a job with a felony conviction, especially a working class job — a middle class person may live down a jail interlude, if it had a "pacifist" character). And there is not a strong anti-war movement among the working class. For all of these reasons, it was never expected that draft refusal would take hold among working class youth.

Under these conditions, it is clear that burning or turning in one's draft card takes on a decided anti-working class character if done as a public ceremony. Working people are deeply alienated by these tactics — indeed, the image of the draft-card burner has been used to discredit the whole movement. Partly, working people are alienated for bad reasons — because they are confused about the war, and about patriotism. But partly they are alienated for the very reasons we have discussed: because they intuitively feel the elitist character of the action, the attitude of moral superiority to them, and of appeal to the ruling class. What the people need is not somebody's moral superiority. In fact, the people are already engaged in a variety of struggles with their oppressors: wildcat strikes, black rebellions, etc. Our pressing need is to link up with them and to arrive with them at a general perspective of overthrowing the ruling class and setting up a just society.

Induction refusal has a somewhat in-between character. If one did not deliberately place oneself in jeopardy by turning in one's draft card, then induction refusal is a more individual action, and not necessarily a case of relying on moral witness as a way of fighting. As I have already indicated, we must support the man who, when faced with the decision, decides to refuse induction. But the fact is that by sitting in jail he does not fight the war, whereas in the army he could fight the war in a variety of ways. Moreover, if he is a middle class student he separates himself from the people by going to jail (and coming out as a kind of martyr), whereas going in the army would be accepting the experiences that working class people have no choice but to accept. On this ground alone, I think it is clear which decision a revolutionary should reach.

Many students feel, however, that they cannot possibly organize inside the army. Part of the answer to this is to debunk the idea of organizing. Not everyone can, say, start an anti-war base newspaper which comes out in 500 copies every issue, and win over his fellow soldiers so that not one would admit to having received the newspaper from him. (One G.I. actually did this.) For some organizing inside the army must take the more modest form of just talking honestly about the war with their buddies. For some it takes the form of distributing some copies of Vietnam G.I. (an anti-war newspaper for soldiers). Some students will feel that they could not take the risks associated with even the most cautious type of anti-war work inside the army, and that they must refuse induction or go to Canada. As I have been repeating, this is a decision we must accept and support. But anti-war work inside the army *is* possible; people are doing it — people who never thought they possibly could; and it is terribly important work.

By contrast, some people in the student movement want to organize G.I.s from outside. This is usually disastrous. Not only is it a violation of a general rule that one should organize people like oneself (so that if you want to organize G.I.s you should become one); but, at least in the Boston area the effect has been to get soldiers in trouble — say, by involving them in Resistance "sanctuaries" (i.e., in another form of moral witness). Increasingly, these people who organize G.I.s from outside are concentrating on legal defense of people who would not be in trouble if it were not for their defenders.

The Errors of the Resistance

If we contrast the perspective of worker-student alliance with the perspective of moral witness on which the Resistance was originally founded,[6] we can see why the organizational collapse of the Resistance was not an accident. The Resistance never had a strategy for winning anything, other than the losing strategy of moral witness, and it never engaged in more limited struggles in which there was a strategy for winning something. Since its members all looked forward to going to jail, there was no long term perspective of organizing, in or out of the army. And since the Resistance never developed a serious counseling program, it could not serve as an educational force for men facing the draft. All of these problems have the same source: the Resistance was a group of men who were in fundamental agreement only on "the war is bad" and on one *tactic*. In other cities the Resistance developed a more stable organization by becoming more explicitly pacifist and moral witness-y; i.e., the implicit politics of the tactic became the explicit politics of the organization. In Boston, the Resistance attempted to become a "radical" group, and to reject "mere" moral witness. But then there was nothing at all (except "the war is bad") on which its members were united. If the leadership had had good radical ideas, and had made a very early effort to take them to the membership and win the membership over (of course, this would have involved giving up the tactic of mass draft-card turn-ins), the situation might perhaps have been saved. But the leadership did not have student-worker alliance politics; they had the politics of anti-authoritarianism in the abstract, of "disruption" without base building, of "youth culture." Those politics *cannot* lead to a strategy for fighting and winning. The political style I described early in these pages, the political style associated with student-worker alliance politics, is also not an accident. Unity on the basis of ideas which have been discussed and understood and accepted by a group of people; collective struggle, leading to better

ideas leading to better struggle; criticism and self criticism; these
are not organizational forms which go with just any content. It is
no accident that people whose politics springs from petty bourgeois
individualism never form groups which exhibit these organizational
forms. Only on the basis of a serious identification with oppressed
people, with the great majority of mankind, and a serious desire
to serve the people can one develop this kind of organization. The
Resistance failed as an organization; but it speaks well for the
fundamental impulse that led young people to support it that a
number of them have gone on to this kind of identification, and to
the politics of student-worker alliance. On the basis of those
politics a movement is being built that will change this country
and change the world.

Notes

[1] In a "sanctuary" an AWOL publicly takes refuge in a church or university,
along with a crowd of supporters. The idea is that the entire group waits —
for days, if necessary — until the police come and bust the AWOL. For a
critique of this tactic, see my article in *New Left Notes*, Dec. 2, 1968.

[2] Henceforth, I will write simply "the Resistance" for "the New England
Resistance"; the reader should remember that I am not discussing the Resistance in other cities, although the remarks made later about moral witness
apply to the politics of these other groups as well as to the New England
Resistance.

[3] David Harris is a leader of the Berkeley Resistance, and one of the founding fathers of the national Resistance.

[4] The Progressive Labor Party is a Marxist-Leninist party whose ideas are
currently under intense discussion in the student movement. The party is
characterized by a Maoist theoretical outlook. In my brief acquaintance with
Progressive Labor people, I have been struck by the very good political work
they do, and by the high degree of honesty they display.

[5] The term "special admissions" is used both for admissions ahead of other
students and for admissions waiving various customary "qualifications."

[6] The New England Resistance has tried recently to get away from this
perspective, but without any clear result.

PRISON NOTES

PETER IRONS

The following notes were taken from letters written from prison-Ed.

March 13, 1967 — Life in a federal prison has a certain unreality about it, although in many respects it rips aside the polite veneer on life. What it exposes most clearly is that the "law-abiding" middle-class, refusing to face up to the social chaos it has created, only sweeps under the rug, safely out of sight, the products of its callousness. For the men in here are not stupid or inherently evil, but the end product of a system which delegates all the fruits of its abundance to those who bend to its rules of social status and "knowing your place."

The men in here have been exposed to all the lures of middle-class life — fancy cars, easy money, white-collar jobs and the "making it" which is the goal of middle-class adolescents — but they have been denied the opportunities to share in the middle-class cornucopia. They go to the worst schools, their parents work in crummy jobs, and they are taught not to aspire to college and the magic ticket of admission to the middle-class. In other words, the goodies are held out in front of them and then jerked away, out of reach. As a consequence, they become bitter and react by grabbing what they can, stealing cars and forging checks. All those who blithely believe this is a classless society, a land of opportunity, should spend some time in a slum school or better still, in a jail. Written over the doorways of both should be the words "Abandon all hope, all ye who enter here."

Those who (or whose parents) have the price to pay for a ticket of admission spend much time bemoaning the lack of willingness to work which is alleged to cause crime. Why not steal, if you're

335

too lazy to work or study, they assume. But work has little meaning if it involves the drudgery of washing cars or bussing dishes. It is not so much that they have failed society, as that society has failed them by relegating them to wretched schools, a cultural vacuum and the prospect of inferior jobs. The only surprise is that more of them do not end up in jail. Many of the men here have real potential and intelligence, and realize the phoniness of a society which demands a degree, polished grammar and a "yes, boss" approach to life.

June 13, 1967 — There is a red and purple glow in the west, out the window over my bed, and once in a while I can watch the pheasants pecking around in the cornfield. But I can't walk around in the field; I must watch through the window. I will have many years to do so but it is now that I feel. If I had the fire-breathing certainty of the fanatic, the true believer, or the resignation of the cynic, I don't think I would miss as much the simple pleasures I am denied. But I am neither; I cannot say without the slightest twinge of doubt that this is where I should be. My doubts have been answered by reasonable arguments, but they do occasionally intrude upon me, questioning my motives or my tactics. This is healthy; the man without doubt is a man incapable of choosing between alternatives and changing his course when the landscape of reality changes.

July 4, 1967 — This whole prison system is built on a basis of lack of trust and denial of humanness. Individuals — hacks, inmates and staff, can relate as persons, but there is always the grim, grey reality of the system, more solid and concrete than the walls. Real relationships must be built on equality and trust, but everyone here is conscious of the hierarchy and the lack of trust that pervades this place. And without trust, the inmate reasons or apprehends, why should I act trustfully?

November 1, 1967 — . . . the futility of war is not only that it kills the young men who do not really understand it, but that it kills the joy of life in all those who are touched by it and swept up in it. And it will cripple us until we break out of the limits of "taking sides" and fight for life. Fight against the war, yes, as hard as we can, but also live and create in the face of it. Make love, not war. "Make" love by building it between people and in ourselves. "Making" love, learning how to craft it and mold it and decorate it should be the trade we teach our children. Everything else is meaningless without it . . . So there's my speech to the parole board if I had not been locked into my convict role. But speeches don't mean much; what I do to create and sustain love is what counts.

November 2, 1967 — Most of my day was spent in those little skirmishes against the armadillo-bureaucracy that make life both frustrating and funny. You just have to laugh at the ways in which people let rules and regulations push them around like rubber balls. For instance, my box of belongings finally arrived from Terre Haute after two months in limbo. So we make a list of what I can keep and what has to be sent home. Can't keep the letters, of course. Of course? Can't keep the tennis shoes; only hightop sneakers allowed here. What? Good grief, Charlie Brown. The officer flipped through the books looking for contraband; people have been known to smuggle guns in hollowed-out books. Never thought that the book itself could be a high explosive. How many people were killed in the Crusades because the Bible told them that they were better than the "infidels"? Oh well. The only thing that caught his eye was a picture of a nude in Marshall McLuhan's book. He let it pass, but he looked long at it.

November 7, 1967 — So at last it is winter, with the first snow, and I have completed a full cycle of the seasons in prison. It was snowing when I went in, and it is snowing again. I have not shared the spring and summer and fall with you, although we have shared it in our separate ways. But one or even two cycles of the earth round the sun are really insignificant in a larger span of time. If I am right in being in here, then all the cycles of the seasons we will share later will be more deeply felt, and the snow we walk through and the sun we lie in will make us more aware that time means only what you make it mean. Without living it, time does not exist, and we have lived together this year.

November 13, 1967 — Since a prison is an artificial community, the inmates are stripped of all the ties of family, neighborhood and common goals. Each man is an island and we have only the most superficial and transitory bonds between us. We are really atoms with nothing to link us together save our common criminal status. With no goals and no permanence, we gradually loose the bonds we bring with us and become no more than a collection of penned animals. At least this is true of most men in prison.

September 4, 1968 — The most redeeming feature of today is that it is almost over and that I'm down to 170 days left. Ever since the 200 day mark, every ten days closer to freedom is like one of the bigger beads on a rosary — a reminder that you are closer to the end of your penance. And with only seventeen big beads to go I feel like an impatient Catholic paying off a mortal sin imposed by the men in the confessional, sort of like a judge, hidden from view behind a screen of laws and prejudices, but real in his power to inflict pain and penance.

September 17, 1968 — . . . a prison society forces all of its members, jailers and inmates, into a trivial and absurd condition which is both a tragic and profound commentary on the inability of a repressive system to allow people their humanity. It is funny in the sense that *Catch-22* is funny — a humor that has underneath it the bitter mocking laughter of the man condemned to futility and desperation. Like flies trapped in honey, we all buzz and struggle and finally sink back, telling ourselves that at least we can enjoy the sweet taste of honey. Never mind that it will mean our death. No one, while in this system, can escape the bondage it imposes, and the worst bondage is that we cannot relate to each other as real human people. It is painful to be reminded of this, and the fly, still savoring the honey, will nonetheless beat his wings to escape it.

December 25, 1968 — Well, we got our brown paper bags again this year, but instead of doling them out from a laundry cart in the dorms, we were herded, one dorm at a time, over to the mess hall. Much more efficient; in one door, literally at a run, grab a bag, then out the other. Two packs of Pall Malls, two cans of Coke, two small boxes of ginger snaps, a candy bar, a bag of hard candy and a bag of assorted nuts. Followed by a noisy session of trading cigarettes for Cokes, etc. Christmas evening in prison. Grab and run. Christ would have thrown it on the floor. I ate the nuts and drank the Cokes and gave away the cigarettes and went to bed early.

IV

THE NEW SOCIETY: A BEGINNING

THE TRIPLE REVOLUTION

This statement is written in the recognition that mankind is at a historic conjuncture which demands a fundamental reexamination of existing values and institutions. At this time three separate and mutually reinforcing revolutions are taking place:

The Cybernation Revolution: A new era of production has begun. Its principles of organization are as different from those of the industrial era as those of the industrial era were different from the agricultural. The cybernation revolution has been brought about by the combination of the computer and the automated self-regulating machine. This results in a system of almost unlimited productive capacity which requires progressively less human labor. Cybernation is already reorganizing the economic and social system to meet its own needs.

The Weaponry Revolution: New forms of weaponry have been developed which cannot win wars but which can obliterate civilization. We are recognizing only now that the great weapons have eliminated war as a method for resolving international conflicts. The ever-present threat of total destruction is tempered by the knowledge of the final futility of war. The need of a "warless world" is generally recognized, though achieving it will be a long and frustrating process.

The Human Rights Revolution: A universal demand for full human rights is now clearly evident. It continues to be demonstrated in the civil rights movement within the United States. But this is only the local manifestation of a worldwide movement toward the establishment of social and political regimes in which every individual will feel valued and none will feel rejected on account of his race.

We are particularly concerned in this statement with the first of these revolutionary phenomena. This is not because we under-estimate the significance of the other two. On the contrary, we affirm that it is the simultaneous occurrence and interaction of all three developments which make evident the necessity for radical alterations in attitude and policy. The adoption of just policies for coping with cybernation and for extending rights to all Americans is indispensable to the creation of an atmosphere in the U.S. in which the supreme issue, peace, can be reasonably debated and resolved.

The Negro claims, as a matter of simple justice, his full share in America's economic and social life. He sees adequate employment opportunities as a chief means of attaining this goal: the March on Washington demanded freedom *and* jobs. The Negro's claim to a job is not being met. Negroes are the hardest-hit of the many groups being exiled from the economy by cybernation. Negro unemployment rates cannot be expected to drop substantially. Promises of jobs are a cruel and dangerous hoax on hundreds of thousands of Negroes and whites alike who are especially vulner-able to cybernation because of age or inadequate education.

The demand of the civil rights movement cannot be fulfilled within the present context of society. The Negro is trying to enter a social community and a tradition of work-and-income which are in the process of vanishing even for the hitherto privileged white worker. Jobs are disappearing under the impact of highly efficient, progressively less costly machines.

The U.S. operates on the thesis, set out in the Employment Act of 1964, that every person will be able to obtain a job if he wishes to do so and that this job will provide him with resources adequate to live and maintain a family decently. Thus job-holding is the general mechanism through which economic resources are dis-tributed. Those without work have access only to a minimal in-come, hardly sufficient to provide the necessities of life, and enabling those receiving it to function as only "minimum con-sumers." As a result, the goods and services which are needed by these crippled consumers, and which they would buy if they could, are not produced. This in turn deprives other workers of jobs, thus reducing their incomes and consumption.

Present excessive levels of unemployment would be multiplied several times if military and space expenditures did not continue to absorb 10% of the gross national product (i.e., the total goods and services produced). Some 6 to 8 million people are employed as a direct result of purchases for space and military activities. At least an equal number hold their jobs as an indirect result of military or space expenditures. In recent years, the military and space budgets have absorbed a rising proportion of national production and formed a strong support for the economy.

However, these expenditures are coming in for more and more criticism, at least partially in recognition of the fact that nuclear weapons have eliminated war as an acceptable method for resolving international conflicts. Early in 1964 President Johnson ordered a curtailment of certain military expenditures. Defense Secretary McNamara is closing shipyards, airfields, and Army bases, and Congress is pressing the National Space Administration to economize. The future of these strong props to the economy is not as clear today as it was even a year ago.

How the Cybernation Revolution Shapes Up

Cybernation is manifesting the characteristics of a revolution in production. These include the development of radically different techniques and the subsequent appearance of novel principles of the organization of production; a basic reordering of man's relationship to his environment; and a dramatic increase in total available and potential energy.

The major difference between the agricultural, industrial and cybernation revolutions is the speed at which they developed. The agricultural revolution began several thousand years ago in the Middle East. Centuries passed in the shift from a subsistence base of hunting and food-gathering to settled agriculture.

In contrast, it has been less than 200 years since the emergence of the industrial revolution, and direct and accurate knowledge of the new productive techniques has reached most of mankind. This swift dissemination of information is generally held to be the main factor leading to widespread industrialization.

While the major aspects of the cybernation revolution are for the moment restricted to the U.S., its effects are observable almost at once throughout the industrial world and large parts of the non-industrial world. Observation is rapidly followed by analysis and criticism. The problems posed by the cybernation revolution are part of a new era in the history of all mankind but they are first being faced by the people of the U.S. The way Americans cope with cybernation will influence the course of this phenomenon everywhere. This country is the stage on which the machines-and-man drama will first be played for the world to witness.

The fundamental problem posed by the cybernation revolution in the U.S. is that it invalidates the general mechanism so far employed to undergird people's rights as consumers. Up to this time economic resources have been distributed on the basis of contributions to production, with machines and men competing for employment on somewhat equal terms. In the developing cybernated system, potentially unlimited output can be achieved by systems of machines which will require little cooperation from human beings. As machines take over production from men, they absorb an increasing proportion of resources while the men who are displaced become dependent on minimal and unrelated government measures — unemployment insurance, social security, welfare payments.

These measures are less and less able to disguise a historic paradox: that a substantial proportion of the population is subsisting on minimal incomes, often below the poverty line, at a time when sufficient productive potential is available to supply the needs of everyone in the U.S.

Industrial System Fails to Provide for Abolition of Poverty

The existence of this paradox is denied or ignored by conventional economic analysis. The general economic approach argues that potential demand, which if filled would raise the number of jobs and provide incomes to those holding them, is underestimated. Most contemporary economic analysis states that all of the available labor force and industrial capacity is required to meet the needs of consumers and industry and to provide adequate public services: schools, parks, roads, homes, decent cities, and clean water and air. It is further argued that demand could be increased, by a variety of standard techniques, to any desired extent by providing money and machines to improve the conditions of the billions of impoverished people elsewhere in the world, who need food and shelter, clothes and machinery and everything else the industrial nations take for granted.

There is no question that cybernation does increase the potential for the provision of funds to neglected public sectors. Nor is there any question that cybernation would make possible the abolition of poverty at home and abroad. But the industrial system does not possess any adequate mechanisms to permit these potentials to become realities. The industrial system was designed to produce an ever-increasing quantity of goods as efficiently as possible, and it was assumed that the distribution of the power to purchase these goods would occur almost automatically. The continuance of the income-through-jobs link as the only major mechanism for distributing effective demand — for granting the right to consume — now acts as the main brake on the almost unlimited capacity of a cybernated productive system.

Recent administrations have proposed measures aimed at achieving a better distribution of resources, and at reducing unemployment and underemployment. A few of these proposals have been enacted. More often they have failed to secure congressional support. In every case, many members of Congress have criticized the proposed measures as departing from traditional principles for the allocation of resources and the encouragement of production. Abetted by budget-balancing economists and interest groups, they have argued for the maintenance of an economic machine based on ideas of scarcity to deal with the facts of abundance produced by cybernation. This time-consuming criticism has slowed the workings of Congress and has thrown out of focus for that body the inter-related effects of the triple revolution.

An adequate distribution of the potential abundance of goods and services will be achieved only when it is understood that the major economic problem is not how to increase production, but how to distribute the abundance that is the great potential of cybernation. There is an urgent need for a fundamental change in the mechanisms employed to insure consumer rights.

Facts and Figures of the Cybernation Revolution

No responsible observer would attempt to describe the exact pace or the full sweep of a phenomenon that is developing with the speed of cybernation. Some aspects of this revolution, however, are already clear:

• The rate of productivity increase has risen with the onset of cybernation.

• An industrial economic system postulated on scarcity has been unable to distribute the abundant goods and services produced by a cybernated system or potential in it.

• Surplus capacity and unemployment have thus co-existed at excessive levels over the last six years.

• The underlying cause of excessive unemployment is the fact that the capability of machines is rising more rapidly than the capacity of many human beings to keep pace.

• A permanent impoverished and jobless class is established in the midst of potential abundance.

Evidence for these statements follows:

1. The increased efficiency of machine systems is shown in the more rapid increase in productivity per man-hour since 1960, a year that marks the first visible upsurge of the cybernation revolution. In 1961, 1962 and 1963, productivity per man-hour rose at an average pace above 3.5% — a rate well above both the historical average and the postwar rate.

Companies are finding cybernation more and more attractive. Even at the present early stage of cybernation, costs have already been lowered to a point where the price of a durable machine may be a little as one-third of the current annual wage-cost of the worker it replaces. A more rapid rise in the rate of productivity increase per man-hour can be expected from now on.

2. In recent years it has proved to increase demand fast enough to bring about the full use either of men or of plant capacities. The task of developing sufficient additional demand promises to become more difficult each year. A $30 billion annual increase in gross national product is now required to prevent unemployment rates from rising. An additional $40 to $60 billion increase would be required to bring unemployment rates down to an acceptable level.

3. The official rate of unemployment has remained at or above 5.5% during the Sixties. The unemployment rate for teenagers has been rising steadily and now stands around 15%. The unemployment rate for Negro teenagers stands at about 30%. The unemployment rate for teenagers in minority ghettos sometimes exceeds 50%. Unemployment rates for Negroes are regularly more than twice those for whites, whatever their occupation, educational level, age or sex. The unemployment position for other racial minorities is similarly unfavorable. Unemployment rates in depressed areas often exceed 50%.

Unemployment Is Far Worse Than Figures Indicate

These official figures seriously underestimate the true extent of unemployment. The statistics take no notice of underemployment or featherbedding. Besides the 5.5% of the labor force who are officially designated as unemployed, nearly 4% of the labor force sought full-time work in 1962 but could find only part-time jobs. In addition, methods of calculating unemployment rates — a person is counted as unemployed only if he has actively sought a job recently — ignore the fact that many men and women who would like to find jobs have not looked for them because they know there are no employment opportunities.

Underestimates for this reason are pervasive among groups whose unemployment rates are high — the young, the old, and racial minorities. Many people in the depressed agricultural, mining and industrial areas, who by official definition hold jobs but who are actually grossly underemployed, would move if there were prospects of finding work elsewhere. It is reasonable to estimate that over 8,000,000 people are not working who would like to have jobs today as compared with the 4,000,000 shown in the official statistics.

Even more serious is the fact that the number of people who have voluntarily removed themselves from the labor force is not constant but increases continuously. These people have decided to stop looking for employment and seem to have accepted the fact that they will never hold jobs again. This decision is largely irreversible, in economic and also in social and psychological terms. The older worker calls himself "retired"; he cannot accept work without affecting his social security status. The worker in his prime years is forced onto relief: in most states the requirements for becoming a relief recipient bring about such fundamental alterations in an individual's situation that a reversal of the process is always difficult and often totally unfeasible. Teenagers, especially "drop-outs" and Negroes, are coming to realize that there is no place for them in the labor force but at the same time they are given no realistic alternative. These people and their dependents make up a large part of the "poverty" sector of the American population.

Statistical evidence of these trends appears in the decline in the proportion of people claiming to be in the labor force — the so-called labor force participation rate. The recent apparent stabilization of the unemployment rate around 5.5% is therefore misleading: it is a reflection of the discouragement and defeat of people who cannot find employment and have withdrawn from the market, rather than a measure of the economy's success in creating jobs for those who want to work.

4. An efficiently functioning industrial system is assumed to provide the great majority of new jobs through the expansion of the private enterprise sector. But well over half of the new jobs created during 1957–1962 were in the public sector — predominantly in teaching. Job creation in the private sector has now almost entirely ceased except in services; of the 4,300,000 jobs created in this period, only about 200,000 were provided by private industry through its own efforts. Many authorities anticipate that the application of cybernation to certain service industries, which is only just beginning, will be particularly effective. If this is the case, no significant job creation will take place in the private sector in coming years.

5. Cybernation raises the level of the skills of the machine. Secretary of Labor Wirtz has recently stated that the machines being produced today have, on the average, skills equivalent to a high school diploma. If a human being is to compete with such machines, therefore, he must a least possess a high school diploma. The Department of Labor estimates, however, that on the basis of present trends, as many as 30% of all students will be high school drop-outs in this decade.

6. A permanently depressed class is developing in the U.S. Some 38,000,000 Americans, almost one-fifth of the nation, still live in poverty. The percentage of total income received by the poorest 20% of the population was 4.9% in 1944 and 4.7% in 1963.

Secretary Wirtz recently summarized these trends: "The confluence of surging population and driving technology is splitting the American labor force into tens of millions of 'haves' and millions of 'have-nots.' In our economy of 69,000,000 jobs, those with wanted skills enjoy opportunity and earning power. But the others face a new and stark problem — exclusion on a permanent basis, both as producers and consumers, from economic life. This division of people threatens to create a human slag heap. We cannot tolerate the development of a separate nation of the poor, the unskilled, the jobless, living within another nation of the well-off, the trained and the employed."

New Consensus Needed

The stubbornness and novelty of the situation that is conveyed by these statistics is now generally accepted. Ironically, it continues to be assumed that it is possible to devise measures which will reduce unemployment to a minimum and thus preserve the over-all viability of the present productive system. Some authorities have gone so far as to suggest that the pace of technological change should be slowed down "so as to allow the industrial productive system time to adapt."

We believe, on the contrary, that the industrial productive system is no longer viable. We assert that the only way to turn technological change to the benefit of the individual and the service of the general welfare is to accept the process and to utilize it rationally and humanely. The new science of political economy will be built on the encouragement and planned expansion of cybernation. The issues raised by cybernation are particularly amenable to intelligent policy-making: cybernation itself provides the resources and tools that are needed to ensure minimum hardship during the transition process.

But major changes must be made in our attitudes and institutions in the foreseeable future. Today Americans are being swept along by three simultaneous revolutions while assuming they have them under control. In the absence of real understanding of any of these phenomena, especially of technology, we may be allowing an efficient and dehumanized community to emerge by default. Gaining control of our future requires the conscious formation of the society we wish to have. Cybernation at last forces us to answer the historic questions: What is man's role when he is not dependent upon his own activities for the material basis of his life? What should be the basis for distributing individual access to national resources? Are there other proper claims on goods and services besides a job?

Because of cybernation, society no longer needs to impose repetitive and meaningless (because unnecessary) toil upon the individual. Society can now set the citizen free to make his own choice of occupation and vocation from a wide range of activities not now fostered by our value system and our accepted modes of "work." But in the absence of such a new consensus about cybernation, the nation cannot begin to take advantage of all that it promises for human betterment.

Proposal for Action

As a first step to a new consensus it is essential to recognize that the traditional link between jobs and incomes is being broken. The economy of abundance can sustain all citizens in comfort and economic security whether or not they engage in what is commonly reckoned as work. Wealth produced by machines rather than by men is still wealth. We urge, therefore, that society, through its appropriate legal and governmental institutions, undertake an unqualified commitment to provide every individual and every family with an adequate income as a matter of right.

This undertaking we consider to be essential to the emerging economic, social and political order in this country. We regard it as the only policy by which the quarter of the nation now dispossessed and soon to be dispossessed by lack of employment can be brought within the abundant society. The unqualified right to an income designed to ensure that no citizen or resident of the U. S. actually starves, would take the place of the patchwork of welfare measures, from unemployment insurance to relief.

We do not pretend to visualize all of the consequences of this change in our values. It is clear, however, that the distribution of abundance in a cybernated society must be based on criteria strikingly different from those of an economic system based on scarcity. In retrospect, the establishment of the right to an income will prove to have been only the first step in the reconstruction of the value system of our society brought on by the triple revolution.

The present system encourages activities which can lead to private profit and neglects those activities which can enhance the wealth and the quality of life of our society. Consequently, national policy has hitherto been aimed far more at the welfare of the productive process than at the welfare of people. The era of cybernation can reverse this emphasis. With public policy and research concentrated on people rather than processes, we believe that many creative activities and interests commonly thought of as non-economic will absorb the time and the commitment of many of those no longer needed to produce goods and services.

Society as a whole must encourage new modes of constructive, rewarding and ennobling activity. Principal among these are activities such as teaching and learning that relate people to people rather than people to things. Education has never been primarily conducted for profit in our society; it represents the first and most obvious activity inviting the expansion of the public sector to meet the needs of this period of transition.

We are not able to predict the long-run patterns of human activity and commitment in a nation when fewer and fewer people are involved in production of goods and services, nor are we able to forecast the over-all patterns of income distribution that will replace those of the past full employment system. However, these are not speculative and fanciful matters to be contemplated at leisure for a society that may come into existence in three or four generations. The outlines of the future press sharply into the present. The problems of joblessness, inadequate incomes, and frustrated lives confront us now; the American Negro, in his rebellion, asserts the demands — and the rights — of all the disadvantaged. The Negro's is the most insistent voice today, but behind him stand the millions of impoverished who are beginning to understand that cybernation, properly understood and used, is the road out of want and toward a decent life.

The Transition

This view of the transitional period is not shared by all the signers. Robert Theobald and James Boggs hold that the two major principles of the transitional period will be (1) that machines rather than men will take up new conventional work openings and (2) that the activity of men will be directed to new forms of "work" and "leisure." Therefore, in their opinion, the specific proposals outlined in this section are more suitable for meeting the problems of the scarcity-economic system than for advancing through the period of transition into the period of abundance.

We recognize that the drastic alternations in circumstances and in our way of life ushered in by cybernation and the economy of abundance will not be completed overnight. Left to the ordinary forces of the market such change, however, will involve physical and psychological misery and perhaps political chaos. Such misery is already clearly evident among the unemployed, among relief clients into the third generation, and more and more among the young and the old for whom society appears to hold no promise of dignified or even stable lives. We must develop programs for this transition designed to give hope to the dispossessed and those cast out by the economic system, and to provide a basis for the rallying of people to bring about those changes in political and social institutions which are essential to the age of technology.

The program here suggested is not intended to be inclusive but rather to indicate its necessary scope. We propose:

1. A massive program to build up our educational system, designed especially with the needs of the chronically under-educated in mind. We estimate that tens of thousands of employment opportunities in such areas as teaching and research and development, particularly for younger people, may be thus created. Federal programs looking to the training of an additional 100,000 teachers annually are needed.

2. Massive public works. The need is to develop and put into effect programs of public works to construct dams, reservoirs, ports, water and air pollution facilities, community recreation facilities. We estimate that for each $1 billion per year spent on public works 150,000 to 200,000 jobs would be created. $2 billion or more a year should be spent in this way, preferably as matching funds aimed at the relief of economically distressed or dislocated areas.

3. A massive program of low-cost housing, to be built both publicly and privately, at a rate of 700,000-1,000,000 units a year.

4. Development and financing of rapid transit systems, urban and interurban; and other programs to cope with the spreading problems of the great metropolitan centers.

5. A public power system built on the abundance of coal in distressed areas, designed for low-cost power to heavy industrial and residential sections.

6. Rehabilitation of obsolete military bases for community or educational use.

7. A major revision of our tax structure aimed at redistributing income as well as apportioning the costs of the transition period equitably. To this end an expansion of the use of excess profits tax would be important. Subsidies and tax credit plans are required to ease the human suffering involved in the transition of many industries from man power to machine power.

8. The trade unions can play an important and significant role in this period in a number of ways:

   a. Use of collective bargaining to negotiate not only for people at work but also for those thrown out of work by technological change.

   b. Bargaining for perquisites such as housing, recreational facilities, and similar programs as they have negotiated health and welfare programs.

c. Obtaining a voice in the investment of the unions' huge pension and welfare funds, and insisting on investment policies which have as their major criteria the social use and function of the enterprise in which the investment is made.

d. Organization of the unemployed so that these voiceless people may once more be given a voice in their own economic destinies, and strengthening of the campaigns to organize white-collar and professional workers.

9. The use of the licensing power of government to regulate the speed and direction of cybernation to minimize hardship; and the use of minimum wage power as well as taxing powers to provide the incentives for moving as rapidly as possible toward the goals indicated by this paper.

These suggestions are in no way intended to be complete or definitively formulated. They contemplate expenditures of several billions more each year than are now being spent for socially rewarding enterprises, and a larger role for the government in the economy than it has now or has been given except in times of crisis. In our opinion, this is a time of crisis, the crisis of a triple revolution. Public philosophy for the transition must rest on the conviction that our economic, social and political institutions exist for the use of man and that man does not exist to maintain a particular economic system. This philosophy centers on an understanding that governments are instituted among men for the purpose of making possible life, liberty, and the pursuit of happiness and that government should be a creative and positive instrument toward these ends.

Change Must Be Managed

The historic discovery of the post-World War II years is that the economic destiny of the nation can be managed. Since the debate over the Employment Act of 1946 it has been increasingly understood that the federal government bears primary responsibility for the economic and social well-being of the country. The essence of management is planning. The democratic requirement is planning by public bodies for the general welfare. Planning by private bodies such as corporations for their own welfare does not automatically result in additions to the general welfare, as the impact of cybernation on jobs has already made clear.

The hardships imposed by sudden changes in technology have been acknowledged by Congress in proposals for dealing with the long- and short-run "dislocations," in legislation for depressed and "impacted" areas, retraining of workers replaced by machines, and the like. The measures so far proposed have not been "transitional" in conception. Perhaps for this reason they have had little effect on the situations they were designed to alleviate. But the primary weakness of this legislation is not ineffectiveness but incoherence. In no way can these disconnected measures be seen as a plan for remedying deep ailments but only, so to speak, as the superficial treatment of surface wounds.

Planning agencies should constitute the network through which pass the stated needs of the people at every level of society, gradually building into a national inventory of human requirements, arrived at by democratic debate of elected representatives.

The primary tasks of the appropriate planning institutions should be:

• To collect the data necessary to appraise the effects, social and economic, of cybernation at different rates of innovation.

• To recommend ways, by public and private initiative, of encouraging and stimulating cybernation.

• To work toward optimal allocations of human and natural resources in meeting the requirements of society.

• To develop ways to smooth the transition from a society in which the norm is full employment within an economic system based on scarcity, to one in which the norm will be either non-employment, in the traditional sense of productive work, or employment on the great variety of socially valuable but "non-productive" tasks made possible by an economy of abundance; to bring about the conditions in which men and women no longer needed to produce goods and services may find their way to a variety of self-fulfilling and socially useful occupations.

• To work out alternatives to defense and related spending that will commend themselves to citizens, entrepreneurs and workers as a more reasonable use of common resources.

• To integrate domestic and international planning. The technological revolution has related virtually every major domestic problem to a world problem. The vast inequities between the industrialized and the underdeveloped countries cannot long be sustained.

The aim throughout will be the conscious and rational direction of economic life by planning institutions under democratic control.

In this changed framework the new planning institutions will operate at every level of government — local, regional and federal — and will be organized to elicit democratic participation in all their proceedings. These bodies will be the means for giving direction and content to the growing demand for improvement in all departments of public life. The planning institutions will show the way to turn the growing protest against ugly cities, polluted air and water, an inadequate educational system, disappearing recreational and material resources, low levels of medical care, and the haphazard economic development into an integrated effort to raise the level of general welfare.

We are encouraged by the record of the planning institutions both of the Common Market and of several European nations and believe that this country can benefit from studying their weaknesses and strengths.

A principal result of planning will be to step up investment in the public sector. Greater investment in this area is advocated because it is overdue, because the needs in this sector comprise a substantial part of the content of the general welfare, and because they can be readily afforded by an abundant society. Given the knowledge that we are now in a period of transition it would be deceptive, in our opinion, to present such activities as likely to produce full employment. The efficiencies of cybernation should be as much sought in the public as in the private sector, and a chief focus of planning would be one means of bringing this about. A central assumption of planning institutions would be the central assumption of this statement, that the nation is moving into a society in which production of goods and services is not the only or perhaps the chief means of distributing income.

The Democratization of Change

The revolution in weaponry gives some dim promise that mankind may finally eliminate institutionalized force as the method of settling international conflict and find for it political and moral equivalents leading to a better world. The Negro revolution signals the ultimate admission of this group to the American community on equal social, political and economic terms. The cybernation revolution proffers an existence qualitatively richer in democratic as well as material values. A social order in which men make the decisions that shape their lives becomes more possible now than ever before; the unshackling of men from the bonds of unfulfilling labor frees them to become citizens, to make themselves and to make their own history.

But these enhanced promises by no means constitute a guarantee. Illuminating and making more possible the "democratic vistas" is one thing; reaching them is quite another, for a vision of democratic life is made real not by technological change but by men consciously moving toward that ideal and creating institutions that will realize and nourish the vision in living form.

Democracy, as we use the term, means a community of men and women who are able to understand, express and determine their lives as dignified human beings. Democracy can only be rooted in a political and economic order in which wealth is distributed by and for people, and used for the widest social benefit. With the emergence of the era of abundance we have the economic base for a true democracy of participation, in which men no longer need to feel themselves prisoners of social forces and decisions beyond their control or comprehension.

Donald G. Agger
Donald B. Armstrong, M.D.
James Boggs
W. H. Ferry
Todd Gitlin
Roger Hagan
Michael Harrington
Tom Hayden
Ralph L. Helstein
Dr. Frances W. Herring
Brig. Gen. Hugh B. Hester
  (Retired)
Gerald W. Johnson
Irving F. Laucks
Gunner Myrdal
  "I am in broad agreement with
  this Statement, though not
  entirely so."
Gerard Piel
Michael D. Reagan

Ben B. Seligman
Robert Theobald
William Worthy
Alice Mary Hilton
Maxwell Geismar
Philip Green
H. Stuart Hughes
Linus Pauling
John William Ward
A. J. Muste
Dr. Louis Fein
Stewart Meacham
Everett C. Hughes
Robert L. Heilbroner
Irving Howe
Bayard Rustin
Norman Thomas
Dwight Macdonald
Carl F. Stover
Ron M. Linton
Erich Fromm

ON COMMUNITY BUILDING

RICK MARGOLIES

What do we do when we're white and affluent, in a world of starvation and colored revolution? Sent to the best schools, for what? To make more money and spend how many vapid Sundays by the pool? Toward what distant goal?

Yes, we've been raised with the best the age could buy: clothes, cars, trips, maids, colleges. And still we're not satisfied. The children of affluence, playing the games of the age. The world prostrate before us, why not rise to the rape? Perhaps, we're afraid to lie, perhaps we learned our families' spoken moralisms too well. Yes, afraid to call cynicism wisdom, label resignation reality. And now, a bit unsure, we stand in beards and old army shirts, having cut loose our buttoned-down minds just a bit. We've marched against the war only to find our parents won't let us come home. We've refused to cooperate with the draft and are in court. For what? Whose battles are we fighting? Deep down, we don't really believe we're making a revolution. We: lily-white, pampered sons and daughters of the suburbs, with our puffy, soft bodies which may never know what labor means. But for all our self-doubts this much we know: we can never go back again. 10,000 kids out to change the world. Now the years of dreaming and visionary phrase-making are over and we stand face-to-face with ourselves. Wrestling with the demons within, striking at the devils without, we must fill the void of this plastic pleasure world or become a vacuum in it.

Several years ago community was the cop-out of those who couldn't cope with our political struggles. Today we find our political and psychic renewal in the creation of community. Our hardships in the past few years have shown the road that supports us in helping each other work things out emotionally and intellectually is the path of greatest political relevancy as well. For most cry out for a better way to live together but are too emotionally and economically locked up in their present style of living. Young people can talk with us freely about our concerns because they have not yet invested their lives in an entrapping mode of existence. Parents and older people, quietly sympathetic to our concerns and criticisms, demand to know our "program." Our "program" is what we are already about: the discovery of our true selves and our need for new relationships, which is the creation of community where there was just alienation.

Thus, our task in the years ahead is to restructure our lives into these new forms of relatedness to each other and the greater society. Our concern is to destroy the master-slave relationship in all its corporate and psychic manifestations and to build in its place non-hierarchic communities. Wherever people are living or working and are not the initiators and final arbitors of that life process, we must lead people to restructure their situation so that where there was a pyramid of command there is now a non-hierarchic democratic body or community. Thus, our politics is mediated to us through our own relationships, whether we be in a family, a work group, or a learning situation.

The Failure of Contemporary Politics

In order to see our task clearly we must understand how the political process rationalizes the mainstream of American life. The failure of contemporary politics is that it accepts as given the atomization, alienation, and fragmentation of existence in an advanced capitalist society. Both conservatives and liberals are corporate capitalists, for their lives are determined by the organizational mode and existential style of the corporation and the city. Lives are atomized in careers and families, each man/family an individual unit viewing itself in competition with all other such units. Sharing and cooperation become superficial. One expends life's energy in accumulating money and consumer objects toward making one's home a privatized utopia. One's personal success and worth are soon equated with accumulated property and people find themselves isolated in their home or apartment with two or three locks on the door. People become threats.

The city fragments our lives by separating work, service and residential sections by considerable distances. People work miles from their homes and develop two sets of acquaintances: those on the job and those at home. At work one relates to those around through the corporate role one has achieved; one knows who is inferior and can be ordered around and whom one must obey. At home, after the psychic death of commuting, one's relationship increasingly takes on the same master-slave character: the wife must keep her place as cook/housekeeper and the kids are ordered around like administrative assistants. People conform to their roles, and as the saying goes, "just do the job." People become objects.

The city is built for commerce and travel. The roads are laid out for auto and truck traffic, not for people. The neighborhoods are segregated as either business or residential by bureaucratic zoning boards that are little influenced by the people who live in the area. The idea of reconstructing the city into humanly-scaled communal neighborhoods in which people can walk or bicycle to stores and services is a threat to the propertied class which controls the zoning and redevelopment boards. People become nuisances.

A man's politics is truly alienated from him if it is a concern he has outside of his everyday existence. No matter whether he is a conservative, a liberal, or a radical, he relates to those around him as threats, objects, and nuisances. The exploitative nature of our lives will remain if we resign ourselves to this alienated politics which is not grounded in a new economic and social reality.

Beyond Resistance: The Integration of Political, Economic and Social Spheres

If we were truly free we would set our own terms. This would mean to work for a new wholeness in our lives. Resistance and protest are basically forms of alienated politics because they do not embrace the total man as he lives his life; they never transcend outrage. We should, of course, resist when we are pushed and protest when outraged, but it is clear that this does not teach us how to live our lives anew. I am far from arguing for the end of protest and resistance, rather for the integration of this vitally necessary consciousness-building activity into a non-frenetic philosophy of our life's work. For personal frustration and psychic

exhaustion are endemic to resistance politics. If a fuller comprehension of what we are about is not grasped we will all become
cynical, bleary-eyed nihilists. The New York City Resistance (an
anti-draft group) has discovered this through its own struggle. In
a recent mailing they counseled "The concept of communal living
is an important element in the lives of people who see themselves
in the struggle for social change on a long-term basis. Development of community and dealing with inter-personal relations are
very important in facilitating working together. Experiments with
new forms of living are crucial to the development of a vision of
the new society that must be built."

The liberal, with his do-your-own-thing pluralism, has no such
socialist vision of a common life together, for his life is rooted deep
in the class and caste system of capitalism, as are his myriad
neuroses. If we know the psychological destructiveness of a
bourgeois existence built around property, how can we but share
what money and property we have? If we see the human perversity
of treating children as private property, how can we but raise our
children in communal families as the kibbutzim do? A marriage
easily becomes a vapid box trapping man, wife and children in a
circle of distrust. Did you know that the Oneida Community over
110 years ago had a highly successful community marriage in which
each was married to all?

As we come together and restructure our relationships, we create
the germ cells of a renewed social organism, growing from the
ground up, into the institutions which sit heavy on our lives. Thus,
as we build out from our own privatized existences into small
communal families living in one house together, sharing the work
necessary to maintain life (meals, sanitation, income) and raising
children . . . so must we build out from our communal houses to
create new communal economic and political institutions in our
neighborhoods.

Our struggle must be based on this process of community building.
We must avoid the false glorification of struggle which comes from
the frustration of seeing no results of resistance and mobilization
politics but bleary eyes, bloodied heads, and pictures in the daily
papers. What is needed now is more programmatic and structural
thinking if we are to avoid an escalating spiral of street confrontations which will psychically and physically destroy our people.
The question is not whether we can face down the police at a confrontation, but rather whether we can decentralize the police

establishment so that neighborhoods can elect and recall police officers and generally set their own moral standards of what is legal and what is not. And that is a question of first getting ourselves together where we live.

Learning From History

The past 150 years have provided us with a rich history of building decentralized socialism within a capitalist society. Of the three major branches of that history, the French Communities of Work, the American communities of the 19th century, and the Israeli kibbutzim, the latter two can teach us more, partly because there is more substantial material on them. My remarks here are generalized and are intended only to excite the reader's curiosity to discover more for himself: a bibliography follows this essay.

During the last century approximately 100,000 people lived in small communitarian societies throughout the wilderness areas of a rapidly industrializing, urbanizing America. Those who forged out these communities were the most imaginative of the pioneer stock. For them the freedom of the new country meant the chance to experiment and innovate toward a more just society, rather than the opportunity for fortune-hunting in the cities.

The kibbutzim represent the end result of the fusion of the religious and socialist traditions of communitarianism in the German youth movements at the turn of the century. They were not as idealistically utopian in their conception as the American communities, for the task was as much forging a new nation out of a desert wilderness as it was to build the micro-units of a just society. In Israel they say the revolution is the color of the ground, for in making the desert fertile they changed the earth from yellow to green. In the American communities the concern from the beginning was self-sufficiency and independence, so the primary question of their role in the developing macro-economic-political structure did not concern them. But from the beginning the various kibbutzim pursued ways of helping each other and the needs of nascent Israel, so their focus while building internally was outward, toward federation. Today there are four kibbutz federations serving 82,000 people in a total of 230 communities. The various federations are allied with political parties and provide, in proportion to their numbers, a remarkably high percentage of government leaders in the Knesset (parliament), the ministries, and the military. With one-third of the nation's total agricultural production, the kibbutzim are an integral part of the economic and political structure of Israel. Whether they will go on to rid their country of corporate capitalism and militarization remains to be seen.

Perhaps the first lesson of this history is the need to develop a communal life style which is continually sensitizing people to the larger task they are about in the society as a whole — a philosophy which leads the people to intentionally build toward the larger task. Whether the kibbutz federations (one is avowedly Marxist) will act to maintain their safe position in a hostile society or take risks to revolutionize the country is an open question. The failures of the American communities show that the critical style was never found. For these communities sought isolation; from the beginning they imagined themselves apart from their society so that as they grew their activity reflected this myopic self-definition. They willingly became encapsulated as their hostility toward outsiders turned in on them, from the local townfolk refusing to trade with them, to outright attacks. But the greatest danger of this selfish concern with internal welfare is the stagnation of increasingly incestuous relationships. The communities became inbred and self-satisfied and in the process destroyed the creative energy of building a new society. It is this complacency, rooted in the static and narrow-minded view of what they were about, that placed them outside the historical forces that were determining the shape of the embryonic nation. The failure is in not seeing that a community's welfare, in the broadest sense, is inextricable from the society's economic and political realities.

The Need for An Experimental Approach

History has also shown us that rigidity of outlook and approach to what a community is about is destructive and inhibiting. As we come together to live or work we must grow toward an ideal, always grounding our action in the compost pile of present realities. Different forms of community will arise for different human types and personalities. This is natural and good as long as the various forms strive for continual growth and further development. Internal development toward human relatedness which is truly liberating, and externally, toward the creation of new communal institutions where the power is vested in the people, not in absentee lords of the propertied class. The goal is a new social dispensation and a New Man. We must keep an open mind and avoid the dogmatic and the fanatic, for the organizational form must begin where people are and grow along a path all can follow in trust and understanding. Let us be clear about dogmatism. One is dogmatic when he imposes what he believes to be true or right on a situation and demands acquiesance and allegiance from others, instead of working through mutual prejudices and fears with them, always willing to change himself, so that all arrive at the apparent truth existentially, in the fullness of self-knowledge.

Mutual Criticism and Dialogue

Our growth, individually and collectively, will take place not in a vacuum but in the dialectic of conflicting ideas and perspectives. And this must be based on a willingness to learn from each other, a willingness to change and grow. A lesson, sad to tell, the American socialist communities never learned. Most died a premature death because of endless internal bickering and factionalism. The need is for a mechanism of some kind which facilitates regular dialogue, such as a weekly meeting for this express purpose. The meeting will truly be mechanical however, if there is no trust between the people.

Oneida, perhaps the most successful of the American intentional communities, had such a session, called "mutual criticism" (an early form of encounter group or group therapy). Charles Nordoff, a journalist who visited Oneida in 1875, noted that mutual criticism was ". . . a most ingenious device, which Noyes (founder of Oneida) and his followers rightly regard as the cornerstone of their practical community life. It is in fact their main instrument of government; and it is useful as a means of eliminating uncongenial elements, and also to train those who remain into harmony with the general system and order." A mutual criticism encounter could be requested by a member who wanted personal council and advice or it could be administered for correction of a delinquency. The important thing to note is that the criticism was not authoritarian and thus was understood to be an aide and guide. No ill feeling was provoked in the "victim." I find this especially striking in that a person's intellectual and spiritual advancement was a community concern. It was the concern of all to uplift each and every member of the community in a real spirit of love and compassion.

Community with Two Poles: Urban and Rural

Another vivid lesson from past community failures is how a community situated in the country, devoted entirely to agriculture and the soil, becomes completely encapsulated and stagnant. Our communities must provide two environments, with houses and work to be done in the cities, as well as land and labor in the country. Perhaps the perfect distance could be measured by an hour or an hour and a half's travel time: close enough to be convenient, but distant enough to limit frivolous trips.

To see community building as our life task is to seriously develop economic means of support which represent our concerns and at the same time free much of our time to be active at other tasks. We must, of course, simplify our living, minimizing bourgeois self-indulgences and expensive tastes. Kropotkin argued well for villages of mixed agriculture and manufacture, a good mind-picture of the rural commune pole of our communities. Full-scale agriculture is too time-consuming; we must develop "truck gardening" (raising vegetables and fruit for immediate sale in near-by cities and towns). In manufacturing, as in agriculture, one of the rules to be followed is how easily can people be trained in the necessary skills; this facilitates more people doing shorter work shifts, a goal in this regard might be everyone doing four hours of work each day in the community's industry, houses, or fields. Possible industries include furniture making, pre-fabricated housing (construction of structural components, as well as completed houses), printing and publishing, graphics and film-making, and the stand-bys of the underground: pottery and leather goods. The work should grow out of what each group finds fulfilling and hopefully can be related to the activity of the community's city terminus. Perhaps selling products on campuses or in depressed neighborhoods would also provide an entree to talking to people about community and concerns of the movement.

Questions of Internal Organization

There are several issues which will arise concerning internal organization. The more openly discussed and understood these inherent questions are, the more stable will be the group. For our purpose here, I wish to deal with the questions of leadership, discipline, new members, child-rearing and women's liberation.

Leadership — Leaders come organically out of a group which is together emotionally and intellectually. The important difference is between a coercive leader and a natural one. The coercive leader bases his authority on a position in a hierarchy which has power over your life or on his own manipulative powers of persuasion over the group. Humor is often used in a face-to-face group by a would-be leader to subtly cause an opposing member to appear foolish. A natural leader gains the personal confidence of members of the group who know him well from living with him, but do not submit to him. It is my experience that the natural leader is the one most willing or devoted to doing the work that must be done. Leaders should not assume too much of the work, however, to avoid the community becoming dependent on their contributions. A genuine leader makes himself superfluous by drawing forth the leadership potentials of others.

Discipline — Discipline in a hierarchic institution is punishment. People in such situations are victims, rather than captains, of their fate. But in a decisional community where all are equal members it is the way they constitute themselves so as to get their work done. Which is to say, where all are life-dedicated to a task, discipline becomes the question of how to organize ourselves toward that goal. And this depends largely on the scale and intimacy of the group. A simple mechanism might be the "period of commitment" in which the community decides to accomplish so many tasks within a certain time period and then members voluntarily pledge themselves to do specific things.

Group responsibility (discipline) should be discussed in the light of the wheelie-feelie polarization. The wheelies are the politicos, the wheeler-dealers of our movement who study history, economics, and politics and consequently see most of the movement's concerns in structural and programmatic ways. The feelies are the artists of the movement who are into the occult, the mystical, and various schools of psychology, and thus see most of the movement's concerns in psycho-dramatic terms of people being more gentle and expressive with each other. Each perspective has a valuable contribution to make to the other; in fact, one of the major failures of the radical movement after the First World War was the estrangement between those doing cultural things and those doing politics. There is now a marked tendency for the wheelies and the feelies to be unable to communicate with each other, let alone work together closely. How they get together over common concerns will depend largely on openly discussing their unique perceptions in mutual criticism encounters.

Discipline is a problem in the movement because most of us have personally rebelled against the perversity of authoritarian families and schools where discipline was a punishment or a means to get us to someone else's end. Now that self-discipline is required to free us further from this societal quagmire, we flounder. But the fact is that in the years ahead we must study and work much harder than we have to this point, for ours is a long march, not an acid trip, through the institutions. And through the creation of new institutions.

New Members — Several of the American communities had a complete open door policy about new members. In each case it was a principle cause for their demise. For such community experiments often attract free-loaders, cranks, and crashers of all kinds who have little interest in the people of the community or commitment to the socio-political task they are about. If the community feels dedicated to the therapeutic task of rejuvenating people to full active and independent communitarians, all well and good, but the history of such situations has been that it requires so much time and effort that it exasperates and destroys the community's mission. In reality, such new members change the personality of the community more than the community does them.

Which is not to say that only exact carbon-copies of present community members should be admitted. Far from it, for such a process will develop an ingrown homogeneity which equally subverts the life of the group. For we are intentionally living a particular communal way and we are purposely about the socio-political reconstruction of a capitalist, racist society. New members should be in joyous agreement with our style of life and our purpose. This is of paramount importance for it means they fully understand and articulate with their own lives what we are about.

A good means for the selection of new members is a less stringent variant of the one the kibbutzim have perfected. A person would simply live and work as a full member in the community for approximately three months. This would provide ample time to get to know a person in many intimate situations and also to fully acquaint the new member with the people and way of life of the community. During the period of mutual familiarization, dialogue encounters might be held so that the new member can confront the community and vice versa. In this way, real existential problems can be worked through to everyone's understanding and satisfaction. This may seem very rigorous and perhaps harsh on the aspirant, but radical communities such as we are building toward are integral, organic bodies and we cannot be too careful in choosing new brothers and sisters. This will seem unnecessary for transient, casual groups that are not building for a *life* together, however.

Child-rearing and Women's Liberation — Community without children is an immature affair. Children are the leaven and spice of group living, if the flour of the loaf is pure. Which is to say, that in a radical community where men and women respond to each other openly and lovingly and where women are not relegated to the caste of dishwasher/child-raiser, children are essential for a full life.

Women's Liberation is the first movement group to emphatically articulate the need for consonance between interpersonal harmony and so-called "radical" politics. In a community of trust, growth and action are based on complete responsiveness to every person's sensitivities and contribution. Our sisters cannot be passed over in what they are feeling and saying in group dialogue and decision-making. Women cannot be treated as second-class citizens who must keep their place as cook, nursemaid, and geisha girl. And this means a reconstitution of how men act, as well as women. Nursing, feeding, cleaning up after the communities' children, is as much man's work as woman's. For in the communal raising of children, where men and women share the work equally, men's so-called "realistic" view of how to deal with people and situations will be humanized, while women's time will be freed up and their perspective broadened. Only through the building of communities of trust and shared responsibility will women (and men) find liberation, and only through communal child-rearing and the liberation of women will we achieve true community. Women looking for liberation without community are souls searching for a body, and a community in which women are not free is a body without a soul.

The Illusion of Community

It is most common for people who live together, whether that be a family, a group of friends, or a larger community, to adjust to each other's sensitivities and peculiarities at the surface, as if they were borders that could not be crossed. Learning how not to irritate other people often passes for a deep relationship. But to really know and be a part of another is to respond to his sufferings and joys, as if they were your own. As if the rich oil of your souls constantly flowed between you, back and forth, and you had no bodies to physically harbor the spirit.

A negative form of community develops when the members become psychologically dependent upon the group. When being together becomes a goal in itself; when everyone feels threatened when one or two members choose not to participate, then a destructive dependency has developed. For the group must free up the individuals in it and this will only happen when everyone helps each other to know his own fears, weaknesses, and strengths so that each person will act out of a strong, honest sense of his being, rather than a weak dependent submission. A seeming paradox: each must be stronger than the group, yet draw his ultimate strength and direction from it.

Some of the so-called "hip" communes evidence this emasculating form of community. Much time is spent just being together, listening to music, rapping endlessly, or sitting around. The ultimate rule of such a community is being gentle with each other, touching each other and generally not violating where a person "is at." It is a regression toward the safe, tactile environment of the womb. This is a serious situation when the supportive group becomes emasculating to the vitality and independence of its members, for the group experience should advance and develop individual potential.

Another community of illusion develops where people settle into living together without truly responding to each other. Mechanisms for mutual defense soon develop, such as a recurring joke, a shared stereotype, scapegoat, or cliche, which defuse the tension when people begin to get into each other. For we are all scarred with the inhibitions and defenses from being dealt with by parents and teachers who manipulated our desires and fears, albeit unknowingly, because they were unresponsive and afraid of themselves. Most people are afraid to be known and know themselves, partly because of the pain of confronting their fears and weaknesses and partly because they may have to change as a result. But in a radical socialist community, the intention is to create new men and women who are strong and loving in the task they are about. And this comes only from being open, accepting, and willing to learn from each other. Only those who are sensitive and probing, only those who are receptive and willing to change will be broken out of the prison of their defenses, like a strong oak shooting up after the hard nut is consumed by the growing seedling.

The Act of Initiation

I think it important to suggest some models of community building for different situations. They will remain incomplete, however, because it is of paramount importance to build community to the situation and needs of the people involved. Perhaps the value of these models is in what they illustrate about the process of initiation.

Initiation is, in a sense, a question of scale and intimacy, for the intensity of the group's life is established in the formative period, just as a person's spirit (faith, hope, vision) which he will carry throughout his life is primarily formed as in infant. For an infant to become a psychically whole organism it must grow in an environment of trust and common concern. It is said that one of the first psychic imprints on a child's mind is the face of his mother as he looks up from suckling her breast. If the face is lovingly approving he is more likely to be secure and hopeful throughout his life. If the child perceives hostility or disapproval, however slight, as he is at his mother's breast, then he will carry the scars of insecurity and indecision with him as he grows. And it is on this early foundation of trust and faith that the child interprets and integrates into his worldview new and more challenging experiences and people.

And so it is with the generation of community. When the first people come together to work out their concerns, as they seek for a common vision, they build the foundation on which the larger community will stand or crumble. For as they widen their circle the hope and spirit of their vision will be unmistakably transmitted to the new people. For communication is more than words, it is the totality of mind-body sensitivity: eye contact, body movement, speed of delivery and response, voice tonality and loudness, and ego diffusion. Thus, the fervor and unity of the core group, what the kibbutzniks call a "garin" (nucleus), will be transmitted to the new members in its true strength and fullness.

If the environment is spiritually whole, if there is understanding and hope, the organism will be strong; if not, the structure will be too brittle and incohesively thrown together to weather the storms and buffetings of its future. It is this communion of inner cohesion, collaboration and mutual stimulation that Martin Buber calls "the center." "The real essence of community is to be found in the fact — manifest or otherwise — that it has a center. The real beginning of a community is when its members have a common relation to the center overriding all other relations: the circle is described by the radii, not the points along its circumference."[1]

Some Models

The communion at conception is a universal prerequisite. The acts of commission which follow, however, might be quite different in varying situations. The spiral of community must generate out from the initial moment of conception into the material world of the present. This would obviously involve a different activity for a middle class residential area, a college campus, or an urbutz (an urban kibbutz).

A Middle Class Neighborhood

On a middle class block, the community building process might begin by two or three neighbors, whose previous contact was casually social and sporadic, coming together to dialogue about what they might do to help each other toward a common life. The discussions might alternate from home to home once or twice a week. They should include all members of the families, for the community they are prefiguring must be an extended family. A common meal, in which all help, gives substance to the ensuing dialogue. During the discussion you should occasionally reverse positions by vocalizing in your own words each other's concerns, to see if you are really sensitive to what each other is saying. In the regular meeting and dialogue, the pooling of money for the meal, and the cooking and cleaning up you will have a slight taste of communal responsibility and responsiveness.

The renting or buying of a house on the block or near-by might be the next important step. This would truly be a communal space, owned and shared by the whole neighborhood, for common meals, dances, drama and satire, meetings, film and music facilities, organizing projects, and community seminars and celebrations. It should be the home and center of the community's life. During the day it might be a daycare center to free up the women's time; it should be staffed by the community's men and women, especially teenagers, for whom exposure and sensitivity to young children is an important orienting and stabilizing element.

Increasingly, by intention or not, the growing community will confront the propertied political powers that be: zoning and licencing boards, redevelopment authorities, realtors, business owners, and school bureaucracies. The children are a case in point. Clearly, we must free the children from the custodial authoritarianism which kills curiosity and eagerness to discover and bring them back into the community, on the streets, and in neighborhood minischools (see Goodman's "Minischools" in the *N.Y. Review of Books*, Jan. 4, 1968). This is but another facet of political decentralization where the power (and the glory) of controlling your own life will have to be won through institutional struggle.

And this freeing of the children is linked to the freeing of the mothers, who must deny their own eagerness to discover new things outside the home because they are imprisoned in the role of custodian while the children are home and the men are away pursuing their horizons. The creation of a minischool/daycare center where all care for the young on a rotating basis is perhaps the most revolutionary beginning act of community building in a middle-class neighborhood, partly because child-rearing is the greatest rationalization for that style of life and partly because the freeing of women will generate enormous creative energy. For it is truly destructive of the exploitative, privatistic life-patterns while at the same time constructing an alternative pattern.

This is not the rhetorically revolutionary, alienated politics of so many today, but the substantive socio-political reconstruction which must be the cell-tissue and the bone structure of any new social body.

After the early accomplishment of a community house, daycare facilities, and a minischool, the group can go on to yet more adventuresome goals: internal revenue sharing, the establishment of a neighborhood food and consumer's co-op, and even the creation or purchase of neighborhood stores and services to be set up as cooperatives. But the really meaty questions involve redesigning the neighborhood into a communal village with ample work, recreation, and residential facilities at hand; planting streets over and making them into village malls; creating small producers' units to be owned by the community, based on the interests of the particular people; setting up a small clothes or furniture producing shop, a bakery, etc. The possibilities are immense. The basic principle is embarrassingly simple: people work great distances from their homes at alienating jobs for which they have been educated, yet at home they have hobbies they truly enjoy doing. The task is to free each other from the money/status rationalizations so that those personally expressive and creative things we do with our hands at home become more and more our activity and source of bread. In the heat and energy of this creation together we will find renewal.

A College Campus

Community building on a campus, whether urban or rural, starts with the control of space. Student power demands are movements to control space, both existentially and environmentally. College administrators believe the dormitories, class buildings, courses, and activities belong to them and are to be "administered" to the students. A doctor "administers" a drug to a disease-ridden patient, but a man cannot administer an education. For to grow and learn in full health is to need nothing administered to you.

The garin, or core group, would start with six to eight men and women, who would go about setting up a cooperative house. It is important to invite sympathetic faculty and their families, as well as non-university people who live in the area, to share your life together. If the house is off campus, the administrators may not let students live there. If it is on campus, they may not let men and women live together. In either case, the struggle to control your own life will be drawn early. In the case of dormitories perhaps the opening act should be what the students of the Free University in West Berlin did recently: a group of forty men packed up their belongings and moved into the previously all-women dormitory, occupying the rooms left vacant by the equal number of women who moved into the men's dorm. The act drew immediate support from the student body and disapproval from the doctoral administrators, but the latter could do nothing when faced with a popularly-supported *fait accompli*.

The direction that all this points to is what community building is all about: the control of your life, the liberation from repressive and exploitative social customs, the creation of democratically (read decentrally) owned and operated institutions and the achievement of communion in our lives. On campus this carries you in the direction of building a non-hierarchic, non-status-enforcing community where all students, faculty, and workers share in maintaining the physical plant, as well as the learning/teaching process. Everyone has something to teach, it is the task of community builders to create the environment where all are sensitive to the wisdom each possesses.

And the fertile ground of this learning environment must be heterosexual, communal living, if future efforts are to bear further fruit.

An Urbutz

In the center of most large cities are growing up loose configurations of people under 30, living in individual houses or apartments of six–twelve, who are beginning to play with the notion of getting together in some communal relationship beyond their own cooperative houses. It is unfortunate, though understandable, that they begin by defining themselves in the predominately ecstatic terms of elysian freedom. It is unfortunate because the vision leads to a rejection of the responsibility facet of freedom, while overemphasizing the liberation side.

Since I work and live in the Washington Free Community, I will use it as a critical example. In January of 1968, a group of twenty young activists and artists came together in an old theater to talk about what they might do to provide facilities and services and generally make the scene for young people more exciting. Plans were hatched for workshops (pottery, sewing, photography, film, acting, dance), exchanges (jobs, cooperative houses), and a food co-op.

A four-page graphics and word explanation of the idea came out in the Washington *Free Press*, whose staff was among the first to conceive of the idea of an "underground" young people's community. But as the weeks went on it became clearer there were few people willing to take on the responsibility of doing the work necessary to make the various new projects happen. Most were too committed to doing their own things, whether that be political organizing, working on the *Free Press* or the American Playground (the community's radical theater: guerrilla, street, and environmental) or otherwise pursuing a privatized vision of what cultural revolution meant. There was in all this a great deal of rationalization and phrase-making, my own included.

Several of the early cooperative houses never congealed because the people were not honest with each other, let alone themselves. Basic questions about how they were to live together (meals, money, decoration of the house, crashers) were never resolved. But today there are eight or so cooperative houses with varying styles, degrees of cooperativeness, and interpersonal communion. There is also a great deal of transience in the houses, with an original group of eight or nine rarely staying together for more than nine months to a year.

Even now there is resistance to any inter-house coordination or organization, which is especially difficult because of the geographic separation of the houses and projects. In the beginning when a few suggested setting up a non-profit corporation (the officers were to be figureheads with all decisions made by a democratic body) so that the community could begin to generate its own funds for projects and to buy cooperative houses, the idea was denounced as a sell-out and as totalitarianism.

Perhaps it is too early to draw conclusions about the experience of the Washington Free Community. Perhaps I am too critical because my hopes were so high, but I think we can learn something valuable from the first year of this experiment. It seems clear that the commitment of the early core group that met at the theater was to an idea, not to each other. This is one of the most destructive aspects to utopian or visionary thinking, for the relationships of the people to each other is filtered and mediated through the mental structure of what they think they should be doing. The relations between the people become rigid. People resort to dogmatic cliches of what it is to be radical and unquestioning allegiance to the original idea of what you are supposedly about. People hide behind political rhetoric and the sanctity of their "thing."

Buber would say there was no community, the people did not " . . . have a common relation to the center overriding all other relations. . . . " For when a true community forms the commitment is to each other first and foremost, and then to a vision of how you are to live together. Where the personal commitment exists there is honesty in expressing one's hopes and reservations, there is trust that you will be respected and not mocked for your views and feelings, and perhaps most importantly there is a willingness to learn from each other. Where there is no honesty, no trust, no willingness to learn and develop, there will be no coordination or organization of joint work (outside of small adhoc groups) and there will be no regular mechanism, such as a weekly meal and meeting, for decision-making. And where there is no center of energy and no magnetism between people who trust each other there will be the continual turn-over of people passing on to other cities and other scenes. Today's mobility is as much a search for a home as a thirst for experience.

Another problem in the Free Community is the absence of a sense of tradition. There is a general feeling that what we are doing is totally new, that there have been few before who have tried such experiments, or that the city, or affluence, or the media have so radically changed our environment there is no previous experience to draw on. As a friend told me, "I've come to the point where I think there is no one who can teach us anything." This anti-intellectualism, this refusal to see ourselves on the cutting edge of the fertile history of socialism, marxist and otherwise, has a deep existential root. All of us in the Free Community have arrived at our present radicalism through a rejection of the imposed teachings and pious moralism of authoritarian families and schools. Wisdom and learning appeared but a rationalization for a repressive social system which was obviously anti-human, manipulative, and plastic. In the process of personal liberation we perhaps over-reacted. This may account for our distrust of the intellectual process and the absence of personal discipline. But perhaps the cause goes deeper into our psychological past in that we really don't trust our own ability to discern sham and pretense from true wisdom. This may tie in with a refusal to be honest about our own perception and intelligence, in that we may have to be willing to admit error or lack of insight and in the process change who we think we are. If we can overcome this existential mistrust and self-doubt we will be greatly enriched by an enormous wealth of wisdom, not only in history, but among ourselves.

But the Washington Free Community is young and hopefully we will see in the coming years its development toward a cohesive micro-socialist urbutz. Such an urbutz might share some of the skeletal forms of the present community but would be much more in the spiritual and socialist tradition of the kibbutzim. There would be the communion of the Buberian center, the essential inner cohesion, collaboration, and mutual stimulation and decision-making of true community. There would be an eagerness to experiment with new modes of organization and coordination of joint work and projects. There would be internal revenue generation and a regular meeting for group planning toward the future. But most important is the sacred commitment to each other in this time and in this place. For it is upon this rock that all we do, both individually and collectively, rests.

Note

[1] Martin Buber, *Paths in Utopia*, Beacon Press Paperback; Boston, p. 135. Should be read in its entirety.

SUGGESTED READINGS

History and Sociology

Holloway, Mark, *Heavens on Earth: Utopian Communities in America, 1680–1880*, Dover, N.Y., 1966.

Noyes, John Humphrey, *History of American Socialisms*, Dover, N.Y., 1966.

Nordoff, Charles, *Communistic Societies of the United States*, Dover, N.Y., 1966.

Hine, Robert, *California's Utopian Colonies*, Huntington Library, San Marino, Calif., 1953.

Beston, A. E., *Backwards Utopia: The Sectarian and Owenite Phases of Communitarian Socialism, 1663–1827*, U. of Pa. Press, Philadelphia, 1950.

Kanovsky, Eliyahu, *The Economy of the Israeli Kibbutz*, Harvard Univ. Press, Cambridge, 1966.

Bishop, Claire, *All Things Common*, Harper, N.Y., 1950. About the French communities of work.

Fromm, Erich, *The Sane Society*, Harper, N.Y., 1955.

Infield, Hendrik F., *Utopia and Experiment: Essays in the Sociology of Cooperation*, F. A. Praeger, N.Y., 1955.
————*Cooperative Communities at Work*, Dryden Press, N.Y., 1945.
————*People in Ejidos: A Visit to the Cooperative Farms of Mexico*, F. A. Praeger, N.Y., 1954.

The Kibbutz

Spiro, Melford E., *Kibbutz: Venture in Utopia*, Schocken, N.Y., 1956.
Ben-Yosef, Avraham C., *The Purest Democracy in the World*, Heryl Press and Thomas Yoseloff, N.Y., London, 1963.
Friedmann, Georges, *The End of the Jewish People*, Anchor Books, Doubleday, N.Y., 1968.
Darin-Drabkin, Haim, *The Other Society*, Harcourt, Brace & World, N.Y., 1963.

Communal Child-Rearing

Spiro, Melford E., *The Children of the Kibbutz*, Schocken Paperback, N.Y.
Bettelheim, B., "Does Communal Education Work?" *Commentary*, 1962, Vol. 33, pp. 117–125.
Neubauer, Peter, *Children in Collectives*, Thomas & Co., Chester, Eng., 1965.

General

Gutkind, E. A., *Community and Environment: A Discourse on Social Ecology*, Philosophical Library, N.Y., 1953.
Buber, Martin, *Paths in Utopia*, Beacon Press, Boston, 1949.
    Highly recommended. Should be read with Engels:
    Socialism Utopian and Scientific.
————*Pointing the Way*, Harper Torchbooks, N.Y., 1963.
    Especially the section "Politics, Community and Peace."
Benello, George, "The Wasteland Culture," *Our Generation*, Vol. 5, No. 2, Sept. 1967. (*Our Generation*, 3837 boul. St. Laurent, Montreal 18, Quebec, Canada.)
Engels, Frederick, *The Origin of the Family, Private Property, and the State*, New World Paperbacks, N.Y., 1942.
Wilson, Edmund, *To The Finland Station*, Anchor Books, Doubleday, N.Y., 1953.

WORKERS' CONTROL

Paul Mattick

According to socialist theory, the development of capitalism implies the polarization of society into a small minority of capital owners and a large majority of wage-workers, and therewith the gradual disappearance of the proprietory middle-class of independent craftsmen, farmers, and small shop-keepers. This concentration of productive property and general wealth into always fewer hands appears as an incarnation of "feudalism" in the garb of modern industrial society. Small ruling classes determine the life and death of all of society by owning and controlling the productive resources and therewith the governments. That their decisions are controlled, in turn, by impersonal market forces and the compulsive quest for capital does not alter the fact that these reactions to uncontrollable economic events are also their exclusive privilege.

Within the capital-labor relations which characterize the prevailing society, the producers have no direct control over production and the products it brings forth. At times, they may exert a kind of indirect control by way of wage struggles, which may alter the wage-profit ratio and therewith the course or tempo of the capital expansion process. Generally, it is the capitalist who determines the conditions of production. The workers have to agree in order to exist, for their only means of livelihood is the sale of their labor power. Unless the worker accepts the exploitative conditions of capitalist production, he is "free" only in the sense that he is free to starve. This was recognized long before there was a socialist movement. As early as 1767, Simon Linguet declared that wage-labor is merely a form of slave labor. In his view, it was even worse than slavery.

"It is the impossibility of living by any other means that compels our farm laborers to till the soil whose fruits they will not eat, and our masons to construct buildings in which they will not live. It is want that drags them to those markets where they await masters who will do them the kindness of buying them. It is want that compels them to go down on their knees to the rich man in order to get from him permission to enrich him. . . . What effective gain has the suppression of slavery brought him? . . . He is free, you say. Ah! That is his misfortune. The slave was precious to his master because of the money he had cost him. But the handicraftsman costs nothing to the rich voluptuary who employs him. . . . These men, it is said, have no master — they have one, and the most terrible, the most imperious of masters, that is *need*. It is this that reduces them to the most cruel dependence."[1]

Two hundred years later this is essentially still the same. Although it is no longer outright misery which forces the workers in the advanced capitalist nations to submit to the rule of capital and to the wiles of capitalists, their lack of control over the means of production, their position as wage-workers, still marks them as a ruled class unable to determine its own destiny.

The goal of socialists was then and still is the abolition of the wage system, which implies the end of capitalism. In the second half of the last century a working-class movement arose to bring about this transformation through the socialization of the means of production. Profit-determined production was to be replaced by one satisfying the actual needs and ambitions of the associated producers. The market economy was to make room for a planned economy. Social existence and development would then no longer be determined by the uncontrollable fetishistic expansion and contraction of capital but by the collective conscious decisions of the producers in a classless society.

Being a product of bourgeois society, however, the socialist movement is bound to the vicissitudes of capitalist development. It will take on varying characteristics in accordance with the changing fortunes of the capitalist system. It will not grow, or it will practically disappear, at times and in places which are not conducive to the formation of proletarian class consciousness. Under conditions of capitalist prosperity it tends to transform itself from a revolutionary into a reformist movement. In times of social crisis it may be totally suppressed by the ruling classes.

All labor organizations are part of the general social structure and, save in a purely ideological sense, cannot be consistently anticapitalistic. In order to attain social importance within the capitalist system they must be opportunistic, that is, take advantage of given social processes in order to serve their own but as yet limited ends. It does not seem possible to slowly assemble revolutionary forces in powerful organizations ready to act at favorable moments. Only organizations which do not disturb the prevailing basic social relationships grow to any importance. If they start out with a revolutionary ideology, their growth implies a subsequent discrepancy between their ideology and their functions. Opposed to the *status quo* but also organized within it, these organizations must finally succumb to the forces of capitalism by virtue of their own organizational successes.

At the end of the century, traditional labor organizations — socialist parties and trade unions — were no longer revolutionary movements. Only a small left-wing within these organizations retained its revolutionary ideology. In terms of doctrine, Lenin and Luxemburg saw the need to combat the reformist and opportunist evolutionism of the established labor organizations and demanded a return to revolutionary policies. While Lenin tried to accomplish this through the creation of a new type of revolutionary party, emphasizing centrally-controlled organized activity and leadership, Rosa Luxemburg preferred an increase in proletarian self-determination generally, as well as within the socialist organizations, through the elimination of bureaucratic controls and the activization of the rank-and-file.

Because Marxism was the ideology of the dominant socialist parties, opposition to these organizations and their policies expressed itself also as an opposition to Marxian theory in its reformist and revisionist interpretations. Georges Sorel[2] and the syndicalists were not only convinced that the proletariat could emancipate itself without the guidance of the intelligentsia, but that it had to free itself from middle-class elements that usually controlled political organizations. Syndicalism rejected parliamentarism in favor of revolutionary trade union activity. In Sorel's view, a government of socialists would in no sense alter the social position of the workers. In order to be free, the workers would have to resort to actions and weapons exclusively their own. Capitalism, he thought, had already organized the whole proletariat in its industries. All that was left to do was to suppress the state and property. To accomplish this, the proletariat was not so much in need of so-called scientific insight into necessary social trends as of a kind of intuitive conviction that revolution and socialism were the inevitable outcome of their own continuous struggles. The strike was seen as the workers' revolutionary apprenticeship. The growing number of strikes, their extensions and increasing duration pointed towards a possible *General Strike*, that is, to the impending social revolution.

Syndicalism and such international offsprings as the *Guild Socialists* in England and the *Industrial Workers of the World* in the United States were, to some extent, reactions to the increasing bureaucratization of the socialist movement and to its class-collaborationist practices. Trade unions, too, were attacked for their centralistic structures and their emphasis upon specific trade interests at the expense of proletarian class needs. But all organizations, whether revolutionary or reformist, whether centralizers or federalists, tended to see in their own steady growth and everyday activities the major ingredient for social change. As regards Social Democracy it was the growing membership, the spreading party apparatus, the increasing number of votes in elections, and a larger participation in existing political institutions which were thought of as growing into the socialist society. As regards the *Industrial Workers of the World*, on the other hand, the growth of its own organizations into *One Big Union* was seen, at the same time, as "forming the structure of the new society within the shell of the old."[3]

In the first twentieth-century revolution, however, it was the unorganized mass of workers which determined the character of the revolution and brought into being its own, new form of organization in the spontaneously arising workers' councils. The Russian councils, or soviets, of the 1905 Revolution, grew out of a number of strikes and their needs for committees of action and representation to deal with the industries affected as well as with legal authorities. The strikes were spontaneous in the sense that they were not called by political organizations or trade unions, but were launched by unorganized workers who had no choice but to look upon their workplace as the springboard and center of their organizational efforts. In the Russia of that time political organizations had as yet no real influence on the mass of workers and trade unions existed only in embryonic form.

"The soviets," Trotsky wrote, "were the realization of an objective need for an organization which has authority without having tradition, and which can at once embrace hundreds of thousands of workers. An organization, moreover, which can unify all the revolutionary tendencies within the proletariat, which possesses both initiative and self-control, and, which is the main thing, can be called into existence within 24 hours." . . . [Whereas] "parties were organizations *within* the proletariat, the soviets were the organization *of* the proletariat."[4]

In essence, of course, the 1905 Revolution was a bourgeois revolution, supported by the liberal middle-class to break Czarist absolutism and to advance Russia via a Constituent Assembly toward the conditions that existed in the more developed capitalist nations. In so far as the striking workers thought in political terms, they largely shared the program of the liberal bourgeoisie. And so did all existing socialist organizations which accepted the necessity of a bourgeois revolution as a precondition for the formation of a strong labor movement and a future proletarian revolution under more advanced conditions.

The soviet system of the Russian Revolution of 1905 disappeared with the crushing of the revolution, only to return in greater force in the February Revolution of 1917. It was these soviets which inspired the formation of similar spontaneous organizations in the German Revolution of 1918, and, to a somewhat lesser extent, the social upheavals in England, France, Italy and Hungary. With the council system a form of organization arose which could lead and coordinate the self-activities of very broad masses either for limited ends or for revolutionary goals, and which could do so independently of, in opposition to, or in collaboration with, existing labor organizations. Most of all, the rise of the council system proved that spontaneous activities need not dissipate in formless mass-exertions but could issue into organizational structures of a more than temporary nature.

The Russian Revolution of 1905 invigorated left-wing oppositions in the socialist parties of the West, but as yet more with respect to the spontaneity of its mass strikes than the organizational form these actions assumed. But the reformist spell was broken; revolution was again seen as a real possibility. However, in the West it would not be a bourgeois-democratic but a pure working-class revolution. But even so, the positive attitude toward the Russian experience was not as yet transformed into a rejection of the parliamentary methods of the reformist parties of the Second International.

II

The prospect for a revival of revolutionary policies in the West proved at first illusory. Not only the "revisionists" within the socialist movement for whom, in the words of their foremost spokesman, Eduard Bernstein, "the movement was everything and the goal nothing," but also so-called orthodox Marxists no longer believed in either the desirability or the necessity of social revolution. While they were still sticking to the old goal — abolition of the wage system — this was now to be reached in piecemeal fashion through the legal means offered by the democratic institutions of bourgeois society. Eventually, with the mass of voters favoring a socialist government, socialism could be instituted by government decree. Meanwhile, trade-union activity and social legislation would alleviate the lot of the workers and enable them to partake in the general social progress.

The miseries of *laissez-faire* capitalism not only produced a socialist movement but also various attempts on the part of workers to ease their conditions by non-political means. Apart from trade unionism, a cooperative movement came into being as a medium of escape from wage-labor and as a vain opposition to the ruling principle of general competition. The precursors of this movement were the early communist communities in France, England and America, which derived their ideas from such utopian socialists as Owen and Fourier.

Producers' cooperatives were voluntary groupings for self-employment and self-government with respect to their own activities. Some of these cooperatives developed independently, others in conjunction with the working-class movements. By pooling their resources, workers were able to establish their own workshops and produce without the intervention of capitalists. But their opportunities were from the very beginning circumscribed by the general conditions of capitalist society and its developmental tendencies, which granted them a mere marginal existence. Capitalist development implies the competitive concentration and centralization of capital. The larger capital destroys the smaller. The cooperative workshops were restricted to special small-scale industries requiring little capital. Soon the capitalist extension into all industries destroyed their competitive ability and drove them out of business.

Consumers' cooperatives proved to be more successful and some of them absorbed producers' cooperatives as sources of supply. But consumers' cooperatives can hardly be considered as attempts at working-class control, even where they were the creation of working-class aspirations. At best, they may secure a measure of control in the disposal of wages, for laborers can be robbed twice — at the point of production and at the market place. The costs of commodity circulation are an unavoidable *faux frais* of capital production, dividing the capitalists into merchants and entrepreneurs. Since each tries for the profit maximum in its own sphere of operation, their economic interests are not identical. Entrepreneurs thus have no reason to object to consumers' cooperatives. Currently, they are themselves engaged in dissolving the division of productive and merchant capital by combining the functions of both in the single production and marketing corporation.

The cooperative movement was easily integrated into the capitalist system and, in fact, was to a large extent an element of capitalist development. Even in bourgeois economic theory it was considered an instrument of social conservatism by fostering the savings propensities of the lower layers of society, by increasing economic activities through credit unions, by improving agriculture through cooperative production and marketing organizations, and by shifting working-class attention from the sphere of production to that of consumption. As a capitalistically-oriented institution the cooperative movement flourished, finally to become one form of capitalist enterprise among others, bent on the exploitation of the workers in its employ, and facing the latter as their opponents in strikes for higher wages and better working conditions. The general support of consumers' cooperatives by the official labor movement — in sharp distinction to an earlier scepticism and even outright rejection — was merely an additional sign of the increasing "capitalization" of the reformist labor movement. The widespread network of consumers' cooperatives in Russia, however, provided the Bolsheviks with a ready-made distributive system which was soon turned into an agency of the state.

The division of "collectivism" into producers' and consumers' cooperatives reflected, in a sense, the opposition of the syndicalist to the socialist movement. Consumers' cooperatives incorporated members of all classes and were seeking access to all markets. They were not opposed to centralization on a national and even international scale. The market of producers' cooperatives, however, was as limited as their production and they could not combine into larger units without losing the self-control which was the rationale for their existence.

It was the problem of workers' control over their production and products which differentiated the syndicalists from the socialist movement. In so far as the problem still existed for the latter, it solved it for itself with the concept of nationalization, which made the socialist state the guardian of society's productive resources and the regulator of its economic life with respect to both production and distribution. Only at a later stage of development would this arrangement make room for a free association of socialized producers and the withering away of the state. The syndicalists feared, however, that the state with its centralized controls would merely perpetuate itself and prevent the working population's self-determination.

The syndicalists envisioned a society in which each industry is managed by its own workers. All the syndicates together would form national federations which would not have the characteristics of government but would merely serve statistical and administrative functions for the realization of a truly collectivist production and distribution system. Syndicalism was predominant in France, Italy and Spain but was represented in all capitalist nations; in some with modifications as in the already noted *I.W.W.* and the *Guild Socialist.* Not only with respect to the final goal, but also in the everyday class struggle, syndicalists differed from parliamentary socialist and ordinary trade unions by their emphasis on direct actions and by a greater militancy.

Although the concern with final goals was premature, it affected nonetheless the actual behavior of their propagators. The rapid bureaucratization of the centralized socialist movement and trade unions deprived the workers in increasing measure of their self-initiative and subjected them to the control of a leadership which did not share their living and working conditions. Trade unions lost their early connection with the socialist movement and degenerated into business-unionism, solely interested in wage-bargaining and, where possible, in the formation of job monopolies. The syndicalist movement was bureaucratized to a far lesser extent, not only because it was the smaller of the two main streams of the labor movement, but also because the principle of industrial self-control affected the everyday class struggle as well.

To speak of workers' control within the framework of capitalist production can mean only control of their own organizations, for capitalism implies that the workers are deprived of all effective social control. But with the "capitalization" of their organizations, when they become the "property" of a bureaucracy and the vehicle of its existence and reproduction, it follows that the only possible form of direct workers' control vanishes. It is true that even then workers fight for higher wages, shorter hours, and better working conditions, but these struggles do not affect their lack of power within their own organizations. To call these activities a form of workers' control is a misnomer in any case, for these struggles are not concerned with the self-determination of the working class but with the improvement of conditions within the confines of capitalism. This is, of course, possible so long as it is possible to increase the productivity of labor at a rate faster than that by which the workers' living standards are raised.

The basic control over the conditions of work and the surplus-yields of production remain always in the hands of the capitalists. When workers succeed in reducing the hours of their working-day, they will not succeed in cutting the quantity of surplus-labor extracted by the capitalists. For there are two ways of extracting surplus-labor — prolonging the working-day and shortening the working-time required to produce the wage-equivalent by way of technical and organizational innovations. Because capital must yield a definite rate of profit, capitalists will stop producing when this rate is threatened. The compulsion to accumulate capital controls the capitalist and forces him to control his workers to get that amount of surplus-labor necessary to consummate the accumulation process. He will try for the profit maximum and may only get the minimum for reasons beyond his control, one of which may be the resistance of the workers to the conditions of exploitation bound up with the profit maximum. But that is as far as working-class exertions can reach within the capitalist system.

III

The workers' loss of control over their own organizations was, of course, a consequence of their acquiescence in the capitalist system. Organized and unorganized workers alike accommodated themselves to the market economy because it was able to ameliorate their conditions and promised further improvements in the course of its own development. Types of organizations effective in such a non-revolutionary situation were precisely reformist socialist parties and centrally-controlled business unions. The enlightened bourgeoisie, too, saw the latter as instruments of industrial peace by way of collective agreements. Capitalists no longer confronted the workers but their representatives, whose existence was based on the existence of the capital-labor market, that is, on the continued existence of capitalism. The workers' satisfaction with their organizations reflected their own loss of interest in social change. The socialist ideology was no longer supported by real working-class aspirations. This state of affairs came dramatically to light in the chauvinism which gripped the working classes of all capitalist nations at the outbreak of the first world war.

Left-wing radicalism had been based on what was designated by their reformist adversaries as the "politics of catastrophe." The revolutionists expected not only deteriorating living standards for the laboring population but also economic crises so devastating as to call forth social convulsions which would, in the end, lead to revolution. They could not conceive of revolution short of its objective necessity. And in fact, no social revolution occurred except in times of social and economic catastrophe. The revolutions released by World War I were the result of catastrophic conditions in the weaker imperialist powers and they raised, for the first time, the question of workers' control and the actualization of socialism as a real possibility.

The Russian Revolution of 1917 was the result of spontaneous movements in protest to increasingly unbearable conditions in the course of the unsuccessful war. Strikes and demonstrations escalated into a general uprising which found the support of some military units and led to the collapse of the Czarist government. The revolution was backed by a broad stratum of the bourgeoisie and it was from this group that the first provisional government was formed. Although the socialist parties and trade unions did not initiate the revolution, they played a greater part in it than had been the case in 1905, As in that year, so also in 1917, the soviets did not intend, at first, to replace the provisional government. But in the unfolding revolutionary process they encompassed increasingly greater responsibilities; practically, power was shared by the soviets and the government. The further radicalization of the movement under deteriorating conditions and the vacillating policies of bourgeois and socialist parties soon gave the Bolsheviks a majority in the decisive soviets and led to the October *coup d'état* which ended the bourgeois-democratic phase of the revolution.

The growing strength of the Bolsheviks within the revolutionary movement was due to their own unconditional adaptation to the real goals of the rebelling masses, that is, the end of the war and the expropriation and distribution of the landed estates by the peasants. Already at his arrival in Russia in April, 1917, Lenin made clear that for him the existence of the soviets superseded the quest for a bourgeois-democratic regime. It was to be replaced by a republic of workers' and peasants' councils. Yet when Lenin demanded preparation for the *coup d'état*, he spoke of the exercise of state power not by the soviets but by the Bolsheviks. Since the majority of the soviet delegates were Bolsheviks, or supported them, he took it for granted that the government formed by the soviets would be a Bolshevik government. And this was the case, of course, even though some left Social-Revolutionaries and left Socialists were given positions in the new government. But to continue the Bolshevik domination of the government, the workers and peasants would have to continue to elect Bolsheviks as their deputies in the soviets. For that there was no guarantee. Just as the Mensheviks and Social-Revolutionaries, once in the majority, found themselves in a minority position, so things could change again for the Bolsheviks. To retain power indefinitely meant to secure for the Bolshevik Party the monopoly of government.

However, just as Lenin equated soviet power with the power of the Bolshevik Party, so he saw in the latter's government monopoly only the realization of the rule of the soviets. After all, there was only the choice between a parliamentary bourgeois state and capitalism and a workers' and peasants' government which would prevent the return of bourgeois rule. Considering themselves the vanguard of the proletariat, and the latter the vanguard of the "people's revolution," the Bolsheviks wished to do for the workers and peasants what they might fail to do for themselves. Unguarded, the soviets were quite capable of abdicating their power positions for the promises of the liberal bourgeoisie and their social-reformist allies. To secure the "socialist" character of revolution demanded that the soviets remain Bolshevik soviets, even if this should require the suppression of all anti-Bolshevik forces within and outside the soviet system. In a short time, the soviet regime became the dictatorship of the Bolshevik Party. The emasculated soviets were only formally retained to hide this fact.

Although the Bolsheviks won with the slogan, "All power to the soviets," the Bolshevik government reduced its content to that of "workers' control." Proceeding at first rather cautiously with its socialization program, the workers were not expected to administer but merely to oversee the industrial enterprises that were still in the hands of the capitalists. The first decree on workers' control extended this control

"over the production, storing, buying and selling of raw materials and finished products as well as over the finances of the enterprises. The workers exercise this control through their elected organizations, such as factory and shop committees, soviet elders, etc. . . . The office employees and the technical personnel are also to have representation in these committees . . . The organs of workers' control have the right to supervise production. . . . Commercial secrets are abolished. The owners have to show to the organs of workers' control all their books and statements for the current year and for the past years."[5]

Capitalist production and workers' control are incompatible, however, and this makeshift affair, whereby the Bolsheviks hoped to retain the aid of the capitalist organizers of production and yet to some extent satisfy the yearnings of the workers to take possession of industry as the peasants had done of the land, could not last very long. "We did not decree socialism all at once throughout the whole of industry," Lenin explained a year after the decree on workers' control,

"because socialism can take shape and become finally established only when the working class has learned to run the economy . . . That is why we introduced workers' control, knowing that it was a contradictory and partial measure. But we consider it most important and valuable that the workers have themselves tackled the job, that from workers' control, which in the principal industries was bound to be chaotic, amateurish and partial, we have passed to workers' administration of industry on a nation-wide scale."[6]

But the change from "control" to "administration" turned out to entail the abolition of both. To be sure, just as the emasculation of the soviets required some time, for it required the formation and consolidation of the Bolshevik state apparatus, so the workers' influence in factories and workshops was only gradually eliminated through methods such as shifting the controlling rights from the soviets to the trade unions, and then transforming the latter into agencies of the state controlling the workers instead. Economic collapse, civil war, peasant opposition to any socialization of agriculture, industrial unrest, and partial return to the market economy, led to various contradictory policies, from the "militarization" of labor to its subordination to the revived free enterprises, in order to secure the Bolshevik government at all costs. The government's dictatorial policies confronted not only its capitalist and political enemies but the workers as well. The basic need was a greater production and because mere exhortation could not induce the workers to exploit themselves to the same or greater extent that they had suffered in the old regime, the Bolshevik state took on the functions of a new ruling class to reconstruct industry and to accumulate capital.

Lenin perceived the Russian revolution as an uninterrupted process leading from the bourgeois to the socialist revolution. He feared that the bourgeoisie proper would rather accept a compromise with Czarism than risk a thorough-going democratic revolution. It was, then, up to the workers and poor peasants to lead the impending revolution, a point of view shared by other observers of the Russian scene, such as Trotsky and Rosa Luxemburg. In the context of World War I, Lenin approached the Russian revolution from an international point of view, envisioning the possibility of its westward extension, which might provide the opportunity to destroy Russian bourgeois rule at the very point of its inception. It was then essential to hang on to power, regardless of compromises and violation of principles which this might involve, until a Western revolution complemented the Russian revolution and allowed for a form of international cooperation wherein Russia's objective unreadiness for socialism would be a less weighty factor. The isolation of the Russian revolution eliminated this perspective. To remain in power under the actually ensuing conditions meant to accept the historical role of the bourgeoisie but with different social institutions and a different ideology.

Of course, to hang on to power was already necessary if only to save the Bolshevik's own necks, for their overthrow would have meant their deaths. But aside from this, Lenin was convinced that the capitalization of Russia under the auspices of the state was more "progressive" and therefore preferable to leaving her development to the liberal bourgeoisie. He was also convinced that his party could do the job. Russia, he once said, "was accustomed to being ruled by 150,000 landlords. Why can 240,000 Bolsheviks not take over the same task?" And so they did, by constructing a hierarchical authoritarian state and its extension into the economic sphere, insisting all the while that economic control by the state meant economic control by the proletariat. Just the same, the foundation of socialism, Lenin declared,

> "calls for absolute and strict *unity of will*, which directs the joint labors of hundreds, thousands, and tens of thousands of people . . . How can strict unity of will be assured? By thousands subordinating their wills to the will of one. Given ideal class-consciousness and discipline on the part of those taking part in the common work, this subordination would be quite like the mild leadership of a conductor of an orchestra. It may assume the sharp form of a dictatorship if ideal discipline and class-consciousness are lacking. But be that as it may, *unquestioning subordination* to a single will is absolutely necessary for the success of processes organized on the pattern of large-scale machine industry."[7]

If this statement is taken seriously, class-consciousness must have been totally lacking in Russia, for control of production and of social life in general took on dictatorial forms exceeding anything experienced in capitalist nations and excluding any measure of workers' control down to the present day.

All this does not alter the fact, however, that it was the soviets which overthrew both Czarism and the bourgeoisie. It is not inconceivable that under different internal and international conditions the soviets might have retained their power and prevented the rise of authoritarian state-capitalism. Not only in Russia, in Germany, too, the actual content of the revolution was not equal to its revolutionary form. But while in Russia it was mainly the general objective unreadiness for a socialist transformation, in Germany it was the subjective unwillingness to institute socialism by revolutionary means which largely accounted for the failure of the council movement.

In Germany, opposition to the war expressed itself in industrial strikes, which, due to the patriotism of Social Democracy and the trade unions, had to be clandestinely organized at the workplace through committees of action that coordinated various enterprises. In 1918, workers' and soldiers' councils sprang up all over Germany and overthrew the government. The class-collaborationist labor organizations found themselves forced to recognize and enter this movement, if only to dampen revolutionary aspirations. This was not difficult because the workers' and soldiers' councils were composed not only of communists, but of socialists, trade-unionists, non-politicals, and even adherents of bourgeois parties. The slogan "All power to the workers' councils," was therefore self-defeating as far as the revolutionists were concerned, unless, of course, the character and composition of the councils should come to change.

However, the great mass of the workers mistook the political for a social revolution. The ideology and organizational strength of Social Democracy had left its mark; the socialization of production was seen as a governmental concern, not as the task of the working class itself. Though rebellious, the workers in the main were such only in a social-democratic reformist sense. "All power to the workers' councils" implied the dictatorship of the proletariat, for it would leave the non-working layers of society without political representation. Democracy, however, was understood as general franchise. The mass of workers desired both workers' councils *and* the National Assembly. They got them both: the councils in a meaningless form as part of the Weimar Constitution — but with it also the counter-revolution, and, finally, the Nazi dictatorship.

It was not different in other nations — Italy, Hungary, and Spain, for example, where workers gave expression to their revolutionary inclinations through the formation of workers' councils. It thus became obvious that workers' self-organization is no guarantee against policies and actions contrary to proletarian class interests. In that case, however, they will be superseded by traditional or new forms of control of working-class behavior by the old or newly-established authorities. Unless spontaneous movements, issuing into organizational forms of proletarian self-determination, usurp control over society and therewith over their own lives, they are bound to disappear again into the anonymity of mere potentiality.

IV

All that has been said relates to the past and seems to be without relevance to either the present or the near future. As far as the Western world is concerned, not even that feeble world-revolutionary wave released by World War I and the Russian Revolution was repeated during the course of World War II. Instead, and after some initial difficulties, the Western bourgeoisie finds itself in full command over its society. It boasts of an economy of high employment, economic growth, and social stability which excludes both the compulsion and the inclination for social change. Admittedly, this is an overall picture, still marred by some as-yet-unresolved problems, as evidenced by the prevalence of pauperized social groups in all capitalist nations. It is expected, however, that these blemishes will be eradicated in time.

It is not surprising then that the apparent stabilization and further expansion of Western capitalism after World War II led not only to the demise of genuine working-class radicalism but also to the transformation of the reformist social-democratic ideology and practice into the ideology and practice of the mixed economy's welfare-state. This event is either celebrated or bewailed as the integration of labor and capital and the emergence of a new, crisis-free, socio-economic system, combining in itself the positive sides of both capitalism and socialism while shedding their negative aspects. This is often referred to as a post-capitalist system in which the capital-labor antagonism has lost its former relevance. There is still room for all kinds of changes within the system, but it is no longer thought to be susceptible to social revolution. History, as the history of class struggles, has seemingly come to an end.

What is surprising are the various attempts which are still being made to accommodate the idea of socialism to this new state of affairs. It is expected that socialism in the traditional concept can still be reached despite the prevalence of conditions which make its appearance superfluous. Opposition to capitalism, having lost its base in the exploitative material production relations, finds a new one in the moral and philosophical sphere concerned with the dignity of man and the character of his work. Poverty, it is said,[8] never was and cannot be an element of revolution. And even if it were, this would no longer be true because poverty has become a marginal issue, for, by-and-large, capitalism is now in a position to satisfy the consumption needs of the laboring population. While it may still be necessary to fight for immediate demands, such struggles no longer bring the entire order into radical question. In the fight for socialism more stress must be laid upon the qualitative rather than the quantitative needs of the workers. What is required is the progressive conquest of power by the workers through "non-reformist reforms."

Workers' control of production is seen as such a "non-reformist reform" precisely because it cannot be established in capitalism. But if this is so, then the fight for workers' control is equivalent to the overthrow of the capitalist system and the question remains how to bring this about when there are no pressing needs to do so. There is also the question of the organizational means to be employed to this end. The integration of existing labor organizations into the capitalist structure has been possible because capitalism was able to provide the majority of the working class with improving living conditions, and if this trend were to continue there is no reason not to assume that the class struggle will cease being a determinant of social development. In that case — man being the product of his circumstances — the working class will not develop a revolutionary consciousness, will not be interested in risking its present relative well-being for the uncertainties of a proletarian revolution. It was not for nothing that Marx's theory of revolution based itself on the increasing misery of the working-class, even though this misery was not to be measured solely by the fluctuating wage-scale of the labor market.

Workers' control of production presupposes a social revolution. It cannot gradually be achieved through working-class actions within the capitalist system. Where it has been introduced as a measure of reform, it turned out to be an additional means of controlling the workers via their own organizations. The legal work councils in the wake of the German Revolution, for instance, were mere appendices of trade-unions and operated within their restricted activities. Although attempts were made to substitute councils for trade-unions, the latter were able, with the aid of the employers and the state, to assert their control over the shop committees. This relationship did not change with the rebirth of the council system after World War II, then implemented by a so-called co-determination law, which was to give labor a voice in decision-making with regard to production and investments. But the spirit of all this labor legislation may be surmised from Article 49 of the German Works Constitution of 1952:

"Within the framework of the applicable collective agreements, employer and works council collaborate in good faith, working together with the trade union and employer associations represented in the enterprise, for the good of the enterprise and of its employees and under consideration of the common welfare. Employer and works council must not do anything which might endanger the work and the peace of the enterprise. In particular, employer and works council must not carry out any measures of labor struggle against each other. This does not affect the labor struggle of parties entitled to conclude collective agreements."[9]

Co-determination did not and does not affect the employer's sole determination over his property, i.e., his enterprise and production. What it was meant to imply was the right of workers' representatives to make suggestions to management — in theory, even regarding the use of profits. But suggestions need not be accepted and, actually, there is no evidence that suggestions running against capitalist interests were ever heeded by management. To be meaningful, co-determination would have to be co-ownership, but that would be the end of the wage system. Co-determination itself merely allows for the usual activities carried on by trade unions, such as wage agreements, plant regulations, and grievance procedures by which industrial peace is maintained.

What has been said about workers' control in Germany, can be repeated, with some unimportant modifications, for any other capitalist nation which legalized shop stewards, works committees, and similar forms of workers' representation within the industrial enterprises. These measures do not point to an unfolding industrial democracy but are designed to safeguard existing production relations and reduce their immanent frictions. They are not a way toward but away from social change. But even social revolutions may not lead to workers' control when workers fail to secure their hold over the means of production and relegate their power to governments as the sole organizers of the social transformation process. This was the case in Russia and, with some modifications, it became the model for the East European "socialist states" which emerged as a consequence of World War II. Yugoslavia, however, seems to be an exception, for there it was the government which offered the workers' councils managerial functions and a measure of control over their production.

Although the Yugoslav Communist government remains the ultimate source of all power, after its break with Russia it decided on a policy of economic decentralization by a return to market relations and the consequent autonomy of individual enterprises under the control of workers' councils. The latter took on competitive entrepreneurial and managerial functions within the framework of a state-determined general developmental plan. Within definite limits set by the government, the councils and

managing boards elected by them, make decisions regarding the
regulation of work, production plans, wage schedules, sales and
purchases, the budget, credit, investments, and so forth. A
director, appointed by a mixed commission of workers' councils
and local governments, presides over each enterprise, managing
its everyday activities with respect to workers' discipline, hiring
and firing, job assignments and the like. He has the right to veto
decisions made by the workers' councils should they conflict with
state regulations.

Government regulations of a rather complicated nature circumscribe the self-regulatory powers of the workers' councils. They
are partly introduced by government decree and partly by local
authorities in conjunction with the workers' councils. A system
of taxation determines that part of the individual enterprises'
income over which it may itself dispose and therewith its range of
decision-making as regards investments and wages. Profits are
siphoned off by government to cover its own expenses and to invest
in government enterprises. The government determines the general
rate of increase of personal incomes, but, while demanding adherence to a minimum wage, it allows for incentive-wages and
bonuses to increase the productivity of labor. The social security
system diminishes the workers' gross income by more than half.
Investments or disinvestments are determined by the profitability
principle and are steered in the desired direction by price, interest,
and credit policies. In brief, in so far as possible under these conditions, overall control of the economy remains in the hands of
the government despite the limited self-control on the part of the
workers' councils. While the latter cannot affect the decisions of
government, the government sets the conditions within which the
councils operate.

What is far more important than the relationship between
councils and government, however, is the objective impossibility
of establishing genuine workers' control of production and distribution within the market economy. It comes up against the
same dilemma which harrassed the early cooperative movement,
even though, in distinction to the latter, it cannot be destroyed
by private capital competition if the government decides otherwise.
"The workers forming a cooperative in the field of production,"
wrote Rosa Luxemburg,

"are faced with the contradictory necessity of governing themselves

with the utmost absolutism. They are obliged to take toward themselves
the role of the capitalist entrepreneur — a contradiction that accounts for
the usual failure of production cooperatives, which either become pure
capitalist enterprises or, if the workers' interests continue to predominate,
end by dissolving."[10]

Operating in a competitive market economy, the Yugoslav workers
have to exploit themselves as if they were still exploited by capitalists. While this may be more palatable, it does not change the fact
of their subordination to economic processes beyond their control.
Profit production and capital accumulation control their behavior
and perpetuate the misery and insecurity bound up with it.
Yugoslav wages are among the lowest in Europe; they can increase
only as long as capital increases faster than wages. The measure
of control granted the workers' councils promotes anti-social
attitudes because fewer workers have to yield larger profits in
order to raise the incomes of those employed. Workers are unemployed because their employment would not be profitable, i.e.,
yield a surplus above their own reproduction costs. They roam all
over capitalist Europe in search for work and payments denied
them in their own "market-socialism." The integration of the
national into the capitalist world market subjects the working
class not only to self-exploitation and to that of a new ruling class,
but to the exploitation of world capitalism by way of trade relations
and foreign capital investments. To speak of workers' control
under these conditions is sheer mockery.

While there cannot be socialism without workers' control,
neither can there be real workers' control without socialism. To
assert that the gradual increase of workers' control in capitalism
is an actual possibility merely plays into the hands of the widespread demagoguery of the ruling classes to hide their absolute
class-rule by false social reforms dressed in terms such as co-
management, participation, or co-determination. Workers' control
excludes class-collaboration; it cannot partake in but instead
abolishes the system of capital production. Neither socialism nor
workers' control has anywhere become a reality. State-capitalism
and market-socialism, or the combination of both, still find the
working class in the position of wage workers without effective
control over their production and its distribution. Their social
position does not differ from that of workers in the mixed or un-
mixed capitalist economy. Everywhere, the struggle for working-

class emancipation has still to begin and will not end short of the socialization of production and the abolition of classes through the elimination of wage labor.

It can hardly be expected, however, that a working-class, satisfied with the social *status quo*, will engage in power struggles in preference to wage struggles for higher incomes within the prevailing system. Although improvements in proletarian living conditions in advanced capitalist nations are highly exaggerated, they have nevertheless been sufficient to extinguish working-class radicalism. Even though the "value" of labor-power must always be smaller than the "value" of the products it creates, the "value" of labor-power may imply different living conditions. It may be expressed in a twelve- or a six-hour day, in good or in bad housing, in more or less consumption goods. At any particular time, however, the given wages and their buying power determine the conditions of the laboring population as well as their complaints and aspirations. Improved conditions become the customary conditions, and continued acquiescence of the workers requires the maintenance of these conditions. Should they deteriorate, it will arouse working-class opposition in the same way that deterioration of less-affluent conditions did previously. It is then only on the assumption that prevailing living standards can be secured and perhaps improved that the social consensus may be maintained.

Though apparently supported by recent experiences, this assumption is not warranted. But to assert its lack of validity on theoretical grounds[11] will not affect a social practice based on the illusion of its permanency. There are indications, however, that the capitalist crises mechanism is reasserting itself despite various modifications of the capitalist system. In view of America's persistent economic stagnation and the levelling-off of West European expansion, a new disillusionment has already set in. With the diminishing potency of government-induced production, the capitalist need to secure its profitability regardless of the ensuing social instability increases. The new economic innovations reveal themselves as being capable of postponing, but not of overcoming, capitalism's built-in crisis-mechanism. This being so, it is only reasonable to assume that when the hidden crisis becomes acute, when the pseudo-prosperity leads to real depression, the social consensus of recent history will make room for a resurgent revolutionary consciousness — the more so as the growing irrationality of the system becomes obvious even to social layers that still benefit by its existence. Apart from pre-revolutionary conditions existing in almost all underdeveloped nations, and apart from the seemingly limited, yet unceasing wars, waged in different parts of the world, a general unrest underlies and undermines the apparent social tranquility of the Western world. From time to time there is a breaking out into the open as in the recent upheavals in France. If this is possible under relatively stable conditions, it is certainly possible under general crisis conditions.

The integration of traditional labor organizations into the capitalist system is an asset to the latter only so long as it is able to underwrite the promised and actual benefits of class collaboration. When these organizations are forced by circumstances to become instruments of repression, they lose the confidence of the workers and therewith their value to the bourgeoisie. Even if not destroyed, they may be overruled by independent working-class actions. There is not only the historical evidence that lack of working-class organizations does not prevent organized revolution, as in Russia, but also that the existence of a well-entrenched reformist labor movement can be challenged by new working-class organizations, as in the Germany of 1918, and by the shop steward movement in England during and after the first world war. Even under totalitarian regimes, spontaneous movements may lead to working-class actions that find expression in the formation of workers' councils as in Poland and in the Hungary of 1956.

Reforms presuppose a reformable capitalism. So long as it has this character, the revolutionary nature of the working class exists only in latent form. It will even cease being conscious of its class position and identify its aspirations with those of the ruling classes. But when capitalism is forced by its own development to recreate the conditions which lead to the formation of class consciousness, it will also bring back the revolutionary demand for workers' control as a demand for socialism. It is true that all previous attempts in this direction have failed, and that new ones may fail again. Still, it is only through the experiences of self-determination, in whatever limited ways at first, that the working class will be enabled to develop toward its own emancipation.

Notes

[1] *Théorie des lois civiles, ou principles fondamentaux de la société*, pp. 274, 464, 470.

[2] *Reflections on Violence*, 1906.

[3] *Preamble of the Industrial Workers of the World.*

[4] *Russland in der Revolution*, Dresden, 1909, pp. 82, 228.

[5] J. Bunyan and H. H. Fisher, *The Bolshevik Revolution*, Stanford, 1934, p. 308.

[6] *Questions of the Socialist Organization of the Economy*, Moscow, p. 173.

[7] *Ibid.*, p. 127.

[8] By André Gorz, for example, in his *Strategy for Labor*, Boston, 1964.

[9] Quoted in A. Sturmthal, *Workers Councils*, Cambridge, 1964, p. 74.

[10] *Reform or Revolution*, New York, 1937, p. 35.

[11] See: P. Mattick, *Marx and Keynes: The Limits of the Mixed Economy*, Boston, 1969.

JOURNEY TO THE PLACE

Amy R. Cass

Age 10

Peter, who was 7 years old, and Clarissa, who was six, lived in a small town called Harringsville with their Mother and Father.

Peter and Clarissa, like all the other children hated what they had to do every day. And this is it: up at 7:00, to school at 8:00; home at 3:00, eat at 5:00; to sleep at 7:30. Do you see why they hated it?

Ever since they were four or five they wanted to go to a place called . . . well, it really doesn't have a name, but I'll tell you about it. It's a place that not everyone knows about, mostly only children. You get there by an animal.

Animals show you the way. Peter and Clarissa really wanted to go. But they had to find the right animal. So they set out to the zoo to find a weird looking or sounding animal. They figured because they are going to such an unusual place, it would have to be an unusual animal to take them there. But they couldn't find any weird looking or sounding animal, so they decided to start without an animal.

They walked and walked and walked.

As they walked along they came to a cat and her kittens. For three hours they sat there and waited to see if they would be lead somewhere or to something.

But they weren't so they went on until they found themselves following a unicorn. By the way, a unicorn is like a horse with one big horn in the middle of his head.

The unicorn led them to a small hole. In the hole there was a key. As Peter picked up the key, the unicorn ran away.

Peter and Clarissa walked on a little more and there was a door. Peter put the key in the keyhole and THERE IT WAS! the place! The place they were looking for . . . everything they wanted right there!

They were the two happiest children I knew.

The Place

This place was beautiful. It had cake and candy, meat and vegetables. Peter and Clarissa loved everything, so did the other children.

Oh yes, there were many, many animals . . . cats, dogs, birds, monkeys, horses and even unicorns.

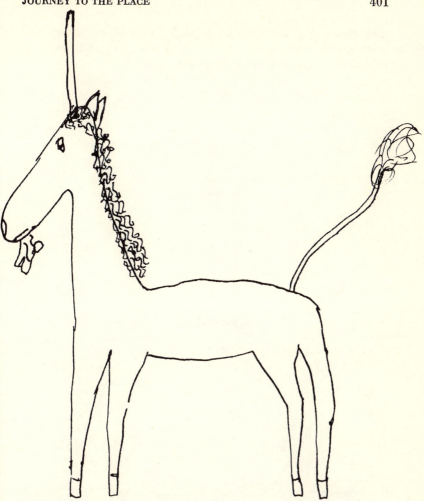

There was something called the Mischief Room where there were glasses of milk to spill, windows to break, hammers and saws to ruin things with, and things to throw around.

There was a Neat Room. That was where you could get pretty clothes and take showers and baths and comb your hair, wash your hands and brush your teeth.

There was a toy store where you didn't need money.

And for a second one might have thought that they didn't learn anything. Well, there is something called a Learning Room. That's where they teach each other how to add and write and read and spell. They had a huge collection of books that children brought with them. And from the books they learnt about history and they learnt about nature and how to do things like tell time and read music. And that is the Learning Room.

One of the favorite rooms of all the children is the Outdoor Room. And that's where there's flowers and trees and animals and streams and lakes and caves to go in, places outside that you can roller skate and jump rope and use a pogo stick and where you can camp out. And for those who like woods, there's woods to walk in.

The Tragedy Of The Door

All the children in The Place were always very cautious not to
be seen opening the door that they came in through, for they
feared that an adult would find out about it. One day, Clarissa
wasn't careful enough, opened the door and was seen by her
Mother. Her Mother asked what was behind the door. Clarissa
was an honest girl, especially after being in The Place, so she told
her Mother the truth.

Her Mother came in, looked around and said it was a very nice
place, but it needed a little tidying and fixing up. So she came in
and started to sweep a little and then went and got a couple of
more mothers to help. When they saw the Learning Room they
thought it was beautiful. So they went and got a teacher who
posted a schedule that said "up at 7:00, to school at 8:00; home at
3:00, eat at 5:00; to sleep at 7:30."

When the teacher saw the Mischief Room, she gasped and said
it was a terrible disaster area and locked it up for good.

As more and more parents came in, making more and more
changes that they thought were good for the children, the children
sneaked out one by one and never came back. All that is left of
The Place now is each child's dream.

PARTICIPATORY DEMOCRACY

AND THE

DILEMMA OF CHANGE

C. George Benello

The founding document of Students for a Democratic Society — the Port Huron Statement — spoke of participatory democracy as the basis for the organization of society:

> As a *social system* we seek the establishment of a democracy of individual participation, governed by two central aims: that the individual share in those social decisions determining the quality and direction of his life; that society be organized to encourage independence in men and provide the media for their participation.

The belief in participatory democracy led SDS in its early days to organize communities of the poor along participatory principles, seeking to create the needed changes in American society from this base. Hayden, Potter, and other SDS leaders spoke of the development of counter-communities and counter-organizations to be used as vehicles to challenge existing structures by withdrawing support and becoming independently legitimate.

The climate in the New Left has shifted. I believe that the sheer magnitude of the problem was what caused New Left organizers to look around for other approaches. Also, other more urgent issues came to dominate the political landscape: particularly the Vietnam war. As the draft escalated the resistance movement grew. The Vietnam war focused attention on U. S. imperialism abroad, and also led to confrontations at home. Radical students did not feel they could allow themselves the luxury of counter-communities when the imperative to resist an unjust war, in which they were directly involved as draftees, was so great.

In part, the change came out of despair. As community organizing laid bare the true extent of poverty in this country, showing it to be a national problem soluble only on the national level, activists came to feel the need of some sustaining vision. There was no evidence of successful counter-communities that had grown to the point where they could claim legitimacy and withdraw support in any significant degree from the surrounding system. As a result, young activists began to align themselves more and more with the Cuban revolution, which represented success. Thus the revolutionary rhetoric was ironically the result of an encounter with a utopian model, but one that came out of a Marxist and revolutionist context. Moreover, the rhetoric matched the mood of the black militants who had come to feel that accommodation of any sort with the white power structure was impossible.

What has become imperiled by the move away from community organizing toward resistance and confrontation is the thin line between resistance and revolutionism. I support resistance when it is seen as a personal and ethical imperative stemming from personal implication in the Vietnam war via the draft, or through studying or teaching at schools whose major funding comes from war research. Its effect, if organized and carried out on a large scale, is to contain the excesses of the war system, and to raise the issue of the war among a wider segment of the American public. But when resistance slips over into revolutionism, or into the rhetoric of revolution, then it goes beyond an ethical position and becomes a strategy for achieving fundamental structural change.

Discussion of revolution is too often befogged by a cloudy use of terms. The word is applied to everything from the Dodge rebellion to the revolution in cybernation and automation. What I hold in question is revolution in its delimited, historical meaning: the overthrow of the existing regime by methods which may not necessarily be violent, but which are essentially extra-legal. Most people on the Left who speak of revolution see it in these terms, and see it as a socialist revolution in which the means of production would be turned over to the people in one way or another. Again, the Cuban model is the one often considered, with its overthrow of the existing elite and its structural changes in the social and economic fabric.

Without getting into a discussion of the existence or non-existence of a revolutionary situation in this country, it should be clear that the government is only one of a number of institutional orders which are intermeshed through common interests and common definitions of reality to a degree which has seldom been present in the past. The Left, on the whole, recognizes that there are ruling elites throughout both the private and the public sector. The military-industrial complex represents only one such conglomeration. There is also a social-industrial complex, and an educational-industrial complex made up of universities which in some cases receive over fifty percent of their funding from the government in the form of research grants, and other lesser coalitions of interest on the state and local level.

These coalitions, taken together, represent a monopoly of the skills necessary to run an industrialized society. The technicians that they employ, the scientists, engineers, administrators and other bureaucrats, represent a mandarinate who agree not so much on common purposes as on a common methodology, and on common definitions of the nature of organization and of efficiency. Moreover, their agreement extends to a common refusal to bring their purposes into question and thus both the direction and the goals of the system remain unquestioned. Viewed in terms of relative pay-offs, these technicians have a large ideological and psychological investment in the system; pay-offs in terms of status and prestige as well as money more than offset any qualms about the depredations brought about by the system as a whole. In short, we are not talking of a ruling junta lording it over a large class of disadvantaged and propertyless peasants, as is often the case in Latin America. Nor is it a matter of the expropriation of property. As Paul Goodman pointed out in his address to the National Security Industrial Association, without the technocratic skills possessed by the mandarins within the present institutional orders, our industrial system would not continue to work. To conceive of a take over which would not simply affect the government, but would also force the other institutional orders to aquiesce to a fundamental restructuring and change of goals, would be to conceive of a centralization of power and a coercive use of it which would be Stalinist in its proportions.

My argument is that revolutionism is inappropriate as an approach to change, and derives from a basic misconception of the problem posed by advanced industrial societies. The original intuition of the New Left, which saw a society of participation as the goal, and sought ways to work toward such a society, was correct, in my view. The trouble is that the intuition lacked any adquate articulation in terms of an analysis of the social order and of how to change it. This is understandable in view of the fact that the only systematic theory which has combined analysis and a theory of change in terms at all acceptable to the New Left has been Marxism. The anarchist and decentralist analyses of people like Goodman and Mumford and some of the English and European anarchists have no built-in theory of change, and in fact anarchism itself has always been ambivalent on the subject of change: some anarchists have been revolutionists, while others have opted for various schemes for building libertarian institutions into the society.

Before indicating the outlines of a theory of social change that is more adequate to the realities of advanced industrial society and at the same time involves a politics of participation, it is best to understand how participatory politics has been understood by the New Left. It can be understood on a number of levels. First, it can be used as a basis of self-organizing. Various accounts indicate the problems involved even at this level. ERAP (the Economic Research and Action Project of SDS) encountered the problem of combining decentralization with coordination and leadership. The students involved were bold to apply their principles to themselves, but they lacked a worked-out theory of participatory organization.

Secondly, participatory democracy can be considered as the goal embodied in the idea of a good society. In this sense it has two dimensions: the requirement that *everyone* be capable of participating in decisions, and the requirement that the participation be continuous and significant, not just a process of voting once a year for tweedledum or tweedledee. As a goal, this is laudable, but couched in these terms it says little about the shape of the existing society, the forces that prevent such participation, and how to overcome them. Thirdly, it could result from an analysis of the basic dynamics of advanced industrial society, basing itself on a systematic critique of the organizational and social structure of that society. In other words, it could relate to the goal of the good society in somewhat the same way that the Marxist socio-historical critique of capitalism relates to the goal of the classless society. This sort of analysis exists at best in bits and pieces, and has not been synthesized into a systematic critique.

Finally, given the existence of an analysis and a vision of the good society, it would then, only after the analysis had captured the fundamental structural dynamics of the present system and laid it bare, be able to delineate a strategy of change. At one level

the New Left has understood — largely as a result of the work of
C. Wright Mills — that our society is organized in terms of elites
and masses and that restructuring it would create a fundamental
change in the values and direction of the society. But it has
tended, in the long tradition of American reformers, to see the
problem in moral terms, which means in terms of individual imper-
fection. The institutional and organizational dimensions of the
problem have consequently been lost, and as a result the lack of
democratic participation in society has been seen by the Left as
one of a number of ills, some of them more blatant, all of which
must be treated.

In part this was the result of the lack of an analysis capable of
indicating the true scope of the problem of participation. As its
critics say, no one seems to quite know what participatory democracy means, and thus they take refuge in invoking various iron
laws of oligarchy, of bureaucracy, of the need for well defined
leadership, in order to prove that participatory democracy is a
hopelessly utopian conception. Indeed, faced with the imperative
of action, there is a strong temptation to sacrifice full participation
to the exigencies of quick decision. This became an important
issue in the May days in France, when the need for efficient
organization to combat the CRS riot police was opposed by the
desire to hash out matters thoroughly in the councils. Also, in
the SDS project in Newark, the desire to operate along the principles of participatory democracy ran into conflict with the need
for efficient administration and effective leadership. Thus, unless
a structural analysis can show that the problem of participatory
organization lies at the root of the ills of modern industrial society,
the temptation is to avoid structural problems of organization in
the interest of the effective attainment of other objectives.

In the work of C. Wright Mills the rise of elites is contrasted
with the early American democracy of small town and rural
countryside where town meetings and the system of geographic
representation were not undercut by the existence of corporate
and other organized forms of power which are national and even
multi-national in their scope. But the analysis, in the tradition of
Weber and Pareto, focuses on the nature of the elites themselves,
rather than on the organizational forms which gave rise to them.
Consequently, this tends to reinforce the moralism of the traditional populist approach to change, which has been influential on
the Left: get rid of the elites, and the people will naturally find

the most suitable forms of self-government. The assumption here is that it is not certain individuals which constitute the problem, it is a ruling class, and when this is replaced with a different class with different values, the problem will be solved.

The difficulty with this approach is that it ignores the extent to which individuals are shaped by the institutions in which they operate. The value of the anarchist analysis, when applied to organizations, is that it is fully conscious of the extent to which organizations shape even those who purport to control them. It is useful to see this in terms of the kinds of structures imposed by the organizational imperative. Faced with a given task requiring group effort, obviously the nature of the task imposes its demands on the form of human organization. However, far too much in the way of technological necessity is ordinarily attributed to the task itself. It is possible, as experiments in England have shown, to assemble a car from the ground up by a single group of workers, and to do this as efficiently as by conventional methods, thus eliminating the assembly line. What has become increasingly evident as a result of such experimentation is that it is not efficiency which dictates the organizational forms of industry so much as efficiency of control. Given a system where, from the start, power is concentrated among a few, much of the centralization of control and specialization of function that exists results from the desire to maintain the system of control, and has nothing to do with efficiency. Studies indicate, in fact, that increasingly the new technology requires decentralization, not concentration. As we progress, this will become clearer.

Beyond the technological imperatives there is always freedom for a number of alternative styles of organizing. What is involved in making the decision on the final organizational plan is a series of trade-offs between short-run and long-run efficiency, between rigid adherence to a pre-conceived plan and a flexibility (which also means unpredictability), between the advantages of control being vested in a small and highly trained elite, and the problems involved in educating all those in the organization to participate in decision-making. It has been the experience of the Rowen Works in England that a system of rotating and elective management is as effective as the traditional system only after a period of five years, at which point all the workers have gained a thorough knowledge of the whole operation.

The fundamental feature of the organizational imperative can be expressed as follows: in the short run it is more efficient to have an elitist structure, dominated by an educated and knowledgeable minority. From this perspective the difficult task of developing a participative structure, and then educating people into using it, is time-consuming and inefficient. It is only in the long run that the values embodied in full participation (which assures work that is non-alienating, by virtue of the degree of control that the worker has over the nature and product of his work) pay off in efficiency. Thus in Yugoslavia, the initial experience in setting up workers' councils was that the workers were impatient at hours spent in discussion and decision-making, and preferred to get on with the job and make money. But now there is general support for democratic self-administration (it is highest in younger workers); moreover it has been extended to all organizations, not just factories.

There are several problems which arise when organizing for participation. The most basic one is that it is always easier to organize in an elitist fashion and then simply dictate to the rest. The organizational form is simpler, less educational effort is needed, and policy can be decided in a simple way by a few. Anyone who has gone through the agonies of broad scale democratic debate is aware of these facts, although often the agonies are caused more by the failure to structure the decision process adequately than by anything inherent in the process itself. Effective decision-making requires small groups which meet regularly and which maintain effective channels of communication with each other. The lesson of the Standard Auto Works in England, where for a period production was entirely under workers' control, was of the primary importance of the careful organization of the work groups, and of the communication between them. It may be easier to organize in elitist fashion, but the psycho-social costs extend far beyond the productive operation. And as modern management research indicates, in the long run alienation produces inefficiency.

Secondly, given a society in which inequalities of class and status are built in, organizations that are formed within such a context will mirror these inequities. However, the organizational imperatives of industrialism have made organization more intensive, and its form more crushing, than ever before. As Robert Nisbet has pointed out, our present organizational forms are closer to an armed camp or a garrison than to anything else.

Thirdly, the process of organizing a productive enterprise initially requires a high level of entrepreneurial skills involving capital accumulation, market research, technological planning, and human organizing. Subsequently, the enterprise can be operated by workers possessing essentially machine-tending and operating skills. This too builds in a class division which is inegalitarian and anti-democratic. Moreover, the power of the machine multiplies vastly the impact of the production organization on the environment. For this reason such organization is very powerful and its authoritarian aspects are reinforced.

Finally, the corporate form developed as a result of its success in meeting the need for rapid industrial expansion, with its promise of plenty in an economy of scarcity. The invention of the limited liability joint stock company ensured that risk-taking was maximally rewarded and minimally penalized for failure. In the absence of broad gauge social planning to develop industry, a premium was placed on the entrepreneurial skills needed to set up factories; rather than hedge the freedom of the entrepreneur by forcing him to confront the problem of social planning and social purposes, either within his plant or in society, he was conveniently left to concern himself with profits. The social structure formed in an earlier age was capable of containing the chaotic effects of this for a while. Subsequent legislation limited the resulting grosser depradations of the system, while allowing the subtler effects — alienation, regimentation, class division, to be perpetuated throughout society. Today the corporation, as a prime locus of power and hence of politics, operates largely unchecked, while the social fabric is torn apart.

I have indicated the seeming naturalness of the evolution of private power, especially in its corporate and productive form. In many ways this evolution took the path of least resistance toward an industrialized, technological society. It suggests that the basic organizational form — here the corporation — is of fundamental importance in determining the social order and its values. But, most important, it indicates that the problem is a systemic one, not to be attributed to the set of elites which arose with the maturing of the system as a whole, but rather to the basic organizational form of the system. Not only is the corporation the prime locus of power, with its capacity to allocate resources, determine productive priorities, delineate the shape of cities and determine where people will work. It is also the model for the other major organizational forms throughout the society: the universities, even the church hierarchies, the professional associations, the unions. Some of these organizations are formally elective, some not. But even where the electoral choice also represents a significant policy choice, there is no continuity of participation by the rank and file, and hence it is easy to argue that they could not participate, simply because they are not trained to. Hence the myth of participation, without the substance, perpetuates itself.

It is possible now to clarify the essential differences in social analysis and social philosophy between the revolutionists and those who advocate that society must be restructured from the ground up, not from the top down. There is no doubt but that the second path would also be revolutionary, but remembering the specific definition of revolution given above, it is evident that the term can be properly applied only to those who wish to *seize* power in order to achieve change. The revolutionists see the basic problem as that of getting rid of the elites — a class whose power is so great as to be qualitatively different from that of other groups. It is true that power is exercised disproportionately at the top, but the question is, is getting rid of the elites going to solve the problem?

I see things differently, from a participatory point of view. I see historical conditions giving rise to certain organizational forms, as a result of pay-offs and trade-offs. A disporportionate reward went to those who possessed the entrepreneurial skills capable of founding productive enterprises. Class and status inequities worsened because a fundamentally different set of relations to the productive apparatus became institutionalized. There is not space here to go into the distinctions between the entrepreneurial class and the managerial class, and how ownership relates to control. However, it can be noted that ownership is entirely analyzable as a form of control. In a worker-controlled enterprise, it disappears as a meaningful category of control. Witness Yugoslavia: a number of groups, including union, workers' council, and commune, exercise varying degrees of control over a productive enterprise, and the union has the power to reorganize the control structure and select new members, in case of business failure. In the modern publicly owned corporation, ownership also means little; ownership of a few shares of stock brings no corresponding control, while ownership of a significant block of shares can bring complete control.

If the history of the development of the productive enterprise is one of elites, it must be remembered that the pay-off for the entrepreneur was high because the pay-off for society in the form of increased goods was also high. And of course the social costs were initially deemed insignificant in comparison to the rewards. Hence, confronted with the fat pay-offs for successful production, even the rudimentary participation of electoral democracy was conveniently forgotten, and the work place became a highly authoritarian and coercive situation. Then, when the workers began to organize, bribery in the form of higher wages was substituted for the possibility of participation. But the entrepreneurs were not exclusively to blame: the whole society was involved. So removing the entrepreneurs would not have solved the problem. A different system with equal incentives would have had to be devised to replace the existing system: and the point is that a system which was more equalitarian in its pay-offs and more participative in its organizational structure would necessarily have been — and would be — far more complicated.

Here we come to the second and most important side of the organizational analysis. Productive organization is one of the most complex forms of human organization, and requires the most extensive planning in view of the technological and industrial requirements. To plan not simply for production but also for extensive participation is even more difficult. The pay-off for a successful planning for production was immediate, and it was and remains high. But for a society to address itself to the unprecedented problem of planning for participation as industry developed, there would have to be a normative system enjoining this kind of equalitarianism, and also some kind of pre-existing model to go by. There were of course neither. Instead the economists and social philosophers busied themselves constructing theories of the innate selfishness of human nature and then showed how the maximizing of individual profit would automatically work out to the greatest good for the greatest number.

Every socio-political system involves a philosophy of man. Where the system is coercive and authoritarian, the philosophy is usually dualistic, seeing man as evil and prone to disobedience. Contemporary philosophies of man have tended to be dystopian and reductionist, seeing the world as absurd, and man as ruled either by his biology or by iron laws of history. One of the major requirements for a society made up of self-administered institutions which are fully participatory is a view of man that extends beyond a dualistic and need-centered psychology. When motivation is reduced to biological drives, it is impossible to understand the role of responsible participation. Psychological research indicates, however, that the opportunity to participate in key decisions affecting one's life is a prerequisite of mental health, and the problem is to fit this within a suitable psychological context. Third force psychology provides such a context, since it posits a set of motives beyond deficiency needs and having to do with the urge toward self-actualization.

Self-actualization can occur when the basic needs — the biological drives, the security needs, the ego's need for recognition — have been met. The person is then free to actualize his potentialities, and this requires that he be able to identify with larger values that transcend himself, and participate significantly in the areas of work and public life that affect his own existence. It also requires that the basic areas of life — work and leisure, private life and public life — be capable of significant integration, since without such objective integration, personal integration is impossible. *This basic viewpoint can be described as the affirmation of the primacy of the person.* Respect for human potentiality and growth under conditions of freedom requires that organizations be seen as tools for the realization of human purposes rather than instruments for the manipulation of human material viewed as personnel. This dictates a policy of total opposition to the current widespread depersonalization imposed by the size, structure, and mindless goals of existing organizations.

It requires that work be re-defined so as to be made meaningful, by allowing everyone involved a say in what is produced, how it is produced, and how income from production is used. The fetishism of commodities, leading to the worship of the GNP, must give way to a respect for the conditions under which human growth and realization are possible. In community life it requires that local units be the locus of decision-making regarding the significant aspects of the physical and social environment, and that such units have a say in the control of productive enterprises within their province. Both of these principles have been employed in the restructuring of the industrial and social organization in Yugoslavia at no expense to the technology. The commune is the basic local unit in Yugoslavia, and its council is made up of representatives of the basic institutions within the commune — the schools, the hospitals, the factories, the unions, the party.

It is possible to oppose a politics of participation to a politics of power, as Robert Pranger has done. Each of these alternatives has a definite psychology behind it. The psychology of participation believes that the self-actualization of an individual is connected with the realization of social purpose and community. This view denies that man is dominated by a need psychology that is innately self-centered, and affirms the possibility of synergy — the correspondence of individual needs with social purpose. On the other hand, the psychology of power posits an unbridgeable gap between the satisfaction of individual needs and the exigencies of the social order. This kind of personal-social dualism mirrors the psychological dualism of the corrupt man who is inwardly split between good and evil drives. It is based on a zero-sum, two-person game view of the social order where one person's gain is inevitably another person's loss. Given such a view, the struggle for power becomes the dominating reality, and conversely, where the physical environment has given rise to a struggle for power, such a view is likely to obtain.

Behind the economic system which developed with the rise of industry, psychological analysis can thus discern another, more fundamental level. The productive organization came to exercise a basic influence on the social order and its values not because historic causation is always and exclusively material, but because the technology of mass production led to opportunities for wealth and power exceeding anything previously imagined. The nearest historical equivalent in terms of opportunities for the deployment of men and resources occurred in warfare, and this was both non-continuous and increasingly a monopoly of the state. It can be argued that Western civilization, at least from the time of the Romans, has always been based on a politics of power, and when power in its blunt military form became a monopoly of the state, it then became more subtle but continued as the pursuit of wealth, thus allowing the power game to continue but under a different form.

But again, notwithstanding the psychological orientation of Western man, the organizational imperative remains: the more extensive the organization, the greater the danger of top-down control, and the more skillful the organizational design must be to avoid this. Hence, far from the populist vision that once the elite is removed from power the social order will naturally become democratic, precisely the reverse is true. The path of least resistance always leads back to elitism; the fundamental problem is how to organize for extensive participation within a context imposed by the technology of extensive organization. The New Left, in talking of participatory democracy, has had an invaluable insight. But for understandable reasons having to do with the magnitude of the problem and the paucity of its own resources, it has been unable to translate the insight into a strategy for achieving change.

At present the typical bureaucracy, whether public or private, is highly organized at the top, but only at the top. Here small committees rule, and decision-making is continuous and constant. As one goes down the hierarchy, group decision-making soon gives way to a machine style of organizing wherein orders flow down from the top and information flows up from the bottom. But the paradigms of complete decision-making are the small face-to-face groups that rule the corporate and bureaucratic worlds: the boards, trustee committees, executive councils and so forth which meet regularly to plan, propose, execute and dispose. The problem thus becomes specific: to design organizations which meet the technological requirements while at the same time embodying the full decision process throughout the organization. Rather than being group-organized only at the top, organizations must embody group structure throughout their own structure so that the one is coterminous with the other.

In those few cases where this has been attempted (some mining companies, and for a while, the aforementioned Standard Auto Works, all in England, come to mind) the result has been higher productivity and, understandably, far higher worker morale. The myth that organizational efficiency requires an authoritarian structure is thus laid to rest. Efficiency is not the problem, but organizational design is. It is true that there is little hope that those now in control of the corporate baronies will be swayed by such arguments, since the pay-offs deriving from the existing system vastly favor them. But it is also true that doing away with the existing elites will not solve the problem. Workers, and certainly their union bosses, have an extensive stake in the system as it is; and a faith in the ideology of hard work for upward mobility into the bourgeois. Job specialization is part of the general apparatus of control, and for the worker with his fragmented and worm's eye view of the whole, the thought of greater responsibility through participation cannot be attractive. The resistance encountered by the Yugoslavs when they set up their workers' councils would probably be magnified, since the level of technology and consequently of organization in the United States is higher, and hence the trained incapacity of the worker is also greater. The question is, if one forsakes revolutionism, how can one achieve change within the context of an advanced industrial society? It should be apparent from what I have said that the problem of participation is a root organization problem for a society deeply involved in technological advance. On its adequate solution depends the question of how power and wealth are distributed throughout the society, for it makes no sense to speak of participation without applying it to the disposition of the capital surplus which comes from production. Moreover, resistance to what would be involved, namely a change in the organizational structure, would come not only from the top, but from all those within the present institutional orders whose main security comes from doing what they know how to do. The ritualized conformism of the bureaucrat is a necessary by-product of the bureaucratic hierarchies, and helps maintain the system of control.

It is true that there are some institutions more amenable to democratization than others. The existing top-down structures of the educational establishments are more obviously dysfunctional, and the students and even some of the faculty are becoming aware of this. But, as I have indicated, fear of change comes not simply from fear of loss of status on the part of those indoctrinated to believe that the existing structures are the only ones that can do the job. While it may be possible to demythologize efficiency a bit, the main job is to prove that participatory organizations work, and so far there are remarkably few examples of such organizations in this country. This means confronting the central organizational dilemma and working toward solutions: planning effective structures that embody participation and educating those in them to take on the responsibility which comes with participation.

It is impossible here to describe in detail how failure to organize participatively lies at the root of the vast problems created by our chaotic and power-ridden industrial and institutional order. At the root of the failure, however, lies the denial that the self-interest of a minority can be equated with the public good of the majority. No such easy out exists; people must participate actively or they will not be heard, and given the existing technology, it is too easy to manipulate and seek justification through various organizational and bureaucratic imperatives. As the system is set up, it cannot operate without being dehumanizing. The importance of the New Left is that it has dared to be utopian and to reject the system, out of an immediate sense of its human wastage and destructiveness. The need now is to show that such a rejection can lead to the development of a liberating and humane use of technology which is capable of affirming the primacy of the person in the face of the organization.

Faced with the prevailing mythology regarding efficiency, only the actual creation of participatory institutions that work can adequately prove that they are viable. And, while it makes sense to start with simpler institutions rather than the productive enterprises, sooner or later such a movement for change must confront the work place. A movement seeking to organize from the ground up to achieve full participation will have the greatest impact when it creates effective productive organizations, *since it is here that social organization confronts most fully the existing technology*. The productive enterprise is the core institution in an advanced industrial society, and hence if it can be self-administering and participative, it takes the ground out from under the supporters of the present authoritarian system.

The objection to full democracy in the work place, as well as in other institutions, is not ideological since the official mythology of course encourages democracy. It is rather practical and psychological; the practical side of the argument is couched in terms of the mythology of efficiency, and in accountants' terms. But social costs are not considered part of cost accounting and the major pay-off is not for comprehensiveness of planning but for getting things done. Psychologically, the question people raise is whether there is an incentive for risk-taking when there is no major pay-off. But the assumption that most people are passive and will not organize except under conditions of bribery is valid only where the prevailing profit ethos and psychology of selfishness is accepted, thus preventing other purposes and values from being realized. But it is precisely the incentive of organizing for broader and more imaginative ends that has stimulated the few existing experiments in self-administration. And a major incentive is surely providing that a self-administering system can work.

Revolutionism tends to personalize the enemy and define it in terms of those with the most stake in the existing system. Corruption of course exists, and venality and self-serving is the rule, but these failures flow from the conjunction of human frailty with institutional structures holding an excess of power with no corresponding accountability. Moreover, the corruption is exacerbated by the critical gap between the myth system of democratic values and the coercive and elitist realities of the major institutions. When an ideology of participation is invoked, and used to build self-administering institutions, the gap is narrowed and the myth system is taken seriously rather than cynically. When asked what it is after, SDS answers that it is merely trying to put into practice what is preached. When people do this in such a way as to humanize the existing technology, rather than renounce it, then the strategy of change operates maximally within social and cultural realities. The specter of the unknown, of a post-revolutionary order in unknown hands serving unknown purposes is put to rest.

Moreover, both the pragmatic and the ideological objections to basic structural change are met: the organizations are built, and are shown to work. And the objection that change must be wrought through the accepted channels is bypassed; rather than resorting to the tweedledum and tweedledee of electoral politics — which can come once the movement has built a sufficient base — structural change is introduced, but introduced specifically for the purpose of democratizing the society. This in no way discounts the importance of resistance to unjust laws, unjust wars, and oppressive policies. But it adds to it another dimension which relates directly to the structural causes of the injustice: to the runaway economy which gives rise to, in fact requires, the military-industrial complex; to the inability to integrate social purpose into the productive process which gives rise to slums and ghettoes; to the resulting social and urban chaos which gives rise to riots and violence. The development of a movement dedicated to the building of self-administering, free institutions is immensely difficult, requiring the collection and coordination of extensive resources. But it is both the most absent and most needed ingredient in a movement for social change.

NOTES TOWARD A RADICAL CULTURE

Louis Kampf

These notes are mainly for the eyes of my brothers and sisters in the movement.* For to discuss radical culture is, at the present time, to discuss the culture of the movement. And what is the movement? Those who know are already a part of this culture: they know its private — and rapidly shifting — language; they understand its physical mannerisms; they are wise to its tensions, loves, divisions, and hatreds. But there are not enough who know; and too many who know are merely voyeurs — celibates of the movement. This is one way of saying that this culture is not deep enough; it is not quite real. Our task is to make its secret language public by realizing words in acts, images in institutions, analyses in practice. If the movement does not become embedded in the general culture, the concept of a radical culture will remain a ghost visible only to the elect.

*　　*　　*

Material need — hunger, lack of shelter, disease — is an oppressive reality for many Americans. In much of the rest of the world people are starving to death. Why, then, the concern over something so seemingly trivial as culture? There are times when I find it difficult not to gag on the word. Yet those who have attained the material comforts which accompany a middle class income know that relative economic security can go hand in hand with profound feelings of social inferiority and an abandonment of will. Such wrenchings of individual sensibilities have a social

---

* When I use the word "movement," I mean *white* radicals in America. The cultural problems of blacks are obviously different.

source; they are an index of cultural failure. Only devotees of the Gross National Product need be surprised, since periods of economic growth have always engendered new individual needs. If the struggle for economic betterment fails to develop a culture which helps individuals to define both themselves and their relation to society, these new needs are inevitably shaped by the pressures of the economic system — that is, of economic growth. Manipulative instruments such as advertising consequently define the individual's new yearnings; the desire for greater — or different — material satisfactions becomes his culture. How to break through this circle of economic motivation? Not much less than a restructuring of our culture seems to be in order. A cultural revolution? Perhaps.

* * *

Amongst radicals one hears much talk of a crisis for capitalist institutions. The very notion of a high Western culture has begun to take a beating. But the doubts about traditional concepts have also created a crisis for the movement. Change hardly ever comes about in the expected ways, and concepts which have been the radicals' bread and butter become as stale and rancid as any capitalist ideology. Thus institutions which have begun to shake disturb our own norms, and force us to reconsider the nature and locus of our activities. How are we to take advantage of loosened foundations? How do we initiate fundamental social change? Often enough our reactions to events are wildly inappropriate because they are given direction by concepts which have turned to stone. We have yet to develop a set of reflexes which would constitute a radical culture. Such reflexes should sustain us, and give our thought and actions continuity; they should be at the center of our lives.

A radical culture is a necessary component of the movement's program, yet we cannot create it by force of will. However, the present historical moment seems favorable. Western culture is in disrepute, some of its central ideas having become masks for the drive toward universal destruction. The pursuit of knowledge, we have assumed, is a good in itself and an agent of progress: it has led to the hydrogen bomb; the concept of rationality is at the foundation not only of scholarship, but of activities relating to work and political and social institutions: it has been used to justify the bureaucratic rationalization typical of industrial states. Intellectuals — the producers of such knowledge and instruments of rationalization — are under serious attack. They have manufactured the ideologies of the Cold War while hiding under the skirts of Western Civilization. The Hudson Institute, we are given to understand, is the natural offspring of Plato's academy. The rootlessness of intellectuals, which in the past has been a sign of independence, has led many to sell themselves to the highest bidder. Such whoring was bound to elicit strong reactions from the young. In the nineteenth century, the most common reaction of young intellectuals and students to rootlessness was a passionate commitment to the culture of nationalism. This commitment to a national culture made revolutionaries of many; unfortunately, it also turned some into the first ideologues of fascism. But today nationalism is not a live option for young movement intellectuals; the rediscovery of a natural culture cannot provide a cure for the individual's sense of separation from society. However, given the movement's stress on community, intellectuals may be able to plant their roots in the movement itself. This implies that the movement must become a culture — that is, a way of life. The very forces which have brought about the alienation of intellectuals and the young have propelled us toward that historical moment appropriate for creating a radical culture.

* * *

These notes are written toward that uncertain end.

Uncertain and puzzling, because the very concept of culture is rooted in social elitism. In the English speaking world it has been given its most typical formulation in Arnold's definition of culture as the study of perfection — that is, of the best that has been thought or said. It is an admirable notion. Who would quarrel with a program which asks us to study both classic and modern masterpieces so that we may become better men? But looked at within a social context, the program turns out to be the property of a privileged class. The best that has been thought or said? Whose best, one is tempted to ask. And what people is this best available to? Whose property are the great masterpieces? What, in fact, do they teach? What interests do they serve?

Some British scholars have begun to look at the notion of culture from a different social perspective. Richard Hoggart and E. P.

Thompson, amongst others, have tried to see what the study of perfection might look like from the bottom. The view is quite different; the very concept of culture is transformed into something else. There are important lessons to be learned from these scholars, but their work does not help us to formulate a radical culture for a movement which is primarily composed of middle-class whites. We are the inheritors, alas, of Arnold's sweetness and light; we are bearers of the tradition which is the property of an elite.

Some have tried to circumvent this traditionalism by inventing new styles. But decoration (of the body, of the mind) is the luxury either of those who can afford it, or of those alienated enough to divest themselves of the past. By itself, the enrichment of surfaces will not create a political culture. Yet who would want a political culture without style?

Radical theorists have insisted often enough that a political revolution must be accompanied by a cultural one. But there is no general theory — or even a set of strategies — to guide us toward that end. We discuss the transformations of culture in terms set by the nineteenth century.

We must find the terms which are our own.

* * *

Let me begin once more — this time at the beginning. What is the meaning of the term "culture"? Perhaps one should ask a different question first: What is the task of a radical culture? Answer: to bring about a social revolution; to make institutions democratic; to make us free; to make life more beautiful and humane.

Such objectives demand that the roots of the state's powers be torn out. These roots ultimately reach down to the *social* division of labor. The division into classes is the foundation — perhaps the substance — of our culture, and therefore must be resisted continually. The partial ruptures we thus effect in the class system will, in turn, become one element in the creation of a different culture.

These tasks, we have ordinarily assumed, are to be performed by the intelligentsia — the technocrats of revolution. But to reach to the roots means to renovate ways of thinking, feeling, looking and, ultimately, acting. This is not quite the same as a vanguard fixing on a particular issue through which it hopes to heighten political consciousness.

Radical culture must be instrumental in obliterating class divisions. Therefore it must lead to a general participation in that culture. The existence of an intelligentsia (of technocrats) has provided some of us with the luxury of privacy. The special skills of the intelligentsia — including those of the revolutionary vanguard — make general participation in the affairs of society unnecessary. But the price we pay for this modern luxury is the domination of our culture by technocrats. Now their existence as a social class is necessarily tied to the existence of industrial society. We cannot wish the intelligentsia away. The real alternative for radical culture is to develop new social functions and contexts for intellectual work. This is not likely to be accomplished by enlightening technocrats about their social responsibility. Considering their involvement with those who hold power, they will have to be fought. One task of a radical culture is to clear our minds of elitist prejudices, so we can see the intelligentsia for what it is.

*   *   *

Why do I — a cultured man, my students and friends might say — choke on the word "culture"? There is the matter of cost. What price has humanity paid for our cultural monuments? For a long time I have been obsessed with the emotional possibilities of baroque architecture. I have traveled, gotten grants, studied, looked and looked — and I have been deeply moved. But at whose expense were my sensibilities deepened by the experience of Rome? And why is the joy of a refined esthetic emotionally available to me — a middle-class academic, an intellectual — but not to others? When I last stood in the Piazza Navona, watching my fellow tourists more than Bernini's fountains, I hardly dared think of the crimes, the human suffering, which made both the scene and my being there possible. I stood surrounded by priceless objects — and I valued them. Yet I hate the economic system which has invested finely chiseled stone with a price. Our esthetics are rooted in surplus value.

Had the advocates of black power who damaged a Rembrandt at the New York Metropolitan Museum been caught, they would have been read a lesson on the values of culture by a philistine judge. More than likely they would have been jailed: a piece of canvas is obviously more valuable than a man's freedom. How could these savages do damage to the Metropolitan? It was built, after all, to bring art to the masses. A million dollars is spent on a painting to improve the lot of the poor. Don't they remember the privilege of museum field trips during grammar school? Oddly enough, some blacks see the culture of the Metropolitan as an instrument of oppression. Culture for the masses! Whose culture?

America's cultural institutions have no more than an incidental relationship to culture — high or low. The most recent version of Roman magnificence, Lincoln Center, was built upon the ruins of a low-cost residential area in midtown Manhattan.

And why not? Magnificence should preside at the center of things. What better place than a depopulated area for the confluence of diverse cultural streams? Besides, entertainment for the rich is at least as important as housing for the poor. But according to a recent story in *The New York Times*, there are difficulties facing this grand attempt at cultural enrichment. I quote Howard Taubman, *The Times'* official keeper of the cultural heritage:

The trouble is that Lincoln Center is running out of operating funds. Working capital as of Jan. 1 was down to $900,000, and a good deal of that was tied up . . . The financial report for fiscal 1968 . . . shows that expenditures were $8.06 million and income amounted to $4.93 million. The deficit . . . was cut . . . by contributions and the use of substantial sums from the Lincoln Center Fund.

An income of $4.93 million! Clearly nothing is too much for the sake of the national esthetic. However, there appear to be extra-esthetic reasons for some of the expenditures. Mr. Taubman continues:

"Consider our security costs," Mr. Ames went on. "We spend $300,000 a year for exterior guarding alone. The spaces — plazas, walks and passageways — at Lincoln Center are so large that we must have many guards, not only when performances are on but also at other times when thousands of visitors come streaming through the center."

But who is Lincoln Center being protected from? The performers? The visitors? The dissatisfied customers? Perhaps it is from the people who were thrown out of their homes so that their esthetic needs might be fulfilled. Alas, the horde does not seem to understand that performances it cannot afford to attend add luster to the national — that is, the horde's very own — culture. How, one wonders, could these misguided souls do damage to something

they own, to a national monument? A bit more of Mr. Taubman's
story might help to explain.

Mr. Ames stressed that Lincoln Center was a significant economic as well as
cultural asset for the city. In an area of 37 blocks radiating from the center
there have been improvements in land use and new buildings that have brought
the city more than $20 million in new taxes, he pointed out, and by 1972 the
taxes in this area will probably be more than $30 million.

So much for the national esthetic. Culture for the masses? It will
no doubt be provided for out of that $30 million in taxes.
    The movement should have harrassed Lincoln Center from the
beginning. Not a performance should go by without disruption.
The fountains should be dried with calcium chloride, the statuary
pissed on, the walls smeared with shit.
    General Maxwell Taylor was the first president of Lincoln
Center, Inc. He left his post — reluctantly, of course — when
President Kennedy issued the call for even higher duty, and
eventually became well-known for his strategic thinking about
Vietnam. The general's career suggests an appropriate designation
for Lincoln Center: a cultural enclave whose freedom is being
protected by $300,000 worth of cops. Counter-insurgency against
undesirable elements in surrounding districts is no doubt next on
the cultural agenda.

                          *   *   *

    The Great Tradition is dead. Does one really need to repeat
Baudelaire's words? It is surely dead for those committed to
radical social change. Each component of the Tradition may be
alive for me as an individual: Pope's late poetry moves me profoundly. Yet *An Epistle to Dr. Arbuthnot* does not exist for me
as part of a humanistic continuum. Indeed, there is an anomaly —
even preciousness — in my reaction to Pope; I have taken an
unnatural leap in time, and embraced someone whose historical
location makes him my enemy. Pope, the last major voice of
Renaissance Humanism! How is that textbook category a part
of my culture?
    The Great Tradition is dead because it assumes that cultural
continuity lies solely in books. And so it does — for some. For
the educated middle class *The Communist Manifesto* is a cultural
object, an anthology piece which appears at some point after the

selection from Hegel, very near that of Darwin's, and before the one from Ruskin. The cultural tradition enbalmed in this anthology is the property of a privileged class. Worse, it is an instrument of oppression. The anthology, we are told, is the repository of our spiritual values. But as Jan Myrdal has observed, spiritual values are the ideology of the ruling class.

The sense of tragedy, it is most commonly agreed, is the most profound of our spiritual values. The experience of classical tragedy ennobles us because it teaches us to accept our fate. Those who reap the benefits of a society can readily afford to accept their fates; they can even afford to elevate suffering to a peerage, and endow it with hereditary nobility. The meek poor, we all know, are rich in spirit; the unmeek ones are brutes without culture.

Brutes, we all know, should be humanized. And what better instruments of humanization, what better repositories of the great tradition, than our colleges? We deposit the uncultured in one for four years so they may become imbued with the tragic sense before venturing into the arena to discover their inevitable fate. They sit and study their grammar and their Homer, swallowing their bad medicine, but only half believing that the mastery of a culture alien to their lives will lift them from their own class, assuring them of membership in a ruling elite. The poor trapped instructor becomes the convenient object of hatred, for he is the most visible symbol of their oppression. However, there is little to fear. Culture, Freud has assured us, is civilization's chief instrument of conflict resolution. It conveniently transforms anger into self-hatred and belligerence into feelings of guilt.

But does the imposition of the great tradition really resolve conflicts? Does it not merely suppress them? Radicals must find ways of allowing such conflicts to be expressed. These conflicts are embedded in a cultural tradition which is not necessarily expressed in our official masterpieces or in our spiritual values. But they do represent a spiritual actuality. The task of radical culture is both to divest tragedy of its nobility, and to direct cultural conflict toward a deeper understanding of the individual's social role — an understanding which leads beyond the limiting hatred of the instructor to the ultimate sources of oppression.

*   *   *

Let me repeat an earlier question: What do I mean by the term "culture"?

First, there is Culture (I shall capitalize it) in the larger sense. A partial list of its components includes the way we live, our manners and rituals, our habits of work and play, what we do with our leisure time. A significant feature of our own Culture, for example, is the relation leisure bears to the notion of efficiency. I might ask, while investigating the relationship, why industrial workers tend to give up their leisure and work overtime. I would learn that in our Culture people need to escalate their consumption of goods if they are to maintain a sense of their own value and uphold their self-respect. Investigating further, I would discover that the leisure activities most common to our Culture are, in fact, attempts to escape from society, to get away. Such attempts lead, of course, to the purchase of consumer goods necessary for the escape. And the purchase leads to further production, and that leads to capital investment, and that to long-range financing and research, and so on and so forth. Underlying the whole process is the feeling of alienation from work; the feeling that work deprives human beings of control — over the means of production and over their own lives.

To understand, then, the relationship of leisure to efficiency — that is, a single element in a definition of the larger Culture — one should study the history of industrialism. Most important for the state of the Culture is industrialism's increasing need for ever more subtle forms of rationalization, and the consequent formation of a large bureaucratic force, headed by a technocratic elite, to implement that rationality.

Though not always practiced, devotion to the principles of efficiency and rationality has been fervent for over a century. These principles demand that the productive process be totally separated from all other aspects of life. Work is performed during a designated part of the day, at a designated place, and in a predetermined manner. The time not used for sleeping or for performing household tasks is called leisure. Leisure is — just time; it is time divorced from all the ordinary activities, just as work is divorced from the rest of life. Leisure creates the necessity for culture (lower case) in the smaller sense: the autonomous arts, pure scholarship, and the various forms of entertainment — all of them unproductive activities. Historically (and quite logically) the smaller culture has become increasingly dissociated from the larger. Indeed, the former has become an independent entity with its own history and its own internal logic. Most of us seek to fulfill ourselves through culture: it is what we live for. Not unexpectedly, there are some forms of culture which are more prestigious — and desirable — than others.

Culture in the smaller sense seems to stand in opposition to the rationalization of the productive process — indeed, to the very nature of our work. It is at war with the larger Culture. Since culture in the smaller sense is the primary source of human fulfillment, our very beings become split. This separation, both in society and in our minds, leads to the arts having the life squeezed out of them for they have lost their connection to the larger Culture: they become a self-indulgent irrelevance, a search for more refined sensations or more exquisite techniques. As for the larger Culture, being deprived of the arts, it survives (perhaps perishes) by the inhuman spirit of rationalization.

Like any warrier resorting to diplomacy, the larger Culture attempts to neutralize — indeed, use — the smaller by rationalizing it. The social task of culture is not to make us more noble, though it may do so incidentally, but to facilitate the wider reproduction of labor. André Gorz, in his *Strategy for Labor*, has put the matter well:

It is impossible in a modern production unit, even of medium size, to be on top of one's job without becoming familiar with world history in the process. And it is impossible to be ignorant of political, scientific, technical, socio-economic, and cultural evolution in the largest sense, or else one will lose the ability to enter into relationships with others, however close, or of suffering that absolute oppression which consists of knowing that one does not know what others know.

That is why cultural activity is an integral part of the necessarily broad reproduction of labor power, that is, of the ability of individuals to cooperate in a given common task. That also is why cultural activity is a *need*.

But this need of the industrial system may be exploited by radicals. The condescending imposition of an official high culture must be discredited. We should demand that various constituencies be allowed to control their own cultural activities, developing those forms and styles which emerge from or relate to their own lives and their own traditions. Thus culture might once again become an instrument for defining class interests, rather than one for their obliteration.

* * *

I shall briefly sketch the fate of one performing art, "serious" music, in industrial society, in the hope of locating the source of some of our cultural difficulties.

The development of large cities and their appropriation by the middle class clearly had an enormous influence on the conditions of musical performance. From the Renaissance through much of the eighteenth century, most "serious" music developed as an integral expression of the aristocratic milieu within which it was performed. Concerts were court occasions, primarily concerned with performance of new compositions. Since the music was always new, and since it was generally performed by some members of the court along with the composer and the hired musicians, it had a most immediate relationship to the cultural assumptions of the audience. In the eighteenth century large cities began to develop cultural institutions for the middle class. Concert halls were built. They became the homes of large orchestras and opera companies which developed historical repertoires that are repeated over the course of generations to the present time. What relationship does this repertoire have to the living culture of the audience? The hall, the orchestra, the opera, the conductor and the singer all become exhibition pieces in a museum. And museums are commodities. People buy their tickets, they sit down and listen passively, because attending a musical performance is one mode of consumption, one way of filling one's leisure time.

Such conditions of musical performance necessarily affect the possibilities of composition. Composers begin to write for the repertoire; they relate not to the cultural suppositions of a specific audience, but to a musical tradition or to the market. The most honest stance becomes the composition of repeated variations on one's musical autobiography: sincere, often moving and brilliant, but almost inevitably self-indulgent.

There is a way out, however, in twentieth century America. The academy has become a new haven for musical genius, and produced the professor-composer-computer expert. The implications of this development for our culture are immense. The recent Lincoln Center performance of Professor Milton Babbitt's *Relata II* prompted the composer to make some crucial remarks on the subject. I quote a few of them from *The New York Times:*

Finally there's the question: who will hear this piece? No one is concerned about my interested musical colleagues, those for whom I really offer it. . . . My associates across the country will not have any opportunity to hear it . . .

On the other hand, the regular Philharmonic audience does not want to hear this piece. And why should they have to? How can it be coherent for them? It's as though a colleague of mine in the field of philosophy were to read his paper on the Johnny Carson show. . . .

The university, the composer's last hope, turns with delight to the electronic field because it is self-contained, requiring neither performance nor publication. The medium provides a kind of full satisfaction for the composer, too. I love going to the studio with my work in my head, realizing it while I am there, and walking out with the tape under my arm. I can then send it anywhere in the world, knowing exactly how it will sound. My last electronic work . . . has been played hundreds of times in universities. These are the people — the university people — whom we regard as our appropriate colleagues. I feel closer to members of my Philosophy department than to many who regard themselves as musicians.

Composition as a self-contained entity! The artist pushing the stops on his synthesizer and going home with his cultural goods on tape: could there be a more appropriate emblem of the social role of the arts in the industrial state?

*   *   *

Babbitt and his "appropriate colleagues" assume that their fun and games, their stockpiling and incessant refining of "knowledge," in laboratories, libraries, conferences and seminars — most of it, of course, at the expense of the taxpayers — are necessary for the advancement of civilization. But whose advancement? And whose civilization? The leisure of a divinely appointed elite, critics have told us for centuries, is a pre-requisite for the birth and continued good health of culture. But is such a notion anything more than a self-serving ideology for that elite? Culture which is owned and administered by the chosen, the rest watching their mysteries with adoration, can be little else but an instrument of class oppression.

Cultural elitism reveals itself most clearly in the division between high and low culture. Since John Gay's *The Beggar's Opera* became a hit on the London stage in the eighteenth century, artists have consistently used — more accurately, exploited — popular materials for the purposes of high art. One could hardly call this a marriage entered into on equal terms; it is rather like the nobleman condescending to marry the servant girl so she might bear him healthy children; the latter will, in due course, take up their appropriate places in the ranks of the nobility. In America, despite endless protestations, jazz is still thought of and treated like a low art — except when it is raped by the nobles of Lincoln Center. If Archie Shepp and Leonard Bernstein were to get together, it would be a grand occasion for the public relations industry; however, their union would not give birth to an equal partnership in America's cultural enterprise.

Can there really be a culture which transcends all classes? Matthew Arnold taught us that culture, being available to those individuals from all classes willing to express their "best selves," is independent of class origin. But this only means that people from the lower classes are invited to reject their own culture, and exchange it for the more valuable goods of the elite. There can be no culture transcending classes as long as we live in a class society. Consequently, radical culture must for the present be a culture of communities or constituencies.

*   *   *

The cult of the great artist is the cultural myth most natural to a competitive society. The artist's dream is to rise to the heights, to be above mortality, to be more than human. At the least, he strives to be better than all other artists. But in a society where art is a commodity, such dreams get translated into a desire for personal advancement. So the artist allows himself to be packaged along with his art, and to be put on the market. Better yet, he markets himself, thus becoming a manipulator, while being unconsciously manipulated himself. Industrial society is expert at putting individualism to the system's use.

The existence of great figures in the arts is a reflection of social disease. Their disappearance will help to erase the line between the larger and the smaller culture: as art stops being the special province of the great, as it stops being the expression of a competitive individualism, it will have the opportunity to develop as a living part of the larger Culture, rather than continuing to be rationalized by the system as a commodity. But such goals cannot be fully realized until class and property relations have dissolved. Meanwhile, we must stop looking to experts to perform the tasks of culture for us. We should try to engage people in those cultural activities which will allow them to express their "best selves" — their beings — as an integral component of the life of their communities. Art should not be a source of intimidation for the uninitiated; it should not be a cause of social shame; least of all should artists stand in the way of the arts playing a democratizing role in the life of the larger Culture.

Art as the only possible fulfillment of life: the notion is perhaps our most important cultural expression of middle-class individualism. It dominated discussions of culture in the nineteenth century and has since then served as the ideological foundation for those typically modern masterpieces, most notably Proust's, whose subject is the relation of art to the life of the artist. But the possibility of fulfilling oneself through high art, as Ruskin and Morris recognized, is generally available to only a very few members of a privileged class. That we have to look to high art as the devout once looked to their gods points to the failures of the larger Culture: to its failure to develop new communal relationships where the old have disintegrated; to its incapacity for meeting collective needs; to its hardening of the distinction between private and external desires. Such failures impel us to force art into playing a false role. Art cannot be the end of most people's lives. Museums — those monuments to the religion of art — illustrate the point: they afford fulfillment for no-one except the curators; for most a visit to one provides, at best, an occasion for passive absorption. Art may have the power to elevate, but not to fulfill; at its best, it has the capacity to uncover the limitations of our Culture.

*   *   *

A short note on criticism.

We take Tolstoy's *What Is Art?* much too lightly. The standard reaction to his magisterial anger is a guilt-ridden giggle or a pedantic quibble about the logic of his esthetics. Tolstoy's simple — and overwhelming — message is that we must consider, to the exclusion of almost everything else, what art does for the quality of life now, this moment. It is difficult for critics to deal with such a dogmatic insistence on the relation of art to life. The critic is ideally concerned with eternal truths, not with the present conditions of life; his task is to transcend his own time, not to let his judgment be engaged by the needs of the moment. Eternal truths, we all know, are noble. Furthermore, literary criticism is concerned with "human nature," not with the feelings of real men, living at a specific time, and belonging to a specific class.

The humanists of the eighteenth century — Pope, Johnson, Voltaire, Goethe — were the last great upholders of the concept of general nature. They used the notion, quite consciously, in an attempt to keep alive an aristocratic culture which was beginning to take its last gasps. Critics today are not so conscious of their own motives. They cannot deal with Tolstoy, because to even admit the possibility of Tolstoy's moral validity would threaten the self-serving mystifications — eternal truths, human nature, timeless judgments — which uphold the class interests of professional criticism.

*   *   *

America's serious journals have been instrumental in creating an intellectual culture which is founded on the false consciousness of intellectuals. Instead of describing the real conflicts in American life, analyzing the specific attempts to deal with them, and proposing new courses of action, our journals have specialized in creating conflicts between intellectuals. The world is the journal. America's intellectual life is autonomous and divorced from political realities. When shall we produce a theoretical work like Gorz's *Strategy for Labor?* That is, a serious work which directs its proposals for revolutionary change to political activists, not to readers of journals and not to fellow intellectuals. Those young academics who have tried to address themselves to activist constituencies, rather than to their peers, have generally paid the price of professional ostracism.

*   *   *

In conclusion, I must admit to not knowing what a radical culture will really look, sound, smell, or feel like — although I have a clear sense of the contours of the larger Culture in a socialist society. The movement's street theaters, radical newsreels, and musical groups perform an important service. But they are internal to the movement, and beyond having a superficial effect on commercial entertainment, they have little impact on the general culture. New institutions like community galleries and worker-artist alliances do effect structural changes and therefore lay the foundation for radical culture. We are beginning to shoot Niagara, and the social transformations we envision imply something more deep — and hopefully less elitist — than experimentation with new art-forms. What is at stake is a new conception of the relationship of art and knowledge to the larger Culture.

A NEW COMMUNITY

The Elimination of the Difference between Production and Consumption

PAUL AND PERCIVAL GOODMAN

Quarantining the Work, Quarantining the Homes

Men like to make things, to handle the materials and see them take shape and come out as desired, and they are proud of the products. And men like to work and be useful, for work has a rhythm and springs from spontaneous feelings just like play, and to be useful makes people feel right. Productive work is a kind of creation, it is an extension of human personality into nature. But it is also true that the private or state capitalist relations of production, and machine industry as it now exists under whatever system, have so far destroyed the instinctive pleasures of work that economic work is what all ordinary men dislike. (Yet unemployment is dreaded, and people who don't like their work don't know what to do with their leisure.) In capitalist or state-socialist economies, efficiency is measured by profits and expansion rather than by handling the means. Mass production, analyzing the acts of labor into small steps and distributing the products far from home, destroys the sense of creating anything. Rhythm, neatness, style belong to the machine rather than to the man.

The division of economy into production and consumption as two opposite poles means that we are far from the conditions in which work could be a way of life. A way of life requires merging the means in the end, and work would have to be thought of as a continuous process of satisfying activity, satisfying in itself and satisfying in its useful end. Such considerations have led many moralist-economists to want to turn back the clock to conditions of handicraft in a limited society, where the relations of guilds and small markets allow the master craftsmen a say and a hand in every phase of production, distribution, and consumption. Can we

achieve the same values with modern technology, a national
economy, and a democratic society? With this aim, let us reanalyze
efficiency and machine production.

Characteristic of American offices and factories is the severe
discipline with regard to punctuality. (In some states the law
requires time clocks, to protect labor and calculate the insurance.)
Now no doubt in many cases where workers cooperate in teams,
where business is timed by the mails, where machines use a temporary source of power, being on time and on the same time as
everybody else is essential to efficiency. But by and large it would
make little difference at what hour each man's work began and
ended, so long as the job itself was done. Often the work could be
done at home or on the premises indifferently, or part here part
there. Yet this laxity is never allowed, except in the typical instances of hack-writing or commercial art — typical because these
workers have an uneasy relation to the economy in any case. (There
is a lovely story of how William Faulkner asked M-G-M if he could
work at home, and when they said, "Of course," he went back to
Oxford, Mississippi.)

Punctuality is demanded not primarily for efficiency but for the
discipline itself. Discipline is necessary because the work is onerous; perhaps it makes the idea of working even more onerous, but
it makes the work itself much more tolerable, for it is a structure,
a decision. Discipline establishes the work in an impersonal
secondary environment where, once one has gotten out of bed early
in the morning, the rest easily follows. Regulation of time, separation from the personal environment: these are signs that work is
not a way of life; they are the methods by which, for better or
worse, work that cannot be energized directly by personal concern
can get done, unconfused by personal concern.

In the Garden City plans, they "quarantined the technology"
from the homes: more generally, we quarantine the work from
the homes. But it is even truer to say that we quarantine the
homes from the work. For instance, it is calamitous for a man's
wife or children to visit him at work; this privilege is reserved for
the highest bosses.

Reanalyzing Production

In planning a region of satisfying industrial work, we therefore
take account of four main principles:

1. A closer relation of the personal and productive environments, making punctuality reasonable instead of disciplinary, and introducing phases of home and small-shop production; and vice versa, finding appropriate technical uses for personal relations that have come to be considered unproductive.

2. A role for all workers in all stages of the production of the product; for experienced workers a voice and hand in the design of the product and the design and operation of the machines; and for all a political voice on the basis of what they know best, their specific industry, in the national economy.

3. A schedule of work designed on psychological and moral as well as technical grounds, to give the most well-rounded employment to each person, in a diversified environment. Even in technology and economics, the men are ends as well as means.

4. Relatively small units with relative self-sufficiency, so that each community can enter into a larger whole with solidarity and independence of viewpoint.

These principles are mutually interdependent.

1. To undo the present separation of work and home environments, we can proceed both ways: (a) Return certain parts of production to home-shops or near home; and (b) Introduce domestic work and certain productive family-relations, which are now not considered part of the economy at all, into the style and relations of the larger economy.

(a) Think of the present proliferation of machine-tools. It could once be said that the sewing machine was the only widely distributed productive machine; but now, especially because of the last war, the idea of thousands of small machine shops, powered by electricity, has become familiar; and small power-tools are a best-selling commodity. In general, the change from coal and steam to electricity and oil has relaxed one of the greatest causes for concentration of machinery around a single driving-shaft.

(b) Borsodi, going back to the economics of Aristotle, has proved, often with hilarious realism, that home production, such as cooking, cleaning, mending, and entertaining has a formidable economic, though not cash, value. The problem is to lighten and enrich home production by the technical means and some of the expert attitudes of public production, but without destroying its individuality.

But the chief part of finding a satisfactory productive life in homes and families consists in the analysis of personal relations and conditions: e.g., the productive cooperation of man and wife as it exists on farms, or the productive capabilities of children and old folk, now economically excluded. This involves sentimental and moral problems of extreme depth and delicacy that could only be solved by the experiments of integrated communities.

2. A chief cause of the absurdity of industrial work is that each machine worker is acquainted with only a few processes, not the whole order of production. And the thousands of products are distributed he knows not how or where. Efficiency is organized from above by expert managers who first analyze production into its simple processes, then synthesize these into combinations built into the machines, then arrange the logistics of supplies, etc., and then assign the jobs.

As against this efficiency organized from above, we must try to give this function to the workers. This is feasible only if the workers have a total grasp of all the operations. There must be a school of industry, academic and not immediately productive, connected with the factory. Now let us distinguish apprentices and graduates. To the apprentices, along with their schooling, is assigned the more monotonous work; to the graduates, the executive and coordinating work, the fine work, the finishing touches. The masterpiece that graduates an apprentice is a new invention, method, or other practical contribution advancing the industry. The masters are teachers, and as part of their job hold free discussions looking to basic changes.

Such a setup detracts greatly from the schedule of continuous production; but it is a question whether it would not prove more efficient in the long run to have the men working for themselves and having a say in the distribution. By this we do not mean merely economic democracy or socialist ownership. These are necessary checks but are not the political meaning of industrialism as such. What is needed is the organization of economic democracy on the basis of the productive units, where each unit, relying on its own expertness and the bargaining power of what it has to offer, cooperates with the whole of society. This is syndicalism, simply an industrial town meeting. To guarantee the independent power of each productive unit, it must have a relative regional self-sufficiency; this is the union of farm and factory.

3. Machine work in its present form is often stultifying, not a "way of life." The remedy is to assign work on psychological and moral as well as technical and economic grounds. The object is to

provide a well-rounded employment. Work can be divided as team work and individual work, or physical work and intellectual work. And industries can be combined in a neighborhood to give the right variety. For instance, cast glass, blown glass, and optical instruments; or more generally, industry and agriculture, and factory and domestic work. Probably most important, but difficult to conjure with, is the division in terms of faculties and powers, routine and initiation, obeying and commanding.

The problem is to envisage a well-rounded schedule of jobs for each man, and to arrange the buildings and the farms so that the schedule is feasible.

4. The integration of factory and farm brings us to the idea of regionalism and regional relative autonomy. These are the following main parts:

(a) Diversified farming as the basis of self-subsistence and, therefore, small urban centers (200,000).

(b) A number of mutually dependent industrial centers, so that an important part of the national economy is firmly controlled. (The thought is always to have freedom secured by real power.)

(c) These industries developed around regional resources of field, mine, and power.

Diversified farmers can be independent, and small farms have therefore always been a basis of social stability, though not necessarily of peasant conservatism. On the other hand, for the machines now desirable, the farmer needs cash and links himself with the larger economy of the town.

The political problem of the industrial worker is the reverse, since every industry is completely dependent on the national economy, for both materials and distribution. But by regional interdependence of industries and the close integration of factory and farm work — factory workers taking over in the fields at peak seasons, farmers doing factory work in the winter; town people, especially children, living in the country; farmers domestically making small parts for the factories — the industrial region as a whole can secure for itself independent bargaining power in the national whole.

The general sign of this federal system is the distinction of the local regional market from the national market. In transport, the local market is served by foot, bicycle, cart, and car; the national market by plane and trailer-truck.

(Now all of this — decentralized units, double markets, the

selection of industries on political and psychological as well as economic and technical grounds — all this seems a strange and roundabout way of achieving an integrated national economy, when at present this unity already exists with a tightness that leaves nothing to be desired, and an efficiency that is even excessive. But we are aiming at a different standard of efficiency, one in which invention will flourish and the job will be its own incentive; and most important, at the highest and nearest ideals of external life: liberty, responsibility, self-esteem as a workman, and initiative. Compared with these aims the present system has nothing to offer us.)

A Schedule and Its Model

TYPICAL SCHEDULE OF ACTIVITIES FOR
MEMBERS OF A COMMUNE
(*numerals equal months*)

Basic Work	Master Workman	Apprentice Workman	Farmer	Farm Family	Ages 6 to 14	Ages 15 to 18
Factory	8(a)	6				1
Industrial Agriculture		3(d)	2(d)	√		1
Diversified Agriculture			{8	√	√	
Domestic Industry			{8	√ (e)		1
Formal and Technical Learning		2(b)				1(b)
Technical Teaching	1(b)		1(b)			
General Education					√	5
Study and Travel						2(f)
Individual Work (c)	2					
Unscheduled (g)	1	1	1	1	√	1

NOTES ON THE SCHEDULE

(a) The factory work of the master workman and workwoman includes executive and fine work.

sioner — has been connected with the city by remarkable highways on which at peak hours the traffic creeps at four miles an hour, while the engines boil.

Meantime the venturesome poor boys of the city swim daily, as they always have, in the Hudson River and the East River — under the sidelong surveillance of usually reasonable police; it is quite illegal. It is illegal because the water is polluted. No strenuous effort is made by the Park Commissioner to make it unpolluted; and the shore is not developed for bathing. Yet to the boys it seems the obvious thing to do on a hot day, to dive into the nearest water, down the hill at the end of the street, into

> *Our lordly Hudson hardly flowing*
> *under the green-grown cliffs*
> *— and has no peer in Europe or the East.*

The Museum of Art

Suppose again, says our neo-functionalist friend, that a number of mighty masterpieces of painting and statuary were decentralized from the big museum and placed, one in this neighborhood church (as in Rome one encounters astounded, *Moses*), and one on this fountain in a local square, wherever there is a quiet place to pause. A few of the neighbors would come to have a friendly and perhaps somewhat proprietary acquaintance with their masterpiece. Are they not to be trusted so close to the treasure?

One cannot help but think of Florence that has come down to us not as a museum city (like Venice), but as a bustling modern town, yet still a continuous home for those strange marble and bronze monsters of the Renaissance, in the squares. It would be very interesting for a sociologist to study, with his questionnaires, the effect of those things on the Florentines. They have had an effect.

When there is such a work in a neighborhood, a stranger, who from afar has heard of its fame, will come to visit the local square where he would otherwise never have ventured. Then the children notice how carefully and reverently he is looking at the statue they climb on.

Nurses' Uniforms

The washing and ironing of all New York's city hospitals is to be done at a great municipal laundry. And it comes out on investigation) was carried on in relative autonomy, under the loose heading of "general welfare."

The kind of life looked for in this new community depends on the awareness of local distinctness, and this is also the condition of political freedom as a group of industries and farm cooperatives, rather than as a multitude of abstract votes and consumers with cash.

Yet every machine economy *is* a national and international economy. The fraction of necessary goods that can be produced in a planned region is very substantial, but it is still a fraction. And this fact is the salvation of regionalism! For otherwise regionalism succumbs to provincialism — whether we consider art or literature, or the characters of the people, or the fashions in technology. The regional industrialists in their meeting find that, just because their region is strong and productive, they are subject to wide circles of influence, they have to keep up.

Refinement

Let us try to envisage the moral ideal of such a community as we are describing.

In the luxury city of consumers' goods, society was geared to an expanding economy — capital investment and consumption had to expand at all costs, or even especially at all costs. In the third community that we shall describe in this book,* "maximum security, minimum regulation," we shall find that, in order to achieve the aim of social security and human liberty, a part of the economy must never be allowed to expand at all.

SOME ELEMENTARY PRINCIPLES
FOR THE
MORAL SELECTION OF MACHINES

1. **Utility** (Functionalist beauty)
2. **Transparency of Operation**
   A. Repairability by the average well-educated person (Freedom)
   B. Constructivist beauty
3. **Relative independence of machine from non-ubiquitous power**
4. **Proportion between total effort and utility** (Neo-Functionalist beauty)

* *Communitas*, from which this essay is taken. Ed.

But in this present, middle-of-the-road, plan there is no reason why the economy either must expand or must not expand. Every issue is particular and comes down to the particular question: "Is it worthwhile to expand along this new line? Is it worth the trouble to continue along that old line?"

This attitude is a delicate one, hard for us Americans to grasp clearly: we always like to do it bigger and better, or we jump to something new, or we cling. But when people are accustomed to knowing what they are lending their hands to, when they know the operations and the returns, when they don't have to prove something competitively, then they are just in the business, so to speak, of judging the relation of means and ends. They are all efficiency experts. And then, curiously, they may soon hit on a new conception of efficiency itself, very unlike that of the engineers of Veblen. When they can say, "It would be more efficient to make it this way," they may go on to say, "And it would be even *more* efficient to forget it altogether."

Efficient for what? For the way of life as a whole. Now in all times honorable people have used this criterion as a negative check: "*We* don't do that kind of thing, even if it's convenient or profitable." But envisage doing it positively and inventively: "Let's do it, it becomes us. Or let's omit it and simplify, it's a lag and a drag."

Suppose that one of the masters, away on his two months of individual work, drafting designs for furniture, should, having studied the furniture of the Japanese, decide to dispense with chairs. Such a problem might create a bitter struggle in the national economy, one thing leading to another.

The economy, like any machine economy, would expand, for it creates a surplus. It would expand into refinement. The Japanese way is a powerful example. They cover the floor with deep washable mats and dispense with chairs and dispense with the floor. It is too much trouble to clutter the room with furniture. It is not too much trouble to lavish many days' work on the minute carving on the inside of a finger pull of a shoji. They dispense with the upholstery but take pains in arranging the flowers. They do not build permanent partitions in a room because the activities of life are always varying.

When production becomes an integral part of life, the workman becomes an artist. It is the definition of an artist that he follows the medium, and finds new possibilities of expression in it. He is

not bound by the fact that things have always been made in a
certain way, nor even by the fact that it is these things that have
been made. Our industrialists — even International Business
Machines — are very much concerned these days to get "creative"
people, and they make psychological studies on how to foster an
"atmosphere of creativity"; but they don't sufficiently conjure
with the awful possibility that truly creative people might tell them
to shut up shop. They wish to use creativity in just the way that
it cannot be used, for it is a process that also generates its own ends.

Notes on Neo-Functionalism: the Ailanthus and the Morning-Glory

In the Introduction to this book, we called this attitude neo-
functionalism, a functionalism that subjects the function to a
formal critique. The neo-functionalist asks: Is the use as simple,
ingenious, or clear as the efficient means that produce it? Is the
using a good experience? For instance, these days they sell us
machines whose operation is not transparent and that an intelligent
layman cannot repair. Such a thing is ugly in itself, and it enslaves
us to repairmen.

There is one abuse of present-day production, however, that is
not only ugly and foolish but morally outrageous, and the per-
petrators should be ostracized from decent society. This is building
obsolescence into a machine, so it will wear out, be discarded, and
replaced. For instance, automobile-repair parts are now stocked
for only five years, whereas previously they were stocked for ten.
Does this mean that the new cars, meant to last a shorter time, are
cheaper? On the contrary, they are more expensive. Does it mean
that there are so many new improvements that there is no point in
keeping the older, less efficient models running? There are no such
improvements; the new models are characterized merely by novel
gimmicks to induce sales — just as the difficulty of repair and the
obsolescence are built in to enforce sales.

Neo-functionalists are crotchety people, for they are in love with
the goddess of common sense, and the way we do things catches
them by the throat. They take exception to much that is universally accepted, because it doesn't add up; they stop to praise many
things universally disregarded, such as the custom of sitting on
slum stoops and sidewalks, with or without chairs: Park Avenue
does not provide this amenity. To a neo-functionalist, much that
is insisted on seems not worth all that bother, and he is often easy-

going; his attitude is interpreted as laziness, but he sees no reason to be busy if he is not bored. He praises the ailanthus.

Of all trees and shrubs it seems to be only the locust and especially the ailanthus that flourish of themselves in the back alleys and yard-square plots of dirt that are the gardens of Manhattan Island. They bloom from the mouths of basements. But the maple saplings and the elms that are transplanted there at large expense and are protected from pests with doses of a nauseating juice, languish and die in that environment of motor fumes and pavements.

MEANS AND ENDS

Emphasis on physical ends	Interpenetration of physical	Emphasis on moral ends
Maximum exploitation of physical means	and moral ends Selection of physical means	Freedom from physical means
TECHNICAL EFFICIENCY	PSYCHOLOGICAL EFFICIENCY	BIOLOGICAL EFFICIENCY

A Neo-functionalist Analysis Of The Three Paradigms

Should our native city not, out of simple respect and piety, exalt the ailanthus to be our chief ornamental scenery, and make places for it everywhere? For the ailanthus loves *us* and thrives in our balance of nature. Our city is rich enough, it could become elegant enough, to flaunt a garden of native weeds. There is everywhere a prejudice against the luxuriating plantain weed, which as abstract design is as lovely as can be. Why should not this weed be raised to the dignity of grass — it is only a matter of a name — and then carefully be weeded in, in rows and stars, to decorate the little sidewalk plots?

The Rivers of New York

Trained in the New Commune, the neo-functionalist mentions also the ludicrous anomaly of New York's bathing places. During the heat of summer tens of thousands of Manhattanites daily travel from two to three hours to go swimming and boating on far-off shores. Many millions of dollars were spent in developing a bathing place no less than 40 miles from midtown Manhattan, and this place — it is the darling of our notorious Park Commissioner — has been connected with the city by remarkable highways on which at peak hours the traffic creeps at four miles an hour, while the engines boil.

Meantime the venturesome poor boys of the city swim daily, as they always have, in the Hudson River and the East River — under the sidelong surveillance of usually reasonable police; it is quite illegal. It is illegal because the water is polluted. No strenuous effort is made by the Park Commissioner to make it unpolluted; and the shore is not developed for bathing. Yet to the boys it seems the obvious thing to do on a hot day, to dive into the nearest water, down the hill at the end of the street, into

> Our lordly Hudson hardly flowing
> under the green-grown cliffs
> — and has no peer in Europe or the East.

The Museum of Art

Suppose again, says our neo-functionalist friend, that a number of mighty masterpieces of painting and statuary were decentralized from the big museum and placed, one in this neighborhood church (as in Rome one encounters astounded, *Moses*), and one on this fountain in a local square, wherever there is a quiet place to pause. A few of the neighbors would come to have a friendly and perhaps somewhat proprietary acquaintance with their masterpiece. Are they not to be trusted so close to the treasure?

One cannot help but think of Florence that has come down to us not as a museum city (like Venice), but as a bustling modern town, yet still a continuous home for those strange marble and bronze monsters of the Renaissance, in the squares. It would be very interesting for a sociologist to study, with his questionnaires, the effect of those things on the Florentines. They have had an effect.

When there is such a work in a neighborhood, a stranger, who from afar has heard of its fame, will come to visit the local square where he would otherwise never have ventured. Then the children notice how carefully and reverently he is looking at the statue they climb on.

Nurses' Uniforms

The washing and ironing of all New York's city hospitals is to be done at a great municipal laundry. And it comes out on investigation that the great part of the work can be done by a small fraction of the labor and machinery, but the small remainder of the work requires all the rest of the labor. It is the kind of situation that puts a neo-functionalist on the alert. It is that most of the labor goes into ironing the uniforms of doctors and nurses, but especially into ironing the frilly bonnets and aprons. The washing and the flat-work is done by machine and mangle, but the frills require hand-finishing.

It's not worth it. Make the uniforms of seersucker or anything else that doesn't need ironing. Make the hats in the form of colored kerchiefs that could equally well indicate the schools from which the nurses have come.

These conclusions are offered to the city fathers who have ordered a functional laundry to be designed; but they decide that they're not practical.

The Morning-Glory

Yet our neo-functionalist friend, who is a great lover of oriental anecdotes, also approvingly tells the following story.

"In the sixteenth century, the morning-glory was as yet a rare plant in Japan. Rikiu had an entire garden planted with it, which he cultivated with assiduous care. The fame of his convolvuli reached the ear of the Taiko, and he expressed a desire to see them; in consequence Rikiu invited him to a morning tea at his house. On the appointed day the Taiko walked through the garden, but nowhere could he see any evidence of the flower. The ground had been leveled and strewn with fine pebbles and sand. With sullen anger the despot entered the tearoom, but a sight restored his humor. In the tokonoma, in a rare bronze of Sung workmanship, lay a single morning-glory — the queen of the whole garden." (Kakuzo Okakura)

The Theory of Packages

In general, when the consumption of a product is removed from its production, by the geographical distance between factory and home, by the economic distance of sale and resale up to retail, and the temporal distance between making and use, the product is encased in a series of packages. There are the shipper's crate and the wholesaler's case and the middleman's carton and the retailer's box and the waterproof, airtight cellophane wrapper that must be kept inviolate and untouched except by the ultimate eater.

These packages are the career of physical goods as a commodity, and once the last wrapper is broken, the commodity is destroyed, it is unsaleable. It has been corrupted by the moisture and air and germs of life, by the passionate fact that someone wants the thing enough to touch it rather than sell it. Economically, then, this is a sacramental moment, when a man or woman brutally breaks the wrapper and takes the bread out of circulation. (From any point of view, the insipid taste is less interesting.)

The principle of packages is a corollary of Ralph Borsodi's blanket principle that as the cost of production per unit decreases by mass production, the cost of distribution increases because of the intermediaries involved in mass distribution. From this principle he derives the paradox of prosperity and insecurity: the copiousness of commodities entails the subordination of the consumer to a vast economic machine which can become deranged in different parts and leave him without elementary necessities. Borsodi's principle does not mean that machine production and labor-saving devices are humanly inefficient, but only when they become too geographically and economically centralized. Borsodi himself is an enthusiast for domestic machines and home industries, but there is also the possibility of a reasonably large community of integrated industrial, agricultural, domestic and cultured life, where the efficiency of machines can be exploited without insecurity.

Time

At present, a man's time of life is also put into packages. We speak, as the British anarchist Woodcock has pointed out, of "lengths of time as if they were lengths of calico." He concludes that the clock, the time clock that the worker aggressively "punches," is the chief machine of industrial exploitation, for it enables human labor to be quantified and priced as a commodity.

This commodity-time is the time of not-life that people step into when they take leave of their hearts, their homes, and even their heads, early in the morning. It is the time of a secondary environment which is, however, still loud with the authoritative but inner and forgotten voice of parents who seemed to wish (so children get to think) to deprive one of pleasure and ease. Especially in the morning at twenty to eight, and late in the afternoon at twenty after four, the fatherly face of the clock is frowning, deeper first on the left side, then on the right.

Advertising

Every one of the packages is printed with its own mumbo-jumbo of words.

In the nature of the case, when the consumer is far from the producer; has not ordered the production nor handled the means of it; nor estimated the cost of the means in proportion to the satisfaction enjoyed; it is necessary to *interest* him in the product, to create a want for it that has not been fired by any previous activity. (When we make or command something to be made, there are goal gradients toward the use.) Also, he must be persuaded to buy it if it is something that is, perhaps, not absolutely indispensable. All these functions are fulfilled by advertising, which draws less and less on the direct relation between the excellence of the product and the cost of its making — the word "cheap" is never used — but more and more on the comparative estimates of social opinion, emulation, fear of inferiority or not belonging. These drives require a handsome fund of insecurity to begin with.

Pictures and slogans are repeated again and again, and it is now classical theory, and perhaps even somewhat true, that repetition leads to belief and even overt action. This theory is true under certain conditions, namely that the use of words is reflex behavior, rather than an action of need, passion, invention, observation, and reflection. It is a poor use of speech, and unfortunately it does damage to English, for free poets must now take pains to use outlandish ways of speech to make sure that their words will not be taken in the meanings to which people have become accustomed, instead of relying on, and striving to reach, the meanings to which people are accustomed.

The Theory of Home Furnishings

The furniture of a home expresses, in its quantity and kind, the division of the concerns of the soul; in different community arrangements this division falls in different places.

On the principle of neo-functionalism, the place where the chief material outlay is made should give the chief satisfaction, otherwise why bother? If this rule is neglected, the material outlay becomes a dead weight, discouraging by its initial cost and even more by its continuing presence.

Now except in the woods, the chief mateiral outlay we see about us is the public city with its services. But in America these streets, squares, and highways do not pretend to compete in satisfaction with the private homes or the theaters of fantasy. They are a dead weight on these other satisfactions. One emerges from the theater into an environment that is less exciting, and one emerges from home into an environment that is quite impersonal and uninteresting. In late medieval times, they spent no effort on the streets, but burgher and baron adorned their homes.

Let us rather take a lesson from the Greeks who were often practical in what concerned the chief end and did not complicate their means. An Athenian, if free and male, experienced in the public places, the market, the law court, the porticoes, the gymnasia, most of the feelings of ease, intimacy, and personal excitement that we reserve for home and private clubs. He lived in the city more than at home. He had for his public objects the affairs of empire, civic duties, and passions of friendship. There was no sharp distinction between public and private affairs.

On the civic places and public institutions, then, they lavished an expense of architecture, mulcted from an empire and slaves in the silver mines, that with us would be quite deadening in its pretentiousness. But the thousands of free men were at home there.

An Athenian's domestic home was very simple; it was not an asylum for his personality. It did not have to be filled with furniture, mirrors, keepsakes, curiosa, and games.

But a bourgeois gentleman, when he is about to leave his home in the morning, kisses his wife and daughter, steps before a mirror and adjusts his tie, and then, the last thing before emerging, puts on a public face.

The most curious examples of heavily furnished homes that are the insane asylums of the spirit frozen and rejected in the city square can be found among the middle classes at the beginning of the twentieth century. And the most curious room of this most curious home was not the bedroom, the dining room, or the parlor, where after all there existed natural and social satisfactions, but the master's den, the jungle and the cavern of his reveries. In our decade, this den of nostalgic revery is in print in the stories of *The New Yorker* magazine.

454   PAUL AND PERCIVAL GOODMAN

Public Faces in Private Places

It is always a question whether the bourgeois den is worse or better than no private home at all, the norm of the states ancient and modern which consider men as public animals, and homes as army barracks.

But it has remained for our own generation to perfect the worst possible community arrangement, the home of the average American. This home is liberally supplied with furniture and the comforts of private life, but these private things are neither made nor chosen by personal creation or idiosyncratic taste, but are made in a distant factory and distributed by unresisted advertising. At home they exhaust by their presence — a bare cell would give more peace or arouse restlessness. They print private life with a public meaning. But if we turn to read this public meaning, we find that the only moral aim of society is to provide private satisfactions called the Standard of Living. This is remarkable. The private places have public faces, as Auden said, but the public faces are supposed to imitate private faces. What a booby trap!

A Japanese Home

"One of the surprising features that strikes a foreigner as he becomes acquainted with the Japanese house is the entire absence of so many things that with us clutter the closets and make squirrels' nests of the attic. The reason for this is that the people have never developed the miserly spirit of hoarding truck and rubbish with the idea that some day it will come into use." (Edward Morse)

"Swallows are often encouraged to build nests in the home, in the room most often used by the family. A shelf is built below the nest. The children watch the construction of the nest and the final rearing of the young birds." (Ibid.)

"One comes to realize how few are the essentials necessary for personal comfort . . . and that personal comfort is enhanced by the absence of many things deemed indispensable. In regard to the bed and its arrangement, the Japanese have reduced the affair to its simplest expression. The whole floor, the whole house indeed, is a bed, and one can fling oneself down on the soft mats, in the draft or out of it, upstairs or down and find a smooth, firm and level surface upon which to sleep." (Ibid.)

"When a tea master has arranged a flower to his satisfaction, he will place it in the tokonoma, the place of honor in a Japanese room. Nothing else will be placed near it which might interfere with its effect, not even a plant; unless there be some special esthetic reason for the combination. It rests there like an enthroned prince, and the guests or disciples on entering the room will salute it with profound bows." (Okakura)

A Japanese house is essentially one big room, divided by sliding screens as desired, for the activity of life is every varying. Outside and inside are also open to one another.

BIOGRAPHICAL NOTES

Michael Appleby was born on September 24, 1938, in Burbank, California. Upon graduating from the University of California in 1960 he joined the American Friends Service Committee's Development Program, and spent six months doing village development work in Mexico. He attended M.I.T. from 1961-68, where in 1965 he was a research assistant for Project Transport. While in New York, he served as a consultant for Mobilization For Youth. During 1967-69, he was an instructor in the Department of City and Regional Planning at M.I.T. He is now with the Bread and Puppet Theater.

Richard J. Barnet has combined an academic interest in international politics with practical experience. After graduation from Harvard College and Harvard Law School, he served in the United States Army as specialist in international law and later was a Fellow of the Harvard Russian Research Center and the Center for International Studies at Princeton. In addition to his books, Mr. Barnet is the author of a number of articles on international law and politics which have appeared in scholarly journals and popular magazines. He lives in Washington with his wife, Ann, who is a neurologist, and their three children. He is the co-director of the Institute for Policy Studies.

C. George Benello was born in 1926. He received his A.B. at Harvard in 1949 and did graduate work in philosophy at Université Laval, Quebec, and Brown University. He received his M.A. at San Francisco State in 1961. He was the director of Adult Education at Goddard College and from 1965-68 was professor of sociology there. He is an authority on Japanese culture and the author of numerous articles. He is now writing a book entitled *Wasteland Culture*.

Father Daniel Berrigan, S.J., 47, is a poet, theologian, editor and lecturer, whose published works include *They Call Us Dead Men, No One Walks Waters, Consequences, Truth and . . .* and *Love, Love at the End*. He recently returned from Hanoi with three U. S. pilots released into his custody by the North Vietnamese government. He is one of the Catonsville Nine and his case is on appeal.

Amy Cass was 10½ when she wrote and illustrated "A Journey to the Place." She is now 13 and has not been part of any Establishment of Education since third grade. This essay is one of two written in the years she lived aboard a boat with her family. Amy is now at Lewis-Wadhams in upper New York State, a Free school organized by Herb Snitzer which functions to meet the needs of its students.

456

Noam Chomsky was born December 7, 1928, in Philadelphia, Pennsylvania. He joined the staff of M.I.T. and in 1961 was appointed full professor in the Department of Modern Languages and Linguistics and the Research Laboratory of Electronics. He is the author of books and articles on linguistics, philosophy, intellectual history and contemporary issues. He is a member of the American Academy of Arts and Sciences, and numerous professional societies. He is on the steering committee of Resist. His major books are *Aspects of the Theory of Syntax, Syntactic Structures, Cartesian Linguistics* and *American Power and the New Mandarins.*

Barbara Deming was born in New York City in 1917. She received a B.A. from Bennington College and an M.A. from Western Reserve University. Her stories, poems, and essays about the theater and films have appeared in *Partisan Review, New Directions, The New Yorker, The Nation, Liberation* and countless other magazines. Her book *Prison Notes* was published in 1966 by Grossman Publishers. She took part in the first peace walk through the South and was one of six radical pacifists headed by A. J. Muste who went to Saigon in 1966. She is on the editorial board of *Liberation.*

Charles Denby calls himself a Marxist-Humanist. He is a black production worker in Detroit who has been editor of *News & Letters*, a unique combination of workers and intellectuals, since its beginning in June, 1955. Born and raised in the Deep South, he came North to find work in the auto plants, and has been an active participant in rank and file struggles against both management and the labor bureaucracy, as well as in the freedom movement in the North and South.

Dave Gilbert began his radical activities in CORE at Columbia University. Since 1965 he has been an organizer in the SDS regional staff in New York City.

Evelyn Goldfield is one of the organizers of Women's Liberation Group on the University of Chicago campus. She worked with Radical Education Project for a year, and has done S.D.S. work. She has an M.A. in Philosophy.

Paul and Percival Goodman. Paul was born in 1911, received a B.A. from The City College of New York and a Ph.D. from the University of Chicago. He is a novelist, poet, critic and playwright. He is the author of many books, including *The Facts of Life, The Structure of Literature, Kafka's Prayer, The Empire City* and *Growing Up Absurd.* Percival is Associate Professor of Architecture at Columbia University in New York and a practicing architect there. He was born in 1904 and attended the Ecole des Beaux Arts in Paris.

Barbara and Alan Haber have been associated with the New Left from its beginnings. Al was a founder of SDS and was its first president, 1960-62. The Habers worked together in founding the Radical Education Project and then at the Institute for Policy Studies in Washington, D.C. Barbara is now doing art work and writing. Al is doing research on ghetto economic development programs. They live in Berkeley, California.

Steve Halliwell is a graduate from Wesleyan University and completed an M.A. in Russian History at Columbia in 1967. During the summer of 1967, he served as Assistant National Secretary of SDS and was a member of the SDS National Interim Committee for 1967-1968. As a result of his involvement in the revolt, he was suspended from the doctoral program at Columbia in May 1968 and is currently working for the radical-controlled student government at New York University.

Peter Irons has recently completed a three year sentence in a federal prison for refusing military service. He is a graduate of Antioch College and for several years lobbied for the UAW in Washington, D.C., and edited their newspaper. He was an active member of the Student Peace Union in Washington, D.C., and began an SDS chapter at the University of New Hampshire. He refused the teachers' loyalty oath at UNH and was responsible for it being declared unconstitutional in New Hampshire. He has had articles in *Progressive Magazine*. He is now a graduate student at Boston University and is married to Priscilla Long.

Frank Joyce was born in Detroit, Michigan, in 1941. He graduated from Royal Oak Dondero High School in 1959 where, during his senior year, he was president of the Student Government. He studied Political Science at Wayne State University. In 1963 Mr. Joyce, along with two others, was instrumental in the creation of the Detroit Education Project. He served as chairman of Northern Student Movement (NSM) until it evolved into People Against Racism (PAR). Some of his writings have appeared in *The New York Free Press*, *Los Angeles Free Press*, *Social Progress* and others. He is the national director of People Against Racism.

Louis Kampf is the head of the Literature Section at M.I.T. He is Associate National Director of Resist, a founder of the New University Conference and President of the Modern Language Association. He is the author of *On Modernism; The Prospects for Literature and Freedom*.

Priscilla Long is a graduate of Moravian Seminary for Girls and Antioch College, where she was active in the Student Peace Union and started a co-educational co-operative dorm. She originally comes from Chestertown Md. This is her first book. She is married to Peter Irons.

Staughton Lynd was born in Philadelphia in 1929. He received his B.A. from Harvard and his M.A. and Ph.D. from Columbia. He is the author of: *Nonviolence in America: A Documentary History; Constitution: Ten Essays; Intellectual Origins of American Radicalism*. He has taught at Spelman College, Yale, and presently is teaching part-time at Columbia College. He works in *The Resistance* in the Chicago area.

Rick Margolies is a three year probate for non-cooperation with the draft. He is an Associate Fellow of the Institute for Policy Studies in Washington, D.C., and lives in the Washington Free Community. He is bearded, has long hair, and drives a black motorcycle.

Paul Mattick, who was born in Germany, came to the United States in 1926. He lives in Cambridge, Massachusetts. He has been active in the radical labor movement here and abroad, and from 1934 to 1943 was the editor of the journals *Living Marxism* and *New Essays* (Chicago). His numerous economic and political articles have appeared in academic and political journals in Europe, the United States and South America. He is the author of essays and monographs on socio-economic issues published by the *Etudes de Marxologie* of the French *Institute de Science Economique Appliquee*.

John McDermott is a field secretary for the New University Conference, an organization of New Left faculty and graduate students. He lectures on politics and international relations at the New School for Social Research in New York and was associate editor and founder of *Viet-Report*, has written for the *New York Review*, *The Nation*, and *Dissent*, and is working on a book on technology and society. He spent six weeks in Cambodia and South Vietnam in January and February, 1967, as correspondent for *Viet-Report*.

C. Wright Mills was a leading critic of American civilization and one of America's most stimulating social analysts. He was a professor of sociology at Columbia University and taught at the William A. White Institute of Psychiatry in New York City. He is the author of many articles and has also written *The New Men of Power: America's Labor Leaders*, *White Collar: The American Middle Classes*, *The Power Elite* and others. He died in 1962.

Sue Munaker is one of the organizers of Women's Liberation Group on the University of Chicago campus. She was assistant to the director of Student Activities Union. She and Evelyn Goldfield worked on a hot dog stand together.

Truman Nelson, novelist and historian, is the author of six books on revolutionary themes, among them *The Surveyor* (John Brown in Kansas) and *The Sin of the Prophet* (Theodore Parker and the Boston Slave Riot). He is a frequent contributor to *Ramparts* and various scholarly journals.

Hilary Putnam is a philosopher of science and a logician. His activity in the peace movement began in 1965, and he has most recently been active with the Cambridge Peace and Freedom Party. He is a Professor of Philosophy at Harvard, where he is currently involved in the campaign to abolish R.O.T.C.

Rudolf Rocker was born at Mainz, Germany, on March 25, 1873. He is considered one of the most brilliant and inspiring anarchist thinkers of his generation. He edited a Yiddish paper, the *Arbeiter Freund*, and a Yiddish literary monthly, *Germinal*. He founded the first Jewish labor unions in England. In 1937, *Nationalism and Culture* was published and was the most widely read and successful fruit of his labors. The last two decades of his life were immensely productive, his writings appearing all over the world. These included some exceedingly important autobiographical material which described in part his relations with the famous anti-statist libertarians, especially of the era of 1890-1920. Rudolf Rocker died on September 10, 1958.

Richard Rothstein was an SDS member while in college. He participated in formulating plans for the ERAP community projects. In August, 1964, he left graduate school to work with the JOIN project in Chicago. He remained with JOIN until the summer of 1967. Since that time he has been active in other organizing attempts in the Chicago area.

Naomi Weisstein received her Ph.D. at Harvard, graduating at the top of her class, and was subsequently told by ten leading academic institutions that she did not have the proper qualifications for an appointment in their psychology departments. She has since found out what those qualifications are. She is currently teaching psychology at Loyola University in Chicago and plays in a Women's Liberation Rock Band.

Howard Zinn is Professor of Government at Boston University, author of six books (the latest: *Disobedience and Democracy*), and many articles.

BIBLIOGRAPHY

Socialism

Dunayevskaya, Raya, *Marxism and Freedom*, News & Letters, 415 Brainard St., Detroit, Mich.
Fromm, Eric, ed., *Socialist Humanism*, Anchor Books, Doubleday, N.Y., 1965.
Kolakowski, Leszek, *Toward a Marxist Humanism: Essays on the Left Today*, Grove Press, N.Y., 1968.
Mandel, Arthur, ed., *Essential Works of Marxism*, Bantam Books, N.Y., 1961.
Marx, Karl and Friedrich Engels, *Selected Works*, International Publishers, N.Y., 1968.

Anarchism

Drinnon, Richard, *Rebel in Paradise*, University of Chicago Press, Chicago, 1961.
Joll, James, *The Anarchists*, Atlantic Monthly Press, Boston, 1965.
Krimerman, Leonard and Lewis Perry, *Patterns of Anarchy*, Anchor Books, Doubleday, N.Y., 1966.
Kropotkin, Petr, *Mutual Aid*, Porter Sargent Publisher, Boston, 1955.
———*Memoirs of a Revolutionist*, Houghton Mifflin, N.Y., 1899.
Woodcock, George, *Anarchism*, The World Publishing Co., Cleveland and N.Y., 1962.

Vietnam

Gettleman, Marvin, *Vietnam*, Fawcett Publications, Conn., 1965.
Kahin, George and John W. Lewis, *The United States in Vietnam*, Delta, N.Y., 1967.
Raskin, Marcus and Bernard Fall, eds., *Vietnam Reader*, Vintage Books, Random House, 1965.
Zinn, Howard, *Vietnam: The Logic of Withdrawal*, Beacon Press, Boston, 1967.

Imperialism and the Cold War

Alperovitz, Gar, *Atomic Diplomacy*, Simon and Schuster, N.Y., 1965.
Fanon, Franz, *The Wretched of the Earth*, Grove Press, N.Y., 1965.
Greene, Felix, *Awakened China, The Country Americans Don't Know*, Doubleday, N.Y., 1961.
Oglesby, Carl, *Containment and Change*, The Macmillan Co., N.Y., 1967.
Schurmann, Franz, *Ideology and Organization in Communist China*, University of California Press, Berkeley, 1966.

Capitalism and American Society

Baran, Paul and Paul Sweezy, *Monopoly Capital*, Modern Reader Paperbacks, N.Y., London, 1966.

Marcuse, Herbert, *Eros and Civilization*, Beacon Press, Boston, 1955.

——— *One Dimensional Man*, Beacon Press, Boston, 1964.

Mattick, Paul, *Marx and Keynes: The Limits of the Mixed Economy*, Porter Sargent Publisher, Boston, 1969.

Mills, C. Wright, *The Power Elite*, Oxford University Press, London, 1965.

White Racism

Disch, Bob, *White Racism in America* [to be published by Dell].

Ellison, Ralph, *The Invisible Man*, Random House, N.Y., 1952.

Gossett, Thomas, *Race: The History of an Idea in America*, Schocken, N.Y., 1963.

Hernton, Calvin, *Sex and Racism in America*, Grove Press, N.Y., 1965.

Jordan, Winthrop, *White Over Black*, University of North Carolina Press, Chapel Hill, 1968.

Litwack, Leon, *North of Slavery: The Negro in the Free States 1790-1860*, University of Chicago Press, Chicago, 1961.

Osofsky, Gilbert, *The Burden of Race: A Documentary History of Negro-White Relations in America*, Harper and Row, N.Y., 1967.

Duberman, Martin, *In White America: a Documentary Play*, Houghton Mifflin, Boston, 1964.

Black Power

Barbour, Floyd B., ed., *The Black Power Revolt: A Collection of Essays*, Porter Sargent Publisher, Boston, 1968.

Carmichael, Stokely and Charles V. Hamilton, *Black Power*, Vintage Books, Random House, N.Y., 1967.

Malcolm X, *The Autobiography of Malcolm X*, Grove Press, N.Y., 1965.

Williams, Robert, *Negroes With Guns*, Marzani and Munsell, N.Y., 1962.

Education

Friedenberg, Edgar, *Coming of Age in America*, Vintage Books, Random House, N.Y., 1963.

Goodman, Paul, *Growing Up Absurd*, Vintage Books, Random House, N.Y., 1956.

——— *Compulsory Miseducation*, Vintage Books, Random House, N.Y., 1962.

Kohls, Herbert, *36 Children*, New American Library, Jackson, Ill., 1967.

Kozol, Jonathan, *Death at an Early Age*, Houghton Mifflin, Boston, 1967.

Neill, A. S., *Summerhill: A Radical Approach to Child Rearing*, Hart Publishing Co., N.Y., 1960.

North American Congress on Latin America, *Who Rules Columbia?*, N. Y., 1968. Copies available from: NACLA, P. O. Box 57, Cathedral Park Station, N.Y., N.Y. 10025.

Culture

Ibsen, Henrik, *Doll's House*, Dutton, Everyman's reprint, N.Y., 1954.
Jules, Henry, *Culture Against Man*, Vintage Books, Random House, N.Y., 1963.
Kampf, Louis, *On Modernism*, M. I. T. Press, Cambridge, 1968.

Other

de Beauvoir, Simone, *The Second Sex*, Alfred Knopf, N.Y., 1953.
Fromm, Eric, *The Revolution of Hope*, Harper and Row, 1968.
Gregg, Richard, *The Power of Nonviolence*, Schocken, N.Y., 1935.
Lynd, Alice, *We Won't Go*, Beacon Press, Boston, 1968.
Lynd, Staughton, *Nonviolence in America: A Documentary History*, Bobbs Merrill, 1966.
Menninger, Karl, *The Crime of Punishment*, Viking Press, N.Y., 1968.
Mumford, Lewis, *Technics of Civilization*, Harcourt, Brace and World, N.Y., 1932.
See also the Bibliography on p. 374.

INDEX

Abortion, 268

Acheson, Dean; 108

Adams, Brooks; quoted, 184

Adams, John; quoted, 84

Adams, John Quincy; quoted, 84

ADC, *see* Aid to Dependent Children

Advertising: as agent of domestic imperialism, 32, 35; aimed at women, 243-246

Agency for International Development, U. S.; **182-183**

Agency of change, historic: viewpoint of "the end of ideology" on, 19; collapse of in advanced capitalist countries, 21-22; socialist view of, 21; the "working class" as most important, 22-23; the intelligentsia as, 23-25; liberal views on criticized, 66-67; traditional Marxist views on criticized, 66-67; proletariat as, 66; Negroes as, 66; students as, 66; *See also* Strategy, revolutionary; Strategy, New Left

AID, *see* Agency for International Development, U. S.

Aid to Dependent Children (ADC), 265-267

Alabama, Montgomery; bus boycott: *see* bus boycott

Alabama, Selma; march in: *see* Selma, Alabama

Alcorn, Robert H.; quoted, 104

Ali, Muhammad; 138

Alinsky, Saul; 274

Alsop, Stewart; 105

Alstyne, R. W.; quoted, 116

Alternative institutions, 67, 305. *See also* Parallel organizations

America and the New Era, SDS policy statement (1963); 275-276, 278. *See also* Students for a Democratic Society

Anarchism, 43-55, 319, 325, 406, 409; ideology of, 43-52. *See also* Anarcho - syndicalism; Socialists, guild; Syndicalism

Anarchist revolution in Spain, 178

Anarcho-syndicalism, 11. *See also* Anarchism; Socialists, guild; Syndicalism

Arendt, Hannah; argument on Eichmann, 108

Aristotle, economics of; 437

Arnold, Matthew; 422-423, 432

Atlantic Monthly (periodical), Arthur Schlesinger quoted from; 77-78

Atomic bomb, dropping of; 107-108

Auden, W. H.; quoted, 454

Automation: origin of term, 152, introduction of, 153, *See also* Cybernation; Technology, cybernated

"Automation and the Abolition of the Market," E. J. Nell; 41

Babbitt, Milton; quoted, 430-431

"Backlash," white working class; 280-282

Bakunin, Michael; disagreement with Marx, 62; quoted, 176. *See also* Anarchism

Ball, George; 90; quoted, 180, 184

Baran and Sweezy, *Monopoly Capital;* 64-65

Base, problems of: *see* Agency of change; Strategy, New Left; Strategy, revolutionary

chist (in Spain), 178; pluralistic, 221-222, 300-301; Russian (1905), 379-380; German (1918), 380, 389-390; Russian (1917), 385-389; isolation of Russian, 388; Cuban (as model for New Left activists), 405; definition of, 405
Revolution, right of: defined, 75-76; Arthur Schlesinger on, 77-78; Justice Douglas on, 78; Declaration of Independence on, 81; Abraham Lincoln on, 83; Thomas Jefferson on, 72, 84; Pennsylvania Declaration of Rights on, 84; Henry Clay on, 84; John Adams on, 84; Henry Thoreau on, 84; Maryland Declaration of Rights on, 84-85; U. S. Grant on, 85; Emerson on, 85; Justice Jackson on, 85
Right, the; definition of by C. Wright Mills, 19
Rights, political; origin of, 52
Right to bear arms, implications of; 76
Riots, student: influence of on governments, 23-24; in Japan, 24
Rhee, Syngman; overthrow of in South Korea, 23-24
Roosevelt, Franklin D.; State Department under, 98-103
Rostow, Walt; 87, 95
ROTC, see Reserve Officers Training Corps
Rousseau, *Social Contract*: 45-46
Rudd, Mark; 209
Rusk, Dean; 87; view on Vietnam, 93; view on China; 96; comment on his job, 106
Ruskin, John; 433
Russell, Bill; 134
Russell, Lord; Committee for Nuclear Disarmament, 7
Russia, criticism of dictatorship of the proletariat in; 48. See also Bolshevism, etc.
Rustin, Bayard; 4

SAC, see Strategic Air Command

Saint-Simon, quoted; 47
Sanctuary, 318, 333
Sandman, Charles W. Jr.; 83-84
Sands, Diana; 134
San Francisco State Strike, 327-328
Sartre, Jean Paul; 5, 123; break with Communist Party, 2-3; "Ideology and Revolution," 4; on French Resistance, 79; *Anti-Semite and Jew*, 135
Savio, Mario; quoted, 9
Schlesinger, Arthur; 17, 77-78
SCLC, see Southern Christian Leadership Conference
SDS, see Students for a Democratic Society
Selective Service System, 10
Self-immolation of Buddhists, see Buddhists, self-immolation of
Selma, Alabama; march in 1964-65, 1
Sex, used to sell products; 33-34
Shepp, Archie; 432
Slavery in U. S., 131-133
Single woman, the; 255-257
Sit-in: first by predominantly black students, 3; Greensboro, North Carolina, 3-4; by SDS at Chase Manhattan Bank, 7
Sitte, Camillo; 441, 443
Smith, Adam; quoted, 206
SNCC, see Student Nonviolent Coordinating Committee
Social Contract, Rousseau; 45-46
Socialism: as source of anarchism, 45-46; development of modern, 45
"Socialist Realism" of the Soviet Union, 16-17
Socialists, Guild; 379, 383. See also Anarchism, Anarcho-syndicalism, Syndicalism
Social strike, see Strike, social
Sorel, Georges; 378
Southern Christian Leadership Conference (SCLC), Vincent Harding quoted on; 3
South Korea, overthrow of Syngman Rhee in; 23-24